S0-BZI-608

A BOOK OF

FAVORITE

Recipes

Compiled by

THE SISTERHOOD

OF

ST. JOHN'S UKRAINIAN ORTHODOX CHURCH

Johnson City, New York

ISBN 0-9729629-0-5

Copyright © 2003

Published and Printed By
Cookbook Publishers, Inc.
P.O. Box 15920
Lenexa, Kansas 66285-5920

Recipes and menus copyrighted 2003 by
St. Mary's Sisterhood of St. John's Ukrainian Orthodox Church
Johnson City, New York

Dear Friends,

It is with great pride that we present **Favorite Recipes From Our Best Cooks, Volume II.*** Recipes feature a combination of old family favorites and popular new creations, some with a Ukrainian flair. This new book is a "must have" for cooks who appreciate recipes that are easy to follow, made with ingredients found in most kitchens, and that taste delicious!

Our Sisterhood is known throughout Broome County, New York, for our baked goods, a focus of this volume. Try some cake and cookie recipes and you will understand what makes our Holiday Bake Sales sell out in two hours.

To those who purchased and made Volume I such an astounding success, we thank you for embracing our first attempt and for encouraging us in this new endeavor. While the first volume was compiled with recipes from our first generation of cooks, this volume is a gift from the second generation to be used and cherished by generations to come.

Cooking and baking is central to our heritage, traditions and family. We are pleased to share these recipes with you and hope that they will, in turn, become some of your favorites.

Happy cooking and baking!

St. Mary's Sisterhood of St. John Ukrainian Orthodox Church
Johnson City, New York

* *All proceeds from the sale of this book will be used to support our Church. To learn more about our church and our traditions, please visit our web site at http://www.stjohnuoc.org.*

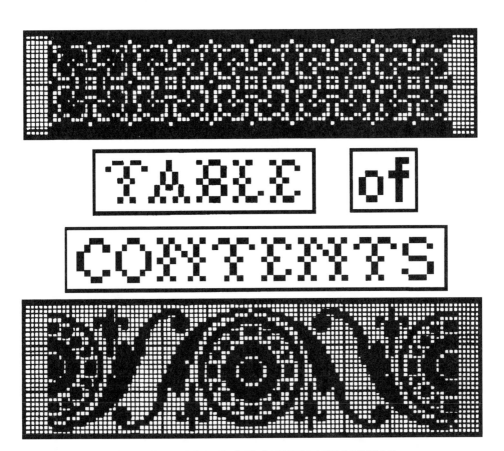

TABLE of CONTENTS

EXPRESSION OF APPRECIATION

The overwhelming response to our first cookbook, *Favorite Recipes From Our Best Cooks,* Volume I, encouraged the Sisterhood of St. John's to compile Volume II. We thank the Cookbook Committee for their untiring efforts in preparing another valuable cookbook filled with new recipes. To all members who shared their favorite recipes, THANK YOU, without this there could be no publication. We have endeavored to combine the traditional with the unusual to provide an interesting assortment of foods that will be treasured and enjoyed by all.

SMACHNOHO!

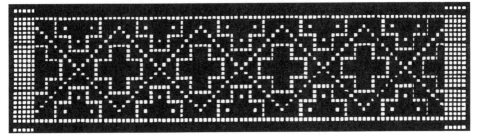

TABLE OF CONTENTS

Appetizers

Beverages

BAGNA CAUDA APPETIZERS

Sue Blue

4 Tbsp. butter
4 cloves garlic
2 Tbsp. flour

16 chopped anchovy fillets, drained
2 c. whipping cream

Melt butter; add garlic. Saute a few minutes. Gradually stir in flour and chopped anchovies, then cream over low heat. Stir until sauce is quite thick. Remove garlic. To serve, keep sauce warm with one candle warmer. Use baby carrots, celery, zucchini, cauliflower, broccoli, tomatoes, radishes, scallions, and Italian bread cubes to dip.

DRIED BEEF DIP I

Olga Gooley

2 c. sour cream
2 c. mayonnaise*
3 tsp. dill seed
2 Tbsp. chopped parsley
3 Tbsp. finely chopped onion

1 (2½ oz.) pkg. dried beef, shredded
2 (2½ oz.) pkg. corned beef, diced
1 medium round rye bread

Combine all ingredients except the bread. Hollow out the bread; break the hollowed out section into pieces to use with dip. Pour dip into hollowed bread.

* Do not use salad dressing.

DRIED BEEF DIP II

Helen Rucky

¼ c. chopped onion
1 Tbsp. oleo
1 c. milk
1 (8 oz.) pkg. cream cheese, cubed
1 (3 oz.) pkg. dried beef, chopped

1 (14 oz.) can mushrooms, drained and chopped
¼ c. grated Parmesan cheese
2 Tbsp. chopped parsley

Saute onion in oleo; add milk and cream cheese. Stir over low heat until cream cheese is melted. Stir in beef, mushrooms, Parmesan cheese, and parsley; heat. Serve hot. Makes 2½ cups.

DOT'S HOT DRIED BEEF DIP III

Jean Geresi
Martha Maliwacki

1 (8 oz.) pkg. cream cheese
2 Tbsp. milk
1 (3 oz.) pkg. dried beef
2 Tbsp. instant onion flakes

2 Tbsp. green pepper, diced
½ tsp. pepper
½ c. sour cream
¼ c. chopped nuts

Soften cream cheese. Add remaining ingredients; mix. Turn mixture into an ungreased 6x8 inch Pyrex dish. Sprinkle with nuts. Bake at 325° for 25 minutes. Serve with crackers.

BLINI

Jane Ellsworth

1 large loaf sandwich bread
2 (8 oz.) pkg. cream cheese
½ c. sugar
1½ tsp. vanilla

2 egg yolks
Margarine, melted
Sugar-cinnamon mixture

In a medium bowl, blend cream cheese, sugar, vanilla, and egg yolks with a wooden spoon. Cut crusts from bread; roll each slice flat with a rolling pin. Spread 1 to 2 teaspoons cream cheese mixture over each slice. Roll up jelly roll style; dip in melted margarine, then roll in sugar-cinnamon mixture. Cut each into thirds; place on cookie sheet. Freeze. Bake frozen Blini at 350° for 15 minutes.

AVOCADO-CHEESE DIP

Evelyn Kanazawich

1 ripe medium avocado
¼ c. mashed Blue cheese

1 Tbsp. lemon juice
Salt and pepper

Peel avocado; mash fine. Add Blue cheese, lemon juice, and salt and pepper to taste. Chill. Serve with crackers. Makes about 1 cup.

BLACK OLIVE CHEESE BALL

Marion Kaspryk

8 oz. cream cheese
4 oz. Blue cheese
¼ c. margarine

⅜ c. chopped black olives
1 Tbsp. minced onion
Ground walnuts

Let cheeses and margarine stand in a bowl at room temperature until soft. Blend with a wooden spoon. Add olives and onion; mix until all ingredients are thoroughly blended. Refrigerate in a covered bowl for several hours. Form into 1 large or 2 small balls. Roll balls in ground nuts; wrap and refrigerate or freeze.

CHEDDAR CHEESE BALL

Marion Kaspryk

4 oz. Roquefort or Blue cheese
1 lb. cream cheese
1 (10 oz.) pkg. Wispride sharp
Cheddar flavor cheese (with
or without wine)

2 Tbsp. minced onion
2 Tbsp. Worcestershire sauce
Garlic salt
Ground walnuts or pecans

Let cheeses stand in bowl at room temperature until soft. Blend with a wooden spoon. Add onion, Worcestershire sauce, and garlic salt to taste; mix until thoroughly blended. Refrigerate in covered bowl for several hours. Form into 2 or 3 balls. Roll balls in ground nuts; wrap and store in refrigerator or freezer.

DIANE'S CHEESE BALL

Sally Shirk

1 (8 oz.) pkg. cream cheese
1 (8 oz.) container Wispride
sharp Cheddar cheese

Garlic powder
¼ c. chopped nuts

Let cheese stand in bowl at room temperature until soft. Sprinkle (two shakes) with garlic powder; mix with wooden spoon until thoroughly blended. Form into a ball; roll in chopped nuts. Wrap in plastic wrap and store in refrigerator.

HOLIDAY CHEESE BALL

Helen Kaspryk

¼ c. milk
3 oz. Blue cheese, cubed
¼ c. Cheddar cheese, cubed
1 small wedge onion

½ tsp. Worcestershire sauce
6 oz. cream cheese, cubed
½ c. pecans
4 sprigs parsley

Put milk and Blue cheese in blender; blend. Add Cheddar cheese, onion, Worcestershire sauce, and cream cheese; blend until smooth. Shape into ball and refrigerate overnight.

Put pecans and parsley into blender; chop. One hour before serving, roll cheese ball in mixture of pecans and parsley. Serve with crackers.

PEPPER CHEESE BALL

Pam Scannell

2 (8 oz.) pkg. cream cheese,
softened
3 Tbsp. finely chopped green
pepper
1 small onion, grated

1 small pkg. dried beef,
chopped
Dash of Tabasco
Coarse ground black pepper

Combine cream cheese, green pepper, onion, chopped dried beef, and Tabasco; mix thoroughly. Form into 2 balls. Roll in coarse pepper until coated completely. Chill 2 hours. Serve with crackers.

SAUSAGE AND CHEESE BALLS
Mary Buckingham
Mary Kostyun

8 oz. cheese, grated (medium sharp)
1 lb. hot or sweet sausage (breakfast kind)

3 c. Bisquick

Mix well and form into small balls. Freeze until ready to use, then bake frozen about 35 minutes at 350°. Serve.

BLUE CHEESE WHIP
Mary Kostyun

¼ lb. Blue cheese
½ c. butter or margarine
1 Tbsp. Worcestershire sauce

⅛ tsp. paprika or 1 tsp. chopped parsley

Combine all ingredients; whip until fluffy. Use as a spread on crackers or to fill 2 inch lengths of crisp celery.

CHEESE CARROTS
Mary Kostyun

1 (3 oz.) pkg. cream cheese
¼ c. grated carrots
¼ tsp. salt
Dash of cayenne
3 drops Worcestershire sauce

1 Tbsp. chopped chives or onion
Paprika
Parsley sprigs

Mix cream cheese and carrots. Add salt, cayenne, Worcestershire sauce, and chives; mix well. Roll into miniature carrot shapes; sprinkle with paprika. Chill until firm. Put a tiny sprig of parsley into each "carrot" to resemble tops. Makes 10 carrots.

CHEESY SOUR CREAM DIP
Mary Kostyun

1½ c. grated American cheese
1 c. sour cream
½ tsp. instant minced onion

½ tsp. dry mustard
2 Tbsp. catsup
1 tsp. soy sauce

In a small bowl, combine all ingredients; blend well. Chill about 2 hours for flavors to blend.

4

CREAMY CHEESE LOG
Mary Kostyun

½ lb. Cheddar cheese, shredded
2 (3 oz.) pkg. cream cheese
2 oz. Blue cheese, crumbled

2 Tbsp. finely chopped onion
½ c. sour cream
1 c. chopped nuts

Cream cheeses together. Add onion and sour cream; mix well. Chill until firm. Shape into 15 inch log; roll in chopped nuts. Refrigerate several hours before serving.

HORSERADISH CHEESE LOAF
Evelyn Kanazawich

1 unsliced loaf Italian or
  French bread
½ c. butter or margarine,
  softened
1 Tbsp. horseradish
½ tsp. lemon juice

Few drops of hot pepper sauce
1 (8 oz.) pkg. process sharp
  American cheese slices, cut in
  halves diagonally
Salt and pepper

Slice bread into ½ inch thick slices, cutting to, but not through, bottom of crust. In bowl, cream together butter, horseradish, lemon juice, hot pepper sauce, and salt and pepper to taste. Spread lightly on all cut surfaces of bread. Starting with end slices, place a triangle of cheese in every cut of bread. Wrap loaf in foil. Bake at 400° for 15 to 20 minutes or until cheese is melted. Makes 8 to 10 servings.

HOT CHEESE AND ONION DIP
Phyllis Hatala
Adrian Mihalko

8 oz. sharp Cheddar cheese
1 c. mayonnaise

1 small onion

Grate cheese on grater. Combine with mayonnaise; mix well. Chop onion finely. Add to rest of mixture. Turn into small casserole dish with cover. Bake, covered, at 400° for 20 minutes. Uncover. Broil until brown and bubbly. Serve hot with Ritz crackers.

CHEESE AND MUSHROOM CANAPES
Jeanne Sankowski

¼ lb. mushrooms
1 Tbsp. butter
2 (3 oz.) pkg. cream cheese

Sliced white bread
Onion salt

Cut mushrooms into very small pieces; saute in butter a few minutes. Combine mushrooms with softened cream cheese* and onion salt to taste. Cut bread into small rounds; toast on one side. Spread untoasted side with mushroom mixture; refrigerate or freeze. When ready to serve, place under broiler until puffy and brown.

* To soften cream cheese, beat with electric beater and add small amount of cream if too thick.

NIPPY CHEESE FILLING
Evelyn Kanazawich

1 (8 oz.) pkg. process cheese spread

¾ c. chopped cooked salami
½ c. chopped pimiento

Combine all ingredients. Store, covered, in refrigerator. Makes 1½ cups. Serve with crackers.

CHEESE SPREAD I
Marie Pufky

1 lb. Velveeta cheese
1 (5½ oz.) jar horseradish

9 Tbsp. mayonnaise
5 dashes of Tabasco sauce

Melt cheese in double boiler. Remove from heat; add remaining ingredients. Blend well. Place mixture in a crock; refrigerate.

CHEESE SPREAD II
Linda Zapach

3 (8 oz.) pkg. cream cheese, softened
1 env. dry onion soup mix

⅓ c. Roka Blue cheese dressing
Whole almonds

Combine all ingredients; shape into a "pine cone" studded with the almonds. Decorate with a fresh sprig of pine for added effect. Serve with crackers.

APPETIZER CHICKEN PUFFS
Marion Kaspryk

Petite Cream Puffs:

1¼ c. water
¼ c. margarine
1 c. flour
½ tsp. salt

4 eggs
1 c. (4 oz.) shredded Swiss cheese

Bring water and margarine to a boil. Add flour and salt; stir vigorously over low heat until mixture forms a ball. Remove from heat. Add eggs, one at a time, beating until smooth after each addition. Stir in cheese. Drop rounded teaspoonfuls of dough onto greased cookie sheet. Bake at 400° for 30 to 35 minutes or until golden brown. Remove from cookie sheet immediately. Makes approximately 4½ dozen.

Filling:

2 c. finely chopped cooked
 chicken
¾ c. chopped celery
1 Tbsp. chopped onion
1 c. (4 oz.) shredded Swiss
 cheese

½ tsp. prepared mustard
½ tsp. salt
Dash of pepper
Mayonnaise

Combine chicken, celery, onion, cheese, mustard, seasonings, and enough mayonnaise to moisten; mix lightly. Cut tops from Petite Cream Puffs; fill with chicken mixture. Replace tops. Bake at 350° for 15 minutes.

CHICKEN WINGS

Dorothy Skellett

24 chicken wings
½ c. honey
2 Tbsp. Worcestershire sauce

⅓ c. soy sauce
1 clove garlic, minced
Juice of 2 lemons

Place wings in a shallow baking pan; combine remaining ingredients. Pour over wings. Bake at 325° for 1 hour. Baste wings while baking.

HOT WINGS

Jody Dimitriou

1 (5 lb.) bag chicken wings
1 (16 oz.) bottle hot sauce
1 (20 oz.) bottle Tabasco sauce

¼ lb. butter
1 tsp. garlic salt
1 Tbsp. cornstarch

Fry wings until crisp. Simmer sauces, butter, and garlic salt; add cornstarch to thicken. Dip fried wings in sauce; layer in a baking dish. Heat in a microwave oven or conventional oven until hot.

* May be baked at 350° up to an hour for a very tender wing. Pour extra sauce over wings as needed.

ROSE'S MARINATED CHICKEN WINGS

Marion Kaspryk

½ c. soy sauce
1 c. pineapple juice
1 clove garlic, minced
2 Tbsp. minced onion
1 tsp. ginger

¼ c. brown sugar
¼ c. salad oil
1 c. beer
36 chicken wings

Combine all ingredients except chicken wings; pour over wings. Marinate in refrigerator overnight. Bake, uncovered, at 400° for 45 minutes.

CLAM DIP I

Helen Rucky

1 (8 oz.) pkg. cream cheese
1 stick oleo
1 tsp. lemon juice
1 Tbsp. minced onion

26 crushed Ritz crackers
1 (6.5 oz.) can minced clams, drained

Saute onion in oleo. Add lemon juice and cream cheese, cooking only until cheese is melted. Remove from heat. Fold in Ritz crackers and drained clams. Put in greased 1 quart casserole dish. Heat at 350° for 10 minutes. Serve with crackers.

CLAM DIP II

Jeanne Sankowski

1 small onion, chopped
1 green pepper, chopped
½ c. butter
2 (7 oz.) cans clams, drained
1 (4 oz.) can mushrooms, drained

¾ c. Velveeta cheese
½ tsp. cayenne pepper
3 Tbsp. red wine
⅔ c. catsup
2 Tbsp. Worcestershire sauce

Saute onion and pepper in butter. Add remaining ingredients; simmer about 30 minutes. Serve hot with corn chips or crackers.

Note: Tuna may be substituted for clams.

PATTY'S HOT CLAM DIP

Sally Shirk

2 (6 oz.) cans minced clams (undrained)
1 Tbsp. lemon juice
¼ lb. butter
1 medium onion, minced
½ green pepper, minced
1 clove garlic, minced

1 Tbsp. fresh parsley, minced
1 tsp. oregano
Dash of red pepper
½ c. seasoned bread crumbs
American cheese, grated
Parmesan cheese
Paprika

In a saucepan, combine clams and lemon juice; simmer for 15 minutes. In another saucepan, melt butter; add onion, green pepper, garlic, parsley, oregano, and red pepper. Saute until onion is soft. Combine both saucepan mixtures; add bread crumbs. Mix. Put mixture in shallow casserole; sprinkle with cheeses and paprika. Bake at 325° for 15 minutes. Serve with a variety of crackers.

CLAMS CASINO

Anna Smyk

½ green pepper, chopped fine
1 small bunch green onions,
  chopped
¾ c. chopped mushrooms
4 Tbsp. bacon bits

3 pieces pimiento, chopped
1 tsp. minced fresh garlic
¼ c. margarine, melted
1 to 1½ doz. clams
Bacon

Combine green pepper, onions, mushrooms, bacon bits, pimiento, garlic, and margarine; mix. Open clams; leave on half shell. Place mixture on clams. Top with bacon strips. Bake at 450° or 500° for 15 minutes.

STUFFED CLAMS

Anna Smyk

2 (46 oz.) cans clams, drained*
1½ lb. margarine
2 green peppers (1¼ c.),
  chopped fine
1 (4 oz.) jar pimentos (¼ c.),
  chopped fine
1 (16 oz.) can mushrooms (2¾
  c.), chopped fine
2 small onions (1 c.), chopped
  fine (1 c.)

1 c. parsley, chopped fine
½ c. chives, chopped
1 Tbsp. oregano
1 bay leaf
1 tsp. rosemary
1 Tbsp. granulated garlic
1 tsp. black pepper
1 c. sherry
9 c. bread crumbs
Romano cheese

Fry clams in margarine for 30 minutes. Add remaining ingredients except bread crumbs; cook 5 minutes. Add bread crumbs to absorb moisture. Turn into a casserole; top with Romano cheese. Bake at 375° for 15 to 20 minutes.

* Three pounds of crabmeat or 3 pounds of shrimp can be used in place of clams.

CRAB CANAPES

Jeanne Sankowski

6 English muffins
1 (7 oz.) can crabmeat
2 Tbsp. margarine

1 (5 oz.) jar Old English cheese
1 tsp. garlic salt

Split English muffin; cut in quarters. Toast. Combine remaining ingredients. Put some crabmeat mixture on toasted muffin; freeze. At serving time, pop canapes under broiler until bubbly.

CRAB DIP 1

Helen Rucky

2 (8 oz.) pkg. cream cheese
1 c. mayonnaise

1 tsp. garlic powder
1 lb. crab sea legs, chopped

Mix together all ingredients. Pour into buttered 2 quart baking dish. Bake at 350° for 30 to 40 minutes.

CRAB DIP II
Helen Rucky

1 (8 oz.) pkg. cream cheese, softened
1 (6 oz.) pkg. crabmeat, chopped
¼ c. milk
2 Tbsp. minced green onion

1 tsp. lemon juice
¼ tsp. salt
¼ c. almonds, chopped
1 tsp. prepared horseradish (optional)

Beat cream cheese until smooth. Add milk, onion, lemon juice, and salt. Stir in crabmeat. Turn into greased 3 cup baking dish. Sprinkle with almonds. Bake, uncovered, at 350° for 20 to 30 minutes or until bubbly. Serve with crackers or bread rounds.

CRABMEAT DIP
Jody Dimitriou

1 c. mayonnaise
½ c. sour cream
1 clove garlic, finely chopped
1 Tbsp. wine
1 Tbsp. chopped parsley
1 Tbsp. onion, finely chopped

1 Tbsp. Worcestershire sauce
½ tsp. salt
⅛ tsp. ground red pepper
2 (6 oz.) cans crabmeat
2 Tbsp. lemon juice

Combine all ingredients except crabmeat and lemon juice. Toss crabmeat with lemon juice; fold crabmeat into the mayonnaise mixture. Refrigerate several hours before serving. Serve with crackers.

HOT CRAB DIP
Jeanne Sankowski

2 (8 oz.) pkg. cream cheese
½ c. mayonnaise
½ tsp. prepared mustard
4 tsp. confectioners sugar

½ tsp. garlic salt
½ tsp. onion juice
2 (6½ oz.) cans crab, drained
3 Tbsp. white wine

Combine first six ingredients in top of double boiler; stir until smooth. Add crabmeat and wine; heat thoroughly. Serve with your favorite dippers.

CON CASO
Jeanne Sankowski

2 lb. Velveeta cheese, grated or cut up

1 (16 oz.) can chili without beans (Hormel brand best)

Melt cheese over low heat. Add chili; mix. Heat thoroughly. Serve in fondue pot. An excellent dip for corn chips.

Note: Can be made in reduced quantity.

CURRY DIP
Marie Pufky

1 c. mayonnaise
1 tsp. minced onion
1 tsp. curry powder
1 tsp. vinegar
1 tsp. horseradish

Combine all ingredients; mix until smooth. Use fresh vegetables for dipping.

DILL DIP
Marie Richardson

1 c. sour cream
1 c. Hellmann's mayonnaise
2 Tbsp. dill weed
2 tsp. minced onion
2 tsp. chopped parsley
2 tsp. seasoned salt

Combine all ingredients. Chill before serving.

DEVILED EGGS
Anna Smyk

6 hard cooked eggs
3 Tbsp. mayonnaise
3 Tbsp. chili sauce
1 small onion, diced fine
½ tsp. salt
¼ tsp. pepper
½ tsp. dry mustard
Paprika

Shell the eggs; cut in halves lengthwise. Scoop egg yolks out from whites, placing yolks in a small bowl; add remaining ingredients. Mix until combined and blended evenly. Fill cavity in egg whites with yolk mixture; sprinkle with paprika.

GUACAMOLE DIP
Carol Wasylko

1 medium avocado (very ripe)
Lemon juice to taste
Hot pepper sauce or jalapeno
  sauce
1½ to 2 Tbsp. Hellmann's
  mayonnaise
1 to 1½ tsp. grated onion

In a blender, process avocado until mashed. Add remaining ingredients; process until combined. Serve with corn chips.

Hamburgers: Season ground beef with onion salt and Worcestershire sauce. Add crushed corn chips; grill. Spread with Guacamole Dip; serve.

HAMBURGER DIP

Marianne Lawryk

1 lb. lean ground beef
½ c. chopped onion
1 (8 oz.) can tomato sauce
1 (8 oz.) pkg. cream cheese
½ c. grated Parmesan cheese

1 clove garlic, minced
1 tsp. oregano
1 tsp. sugar
Salt and pepper to taste

Saute ground beef until brown. Add onion; cook until tender. Add remaining ingredients, stirring over low heat until cheese melts. Spoon into chafing dish. Serve warm with corn chips. Makes 1 quart.

HORSERADISH DIP

Marion Kaspryk

2 (3 oz.) pkg. cream cheese
¼ c. sour cream
¼ c. prepared horseradish, well
   drained

½ tsp. salt
¼ tsp. black pepper
½ tsp. paprika

Beat cheese; add sour cream. Beat. Add horseradish, salt, pepper, and paprika; beat. Chill. Serve surrounded with crisp, raw vegetables. Makes about 1 cup.

HOT DOG DELIGHT

Nell Leska Boser

¾ c. whiskey
1 Tbsp. minced onion
½ c. catsup

½ c. brown sugar
2 lb. party hot dogs

Combine whiskey, onion, catsup, and brown sugar; bring to boiling. Add hot dogs; simmer 2 hours. Serve piping hot.

LIVERWURST DIP

Evelyn Kanazawich

½ lb. liverwurst, mashed
1 c. sour cream
2 tsp. grated onion
1½ Tbsp. finely chopped dill
   pickles

1 tsp. prepared mustard
Dash of pepper
Parsley sprigs

Combine first 6 ingredients; mix thoroughly. Cover and chill. Garnish with parsley. Serve with crackers or cheese flavored sticks. Makes about 2¼ cups.

CREAM CHEESE AND LIVERWURST FILLING

Evelyn Kanazawich

1 (8 oz.) pkg. cream cheese, softened
¾ lb. liverwurst
1 (4 oz.) can chopped mushrooms, drained
1 Tbsp. instant minced onions
2 tsp. Worcestershire sauce
⅛ tsp. pepper
¼ c. undiluted evaporated milk

Mash together cream cheese and liverwurst. Add remaining ingredients; mix well. Cover; refrigerate. Makes about 3 cups. Serve with crackers.

MARINATED MUSHROOM SPRING SALAD PLATTER

Mike Charnetsky

1 lb. fresh mushrooms or 2 (8 oz.) cans whole mushrooms
1 c. celery, sliced thin
½ green pepper, coarsely chopped
½ onion, finely chopped
1 c. olive or salad oil
¼ c. dry red wine or wine vinegar
2 tsp. sweet basil
1 tsp. salt
½ tsp. garlic, minced fine
½ tsp. coarse black pepper
½ tsp. sugar

Rinse, pat dry, and halve fresh mushrooms or drain canned mushrooms. In a large bowl, combine mushrooms, celery, green pepper, and onion; set aside. Combine remaining ingredients; pour over mushroom mixture. Toss well. Refrigerate 6 hours or longer. Serve as an appetizer or as a salad with assorted sliced luncheon meats if desired.

PICKLED MUSHROOMS

Chuck Sarnoski

⅔ c. tarragon vinegar
½ c. salad oil
1 medium clove garlic, crushed
1 Tbsp. sugar
2 Tbsp. water
1½ tsp. salt
Dash of pepper
Dash of bottled hot pepper sauce
1 medium onion, sliced
2 (6 oz.) cans broiled mushroom crowns or 2 pt. fresh mushrooms, washed and trimmed

Combine first 8 ingredients. Slice onion; separate into rings. Add onion and mushrooms to marinade. Cover. Refrigerate 8 hours or overnight, stirring several times. Drain; serve as appetizer.

KAREN'S RAW STUFFED MUSHROOMS

Mary Ann Klish

1 lb. white mushrooms, washed
1 small onion, chopped
¼ c. margarine
1 (8 oz.) pkg. cream cheese,
   softened

Salt
Pepper
Garlic salt
Parsley flakes

Remove stems from mushroom caps. Chop stems; saute stems and onion in margarine. Cool; add cream cheese. Season to taste with salt, pepper, garlic salt, and parsley flakes. Stuff mushroom caps just before serving to prevent from turning brown.

Hint: To prevent mushrooms from discoloration, dip in water to which some lemon juice has been added.

STUFFED MUSHROOMS

Helen Rucky

50 mushrooms
¼ c. oleo
1 Tbsp. flour
½ tsp. salt

½ c. light cream
2 tsp. minced chives
1 tsp. lemon juice
Fine bread crumbs

Wipe mushrooms and remove stems. Chop stems and saute in oleo. Stir in flour and salt. Add cream and stir until thick. Stir in chives and juice. Stuff caps and place on ungreased cookie sheet. Sprinkle with crumbs. Bake at 400° for 8 minutes.

MUSHROOM SPREAD

Helen Rucky

4 slices bacon
8 oz. fresh mushrooms, chopped
   (3 c.)
1 medium onion, finely chopped
   (½ c.)
1 clove garlic, minced
2 Tbsp. flour

¼ tsp. salt
⅛ tsp. pepper
1 (8 oz.) pkg. cream cheese,
   softened
2 tsp. Worcestershire sauce
1 tsp. soy sauce
½ c. sour cream

In skillet, cook bacon until crisp. Drain, reserving 2 tablespoons drippings; crumble. Set aside. Cook mushrooms, onion, and garlic in reserved drippings until most of liquid evaporates. Stir in flour, salt, and pepper. Add cream cheese, Worcestershire sauce, and soy sauce. Heat and stir until cheese is melted. Stir in sour cream and crumbled bacon. Heat through; do not boil. Makes 2½ cups. Serve with rye bread rounds or crackers.

NACHOS

Millie Finch

Tortilla chips or potato chips
Cheddar cheese or any sharp
cheese

Put chips on jelly roll pan. Grate cheese; sprinkle over chips. Bake at 350° until cheese melts.

SPICED NUTS

Millie Finch

1 egg white, slightly beaten
1 tsp. water
1 (8 oz.) jar dry roasted peanuts
½ c. whole almonds
½ c. walnut halves

¾ c. sugar
1 Tbsp. apple or pumpkin pie
spice mix
½ tsp. salt

Combine egg white with water; beat well. *Do not* let whites thicken much. Add all nuts; coat well. Combine sugar, spice, and salt; add to nuts. Coat well again. Place nuts on lightly greased cookie sheet. Bake at 300° for 20 to 25 minutes. Cool on waxed paper; break into small pieces. Serve.

SUGARED PECANS

Mary Kostyun

⅓ c. butter or margarine
¼ c. sugar
½ tsp. cinnamon

¼ tsp. ginger
¼ tsp. nutmeg
1 lb. pecan halves

In a small saucepan, melt butter; stir in sugar and spices. Mix well. Pour over pecans in a large roasting pan; mix well to coat. Bake at 275° for 1 hour, stirring several times during baking. Cool. Store in a tightly covered container.

PARMESAN TWISTS

Millie Finch

¼ c. butter or margarine
1 c. grated Parmesan cheese
½ c. sour cream
1 c. flour
½ tsp. Italian salad dressing
mix (dry)

1 egg yolk
1 Tbsp. water
Caraway seeds
Sesame seeds
Poppy seeds

Cream butter; add cheese. Beat until light and fluffy. Add sour cream; beat. Add flour and Italian salad dressing mix; blend. Roll out dough on lightly floured board to form a 12x7 inch rectangle; cut into 28 (6 x ½ inch) strips. Beat egg yolk with 1 tablespoon of water; brush on cut strips. Sprinkle with any one of the seeds. Twist each strip 2 or 3 times; place on buttered cookie sheet. Bake at 350° for 12 to 15 minutes or until golden. Repeat with remaining half of dough. Makes 56. Good on a party tray served with cheeses, cold cuts, etc.

BURRO'S AND LEVINE'S MINIATURE
PIZZAS
Mary Ann Klish

Party rye bread
Tomato paste
Salami, sliced thin

Mozzarella cheese, sliced
Oregano

Spread each slice of bread with tomato paste; top with slice of salami and slice of Mozzarella cheese. Sprinkle with oregano. Refrigerate or freeze until ready to serve. Before serving, place under broiler until cheese melts and begins to turn brown.

PIZZA TURNOVERS
Helen Rucky

⅓ c. chopped mushrooms
¼ c. chopped green pepper
¼ c. chopped onion
2 Tbsp. oleo
1 (6 oz.) can tomato paste
¼ c. water
1 tsp. oregano

½ tsp. salt
¼ tsp. garlic powder
1 c. (4 oz.) shredded Mozzarella
cheese
Pastry for 2 double crust 9 inch
pies

In skillet, saute mushrooms, green peppers, and onion in oleo. Stir in tomato paste, water, and seasonings; simmer 15 minutes. Stir in cheese. Remove from heat. On lightly floured surface, roll pastry ⅛ inch thick. Cut into 3½ inch rounds. Spoon 1 teaspoon mixture in center of each round. Fold in half; seal edges. Bake on greased tins at 450° for 10 to 15 minutes. Makes about 3 dozen.

OVEN SEAFOOD SPREAD
Marion Kaspryk

12 oz. cream cheese, softened
⅓ c. minced green pepper
⅓ c. chopped green onion
2 Tbsp. lemon juice
½ tsp. Worcestershire sauce
½ tsp. salt

Dash of garlic powder
1 (6 oz.) can crabmeat, drained
1 (4½ oz.) can small shrimp,
drained and rinsed
1 (6½ oz.) can minced clams,
drained

In medium bowl, blend cream cheese, green pepper, onion, lemon juice, Worcestershire sauce, salt, and garlic powder. Stir in crab, shrimp, and clams. Turn mixture into a 1 quart ovenproof serving dish. Bake at 350° for 30 minutes or until bubbly around edges. Serve with assorted crackers.

SHRIMP CHEESE BALL

Marie Pufky

1 (8 oz.) pkg. cream cheese
½ tsp. prepared mustard
1 tsp. grated onion and juice
1 tsp. lemon juice

Dash of salt and pepper
1 (4½ oz.) can small shrimp,
  drained
Chopped nuts

Combine all ingredients; blend. Form into a ball. Roll in chopped nuts. Chill several hours before serving.

SHRIMP COCKTAIL SPREAD

Anna Smyk

1 (8 oz.) pkg. cream cheese

2 (4 oz.) jars shrimp cocktail

Place cream cheese on serving dish. Pour shrimp cocktail over cheese. Do not mix. Serve with crackers.

DIP FOR SHRIMP

Evelyn Kanazawich

1 lb. cottage cheese
1 pt. sour cream
Dill mix or crushed dill

Pimiento, chopped
Garlic salt
Salt and pepper

Beat cheese and sour cream with electric mixer. Add remaining ingredients to taste; continue beating until well blended. Let stand in refrigerator at least ½ hour before serving.

SHRIMP DIP I

Jane Ellsworth

1 (8 oz.) pkg. cream cheese
1 (12 oz.) bottle cocktail sauce

Prepared horseradish to taste
1 (4½ oz.) can shrimp, drained

Place cream cheese, which has been warmed to room temperature, in a serving bowl. Mix together cocktail sauce and horseradish; add shrimp. Pour over cream cheese. Serve with crackers.

PINK SHRIMP DIP II

Mary Kostyun

3 (3 oz.) pkg. cream cheese
1 lb. cooked shrimp, cut fine
3 Tbsp. chili sauce

½ tsp. prepared mustard
2 tsp. lemon juice
¼ tsp. Worcestershire sauce

Soften cheese with fork. Add shrimp; blend. Add remaining ingredients; blend thoroughly. If too stiff, add milk. Use as a dip for chips or crackers.

SHRIMP DIP III

Helen Zellers

1 (8 oz.) pkg. cream cheese
⅔ c. catsup
1 Tbsp. (heaping) chopped
  onion
1 tsp. (heaping) prepared
  horseradish

Dash of Worcestershire sauce
Dash of pepper
2 (4½ oz.) cans shrimp

Place all ingredients in a medium size bowl; beat until creamy. Serve with Ritz crackers.

SHRIMP DIP IV

Marion Kaspryk

3 oz. cream cheese
1 c. sour cream
2 tsp. lemon juice
1 env. Italian salad dressing
  mix

2 Tbsp. chopped green pepper
½ c. chopped shrimp

Beat room temperature cream cheese. Add remaining ingredients; blend. Use as a dip for potato chips or crackers.

SNACK CRACKERS

Shirley Buchma
Dorothy Skellett

2 pkg. Hidden Valley Ranch
  dressing mix
1 Tbsp. dill weed

1 Tbsp. garlic powder
1½ c. salad oil
2 (12 oz.) bags oyster crackers

Combine dressing mix, dill weed, garlic powder, and salad oil. Pour over crackers in a shallow baking pan. Bake at 325° for 45 minutes, stirring every 15 minutes.

SNOWBALL PATE

Anna Smyk

2 (8 oz.) pkg. liver sausage
¼ c. lemon juice
¼ c. mayonnaise
4 tsp. grated onion

2 (3 oz.) pkg. cream cheese
Milk
Pimiento

Combine liver sausage, lemon juice, mayonnaise, and grated onion; form into ball. Refrigerate until firm. Combine cream cheese with enough milk to make spreading consistency. Frost chilled ball; garnish with pimiento. Serve with crackers.

SPINACH BALLS

Helen Rucky

2 boxes chopped spinach, cooked and drained (do not squeeze)
1 c. onion, minced
½ c. grated Romano cheese

2 c. Pepperidge Farm herb cubes
2 eggs, beaten
Dash of garlic powder
Dash of pepper

Mix all ingredients; form into about 40 balls. Place on greased cookie sheet and bake at 325° for 20 minutes.

CHEESY SPINACH BAKE

Helen Rucky

2 pkg. chopped spinach, drained
4 eggs, beaten
1 c. milk

1 c. shredded Swiss cheese
1 c. cubed, firm white bread
½ c. sliced green onion
¼ c. grated Parmesan cheese

Combine all ingredients; pour into 1 quart baking dish. Cover and bake at 375° for 25 to 30 minutes. Yields 6 servings.

SPINACH DIP I

Carol Walling

1 (10 oz.) box frozen chopped spinach
⅓ c. chopped scallions
½ tsp. dill weed
2 tsp. lemon juice

1 tsp. Salad Supreme
1 c. sour cream
1 c. mayonnaise
1 tsp. oregano
1 loaf unsliced rye bread

Thaw spinach; drain thoroughly by squeezing out the water. Combine remaining ingredients; mix thoroughly. Refrigerate overnight to develop flavor. Hollow out bread; cut or tear into pieces. Pour dip into bread shell; surround with bread pieces.

SPINACH DIP II

Linda Zapach

10 oz. chopped spinach, cooked and drained
2 c. sour cream
1 c. mayonnaise

1 pkg. dry onion or leek soup
1 tsp. Good Seasons Italian dressing (powder)

Combine and serve in hollowed out red cabbage head.

TACO DIP I
Jane Ellsworth

1 pt. sour cream
1 (8 oz.) pkg. cream cheese
1 pkg. taco seasoning

Grated cheese
Tomato, cut into small pieces
Tortilla chips

Combine sour cream, cream cheese, and taco seasoning. Place mixture on a flat dish with a ridge. Top with grated cheese and tomato pieces. Surround with chips.

TACO DIP II
Pam Scannell

8 oz. cream cheese, softened
1 c. sour cream
1 packet taco seasoning
1 (8 oz.) jar picante sauce

Diced tomato
Shredded lettuce
Shredded cheese

Combine cream cheese, sour cream, and taco seasoning in a medium bowl. Blend together and spread in a shallow dish. Refrigerate 1 hour. Cover with picante sauce, tomato, lettuce, and cheese. Serve with nachos.

MEAT FILLED TEROPITAS
Anna Smyk

1 small onion, finely chopped
1 Tbsp. olive oil
¾ lb. lean ground chuck
¼ lb. lean ground pork
¼ c. dry red wine
2 Tbsp. tomato sauce

¼ c. water
1 egg, slightly beaten
½ c. Parmesan cheese, grated
2 Tbsp. grated toast
1 lb. filo dough
1 lb. butter, melted

Saute onion in oil. Add meat; brown well. Drain fat. Combine liquids; add to meat. Cover; simmer 30 minutes. Remove from heat; add egg, cheese, and toast. Blend well; cool. Cut dough into long strips. Place one tablespoonful of filling in one corner; fold like you would a flag, corner to corner to make a triangle. Place on a greased cookie sheet. Bake for 35 minutes at 325° until light brown. Remove from pan immediately. Serve hot.

TUNA FISH TREE
Chuck Sarnoski

2 (6 or 7 oz.) cans water packed
 tuna, drained
1 (8 oz.) pkg. cream cheese
2 Tbsp. minced onion
2 Tbsp. chopped green olives

Salt and pepper to taste
Dash of Tabasco sauce
Parsley flakes
Chopped pimento

Blend all ingredients except parsley and pimento. On a tray or flat platter, form into a Christmas tree shape. Sprinkle with parsley; dot with pieces of pimento. Serve with crackers placed around bottom of tree.

FRESH VEGETABLE DIP
Linda Zapach

1 c. sour cream
1 c. mayonnaise
1½ to 2 tsp. dill weed

1 tsp. green onion flakes
1 Tbsp. + 1 tsp. parsley flakes

Combine ingredients; allow to stand in refrigerator overnight. Serve with fresh veggies: Carrots, celery, sliced cucumbers, cauliflower, broccoli, radishes.

YOGURT MINT DIP
Anna Smyk

2 c. plain yogurt
2 Tbsp. finely chopped fresh
    mint or 2 tsp. dried mint

¼ c. orange juice concentrate
2 Tbsp. honey

Combine all ingredients; cover. Chill. When ready to serve, place bowl of dip on crushed ice surrounded by bite size pieces of fresh fruit as dippers. Fruits which make excellent dippers are honeydew melon, strawberries, and pineapple.

ZUCCHINI BAKE
Mary Mihalko

3 c. finely grated zucchini,
    drained
1 c. Bisquick
½ c. vegetable oil
1 clove garlic, minced
½ c. finely chopped onion
4 eggs, slightly beaten

½ tsp. salt
½ tsp. seasoned salt
½ tsp. oregano
2 Tbsp. chopped parsley
½ c. grated Parmesan cheese
½ c. grated sharp cheese
Dash of pepper

Combine all ingredients in a mixing bowl; mix thoroughly. Turn into a greased 9x13 inch pan. Bake at 350° for 25 to 35 minutes until golden brown.

O'S ZUCCHINI PUFFS
Dorothy Skellet

2 c. flour
3 tsp. baking powder
½ c. grated Parmesan cheese
2½ c. grated zucchini

3 eggs, beaten
Garlic powder to taste
Parsley flakes to taste
Basil to taste

Combine flour, baking powder, and cheese; add zucchini. Mix until zucchini is coated. Add seasonings and eggs; mix thoroughly. Drop by teaspoon into hot fat; fry until golden.

APRICOT BRANDY

Millie Finch

1 lb. dried apricots
½ lb. white rock candy

1 fifth vodka

Put all ingredients in a widemouth jar; seal tightly. Place in a cool, dry place for 6 weeks. The apricots will become small chunks. Pour over chipped ice in small cocktail glasses.

BANANA SHAKE

Marie Richardson

2 bananas
8 ice cubes

1 c. water or skim milk
1 to 2 tsp. vanilla

Process ingredients in blender; pour into glasses. Serve.

BANANA SLUSH

Mary Mihalko

3 c. water
1 c. sugar
2 ripe bananas, sliced
2 Tbsp. lemon juice
3 c. unsweetened pineapple
   juice

1 (6 oz.) can frozen orange juice
1 (6 oz.) frozen lemonade
1½ to 2 c. vodka
Club soda

In a saucepan, combine water and sugar; boil 3 minutes. Cool. In blender, combine bananas and 1½ cups pineapple juice; blend. Stir into cooled syrup. Add remaining ingredients except club soda. Put in freezer container; freeze. Serve as slush or fill glass ¾ full and fill with club soda.

BASIC HEALTH DRINK

Helen Kaspryk

1 medium carrot
1 stalk celery (with leaves)
1 slice green pepper

1 cabbage leaf
1½ c. pineapple juice
1 c. crushed ice

Cut carrot and celery into ½ inch pieces. Put all ingredients, except ice, in blender; blend to a smooth liquid. Add crushed ice; blend a few seconds to chill mixture thoroughly. Makes 2½ cups.

IRISH CREAM LIQUEUR

Marsha Finch Smith

6 eggs
1 (13 oz.) can evaporated milk
1 (14 oz.) sweetened condensed
 milk
1 Tbsp. instant coffee
1 tsp. vanilla
1½ c. Irish whiskey

Put all ingredients in a blender; process until thoroughly blended. Refrigerate.

KAHLUA

Millie Finch

4 c. granulated sugar
1 (2 oz.) jar instant coffee
2 c. boiling water
1 vanilla bean
1 fifth vodka

Combine sugar, coffee, and boiling water; stir until sugar and coffee are dissolved. Add vanilla bean which has been split down the middle with a sharp knife. Add vodka; mix well. Pour into a ½ gallon wine bottle; cap tightly. Set aside for 4 weeks in a cool, dry place. *Do not* open cap during the 4 week period.

Kahlua is delicious dribbled over ice cream. It can replace vanilla or other flavorings in cookies and cakes.

ORANGE JULIUS

Mary Mihalko

1 c. milk
½ c. sugar
1 tsp. vanilla
½ c. water
⅓ c. orange juice concentrate
Tray of ice cubes

Combine all ingredients in blender. Blend on high speed until ice is fine.

POPULAR DRINK

Millie Finch

3 jiggers Kahlua
½ c. milk
6 ice cubes

Put all ingredients in a blender; whip until ice cubes don't crunch. Serves 2.

PUNCH

Mary Mihalko

2 (46 oz.) cans Hawaiian Punch
1 (46 oz.) can orange juice
2 c. ginger ale
2 (16 oz.) pkg. frozen, sliced
 strawberries, thawed

Make an ice ring from one can of Hawaiian Punch. Mix the juices in a punch bowl; add ginger ale, strawberries, and ice ring. Serve.

For an alcoholic punch, add 1 quart gin.

CATAWBA FROZEN FRUIT PUNCH   Mary Mihalko

1 (6 oz.) can frozen orange juice
1 (6 oz.) can frozen pineapple
  juice
1 (6 oz.) can frozen grapefruit
  juice

3 (6 oz.) cans frozen lemonade
1 qt. 7-Up or ginger ale
1 pt. pink Catawba*
1 qt. 3-flavor sherbet

In a punch bowl, mix all juices as directed on each can; add remaining ingredients.

* For a non-alcoholic punch, substitute Hawaiian Punch for the Catawba.

DELICIOUS PUNCH   Marion Kaspryk

1 qt. cranberry drink
1 qt. pineapple juice

1½ c. sugar
2 qt. ginger ale

Combine juices and sugar; stir to dissolve sugar. Chill. Pour over ice; add ginger ale. Serve.

ELEGANT CHAMPAGNE PUNCH   Evelyn Kanazawich

12 bottles cognac
1 bottle rum (light or dark)
1 doz. oranges, quartered
1½ doz. lemons, quartered
1 qt. maraschino cherries

Rind of 1 cucumber
36 bottles Brut champagne or
  extra dry
Ice

Empty bottles of cognac and rum into a large crock. Add oranges and lemons; add cherries as well as the juice. Add cucumber rind. Cover crock; set aside for 4 or 5 days. Stir at least once each day. Strain contents of crock through a cheesecloth. Press all the juice from the fruit. Put the juice in bottles.

To serve, pour a bottle of the chilled juice (brandy) over a large cake of ice in a punch bowl. Add 3 bottles chilled champagne. Stir gently. Keep in mind, this punch is not as mild as the first taste leads you to believe. Serves 200.

7-UP PROMENADE PUNCH   Marion Kaspryk

2 qt. apple juice
1 qt. cranberry juice cocktail

2 c. orange juice
2 (28 oz.) bottles 7-Up

Chill ingredients thoroughly. At serving time, combine fruit juices in a punch bowl. Slowly add 7-Up. Makes about 40 (4 ounce) servings.

BRANDY SLUSH

Pauline Klym

1 pt. apricot brandy
9½ c. water
1 (6 oz.) can frozen orange or
   pineapple juice

1 (6 oz.) can frozen lemonade
2 c. sugar
1 medium jar maraschino
   cherries, drained, cut

Combine all ingredients; mix well. Place in a large container. Freeze for 2 days, stirring every once in a while. When you want to serve, put a portion in a punch bowl and add 7-Up or ginger ale, adding more of the slush as needed.

WHISKEY SLUSH

Mary Mihalko

2 c. hot water
3 tea bags
1 (12 oz.) can frozen orange
   juice

1 (12 oz.) can frozen lemonade
1 c. sugar
7 c. water
2½ to 3 c. whiskey or vodka

Combine all ingredients in a large container; put in freezer. Stir after 12 hours and again after 24 hours. To serve, fill glass ½ full with slush; add 7-Up or ginger ale until full or just pour slush over ice.

SPARKLING BURGUNDY BOWL

Helen Charnetsky

1 (46 oz.) can Hi-C wildberry
   drink
2 (10 oz.) pkg. frozen
   raspberries
¼ c. lemon juice

½ c. sugar
⅛ tsp. salt
2 or 3 bottles Andre sparkling
   burgundy

Combine first 5 ingredients in punch bowl; stir until sugar is dissolved and raspberries are slightly thawed. Add ice ring. Pour sparkling burgundy into bowl. Serve. Serves 40.

FRIENDSHIP TEA

Helen Chubinsky
Mary Kostyun, Nancy Tarcha

2 c. orange flavored Tang
½ c. instant tea
2 (3 oz.) pkg. lemonade mix

2 c. sugar
1 tsp. cloves
1 tsp. cinnamon

Combine all ingredients; mix well. Store in jar. Use 2 teaspoons of mixture per 1 cup hot or cold water.

Variation: Use ½ teaspoon each of cloves, cinnamon, and allspice in place of 1 teaspoon each of cinnamon and cloves.

MY SISTER'S UKRAINIAN TEA

Pani Lawryk

2 c. Tang
½ c. Lipton iced tea mix (100% tea)

½ c. Wyler's or Country Time lemonade mix
2 tsp. cinnamon

Pour all ingredients into a clean quart jar. Cover. Shake to mix. Place 2 heaping teaspoons of mix into a pretty cup. Add hot water; mix and savour the moment!

Also may be enjoyed cold. Use cold water; mix well. Add ice cubes and a sprig of mint or slice of lemon for garnish.

WALTER'S CHRISTMAS SOCK

Evelyn Kanazawich

2 Tbsp. unsalted butter
2 Tbsp. honey

½ liter vodka

Melt butter in saucepan; add honey. Cook on low heat 2 minutes. Add vodka; heat. Serve hot.

WASSAIL

Marsha Finch Smith

2 qt. cider
1 c. orange juice
½ c. lemon juice
¾ c. sugar

¼ tsp. nutmeg
3 sticks cinnamon
1 tsp. whole allspice
½ tsp. whole cloves

In a pot, combine cider, orange juice, lemon juice, sugar, and nutmeg. Place cinnamon sticks, whole allspice, and cloves in cheesecloth; add to pot. Bring to a boil; reduce heat. Simmer for 2 hours. Remove spice bag; serve hot.

Variation: A shot of brandy may be added to each serving.

BREADS

Quick

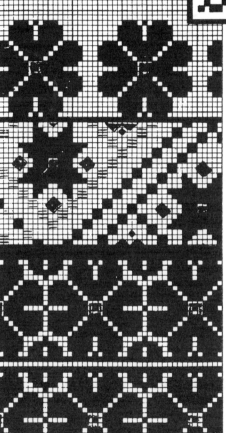

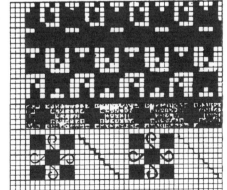

BREADS, QUICK

BASIC QUICK BISCUIT MIX
Anna Smyk

8 c. sifted flour
2 tsp. salt
3 Tbsp. plus 1 tsp. baking
powder

1 c. dry milk
1¾ c. shortening

Sift dry ingredients 3 times. Cut in shortening until mixture resembles coarse cornmeal. Store in an airtight container in a cool place. Can be used in place of Bisquick.

BISCUITS
Sophie Pufky

2 c. flour
3 tsp. baking powder
3 Tbsp. sugar
¾ tsp. salt

½ c. lard or Crisco
1 egg, beaten
⅓ c. milk

Combine flour, baking powder, sugar, and salt. Cut in lard with pastry blender. Combine egg and milk; add to flour mixture. Mix with fork to form a ball. Roll out on lightly floured surface; cut biscuits using biscuit cutter. Bake at 350° on ungreased cookie sheet for about 30 minutes.

Note: To make drop biscuits or muffins, add more milk.

OLGA'S BLUEBERRY RING
Anna Chyl

4 c. biscuit mix
1⅓ c. milk
1 (16 oz.) can blueberries or 15
oz. frozen, defrosted
½ c. butter
¾ c. dry bread crumbs
½ c. coarsely chopped nuts

¼ c. sugar
½ tsp. cinnamon
1 tsp. grated orange rind
Dash of Augostini bitters
1 c. confectioners sugar
2 Tbsp. orange juice

Combine biscuit mix and milk. Prepare dough according to package directions for rolled biscuits. Knead several times on lightly floured board. Roll out to a 10x14 inch rectangle. Drain blueberries. Reserve a small amount of berries for garnish. Melt butter in saucepan; stir in bread crumbs, nuts, sugar, cinnamon, orange rind, and bitters. Cook until lightly browned. Gently stir in blueberries.

Spread blueberry mixture evenly over dough. Roll up like jelly roll, starting at wide end. Shape into ring joining edges. (This is a tricky part - I put my greased 6 quart ring mold over the ring and invert with board.) Bake at 375° for 30 to 35 minutes or until golden brown. Turn out of pan onto serving plate while hot. Combine confectioners sugar and orange juice; beat until smooth. Spread over top of warm ring to glaze. Garnish with reserved berries. Serve warm.

APRICOT PRUNE BREAD   Margaret Klish

1½ c. sugar	1 tsp. salt
½ c. shortening	2 c. milk
4 eggs	½ c. chopped nuts
4 c. sifted flour	1 c. chopped, dried prunes
2 Tbsp. baking powder	1 c. chopped, dried apricots

Cream together sugar and shortening. Add eggs; beat until light. Sift together flour, baking powder, and salt; add to creamed mixture alternately with milk, beating after each addition. Stir in apricots, prunes, and nuts. Bake in two greased and floured 9x5x3 inch loaf pans at 350° for 60 to 65 minutes or until bread tests done. Cool 10 minutes; remove to wire rack to finish cooling. Store overnight before slicing.

A HONEY OF A BLUEBERRY BREAD   Josephine Vimislik

3 c. sifted flour	½ c. water
1 tsp. baking powder	1 Tbsp. instant coffee
½ tsp. baking soda	Grated rind of 1 lemon
1 tsp. salt	½ c. chopped nuts
1 c. sugar	2 c. frozen dry-pack
⅓ c. shortening	blueberries, or 1½ c. well
2 eggs, beaten	drained canned blueberries,
⅓ c. honey	or 2 c. fresh blueberries

Combine first 5 ingredients. Cut in shortening until like coarse cornmeal. Mix eggs, honey, water, coffee, and lemon rind to dry ingredients all at once; stir until just blended. Fold in nuts and blueberries. Pour into a well greased 9x5x3 inch loaf pan. Bake at 350° for 55 to 65 minutes. Can be served with butter or cream cheese.

BARB'S BLUEBERRY BREAD   Dorothy Skellett

3 c. flour	4 eggs
2 tsp. baking powder	½ c. milk
1 tsp. baking soda	1½ tsp. lemon juice
½ tsp. salt	1 c. crushed pineapple
⅔ c. shortening	2 c. blueberries
1⅓ c. sugar	1 c. chopped nuts

Sift together flour, baking powder, baking soda, and salt; set aside. In a large bowl, cream shortening and sugar. Add eggs, milk, and lemon juice; beat. Add crushed pineapple; stir. Add dry ingredients; mix until blended. Fold in blueberries and nuts. Pour into 2 (13 x 9½ x 2½ inch) or 3 (5½ x 9 x 2 inch) greased and floured pans. Bake at 350° for 40 to 45 minutes.

BROWN BREAD
Audrey Klym

1½ c. maple syrup
2 c. buttermilk
½ c. molasses
2 c. white flour
1 tsp. baking soda

1 tsp. baking powder
1 tsp. salt
2½ to 3 c. graham flour
Raisins (optional)

Combine maple syrup, buttermilk, and molasses. Sift together white flour, baking soda, baking powder, and salt; add to previous mixture. Blend. Add graham flour; mix thoroughly. Spoon batter into a greased 9x5x3 inch loaf pan. Bake at 350° for 1 hour.

CHERRY APPLE NUT BREAD
Genevieve Sadowitz

⅓ c. butter or margarine,
    softened
⅔ c. sugar
2 eggs
1 c. applesauce
¼ c. milk
2 c. flour

1 tsp. baking powder
½ tsp. baking soda
½ tsp. salt
1 Tbsp. grated lemon rind
⅔ c. chopped nuts
⅓ c. maraschino cherries,
    chopped

Cream butter and sugar. Add eggs, one at a time, beating thoroughly after each. Add remaining ingredients except nuts and cherries; mix only until blended. Stir in nuts and cherries. Pour into greased 9x5x3 inch loaf pan. Bake at 350° for 1 hour or until done.

DATE BREAD
Eugenia Skarvinko

½ lb. dates, chopped
1 tsp. baking soda
1 c. boiling water
¾ c. sugar
1 egg, beaten

2 c. flour
1 tsp. baking powder
½ tsp. vanilla
½ c. chopped nuts

Combine dates and baking soda in large bowl; add boiling water. Stir to dissolve baking soda. Cool. Add sugar and egg; mix thoroughly. Sift together flour and baking powder; add to previous mixture. Stir to moisten all ingredients. Add vanilla and nuts; stir. Pour into a greased 9x5x3 inch loaf pan. Bake at 350° for 1 hour or until it tests done. When cool, wrap in plastic wrap at least 24 hours before serving.

IRISH SODA BREAD
Olga Gooley

4 c. sifted flour
¼ c. sugar
1 tsp. salt
1 tsp. baking powder
¼ c. margarine

2 c. raisins
1⅔ c. buttermilk
1 tsp. baking soda
1 egg, beaten

In a large bowl, combine flour, sugar, salt, and baking powder. Cut in margarine with pastry blender. Add raisins. Add baking soda to buttermilk. Make a well in dry ingredients; pour in buttermilk and egg. Mix with wooden spoon until all ingredients are moistened. Pour batter in 2 greased 9x5x3 inch pans. Bake at 350° for 45 to 50 minutes.

Note: The real Irish way to bake this bread is to bake it in a round iron skillet or pan.

MONKEY BREAD
Julieanne Rucky

1 c. sugar
2 Tbsp. cinnamon
1 tsp. nutmeg
4 pkg. buttermilk biscuits, cut
   in quarters

½ stick margarine
¾ c. brown sugar
2 tsp. cinnamon
½ c. chopped walnuts

In a bowl, combine 1 cup sugar, 2 tablespoons cinnamon, and 1 teaspoon nutmeg; mix thoroughly. Add quartered biscuits, spooning mixture over biscuits to coat. Arrange in a greased tube pan. Melt margarine; add brown sugar, 2 teaspoons cinnamon, and chopped walnuts. Mix thoroughly; pour over biscuits in tube pan. Bake at 350° for 30 minutes. To serve, pull biscuits from the bread ring.

FROSTED PEACH BREAD
Helen Rucky

½ c. margarine
½ c. sugar
½ c. firmly packed brown sugar
1 (16 oz.) can sliced peaches,
   chopped, save liquid
2 eggs
½ c. sour cream

½ tsp. vanilla
2½ c. flour
1 tsp. baking soda
½ tsp. salt
½ tsp. cinnamon
½ c. finely chopped almonds

In large bowl, cream margarine and sugars until light and fluffy. Add eggs, sour cream, peaches, and vanilla; mix well. Stir in flour, soda, salt, and cinnamon; blend well. Fold in almonds. Pour into greased 9x5 inch loaf pan. Bake at 350° for 60 to 70 minutes. Cool 10 minutes. Remove from pan. Cool completely.

Glaze:

½ c. confectioners sugar
1 Tbsp. reserved peach liquid

1 tsp. corn syrup
¼ tsp. cinnamon

In small bowl, combine glaze ingredients. Beat until smooth. Frost cooled loaf.

PEANUT BUTTER LOAF

Millie Finch

¾ c. peanut butter (smooth or
   chunky)
⅔ c. sugar
¼ c. melted Crisco
1 egg, beaten

1 c. milk
2 c. all-purpose flour
1 Tbsp. baking powder
1 tsp. salt

Combine peanut butter, sugar, Crisco, egg, and milk; beat until smooth. Combine flour, baking powder, and salt; add to peanut butter mixture. Beat on medium speed until blended. Spoon batter into greased 8½ x 4½ x 2¾ inch loaf pan. Let stand 15 minutes. Bake at 350° for 40 to 50 minutes. Cool slightly; remove from pan. Cool completely. Wrap and store in a cool place 24 hours. Delicious when served with peanut butter and jelly spread on a thin slice.

PEAR NUT BREAD

Marie Richardson

3 fresh pears
½ c. salad oil
1 c. sugar
2 eggs
¼ c. sour cream
1 tsp. vanilla
2 c. flour

½ tsp. salt
½ tsp. baking powder
½ tsp. baking soda
½ tsp. cinnamon
¼ tsp. nutmeg
¼ to ½ c. chopped walnuts

Pare and core pears; chop to make 1½ cups. In a large bowl, with electric mixer, beat together oil and sugar until well blended. Beat in eggs, one at a time. Add sour cream and vanilla; blend. Sift together flour, salt, baking powder, baking soda, cinnamon, and nutmeg; add to egg mixture. Beat until blended. Add pears and nuts; mix with wooden spoon. Spoon into a well greased 9x5x3 inch loaf pan. Bake at 350° for 1 hour or until done. Let cool in pan 15 minutes; turn out on cooling rack to finish cooling.

31

PUMPKIN BREAD I

Sue Blue

1 c. honey
1 c. brown sugar
1 c. vegetable oil
3 c. pumpkin
1 c. chopped dates
1 c. chopped walnuts
1 tsp. salt

1 tsp. cinnamon
1 tsp. cloves
4 tsp. baking soda
2 c. white flour
2½ c. wheat flour
½ c. wheat germ

Combine honey, brown sugar, oil, pumpkin, dates, walnuts, salt, cinnamon, cloves, and baking soda in a large bowl; mix well. Stir in remaining ingredients. Spoon batter into 3 well-oiled 8½ x 4½ inch loaf pans. Bake at 350° for 1 hour. Cool in pans 20 minutes before turning onto a rack to finish cooling.

PUMPKIN BREAD II

Tammy Chebiniak

1 c. butter flavored shortening
1 c. sugar
3 eggs
1 lb. solid pack pumpkin
1 tsp. vanilla
3 c. flour
1½ tsp. salt

1 tsp. baking soda
1 tsp. baking powder
1 tsp. cinnamon
1 tsp. cloves
½ tsp. nutmeg
1 c. chopped walnuts

Cream shortening and sugar until very soft and creamy; add eggs. Beat thoroughly. Add pumpkin and vanilla; beat. Sift together flour, salt, baking soda, baking powder, and spices; add sifted ingredients to pumpkin mixture. Blend. Stir in nuts. Pour into 2 greased 9x5 inch loaf pans. Bake at 350° for 45 minutes.

RHUBARB BREAD

Mary Mihalko
Helen Rucky

1½ c. brown sugar
1 c. buttermilk or sour milk*
⅔ c. oil
1 egg
1 tsp. vanilla
2½ c. flour
1 tsp. baking soda

1 tsp. salt
1½ to 2 c. chopped fresh
   rhubarb
½ c. chopped nuts
½ c. sugar
½ tsp. cinnamon
1 Tbsp. margarine, melted

Blend first 5 ingredients until smooth. Sift together flour, baking soda, and salt; add to egg mixture. Blend thoroughly. Stir in rhubarb and nuts. Pour into 2 greased and floured 8x4x3 inch pans. Combine sugar, cinnamon, and margarine to form a crumb mixture; sprinkle over batter. Bake at 325° for 60 minutes. Cool in pan 10 minutes before turning out on cooling racks.

* To sour milk, use 1 tablespoon vinegar and enough milk to equal one cup.

STRAWBERRY BREAD
Helen Rucky

1 (10 oz.) pkg. frozen
strawberries, thawed
¾ c. sugar
⅔ c. oil
2 eggs

1½ c. flour
1 tsp. baking soda
½ tsp. salt
½ tsp. cinnamon
¾ c. chopped nuts

In large bowl, combine strawberries, sugar, oil, and eggs; blend well. Add remaining ingredients; stir just until dry particles are moistened. Pour into greased 9x5 inch loaf pan. Bake at 350° for 50 to 60 minutes. Cool completely.

Glaze:

¾ c. confectioners sugar
1 Tbsp. milk

1 to 2 drops red food coloring

In small bowl, combine glaze ingredients; mix until smooth. Drizzle over cooled loaf.

WHITE NUT LOAF
Sue Blue

¾ c. sugar
2 Tbsp. shortening
1 egg
1½ c. milk

3 c. flour
3½ tsp. baking powder
1 tsp. salt
Nuts

In a large bowl, combine sugar and shortening; beat. Stir in milk. Sift flour, baking powder, and salt into previous mixture; mix until all ingredients are moistened. Add nuts; mix. Pour into a well greased 9½ x 5¼ x 2¾ inch loaf pan; let stand in pan 20 minutes before baking. Bake at 350° for 60 to 70 minutes.

ZUCCHINI BREAD I
Mary Ann Kocak
Eloise Maliwacki

3 eggs
1 c. vegetable oil
2 c. sugar
2 c. shredded zucchini
3 tsp. vanilla
3 c. flour
1 tsp. baking powder

1 tsp. baking soda
1 tsp. salt
3 tsp. cinnamon
1 tsp. cloves
1 c. chopped nuts
1 c. raisins

In a large bowl, beat eggs until foamy. Add oil and sugar; beat. Add zucchini and vanilla; mix. Sift together flour, baking powder, baking soda, salt, cinnamon, and cloves; add to egg mixture. Mix thoroughly. Stir in nuts and raisins. Spoon batter into a greased 9x5x3 inch loaf pan. Bake at 325° for 1 hour.

ZUCCHINI BREAD II
Cheryl Lewkowicz

3 eggs
1 c. oil
1 c. brown sugar
1 c. sugar
2 c. grated zucchini (raw and
  unpeeled)

2 c. flour
¼ tsp. baking powder
2 tsp. baking soda
1 tsp. salt
3 tsp. cinnamon
2 tsp. vanilla

Beat eggs. Add oil and sugar; beat. Mix in zucchini. Sift together dry ingredients; add to egg mixture. Stir in vanilla. Pour into 2 greased 8x4x3 inch loaf pans. Bake at 350° for 60 to 70 minutes or until toothpick inserted in center comes out clean.

ZUCCHINI BREAD III
Mary Buckingham

2 c. sugar
¾ c. oil
2 tsp. vanilla
3 eggs
2 c. flour
2 tsp. cinnamon

1 tsp. baking powder
1 tsp. baking soda
2 c. grated zucchini
1 c. chopped nuts, dates,
  prunes, or cherries (optional)

In a large bowl, combine sugar, oil, vanilla, and eggs; beat thoroughly. Sift together flour, cinnamon, baking powder, and baking soda; add to egg mixture alternately with zucchini. Add nuts; mix to combine. Turn into 3 small or 2 regular size greased and floured loaf pans. Bake at 350° for 45 to 50 minutes or until cake tester comes out clean when poked in center of loaf.

ZUCCHINI BREAD IV
Marion Kaspryk

3 c. flour
1 tsp. salt
1 tsp. baking powder
1 tsp. baking soda
1 Tbsp. cinnamon
3 eggs

1¾ c. sugar
1 c. vegetable oil
2 c. shredded zucchini
1 Tbsp. lemon rind
2 tsp. vanilla
½ c. coarsely chopped walnuts

Sift together flour, salt, baking powder, baking soda, and cinnamon; set aside. Beat eggs lightly in a large bowl; stir in sugar, oil, zucchini, lemon rind, and vanilla. Add flour mixture, blending thoroughly; stir in walnuts. Spoon batter into two well greased 8½ x 4½ x 2½ inch loaf pans. Bake at 350° for 50 minutes. Cool in pans or wire rack 10 minutes. Remove from pans; cool thoroughly.

Variation: Add 1 cup blueberries (fresh or frozen) or 1 cup chocolate chips and ½ cup coconut.

ZUCCHINI BREAD V
Tammy Chebiniak

3 c. flour
1 tsp. salt
1 tsp. cinnamon
1 tsp. baking soda
1 tsp. baking powder
2 eggs
1 c. sugar

1 c. oil
2 c. shredded zucchini
1 Tbsp. water (only if zucchini
  is dry)
½ tsp. vanilla
1 c. chopped walnuts

In a bowl, mix flour, salt, cinnamon, baking soda, and baking powder; set aside. In another bowl, beat eggs, sugar, oil, zucchini, water, and vanilla. Add flour mixture to egg mixture; mix until thoroughly combined. Add nuts; mix. Pour into 2 greased 9x5 inch loaf pans. Bake at 350° about 45 minutes.

1976 ZUCCHINI NUT BREAD
Josephine Vimislik

4 eggs
2 c. sugar
1 c. vegetable oil
3½ c. flour
1 tsp. salt
1½ tsp. baking soda

¾ tsp. baking powder
1 tsp. cinnamon
2 c. grated, unpeeled zucchini
1 c. chopped nuts
1 c. raisins
1½ tsp. vanilla

In a large bowl, beat eggs. Add sugar; beat. Add oil; beat. Sift together flour, salt, baking soda, baking powder, and cinnamon; add to egg mixture alternately with zucchini, mixing until thoroughly combined. Add nuts, raisins, and vanilla; mix. Spoon batter into 2 greased and floured 9x5x3 inch loaf pans. Bake at 350° for 55 minutes. Loaves may be iced with sugar-water glaze when cool.

CHERRY CREPES
Evelyn Kanazawich

1 c. sour cream
⅓ c. brown sugar
1 c. Bisquick
1 egg

1 c. milk
1 can cherry pie filling
½ to 1 tsp. orange extract

Blend sour cream and brown sugar; set aside. Beat Bisquick, egg, and milk with beater until smooth. Spoon 2 tablespoons batter into hot, lightly greased 6 to 7 inch skillet, rotating pan until batter covers bottom. Cook until bubbles appear; gently loosen edge. Turn and cook other side. Spoon 1 tablespoon sour cream mixture onto half of each crepe; roll up. Place crepes, seam side down, on ovenproof platter. Bake at 350° about 5 minutes. Heat pie filling in chafing dish until hot. Pour extract on pie filling. *Do not* stir; ignite immediately and spoon over crepes. Makes 12 to 15 crepes.

BAKED FRENCH DOUGHNUTS   Anna Chyl

5 Tbsp. margarine	¼ tsp. salt
½ c. sugar	¼ tsp. nutmeg
1 egg	½ c. milk
1½ c. flour	6 Tbsp. margarine, melted
2¼ tsp. baking powder	Sugar-cinnamon mixture

Cream margarine and sugar; add egg. Mix well. Sift dry ingredients; add alternately with milk, mixing after each addition. Fill greased muffin tins half full. Bake at 350° for 20 to 25 minutes. Take out of pan immediately. Roll in melted margarine, then in cinnamon mixture. Makes about 14 doughnuts.

PURPLE PLUM DOUGHNUTS   Millie Finch

2 c. diced fresh plums	½ tsp. nutmeg
4 egg yolks	½ tsp. cinnamon
¾ c. sugar	4 tsp. baking powder
1 tsp. grated orange rind	1 c. milk
3 c. sifted flour	Vegetable oil
¼ tsp. salt	

Beat egg yolks until thick and lemon colored. Add sugar and orange rind; beat. Sift together flour, salt, nutmeg, cinnamon, and baking powder; add to egg mixture alternately with milk. Fold in plums. Drop batter by tablespoon into deep oil heated to 375°. Fry until golden, turning once. Take out with slotted spoon; drain on absorbent paper. While hot, roll in a mixture of sugar and cinnamon. Makes about 4 dozen.

SOUR CREAM CRULLERS   Josephine Vimislik

1 c. sugar	1 tsp. baking soda
2 Tbsp. butter	½ tsp. salt
2 eggs, beaten	About 3½ c. flour
1 c. sour cream	

Cream together sugar and butter; add eggs. Dissolve baking soda in sour cream. Add flour and sour cream alternately to egg mixture. (Add salt to the first cup of flour.) Use just enough flour to make dough the right consistency for rolling. Roll dough on floured surface; cut with doughnut cutter. Fry in deep fat at 360° until brown on each side. Dust with powdered sugar.

SWEET CREAM DOUGHNUTS
Josephine Vimislik

3 eggs
½ pt. heavy cream
1 c. sugar
3½ c. sifted flour

3 tsp. baking powder
½ tsp. salt
½ tsp. nutmeg
Fat for frying

In a bowl, combine unbeaten eggs, heavy cream, and sugar. Gradually add flour, baking powder, salt, and nutmeg which have been sifted together; blend well. With a wooden spoon, beat until smooth. Dough will be quite soft. Divide dough in half; roll out on floured board to ½ inch thickness. Cut with doughnut cutter. Fry in deep fat at 360° for 3 to 4 minutes. Makes 3 dozen.

SWEET MILK DOUGHNUTS
Sophie Cox

3 Tbsp. butter
1 c. sugar
1 egg
3 to 4 c. flour

1 tsp. baking powder
½ tsp. salt
½ tsp. cinnamon or nutmeg
1 c. milk

Beat butter, sugar, and egg until light. Sift together 3 cups flour, baking powder, salt, and cinnamon; add alternately with milk. Add enough of the fourth cup of flour to make a soft dough. Roll out dough on floured surface to ⅜ inch thickness. Cut with doughnut cutter. Fry in deep fat at 375° until brown on each side. Drain on absorbent paper. If desired, glaze while warm.

POTATO DUMPLINGS
Anne Pufky

2 medium potatoes
1 tsp. salt

1 egg, beaten
2 c. flour

Grate potatoes; add salt, egg, and flour. If dough is too stiff, add a little water (¼ cup more or less). Drop small portions from tip of spoon into boiling water. Cook 7 to 10 minutes. Drain. Rinse with warm water. Serve with cottage cheese or cabbage (see below).

Cottage Cheese: Heat ¼ cup butter until golden brown. Pour over dumplings; mix. Crumble dry cottage cheese over buttered dumplings. Serve.

Cabbage: Cook a small, chopped onion in ¼ cup butter or bacon fat until lightly browned. Add finely chopped cabbage, salt, and paprika to taste. Cover pan. Cook about 20 minutes or until done. Add dumplings; mix well. Serve.

SUPER FRENCH TOAST

Pani Julia Lawryk

10 slices day-old French bread,
  cut 1 inch thick
6 eggs, well beaten
1½ c. half & half

1 tsp. vanilla
1 tsp. sugar
¼ tsp. salt
Butter for frying

Combine eggs, half & half, vanilla, sugar, and salt; pour over sliced bread arranged in a shallow dish or pan. Turn bread over to soak well; refrigerate overnight. Heat oven to 450°. Meanwhile, fry each slice in butter until golden; place fried slices on a baking sheet. Bake 5 to 7 minutes or until puffed and brown. Serves 5.

HUSH PUPPIES

Patricia Hoover

2 c. corn meal
1 Tbsp. flour
½ tsp. baking soda
1 tsp. baking powder

1 tsp. salt
1 c. buttermilk
1 egg, beaten
3 Tbsp. chopped onion

Mix dry ingredients. Add remaining ingredients; mix. Drop by tablespoon in deep hot fat at 370°. Brown on both sides; drain on paper towels. Serve hot. Makes 36 pups. Good served with fish dishes.

JOHNNY CAKE

Marie Brink

1 c. sour milk
1 c. sweet milk
½ tsp. baking soda
1 egg, beaten

2 Tbsp. sugar*
2 Tbsp. butter
1½ c. cornmeal

Combine sour and sweet milk in a large bowl. Add baking soda; stir to dissolve. Add egg, sugar, and butter; beat. Stir in cornmeal. Pour into a greased 9 inch square pan. Bake at 350° for 30 to 45 minutes.

* More sugar may be added for a sweeter bread.

BLUEBERRY MUFFINS I

Helen Charnetsky

1 c. blueberries (fresh or
  frozen)
2 to 3 Tbsp. sugar
2 c. flour
1 tsp. salt
3 tsp. baking powder

2 Tbsp. sugar
1 egg
1 c. milk
6 Tbsp. salad oil
Granulated sugar

Sweeten berries with 2 to 3 tablespoons sugar. Do not thaw frozen berries. In a large bowl, sift flour, salt, baking powder, and 2 tablespoons sugar; set aside. In a small bowl, beat egg; add milk and salad oil. Beat. Make well in flour mixture; pour in egg mixture. Mix until dry ingredients are moistened, but still lumpy. Fill paper lined muffin cups ¾ full. Put about 6 blueberries in each muffin; sprinkle with sugar. Bake at 425° for 25 minutes or until light brown. Serve hot with butter. Makes 14 (2½ inch) muffins.

BLUEBERRY MUFFINS II
Sophia Pufky

3 c. flour
2 tsp. baking powder
1 tsp. salt
1 c. Crisco
1¼ c. sugar

3 eggs
1 tsp. vanilla
1 c. milk
2 c. blueberries

Mix 1 cup flour to coat blueberries. Sift together flour, baking powder, and salt; set aside. Cream together Crisco and sugar; add eggs, one at a time, beating thoroughly after each. Add vanilla; blend. Add flour mixture alternately with milk, blending after each addition. Fold in blueberries. Fill paper lined muffin pans ¾ full. Bake at 350° for 30 minutes.

BLUEBERRY MUFFINS III
Marion Kaspryk

2 c. flour
2 tsp. baking powder
½ tsp. salt
½ c. margarine
1¼ c. sugar

2 eggs
1 tsp. vanilla
½ c. milk
2 c. blueberries
2 tsp. sugar

Sift together flour, baking powder, and salt; set aside. In a large bowl, cream margarine and sugar. Add eggs; beat. Add vanilla; blend. Add dry ingredients alternately with milk. Stir in blueberries. Fill paper lined muffin pans ¾ full; sprinkle with sugar. Bake at 375° for 25 to 30 minutes.

BRAN MUFFINS
Eugenia Skarvinko

1 c. All-Bran
½ c. milk
¾ c. honey
1 egg

¼ c. vegetable oil
1¼ c. sifted flour
3 tsp. baking powder
¼ c. raisins

Place All-Bran and milk in a medium bowl; stir to combine. Let stand 1 to 2 minutes. Add honey, egg, and oil; beat well. Add flour and baking powder; stir just until combined. Fold in raisins. Portion evenly into 12 greased muffin cups. Bake at 400° for 25 minutes or until golden brown.

BANANA OAT BRAN MUFFINS

Marion Kaspryk

1 egg
¾ c. brown sugar
1⅓ c. mashed ripe bananas
⅓ c. vegetable oil
1 tsp. vanilla
1½ c. flour

½ c. oat bran
2 tsp. baking powder
½ tsp. baking soda
¼ tsp. salt
1¼ tsp. cinnamon

Beat egg and sugar until smooth. Beat in bananas, oil, and vanilla; let stand 1 minute. Combine flour, oat bran, baking powder, baking soda, salt, and cinnamon in a large bowl. Add banana mixture; mix just until dry ingredients are moistened. Fill paper lined muffin cups. Bake at 375° for 20 to 25 minutes. Makes 12 to 14 muffins.

RAISIN BRAN MUFFINS

1 (15 oz.) box Raisin Bran
3 c. sugar
5 c. flour
5 tsp. soda

2 tsp. salt
1 c. melted margarine
4 eggs, beaten
1 qt. buttermilk

Combine dry ingredients in a large bowl. In another bowl, combine liquid ingredients. Add liquid ingredients to dry ingredients; mix. Batter may be kept in refrigerator 6 weeks. Bake at 350° for 25 minutes.

SOURDOUGH MUFFINS

Audrey Klym
Anne Pufky

4 c. Kellogg's All-Bran*
2 c. Nabisco 100% Bran Buds*
2 c. boiling water
1 c. shortening
2½ c. sugar

4 eggs
5 c. flour
5 tsp. baking soda
1 tsp. salt
1 qt. buttermilk

In a 5 quart bowl, place All-Bran and Bran Buds. Add boiling water; stir and set aside. Cream shortening and sugar; add eggs. Beat. Sift together flour, baking soda, and salt; add to creamed mixture alternately with buttermilk. Mix thoroughly. Add to bran mixture, stirring until blended. Fill paper lined muffin cups ¾ full. Bake at 400° for 15 to 20 minutes.

Note: Batter may be stored up to 2 weeks in refrigerator in a covered container. Bake only as many muffins as you need. You can have fresh muffins every day.

* A 15 ounce box of Raisin Bran may be substituted for All-Bran and Bran Buds.

MUFFINS THAT TASTE LIKE DONUTS — Marion Kaspryk

1¾ c. flour
1½ tsp. baking powder
½ tsp. salt
½ tsp. nutmeg
¼ tsp. cinnamon

⅓ c. vegetable oil
¾ c. sugar
1 egg
¾ c. milk
Cinnamon-sugar

In a bowl, combine flour, baking powder, salt, nutmeg, and cinnamon. In another bowl, thoroughly combine oil, sugar, egg, and milk. Add liquid ingredients to dry; stir only to combine. Spoon batter in paper lined muffin cups. Bake at 350° for 20 to 25 minutes. While muffins are hot, dip in melted butter, then in cinnamon-sugar mixture. Makes 12 muffins.

Cinnamon-Sugar: In a shallow bowl, combine ¼ cup sugar with ½ teaspoon cinnamon.

PRUNE-RAISIN-NUT FILLED ROLLS — Annie Schlatz

Filling (make first):

1 c. raisins, cut in halves
2 c. chopped prunes
1 c. chopped nuts
⅓ c. sugar

⅓ c. butter
⅓ c. finely chopped orange
peel* or 1 Tbsp. grated
orange rind

Put raisins in saucepan with a small amount of water; bring to a boil. Cover. Let stand about 5 minutes. Add remaining ingredients; bring to a boil. Remove from heat. Cool.

Dough:

5 eggs
⅔ c. Wesson or Crisco oil
¾ c. sugar
½ tsp. vanilla

4½ c. unbleached Robin Hood
flour
6 tsp. baking powder

Beat eggs, oil, sugar, and vanilla in large bowl. Combine flour and baking powder; add to liquid mixture. Mix thoroughly. Form into 2 balls. Let stand 10 minutes. Divide each ball into 4 or 5 pieces, depending on size of rolls desired. Roll dough quite thin on heavily floured board. Put about ½ cup filling on a little more than half the dough. Roll as a jelly roll; put seam side of roll on bottom. Place rolls on greased cookie sheets. Slit rolls with knife. Bake at 350° for 15 to 20 minutes or until very light brown. *Do not overbake.* Makes 8 to 10 rolls.

* Best flavor with chopped orange peel.

PANCAKES I

Marion Kaspryk

1 c. flour
2 tsp. baking powder
½ tsp. salt
2 tsp. sugar

1 egg
1 c. milk
3 Tbsp. butter or margarine,
   melted

Sift flour, baking powder, salt, and sugar into a medium bowl; set aside. In a small bowl, beat egg; add milk and butter. Beat until thoroughly mixed. Pour liquid mixture into dry ingredients; beat only until combined. Batter will be lumpy. Cook pancakes on hot griddle or fry pan using about ¼ cup batter for each pancake; cook until bubbles form on surface and edges become dry. Turn; cook 2 minutes longer or until nicely browned on underside. Serve with whipped butter and syrup.

PANCAKES II

Marie Brink

1 qt. sour milk or buttermilk
½ tsp. baking soda
3 eggs, well beaten
½ tsp. salt

1 Tbsp. melted butter
1 c. flour
2 c. stale bread cubes

Dissolve baking soda in milk. Add eggs, salt, butter, and flour; beat thoroughly. Add bread cubes! Fry cakes, using about ¼ cup batter for each on a lightly greased hot griddle.

JOHN'S BLINTZES

Vera Cibulsky

Batter:

2 large eggs
2 tsp. sugar
½ tsp. salt
1¼ c. milk

1 c. flour
½ tsp. vanilla
2 level Tbsp. melted butter

Beat eggs slightly; add sugar and salt and mix well. Add milk; blend well. Stir in flour gradually until mixture is smooth. Add vanilla and butter; blend well. Let mixture stand at room temperature at least 15 minutes. Use a 6½ inch cast iron skillet; heat skillet. Brush with butter or margarine. Have 2 tablespoons of batter fill the pan like a thin pancake. Blintz is ready to turn when it is easy to lift with a turner and flip it on the other side. Do not overfry. Regulate heat temperature. Continue making blintzes until all of the batter is used.

Cheese Filling:

12 oz. pot cheese (best) or Farmer's cheese	1 medium egg
12 oz. large curd cottage cheese	Sugar to taste

Combine all ingredients and mix well. When blintzes have cooled enough to handle, place a heaping tablespoon of cheese mixture at one end and roll the pancake to the other end. If ready to bake, place in any buttered baking ware and bake at 350° for 25 to 30 minutes. Brush each layer with melted butter or margarine.

For freezing: Place rolled blintzes in a lightly buttered aluminum foil pan. Can be frozen for 6 months. When ready to bake, first thaw, then bake at 350° for 30 to 40 minutes.

BLUEBERRY BANANA PANCAKES   Josephine Vimislik

2 c. sifted all-purpose flour
¼ c. sugar
4 tsp. baking powder
1 tsp. salt
2 eggs, well beaten
1½ c. milk
¼ c. melted butter or
    margarine

⅔ c. mashed bananas (about 2)
1 tsp. vanilla
2 c. frozen dry-pack blueberries
    or 1½ c. well drained canned
    blueberries or 2 c. fresh
    blueberries

Mix flour, sugar, baking powder, and salt. Add eggs, milk, butter, bananas, and vanilla. Mix until well blended and smooth. Fold in blueberries. Spoon about ¼ cup batter for each pancake on preheated greased griddle. Cook on one side; turn. Brown on other side. Stack and serve with butter and syrup. Yield: 6 to 8 servings.

BUCKWHEAT PANCAKES LIKE MA MADE   Marie Brink

½ pkg. dry yeast
2 c. scalded milk
1 c. buckwheat flour
1 c. white flour
½ tsp. salt

¼ tsp. baking soda
2 Tbsp. molasses
2 Tbsp. warm water
¼ c. melted shortening

Sprinkle yeast over ½ cup of the scalded milk which has been cooled to lukewarm. Let stand 10 minutes or until yeast dissolves. Combine yeast with flour, salt, and rest of lukewarm milk. Let stand overnight. The next morning, combine remaining ingredients; add to mixture made the day before. Cook pancakes on hot griddle using ¼ cup batter for each pancake.

CONTINENTAL PANCAKE

Martha Maliwacki

1 Tbsp. fat
3 eggs
½ tsp. salt
1 Tbsp. sugar
⅓ c. sifted flour
½ c. milk

Butter or margarine
Tart jam, applesauce, cooled,
   sweetened berries, or other
   filling
Confectioners sugar

Place fat in an 8 to 10 inch skillet. Put skillet in oven while ingredients are being mixed and oven temperature is being brought to 450°. Beat eggs and salt until very light. Blend sugar and flour; add to egg mixture. Beat until batter is smooth. Add milk; beat thoroughly. Remove skillet from oven. Spread melted fat to grease bottom of pan. Pour all batter in pan. Bake for 15 minutes or until pancake is puffy, well risen, and brown. Remove from oven; let stand in pan until ready to serve. Dot with butter or margarine; put filling in center. Roll or fold from opposite sides to center, making 3 layers. Turn out on a warm platter; sprinkle with confectioners sugar. Serve promptly.

COTTAGE CHEESE PANCAKES

Patricia Hoover

3 eggs
1½ c. cottage cheese
½ tsp. salt

½ c. flour
¼ tsp. baking powder

Beat eggs until light. Add cottage cheese; beat until almost smooth. Add remaining ingredients; mix well. Drop by tablespoon onto lightly greased griddle. Cook until bubbles form on surface. Turn; cook until nicely browned on underside. Serve with syrup or berries. Makes about 12 (3 inch) pancakes.

DELICIOUS PANCAKES

Mary Ann Klish

1⅓ c. flour
2 tsp. baking powder
½ tsp. salt
1 Tbsp. sugar

2 eggs, separated
1¼ c. milk
2 Tbsp. salad oil
Cooking spray

Combine flour, baking powder, salt, and sugar. In a separate bowl, combine egg yolks, milk, and oil; blend. Add to flour mixture; blend with wire whisk. Beat egg whites until soft peaks form; fold into batter. Spray hot griddle with cooking spray. Using ⅓ cup batter for each pancake, cook until edges are dry. Turn over; cook until golden. Serve with Strawberry Sauce.

Strawberry Sauce for Pancakes:

⅓ c. sugar
1 Tbsp. cornstarch
⅓ c. water

2 Tbsp. lemon juice
2 c. frozen strawberries in
   syrup, thawed

Combine sugar and cornstarch in a small saucepan; mix to separate cornstarch granules. Combine water and lemon juice; slowly add to cornstarch-sugar mixture in saucepan, stirring while adding to prevent lumps. Add thawed strawberries; cook over medium heat, stirring frequently until it boils and thickens. Serve warm over pancakes.

NORWEGIAN PANCAKES

Marie Brink

1 c. small curd cottage cheese
1 c. sour cream
4 eggs, beaten

1 Tbsp. sugar
¾ tsp. salt
¾ c. flour

Combine cheese and sour cream. Add eggs; stir. Add sugar and salt; stir to dissolve. Add flour; mix until flour is moistened. Cook pancakes on a greased hot griddle or fry pan.

To serve, you may: (1) Spread with cream cheese you have beaten until smooth. (2) Fill with berries and then rolled. (3) Spread with whipped cream and then rolled.

SUMMER SQUASH PANCAKES

Sophia Pufky

1 small squash, grated
1 egg

3 Tbsp. flour
Salt and pepper

Mix ingredients together. Fry pancakes, using a tablespoon for each, in a fry pan greased with bacon drippings or oil. Flip and cook on second side.

POPOVERS

Patricia Hoover

2 eggs
1 c. milk
1 Tbsp. butter or margarine,
    melted

1 c. flour
½ tsp. salt

Butter 8 (5 ounce) custard cups or 2 muffin tins. Beat eggs; add milk and butter. Beat until blended. Add flour and salt; beat until smooth. Half fill prepared cups. Bake at 425° for 35 minutes. Cut slit in each side of popover. Bake 5 minutes longer. Serve at once.

WELSH CAKES

Millie Finch

2 c. flour
2 tsp. baking powder
½ c. butter or margarine

½ c. sugar
⅔ c. currants
2 eggs, well beaten

Mix flour and baking powder. Cut in butter. Add sugar and currants; mix. Add eggs; mix. Cook as you would pancakes, in a lightly oiled electric fry pan heated to 350°, using 1 tablespoon for a round cake.

YORKSHIRE PUDDING   Josephine Vimislik

2 eggs   Salt
1 c. flour (scant)   Beef drippings
1 c. milk

Beat eggs until light and fluffy. Gradually beat in flour and milk. Add a pinch of salt and 2 tablespoons beef drippings. Heat a baking pan or ring mold; pour ¼ cup beef drippings over bottom of pan. Pour batter into pan. Bake at 450° for 10 minutes. Reduce heat to 350°; bake 10 to 15 minutes longer or until puffy and delicately browned. Cut in squares or slices to serve.

BREADS

Yeast

BREADS, YEAST

CINNAMON RAISIN BREAD

Patricia Hoover

2 pkg. dry yeast
½ c. warm water
1½ c. lukewarm milk
¼ c. sugar
2 tsp. salt
¼ c. margarine

4½ c. flour
1 egg
1 c. rolled oats
1 c. raisins
½ c. sugar
2 Tbsp. cinnamon

Dissolve yeast in warm water. Combine milk, ¼ cup sugar, and salt; stir to dissolve. Beat in 1 cup flour, margarine, egg, and yeast with electric mixer. Add oats and raisins. Mix in remaining flour with spoon until dough leaves sides of bowl. Turn onto floured surface; knead thoroughly adding only enough flour to make dough smooth and elastic. Place in greased bowl, turning to bring greased side up. Cover. Let rise in warm place until double (about 1½ hours). Punch down; let rise again.

Divide dough into 2 balls. Roll each ball into large rectangle 9x12 inches. Combine ½ cup sugar and cinnamon. Sprinkle over dough surface. Roll dough, starting at short end, jelly roll fashion. Place in greased 9x5x3 inch pan. Brush top with melted butter. Cover. Let rise again in warm place until dough reaches top of pan and fills in corners (1 to 1½ hours). Bake at 350° for 40 to 50 minutes. Cool on rack completely. Slice and toast for breakfast.

EASTER BREAD

Helen Charnetsky

¾ c. milk
½ c. water
½ c. (1 stick) margarine
2 pkg. active dry yeast
¾ c. sugar
½ tsp. salt
1 tsp. cardamom (optional)

1 Tbsp. grated orange peel
1 tsp. grated lemon peel
2 eggs (room temperature)
5¼ to 6¼ c. unsifted flour
½ c. chopped or slivered
    almonds
½ c. golden raisins

Combine milk, water, and margarine in saucepan. Heat over low heat until liquids are very warm (120° to 130°). Margarine doesn't need to melt. Add yeast, sugar, salt, cardamom, and grated orange and lemon peel. Beat. Add eggs; beat. Add 1 cup flour; beat on high speed 2 minutes, scraping bowl occasionally. Stir in enough additional flour to make a soft dough. Turn out onto lightly floured board; knead until smooth and elastic, about 8 to 10 minutes. Place in greased bowl, turning to grease top. Cover. Let rise in warm place until doubled in bulk, about 1 hour.

Punch dough down; turn out onto lightly floured board. Knead in almonds and raisins. Divide in half; shape into 2 smooth balls. Place in 2 greased 8 inch round cake pans or 2 greased 9¼ x 4½ to 2½ inch loaf pans. Cover. Let rise in warm place until doubled in bulk, about 1 hour. Bake at 375° for 35 to 40 minutes or until done. Cover with aluminum foil tent if bread browns too quickly. Remove from pans; cool on wire racks. Frost with confectioners sugar frosting if desired.

OATMEAL MOLASSES BREAD   Patricia Hoover

2 pkg. dry yeast
2 Tbsp. sugar
1 c. lukewarm water
⅓ c. margarine
1 c. boiling water
1 c. rolled oats

½ c. molasses
1 Tbsp. salt
1 egg, beaten
5½ c. flour
Melted margarine

Dissolve yeast and sugar in water. Let stand 10 minutes. Cream margarine. Add boiling water, oats, molasses, and salt. Cool. Add yeast mixture and egg. Add flour gradually; mix. Let rise in warm place until double. Punch down. Divide dough in half. Knead each piece; shape into loaves. Put in 2 greased 9x5x3 inch loaf pans. Let rise until double. Bake at 350° for 40 minutes. Brush tops of warm bread with melted margarine to keep it soft.

PARMESAN GARLIC BREAD   Patricia Hoover

2 c. milk
2 Tbsp. sugar
2 tsp. salt
2 pkg. active dry yeast
2 c. very warm water
1 clove garlic, crushed

2 Tbsp. butter or margarine,
  melted
10 c. flour
1 c. grated Parmesan cheese
Grated Parmesan cheese

Heat milk with sugar and salt in saucepan until lukewarm. In a large bowl, sprinkle yeast in very warm water; stir until dissolved. Add cooled milk mixture, garlic, and butter. Beat in 5 cups flour and 1 cup cheese until blended. Beat in remaining flour gradually to form a soft dough. Turn out on floured surface; knead, adding only enough flour to keep from sticking. Place dough in large, greased bowl, turning once to grease surface. Cover; let rise in warm place for 1 hour or until double. Punch down; knead a few minutes. Divide dough according to size loaves you wish to make.

Also good made into rolls. Let rise in greased pans in warm place for 45 minutes or until double. Brush tops with water; sprinkle lightly with grated cheese. Bake at 400°, large loaves 40 minutes, small loaves 30 minutes, and rolls 20 to 25 minutes. Remove from pans to wire racks. Cool completely.

48

SCANDINAVIAN RYE BREAD

Patricia Hoover

2 pkg. active dry yeast
2½ c. very warm water
¼ c. light molasses
4 tsp. salt

2 Tbsp. shortening
2½ c. rye flour
1 Tbsp. caraway seeds
5½ to 6 c. all-purpose flour

Sprinkle yeast into ½ cup "very warm water" (feels comfortable when dropped on wrist). Stir in 1 teaspoon molasses; keep stirring until yeast dissolves. Let stand until bubbly and double in volume (about 10 minutes). Combine remaining water and molasses with salt and shortening in large bowl. Stir in yeast mixture, rye flour, and caraway seeds. Add enough all-purpose flour to make a soft dough. Turn out onto lightly floured surface; knead until smooth and elastic (about 10 minutes) using only enough flour to keep from sticking. Place in buttered bowl; turn to bring buttered side up.

Cover with towel; let rise in warm place away from drafts for 1 hour or until double in volume. Butter a cookie sheet, 2 (9x5x3 inch) loaf pans or 2 casseroles; sprinkle bottom with corn meal if desired. Punch down dough; knead a few times. Divide in half; knead each piece a few more times. Shape into 2 loaves. If using a cookie sheet, place at least 4 inches apart. Let rise in warm place again until double (about 45 minutes). Brush tops with water. Bake at 400° for 35 minutes or until browned and loaves sound hollow when tapped lightly. Remove from pan to wire rack. Cool completely.

ENGLISH MUFFINS

Marie Pufky

2 pkg. dry yeast
2 c. warm water
1 Tbsp. sugar

4 tsp. salt
½ c. shortening
5 to 5½ c. flour

In a large bowl, dissolve yeast in warm (110° to 115°) water. Add sugar, salt, and shortening; stir. Add 2 cups flour; beat until smooth. Add 3 cups flour; mix thoroughly. The batter will be stiff. Add more flour, if possible, for it to be mixed in. Put dough on lightly floured board; stretch until ½ inch thick. Cut with cookie cutter or glass dipped in corn meal. Place muffins on cookie sheet which is sprinkled with corn meal. Let rise 1½ hours. Fry on electric griddle at 340° until lightly browned on each side. Makes 2 dozen.

CARAMEL NUT BUNS

Patricia Hoover

½ c. milk
½ c. sugar
1 tsp. salt
⅔ c. shortening

2 pkg. active dry yeast
½ c. very warm water
4 eggs, beaten
4½ c. all-purpose flour

Combine milk, sugar, salt, and shortening in saucepan. Heat just until shortening melts. Cool to lukewarm. Sprinkle yeast into very warm water in large bowl; let stand 10 minutes. Add lukewarm egg mixture, eggs, and 2 cups flour; beat until smooth. Add just enough remaining flour to make a soft dough. Turn onto floured surface. Knead until smooth and elastic (about 5 minutes), using only enough flour to keep dough from sticking. Place in greased bowl; turn to bring greased side up. Cover. Let rise in warm place for 1 to 1½ hours or until double in bulk. Punch down; knead a few times. Let rest 5 minutes.

Pour caramel syrup into 2 (9x9x2 inch) pans. Sprinkle with 1 cup walnuts or pecan halves. Roll out dough into 2 large rectangles. Spread entire surface with soft margarine. Sprinkle sugar-cinnamon mixture over margarine. Roll up jelly roll fashion beginning with long side. Pinch to seal seam. Cut each roll into 12 equal slices; place, cut side down, into pan of syrup. Cover. Let rise in warm place until double (about 1 hour).

Bake at 375° for 25 minutes or until golden brown. Immediately upon removal from oven, invert pan onto square of aluminum foil. Leave pan in place a few minutes to allow topping to run over the buns. Lift pan off. Separate buns with fork to serve warm.

Caramel Syrup:

1½ c. packed brown sugar　　　**½ c. margarine**
1 c. light corn syrup　　　**1 c. walnuts**

Combine brown sugar, corn syrup, and margarine in small saucepan. Simmer 2 minutes.

Sugar-Cinnamon:

⅔ c. sugar　　　**1 c. raisins**
1 tsp. cinnamon

Combine sugar and cinnamon; mix to distribute cinnamon throughout sugar. Add raisins; mix.

HEALTHY CHALLAH BREAD　　　Sophia Malowicky

¾ c. very warm water　　　**7 eggs**
3 pkg. active dry yeast　　　**9 c. unbleached flour**
1 tsp. honey　　　**1 c. wheat germ (with sugar**
1 c. very warm water　　　**and honey)**
1 Tbsp. salt　　　**1 egg**
⅓ c. honey (can use more)
1 stick (½ c.) unsalted butter,
softened

Pour ¾ cup very warm water into large bowl; sprinkle yeast over water. Stir in 1 teaspoon honey. Let stand 10 minutes or until bubbly. Combine 1 cup very warm water, salt, honey, and butter in small bowl. Beat into yeast mixture with electric mixer. Add eggs, one at a time, beating well after each egg. Add 4 cups flour; beat 2 minutes with mixer. Stir in wheat germ. Add enough flour to make dough that holds together and pulls away from side of bowl. Turn dough onto floured board. Knead until smooth and elastic, about 10 minutes. Place in large greased bowl; turn to bring greased side up. Cover. Let rise in warm place about 1 hour or more. Punch down; knead a few times to press out bubbles. Divide dough into 4 pieces. Divide each piece into 3 parts. Roll each part into a 13 inch long rope. Braid the 3 ropes together, pinching ends to seal. Place in greased pan. Let rise in warm place until double. Brush with beaten egg. Bake at 375° for 30 minutes.

APPLE KUCHEN

Ann Dobransky

1 pkg. dry yeast
¼ c. warm water
2 Tbsp. sugar
2 Tbsp. butter
1 tsp. salt
¼ c. milk, scalded
1 egg, beaten

2 to 2¼ c. flour
3 c. apple slices (¼ inch thick)
1 c. sugar
1 tsp. cinnamon
2 Tbsp. butter
1 egg yolk
⅓ c. light cream

Soften yeast in warm water. In a mixing bowl, combine 2 tablespoons sugar, 2 tablespoons butter, salt, and milk; cool to lukewarm. Stir in egg and yeast. Gradually add flour, beating well after each addition to form a stiff dough. Cover; let rise in warm place until doubled, about 1 hour. Spread in well-greased 9x13 inch pan. Arrange apples in rows on top of dough. Combine 1 cup sugar, cinnamon, and 2 tablespoons butter. Sprinkle over apples. Cover; let rise in warm place until doubled, about 30 minutes. Bake at 375° for 20 to 25 minutes or until golden brown. Blend egg yolk with cream; spoon over cake. Bake 15 minutes.

PLUM KUCHEN

Ann Dobransky

1 box hot roll mix
2 lb. plums
½ c. sugar

1 c. flour
½ tsp. cinnamon
¼ c. softened butter

Prepare dough according to package directions. Turn dough out onto floured surface; knead until smooth. Let rise until double. Knead a few turns. Press dough into a greased 10 inch square baking pan. Arrange pitted and quartered plums, cut side up, in rows on dough, pressing in firmly. Cover with topping made by combining sugar, flour, cinnamon, and butter. Let rise until almost double. Bake at 375° for 35 minutes. Serve warm.

MINIATURE APRICOT KULICHE
Carol Wasylko

5 to 5½ c. unsifted flour
½ c. sugar
2 pkg. dry yeast
1 tsp. salt
1 c. warm water
½ c. milk
½ c. butter or margarine
3 eggs, beaten (at room
 temperature)
1 tsp. grated lemon peel

½ c. chopped dried apricots
¼ c. chopped candied citrus
 peel
¼ c. chopped blanched almonds
1½ c. confectioners sugar
2 Tbsp. milk
¼ tsp. almond extract
Dried apricot halves for
 garnish
Red and green candied cherries

In large bowl, combine 1½ cups flour, sugar, yeast, and salt. In small saucepan, combine water, milk, and butter; heat on low until liquids are very warm (120° to 130°). (Butter or margarine does not need to melt completely.) With mixer at low speed, gradually add liquids to dry ingredients; beat 2 minutes, scraping bowl occasionally. Add eggs, lemon peel, apricots, citrus peel, and almonds; mix. Add 1 cup flour; mix on medium speed for 2 minutes. With wooden spoon, stir in enough additional flour (about 2½ cups) to make a soft dough.

Turn dough onto lightly floured surface; knead until smooth and elastic, 8 to 10 minutes, adding more flour if necessary. Shape into a ball; place in greased bowl, turning dough over so top is greased. Cover; let rise in warm place until double, about 1½ hours. Grease twelve 2½ x 2½ inch metal babka molds or 12 (6 ounce) clean metal juice cans; place on jellyroll pan. Divide dough into 12 equal pieces; shape to fit into molds. Cover; let rise until double, about 30 minutes. Bake at 375° for 20 minutes or until bread sounds hollow when lightly tapped with fingers. Remove from molds; cool on wire racks.

Combine confectioners sugar, milk, and almond extract until smooth. Frost top of loaves, lettuce some drip down sides. Garnish top with apricots and candied cherries.

SWEDISH LIMPA
Patricia Hoover

2 pkg. active dry yeast
2½ c. very warm water
¼ c. brown sugar
⅓ c. molasses
3 Tbsp. vegetable shortening
1 Tbsp. salt

2 Tbsp. grated orange rind
1 tsp. anise seed, crushed
1 c. cracked wheat
3½ c. whole rye flour
3¾ to 4 c. all-purpose flour

Sprinkle yeast in ½ cup of the warm water. Stir in 1 teaspoon of the brown sugar. Stir until dissolved. Let stand until bubbly and double in volume (about 10 minutes). Combine remaining water and sugar with molasses, shortening, and salt in saucepan. Heat slightly; cool to lukewarm. Combine yeast mixture and molasses mixture in large bowl. Add orange rind, anise seed, cracked wheat, and rye flour. Beat with electric mixer at medium speed for 3 minutes. Gradually stir in enough all-purpose flour to make a soft dough. Turn out onto floured surface; knead until smooth and elastic, using all-purpose flour to keep dough from sticking. Place in greased bowl; turn to grease all sides. Cover with towel. Let rise in warm place for 1½ hours or until double in bulk.

Punch down. Turn out onto floured surface; invert bowl over dough. Let rest 10 minutes. Divide dough in half. Knead each half a few times. Put into 2 buttered 9x5x3 inch pans or shape into ovals and place on buttered cookie sheets. Let rise in warm place 40 minutes or until double.** Bake at 375° for 45 minutes or until golden brown and loaves sound hollow when tapped. Cool on wire racks.

* Bowl with dough may be placed in oven with pan of hot water on shelf below; close oven door.

** Loaves may be glazed with a mixture of slightly beaten egg white plus 1 tablespoon cold water.

NUT ROLL DOUGH
Jane Ellsworth

¾ c. milk
½ c. sugar
1 tsp. salt
1 stick margarine

½ c. warm water
2 pkg. active dry yeast
1 egg, beaten
4 to 5 c. flour

Scald milk. Add sugar, salt, and margarine; stir until margarine is melted. Sprinkle yeast into warm water in large bowl; stir until dissolved. Add lukewarm milk mixture, egg, and half the flour. Mix thoroughly. Add remaining flour; knead to form a soft dough. Cover tightly; refrigerate overnight. Divide dough into 4 equal parts. Roll each part, on very lightly floured surface, into a rectangle; spread with filling. Roll as you would a jelly roll. Place rolls in lightly greased pans. Bake at 350° about 25 minutes.

NUT ROLLS
Josephine Vimislik

2 Tbsp. sugar
½ c. warm milk
1 cake compressed yeast or 1
   pkg. active dry yeast
3½ c. flour
Dash of salt

1 c. margarine
4 eggs, separated
1 c. sugar
Confectioners sugar
Ground nuts
Cinnamon

Dissolve 2 tablespoons sugar in warm milk; crumble yeast into milk. Let stand 3 to 5 minutes. Combine flour and salt in large bowl; add margarine.

Blend with pastry blender. Add beaten egg yolks to yeast. Add liquid mixture to flour; mix thoroughly. Refrigerate 5 hours or overnight.

Beat egg whites, adding sugar gradually, until thick like marshmallow creme. Divide dough into 4 equal parts. Roll dough on waxed paper. Sprinkle with confectioners sugar; spread with beaten egg whites. Sprinkle with nuts and cinnamon. Roll as you would a jelly roll. Place on greased cookie sheet. Let rise 1 hour. Bake at 350° for 25 minutes.

MARY'S FAVORITE NUT ROLLS
Mary Mihalko

Dough:

1 pkg. dry yeast	3 eggs
½ c. warm milk	1 c. sour cream
1 tsp. sugar	1 tsp. vanilla or almond extract
2 sticks butter	5 c. sifted flour
½ c. sugar	

Dissolve yeast in warm milk with 1 teaspoon sugar; set aside. Cream butter and sugar; add eggs, one at a time, beating well after each. Add sour cream and flavoring; add flour alternately with yeast mixture, beating until dough leaves sides of bowl. Knead a few minutes by hand; shouldn't stick to your hand. Form into 6 balls; refrigerate overnight. Roll out each ball of dough; spread with any filling. Roll like a jelly roll; place on a lightly greased 9x13 inch pan or a 9x13 inch pan lined with parchment paper. Place 3 rolls per 9x13 inch pan with a piece of parchment paper between rolls to keep them from sticking. Let rise until double. Bake at 350° for 30 to 35 minutes.

Nut Filling:

1 lb. ground walnuts	1 tsp. vanilla
½ c. sugar	Log Cabin pancake syrup

Combine nuts, sugar, vanilla, and enough pancake syrup to make filling easy to spread on rolled out dough; set aside until ready to spread on dough.

QUICK NUT ROLLS
Mary Kasprowitz

2½ c. warm milk	4 Tbsp. sugar
1 large yeast cake	½ lb. (1 c.) butter, melted
4 Tbsp. sugar	8 c. flour
4 eggs, beaten	2 tsp. salt

Combine first 3 ingredients. Let rise 10 minutes or until foamy. Combine eggs, sugar, and butter; add yeast mixture. Sift together flour and salt; add to liquid ingredients. Mix thoroughly. Divide dough into 8 parts. Roll into rectangles 12x15 inches. Spread with desired filling; roll as a jelly roll. Pinch seam.

Place on greased cookie sheet seam side on bottom. Prick with fork; slit top. Let rise 1 hour. Brush top of rolls with mixture of a beaten egg and 1 tablespoon milk. Bake at 350° for 30 minutes or until brown.

Nut Filling:

1⅓ c. boiling water	2 lb. ground walnuts
3 c. sugar	2 tsp. butter or margarine

Combine ingredients in saucepan. Bring to a boil. Makes enough filling for 8 rolls.

Poppy Seed Filling:

2 lb. poppy seed, ground	3 c. sugar
3 c. milk, scalded	4 Tbsp. margarine
2 eggs, beaten	

Combine ingredients in saucepan. Bring to a boil. Makes enough filling for 8 rolls.

PIZZA DOUGH I
Jane Ellsworth

4 c. flour	1½ c. warm water
1 tsp. salt	1 tsp. sugar
1 small cake yeast or 1 pkg. active dry yeast	½ c. salad oil

Sift together flour and salt; set aside. Sprinkle yeast in warm water; add sugar. Let rise (about 10 minutes). Add salad oil. Add liquids to flour; knead. Grease hands; spread dough on 2 greased baking pans. Spread with your favorite pizza sauce. Bake at 425° about 20 minutes.

PIZZA II
Patricia Hoover

Dough:

1 pkg. active dry yeast	1 tsp. salt
1 c. warm water	2 Tbsp. oil
1 tsp. sugar	2½ c. flour

In a large bowl, dissolve yeast in warm water. Stir in remaining ingredients with fork. Knead slightly. Let dough rest. With floured hands, spread dough onto 2 (10 inch) or 1 (20 inch) greased pizza pan. Bake at 425° about 15 minutes or until *slightly* browned. Spread with sauce; top with your favorite toppings. Bake an additional 10 minutes.

Sauce:*

1 (8 oz.) can tomato sauce	**⅛ tsp. garlic powder**
½ c. chopped onion	**⅛ tsp. pepper**
¼ tsp. salt	

Combine all ingredients. Let stand 5 minutes.

Suggested toppings (any combination):

2 tsp. oregano	**¼ c. Parmesan cheese**
Sliced pepperoni	**2 c. grated Mozzarella**
Chopped peppers	**Sausage slices**
Sliced mushrooms	**Sauteed hamburger**

Note: If using self-rising flour, omit salt in dough.

* Spaghetti sauce can be substituted.

PIZZA DOUGH III

Marie Richardson

½ pkg. active dry yeast	**1 Tbsp. sugar**
2 Tbsp. warm water	**¼ c. milk, scalded**
2 Tbsp. shortening	**1 to 1¼ c. flour**
½ tsp. salt	

In a small bowl, sprinkle yeast into warm water. In a medium bowl, combine shortening, salt, sugar, and milk. Cool to lukewarm. Add dissolved yeast. Add enough flour to form a stiff dough. Cover. Let rise in warm place 45 to 90 minutes. Roll dough to fit small pizza pan. Spread with your favorite filling. Bake at 350° about 20 minutes or until crust browns.

SOFT PRETZELS

Anna Smyk

1 large yeast cake	**4 c. flour**
1 Tbsp. sugar	**1 tsp. salt**
1½ c. warm water	**Coarse salt**

Dissolve yeast and sugar in warm water. Sift flour and salt into large bowl. Add yeast mixture; knead 5 minutes. Shape into pretzels. Brush with beaten egg yolk; sprinkle with coarse salt. Bake at 425° for 12 to 15 minutes.

BUTTERMILK WHEAT BREAD

Patricia Hoover

2 pkg. active dry yeast
½ c. very warm water
¼ c. honey
2 c. buttermilk
2 Tbsp. margarine
1 Tbsp. salt

½ tsp. baking soda
3½ c. whole wheat flour
1 c. cracked wheat
2¼ c. unbleached or all-purpose flour

In a small bowl, sprinkle yeast into very warm water. Stir in 1 teaspoon of the honey. Let stand 10 minutes or until double. Heat buttermilk with margarine, remaining honey, and salt until lukewarm. Add yeast mixture. Stir in baking soda, whole wheat flour, and cracked wheat. Beat in enough unbleached flour to make soft dough. Turn out onto floured surface; knead until smooth using only enough flour to keep dough from sticking. Place in buttered bowl; turn to grease all sides. Cover. Let rise in warm place for 1 hour or until double.

Punch down; knead a few times. Invert bowl over dough; let it rest 10 minutes. Divide dough in half. Roll each section into a 9x18 inch rectangle; roll up jelly roll fashion from the short end. Place in 2 greased 9x5x3 inch pans, seam side down. Let rise 40 minutes or until double. Bake at 375° for 35 minutes or until sound is hollow when tapped. Remove from pans to wire rack. Cool completely.

HONEY WHOLE WHEAT BREAD

Patricia Hoover

3 c. whole wheat flour
½ c. instant dry milk powder
1 Tbsp. salt
2 pkg. active dry yeast
3 c. water

½ c. honey
2 Tbsp. vegetable oil
1 c. whole wheat flour
4 to 4½ c. all-purpose flour

In a large bowl, combine 3 cups whole wheat flour, dry milk powder, salt, and dry yeast. In a small pan, heat water, honey, and oil until warm. Pour warm liquid over flour mixture. Blend at low speed for 1 minute, on medium speed 2 minutes. Using a wooden spoon, stir in 1 cup whole wheat flour and the all-purpose flour. Knead until smooth and elastic. Place in a greased bowl; cover. Let rise 45 to 60 minutes until light and double in bulk. Punch down; divide in half. Shape by rolling into a rectangle; roll up jelly-roll fashion. Place in 2 greased 9x5x3 inch loaf pans. Cover; let rise 30 to 45 minutes or until double. Bake at 375° for 40 to 45 minutes or until top sounds hollow when tapped. Remove from pans; cool completely on wire rack before slicing.

WHOLE WHEAT BREAD

Patricia Hoover

2 pkg. active dry yeast
3 Tbsp. sugar
1½ c. very warm water
1 c. milk
2 Tbsp. butter or margarine
1 Tbsp. salt
¼ c. sesame seeds
⅔ c. instant non-fat dry milk
   powder

⅓ c. soybean powder
3 Tbsp. wheat germ
3 c. whole wheat flour
3 c. unbleached or all-purpose
   flour, sifted
½ c. bran (optional)
1 egg, slightly beaten
Melted butter
Sesame seeds (optional)

In a small bowl, sprinkle yeast into ½ cup very warm water. Stir in 1 teaspoon of the sugar. Let stand 10 minutes or until bubbly and double in volume. Combine remaining water, remaining sugar, milk, butter, and salt in saucepan; heat to melt butter. Pour into large bowl; cool to lukewarm. Stir in yeast. Add sesame seeds. Stir in dry milk, soybean powder, wheat germ, 1½ cups whole wheat flour, 1 cup unbleached flour, and bran. Beat at medium speed with electric mixer 3 minutes.

Stir in remaining whole wheat flour and enough unbleached flour to make stiff dough. Turn out dough on floured surface, kneading until smooth (about 10 minutes) using only enough flour to keep dough from sticking. Place in buttered bowl; turn to grease all sides. Cover. Let rise in warm place 1 to 1½ hours. Punch down. Divide into 2 parts. Knead a few times.

Shape into loaves; place into 2 greased 9x5x3 inch pans. Let rise 45 minutes or until double. Brush tops with butter and beaten egg; sprinkle with sesame seeds. Bake at 375° for 35 minutes or until hollow when tapped. Remove from pans to wire racks. Cool completely.

FAVORITE YEAST ROLLS

Patricia Hoover

1½ c. milk
½ c. margarine or butter
¼ c. sugar
2 tsp. salt
2 pkg. active dry yeast

½ c. very warm water
1 tsp. sugar
2 eggs
8 c. all-purpose flour

Heat milk with margarine, sugar, and salt until margarine melts. Cool to lukewarm. Sprinkle yeast into very warm water. Stir in 1 teaspoon sugar. Let stand 10 minutes. Stir in cooled milk mixture; beat in eggs. Beat in enough flour to make soft dough. Turn out and knead until smooth (5 minutes) adding only enough flour to keep dough from sticking. Place in greased bowl; turn to grease all sides. Cover. Let rise in warm place until double (about 1½ hours).

Punch down. Divide into small portions for shaping. Keep remaining dough covered with an inverted bowl until ready to use. Shape rolls into cloverleafs, knots, crescents, fantans, or any desired shape. Place on appropriate greased pans according to shape. Let rise 45 minutes or until double. Bake at 375° for 20 minutes. Serve hot. Makes about 5 dozen. Rolls may be frozen.

To reheat or freshen leftover rolls, place in paper bag; sprinkle with water. Heat at 350° for 10 minutes. To serve frozen baked rolls, place on cookie sheet. Heat at 300° for 15 minutes or until hot.

Cloverleaf Rolls: Cut off marble size chunks of dough. Roll into balls. Place 3 balls in a greased muffin tin. Continue until pan is full.

Knots: Cut off large egg size chunks of dough. Roll out into a 6 inch rope; "tie a knot." Form a loop; bring one end through loop. Place on greased cookie sheet.

Crescents: Roll out a portion of dough into an 8 inch round (½ inch thick). Cut into 8 or 12 wedges. Roll up each wedge, starting at large end, placing pointed side down on greased cookie sheet, curving ends of rolls slightly to shape like crescents.

Fantans: Roll out a portion of dough into a 9x18 inch rectangle ½ inch thick. Cut into 1½ inch wide strips. Brush with melted butter. Stack 6 strips on top of each other. Cut stack into 1½ inch wide pieces. Place each piece of cut stack, cut side down, in a greased muffin tin.

Notes

Cakes & Tortes

CAKES, TORTES

APPLE CAKE

Ann Dobransky

3¾ c. flour
3 Tbsp. sugar
1½ tsp. salt
1½ c. shortening
2 egg yolks
Milk
1 c. crushed corn flakes

3 lb. apples, sliced thin
2 c. sugar
2 tsp. cinnamon
2 egg whites
1 c. confectioners sugar
4 Tbsp. lemon juice

Sift flour, sugar, and salt together. Cut in shortening as for pie crust. Place egg yolks in measuring cup; add milk to make 1 cup. Beat. Add to flour mixture; mix just enough to shape into a ball. Roll out half the dough to fit a 15½ x 10½ x 1 inch pan. Cover dough with crushed corn flakes. Arrange apple slices over corn flakes. Mix 2 cups sugar and cinnamon; sprinkle on top of apples. Roll out other half of dough; place over apple layer. Beat egg whites until stiff; spread over crust. Bake at 400° for 40 minutes.

Combine confectioners sugar and lemon juice. Drizzle on hot cake. To serve, cut in squares or diamonds. Store in refrigerator; do not cover. It will keep for a week.

APPLE FILLED CRUMB CAKE

Jane Ellsworth

1¼ c. sifted flour
¾ c. sugar
1 tsp. baking powder
¾ tsp. salt
¼ tsp. nutmeg

⅓ c. margarine
⅓ c. milk
2 eggs
1 tsp. vanilla

Sift dry ingredients into bowl. Add margarine and milk; beat 1½ minutes. Add eggs and vanilla; beat 1½ minutes more. Spread half the batter into a greased 8x12 inch pan. Spoon half the apples over batter. Cover apples with remaining batter. Top with remaining apples. Sprinkle Crumb Topping on apples. Bake at 350° for 30 minutes.

Apple Mixture:

5 apples, peeled, cored, and
    sliced
½ c. sugar

1 tsp. cinnamon
1 Tbsp. butter
1 Tbsp. lemon juice

Combine all ingredients in saucepan. Cover; simmer until apples are tender. Cool. Drain thoroughly.

Crumb Topping:

¾ c. brown sugar   ¼ c. margarine
½ c. flour   ½ c. chopped nuts

Combine brown sugar and flour. Add margarine; combine to form crumb mixture. Add nuts.

APPLESAUCE CAKE   Miranda Klish

½ c. shortening   1 tsp. baking powder
½ c. brown sugar   1 tsp. cinnamon
½ c. granulated sugar   ½ tsp. nutmeg
2 eggs   ¼ tsp. cloves
2 c. sifted flour   1½ c. applesauce
1 tsp. salt   ½ c. raisins
1 tsp. baking soda   ½ c. chopped nuts

Cream together shortening and sugars. Add eggs; beat well. Sift together flour, salt, baking soda, baking powder, and spices; add to creamed mixture alternately with applesauce. Beat well after each addition. Stir in nuts and raisins. Bake in a greased 9x13x2 inch pan at 350° for 35 to 40 minutes.

MOTHER'S ONE BOWL APPLESAUCE
CAKE   Olga Gooley

2½ c. flour   1 c. molasses
½ tsp. salt   1 egg
1 tsp. baking soda   1 c. applesauce
1 tsp. cinnamon   ¾ c. raisins
½ c. soft butter   ¾ c. chopped nuts

Combine flour, salt, baking soda, and cinnamon. Add butter, molasses, egg, and applesauce; beat well. Add raisins and nuts. Pour batter into greased and floured 8 x 11½ inch glass pan. Bake at 325° for 40 minutes. Pour Glaze over hot cake.

Glaze:

¾ c. confectioners sugar   1½ Tbsp. lemon juice

Combine sugar and lemon juice; beat until smooth.

CAROB CHOCOLATE CHIP APPLE CAKE

Genevieve Sadowitz

½ c. butter
¾ c. sugar
¾ c. brown sugar
2 eggs
1 tsp. vanilla
2 c. flour
2 c. thinly sliced apples

1 tsp. baking powder
1 tsp. baking soda
½ tsp. salt
½ c. water
½ c. carob chocolate chips
½ c. chopped walnuts

Cream shortening and sugars until light. Add eggs and vanilla; beat well. Dredge apples in 2 tablespoons of the flour; set aside. Combine the remaining flour, baking powder, baking soda, and salt; add to creamed mixture alternately with water. Fold in apples, chocolate chips, and nuts. Pour into a greased 9x13x2 inch pan. Sprinkle with Topping. Bake at 350° for 40 to 50 minutes.

Topping:

¼ c. brown sugar
¼ c. carob chocolate chips

¼ c. chopped walnuts

Combine ingredients.

JEWISH APPLE CAKE I

Anna Chyl

3 c. all-purpose flour
3 tsp. baking powder
1½ c. sugar
1 c. salad oil

4 eggs, beaten fluffy
⅓ c. orange juice
2½ tsp. vanilla
3 large apples, sliced very thin

Combine all ingredients, except apples, in a large bowl; beat until smooth. Spread half the batter in a greased 9x13x2 inch pan. Cover with a layer of half the apples. Sprinkle with cinnamon and sugar to suit you. Spread remaining batter over apples. Arrange remaining apples on batter. Sprinkle with cinnamon and sugar. Bake at 350° for 45 minutes or until done.

JEWISH APPLE CAKE II

Olga Gooley

2 c. sugar
1 c. Crisco oil
4 eggs
2½ tsp. vanilla
3 c. unsifted flour

3 tsp. (heaping) baking powder
¼ c. orange juice
4 large apples, sliced
5 Tbsp. sugar
2 tsp. cinnamon

Combine 2 cups sugar, oil, eggs, and vanilla; beat thoroughly. Combine flour and baking powder; add to egg mixture alternately with orange juice. Spread half the batter in greased 10 inch tube pan. Combine 5 tablespoons sugar and cinnamon; sprinkle over apples. Top batter in pan with half the apple mixture. (*Do not* mix apples through batter.) Spread remaining batter on apples; top with remaining apples. Bake at 350° for 1 hour and 15 minutes.

Note: Batter is heavy.

APPLE KUCHEN
Mary Duby

1 c. margarine
1 c. sugar
4 eggs
2 c. flour
½ tsp. salt
2 tsp. baking powder

2 tsp. vanilla
4 large apples, sliced thin
2 tsp. cinnamon
1 c. sugar
¼ c. chopped nuts (optional)

Cream margarine; add 1 cup sugar gradually, beating until creamy. Add eggs, one at a time, beating well after each. Add flour, salt, and baking powder which have been sifted together; mix thoroughly. Add vanilla; blend. Spread three-fourths of the dough in greased 9x13 inch pan. Place sliced apples over dough. Combine cinnamon and 1 cup sugar; sprinkle over apples. Put small amounts of remaining dough here and there; dough will spread while baking. Bake at 350° for 45 minutes. Cool. Serve sprinkled with confectioners sugar or with a dollop of whipped cream.

SOUR CREAM APPLE CAKE
Marion Kaspryk

1 (2 layer size) pkg. white cake
  mix
½ c. salad oil
½ c. sugar

4 eggs
1 c. sour cream
1 tsp. vanilla
1 c. chopped pecans

Combine all ingredients in a large bowl; mix thoroughly. Pour half of batter into a greased and floured 9x13 inch pan. Sprinkle Filling over batter. Pour remaining batter over Filling. Arrange sliced apples on batter. Sprinkle with Topping. Drizzle melted margarine over Topping. Bake at 325° for 45 minutes. While warm, drizzle icing over cake.

Filling:

2 tsp. cinnamon

4 Tbsp. brown sugar

Combine cinnamon and sugar. Sprinkle over cake batter.

Topping:

1½ c. sliced, peeled apples
⅓ c. sugar
½ tsp. cinnamon

1½ tsp. flour
¼ c. margarine, melted

Arrange apples on batter. Combine sugar, cinnamon, and flour; sprinkle over apples. Drizzle melted margarine over crumbs.

Icing: Combine confectioners sugar with enough milk to make a mixture thin enough to drizzle.

BANANA CAKE
Jane Ellsworth

1 pkg. yellow cake mix
1 (3.4 oz.) pkg. banana instant
  pudding
1 c. sour cream

4 eggs
2 mashed bananas
1 c. chopped nuts

In a large bowl, combine cake mix and instant pudding; mix. Add sour cream and eggs; blend. Add bananas; mix. Add nuts; mix to distribute throughout batter evenly. Turn into a greased and floured Bundt or angel food cake pan. Bake at 350° for 55 to 60 minutes.

LARGE BANANA CAKE
Ann Dobransky

¾ c. shortening
2¼ c. sugar
3 eggs
1½ tsp. vanilla
3 c. cake flour

1 tsp. baking powder
1 tsp. baking soda
6 Tbsp. buttermilk
1½ c. mashed bananas

Cream shortening and sugar. Add eggs, one at a time, beating after each addition. Add vanilla; beat. Sift together dry ingredients. Combine buttermilk and bananas; add alternately with dry ingredients to egg mixture. Pour into greased 9x13x2 inch pan. Bake at 350° for 35 to 40 minutes.

OLGA'S BANANA CARROT CAKE
Anna Chyl

1 c. sugar
1 c. mashed ripe bananas
⅔ c. vegetable oil
2 eggs
1½ c. all-purpose flour
2 tsp. baking powder
1 tsp. salt

1 tsp. baking soda
1 tsp. cinnamon
½ tsp. cloves
1 c. quick oats (uncooked)
1 c. shredded carrots
⅓ c. chopped nuts

Combine sugar, bananas, and oil. Add eggs, one at a time, beating well after each addition. Stir in combined flour, baking powder, salt, baking soda, and spices. Add oats and carrots; mix well. Spread in greased 9 inch square pan. Sprinkle with nuts. Bake at 350° for 40 minutes or until done.

BANANA CHOCOLATE CHIP LOAF

½ c. margarine, softened
¾ c. sugar
1 tsp. vanilla
2 eggs
2 c. sifted all-purpose flour

1 tsp. baking soda
1 tsp. salt
1 c. mashed ripe bananas
1 (6 oz.) pkg. semi-sweet
   chocolate bits

In large bowl, cream margarine, sugar, and vanilla until light and fluffy. Add eggs; beat. Sift together flour, baking soda, and salt; blend into creamed mixture alternately with mashed bananas. Stir in chocolate bits. Turn into greased 9x5x3 inch loaf pan. Bake at 350° for 50 to 55 minutes or until done. Cool in pan 10 minutes. Turn out onto rack to cool completely. Drizzle with White Glaze.

White Glaze:

1 c. confectioners sugar

2 to 3 Tbsp. milk

Mix sugar with enough milk to make a glaze thin enough to drizzle from a spoon.

SOUR CREAM BANANA CAKE

Ann Dobransky

¼ c. butter
1⅓ c. sugar
2 eggs
1 tsp. vanilla
2 c. sifted all-purpose flour
1 tsp. baking powder

1 tsp. baking soda
¾ tsp. salt
1 c. sour cream
1 c. mashed ripe bananas (2
   medium)
½ c. chopped nuts

In a mixing bowl, cream butter. Add sugar gradually, beating until fluffy. Beat in eggs one at a time. Add vanilla. Sift together flour, baking powder, baking soda, and salt; add to creamed mixture alternately with sour cream. Add bananas; blend. Add nuts; mix just until evenly distributed. Turn into greased 9x13x2 inch pan. Bake at 350° for 40 to 45 minutes. Sift confectioners sugar over cooled cake.

BANANA SPLIT CAKE

Julieanne Marra

1 stick margarine, melted
2 c. graham cracker crumbs
2 eggs
2 sticks margarine
2 c. confectioners sugar
4 to 5 medium bananas, sliced
1 (20 oz.) can crushed
   pineapple, drained

2 (10 oz.) pkg. frozen
   strawberries, thawed and
   drained
1 (9 oz.) container Cool Whip
½ c. ground walnuts
¼ c. maraschino cherries,
   quartered

Combine melted margarine and graham cracker crumbs. Press into a greased 9x13 inch pan. Combine eggs, margarine, and confectioners sugar; beat well. Spread on crust. Arrange sliced bananas on filling, then spread drained pineapple on top of bananas. Spread strawberries over pineapple, topping all with the Cool Whip. Sprinkle with walnuts and maraschino cherries. Refrigerate several hours before serving.

BEER CAKE
Marie Pufky

4 c. flour
4 tsp. baking powder
1 tsp. salt
1 c. sugar

1 c. shortening
½ c. beer
2 eggs, beaten
3 (1 lb. 6 oz.) fruit pie filling*

Combine flour, baking powder, and salt. Add shortening; blend with pastry blender until crumbly. Add beer and eggs; mix until blended. Form into 2 balls. Roll (between 2 pieces of waxed paper) one ball to fit an 11x14x1 inch jelly roll pan, bringing dough up the sides. Fill with pie filling. Roll second ball; cover pie filling with dough. Bake at 350° for 45 to 60 minutes.

* Apples mixed with sugar and cinnamon may be substituted for pie filling.

AUSTRALIAN BEER CAKE
Dorothy Skellett

4 eggs
2 c. sugar
1 c. melted butter
2 tsp. cream of tartar

1 tsp. baking soda
1 c. beer
2½ c. sifted flour

Beat eggs and sugar together until blended. Add melted butter; blend. Add cream of tartar and baking soda to ¼ cup beer; set aside. Add remaining beer and flour to eggs; mix thoroughly. Add cream of tartar and baking soda mixture; blend. Pour into greased 9x13x2 inch pan. Top with Streusel Topping. Bake at 375° for 45 minutes.

Streusel Topping:

¾ c. unsifted flour
⅓ c. butter

½ c. sugar

Mix together ingredients with pastry blender. Sprinkle over cake before baking.

HARVARD BEET CAKE
Celia Matias

1 c. salad oil
2 c. sugar
2 eggs, well beaten
2½ c. flour
2 tsp. cinnamon
2 tsp. baking soda
1 tsp. salt

2 tsp. vanilla
1 c. Harvard beets, chopped
  fine
1 c. crushed pineapple
  (undrained)
1 c. cottage cheese
1 c. chopped nuts

In a large bowl, combine oil, sugar, eggs, flour, cinnamon, baking soda, salt, and vanilla; beat well. Add remaining ingredients; mix until thoroughly combined. Turn into greased 9x13 inch pan. Bake at 350° for 60 minutes or until toothpick comes out clean. Cool. Spread Frosting on cake.

Frosting:

½ c. margarine
2 c. confectioners sugar

1 egg white, stiffly beaten
1 tsp. vanilla

Cream margarine and sugar. Add stiffly beaten egg white and vanilla; fold in until thoroughly combined.

Chocolate Frosting: Make frosting same as above, but add 2 ounces melted chocolate.

SPECIAL BIRTHDAY CAKE
Mary Charnetsky

7 eggs, separated
1½ c. sugar
1½ c. sifted flour
2½ tsp. baking powder

½ tsp. salt
7 Tbsp. water
1 tsp. vanilla
¾ c. ground walnuts

Beat yolks seven minutes with electric beater. Add sugar gradually; beat three minutes more. Sift together flour, baking powder, and salt; add alternately with water to egg yolk mixture. Add vanilla and nuts. Beat egg whites until stiff; fold into egg yolk mixture. Pour into ungreased 10 inch tube pan. Bake at 350° for 1 hour or until cake tests done. Invert pan to cool. Frost as desired.

BOURBON NUT CAKE
Anna Chyl

4 c. sifted flour
1 tsp. baking powder
4 tsp. nutmeg
1 c. butter or margarine
2 c. sugar
6 eggs

½ c. bourbon
4 c. pecans, coarsely chopped
1 lb. seeded dark raisins
½ lb. candied cherries, sliced
Confectioners sugar

Sift together flour, baking powder, and nutmeg. Set aside. Cream butter; add sugar gradually. Continue creaming until fluffy. Beat in eggs one at a time. Add dry ingredients alternately with bourbon. Stir in nuts, raisins, and cherries. Turn batter into well-greased 10 inch tube pan lined on bottom with waxed paper. Bake at 300° about 2 hours or until cake tests done. If top of cake begins to brown before done, cover loosely with foil. Cool cake in pan 10 to 15 minutes, then turn out onto rack to cool completely. When cool, sprinkle with additional bourbon; wrap tight in foil or store in airtight tin. Sprinkle with confectioners sugar before slicing.

Hint: For best flavor, age cake at least a week (or even 2 weeks), moistening every few days with additional bourbon.

MABEL WHEELER'S BLUEBERRY COBBLER

Ann Dobransky

2 (21 oz.) cans blueberry pie
   filling
1 (20 oz.) pkg. white cake mix

½ c. butter or margarine
1 egg

In a 9x13 inch baking pan, spread pie filling. In large mixer bowl, cream butter; add dry ingredients (cake mix) and egg. Blend well. Spoon over pie filling. Bake at 350° for 40 minutes or until golden brown. Cut into twelve 3 inch squares.

BLUEBERRY COFFEE CAKE

Jody Dimitriou

4 c. flour
½ c. sugar
1 Tbsp. plus 2 tsp. baking
   powder

½ c. oil
1½ c. milk
2 eggs
2 c. blueberries

In a large bowl, combine dry ingredients. In a small bowl, combine oil, milk, and eggs; beat. Add to dry ingredients; mix until all ingredients are moistened. Fold in blueberries. Pour into a 9x13 inch pan sprayed with Pam. Sprinkle topping on cake. Bake at 375° for 45 to 50 minutes.

Topping:

1 c. sugar
⅔ c. flour

1 tsp. cinnamon
½ c. butter

In a small bowl, combine sugar, flour, and cinnamon; mix. Add butter; work in with a pastry blender, fork, or 2 knives to form a crumbly mixture. Sprinkle on top of cake before baking.

ANN'S BUTTERMILK CAKE

Sophia Malowicky

1 c. shortening
2 c. sugar
4 eggs
3½ c. flour
3 tsp. baking powder

½ tsp. baking soda
Pinch of salt
1½ c. buttermilk
2 tsp. vanilla

Cream shortening and sugar. Add eggs, one at a time, beating after each addition. Sift together flour, baking powder, baking soda, and salt; add to egg mixture alternately with buttermilk. Add vanilla; mix thoroughly. Pour into greased 9x13 inch pan. Bake at 350° for 1 hour. Spread Creole Icing on warm cake. Return to oven; bake 5 minutes.

Note: Yellow food coloring may be added for a yellow cake.

Creole Icing:

½ c. brown sugar
¾ Tbsp. flour
¼ c. melted butter

2 Tbsp. water
⅔ c. chopped nuts

Combine all ingredients; mix thoroughly.

CANDLELIGHT CAKE

Anna Chyl

1 (2 layer size) pkg. yellow cake
   mix
1 (3½ oz.) pkg. instant vanilla
   pudding
4 eggs

1 c. sour cream
½ c. vegetable oil
½ c. water
¼ c. poppy seed
Orange Butter Glaze

Combine cake mix, pudding mix, eggs, sour cream, oil, water, and poppy seed in large mixer bowl. Beat at medium speed for 2 minutes. Pour into greased 10 inch Bundt pan. Bake at 350° for 50 minutes or until cake tests done. Cool in pan 15 minutes. Remove from pan; finish cooling on rack. Spoon Orange Butter Glaze over cooled cake.

Orange Butter Glaze:

1½ Tbsp. milk
1 Tbsp. butter or margarine
1 Tbsp. orange juice

1¼ c. sifted confectioners sugar
½ tsp. grated orange rind

Heat milk, butter, and orange juice until butter is melted. Gradually pour into sugar and orange rind, beating until smooth.

CRANBERRY CARROT CAKE

Josephine Vimislik

3 c. sifted all-purpose flour
2 tsp. baking powder
1 tsp. baking soda
½ tsp. salt
½ tsp. cinnamon
½ tsp. nutmeg
½ tsp. cloves
1 c. grated carrots

1 c. whole cranberry sauce
1 c. light brown sugar
1 c. granulated sugar
1 c. salad oil
4 eggs, well beaten
½ c. chopped candied lemon
   peel

Sift flour, baking powder, baking soda, salt, and spices together into large bowl. Add remaining ingredients; beat until well blended. Pour into well greased and floured 2 quart mold, loaf, or tube pan. Bake at 350° for 1½ hours or until top is brown and springs back when lightly touched.

SWISS CARROT CAKE

Dorothy Skellett

⅔ c. grated carrots, firmly
   packed
1⅔ c. unblanched almonds or
   hazelnuts, chopped
¾ c. fine, dry bread crumbs
1 tsp. cinnamon

¼ tsp. ground cloves
6 eggs, separated
1¼ c. sugar
Grated rind and juice of 1
   lemon
2 Tbsp. sugar

Combine carrots, almonds, bread crumbs, cinnamon, and cloves. Beat egg yolks, 1¼ cups sugar, and lemon rind and juice until thick and creamy. Add to carrot mixture; blend. Beat egg whites until frothy; add 2 tablespoons sugar. Beat until stiff. Carefully fold egg whites into carrot mixture. Grease and line an 8 inch spring form pan with waxed paper. Grease waxed paper; sprinkle with additional bread crumbs. Pour batter into prepared pan. Bake at 350° for 45 to 60 minutes or until cake tests done. Cool. Remove from pan. Drizzle Glaze over cake.

Glaze:

2 c. confectioners sugar
3 Tbsp. water

¼ tsp. lemon extract

Combine ingredients; beat until smooth.

CASHEW NUT AND POTATO CAKE

Mary Kostyun

3 medium potatoes
1½ c. butter
2 c. sugar
2 Tbsp. flour
2 c. roasted, unsalted cashews, chopped

2 tsp. lemon rind
2 tsp. orange rind
9 egg yolks
4 egg whites

Boil potatoes until soft; mash. Set aside to cool. Cream butter and sugar. Add potatoes, flour, cashews, and lemon and orange rind; beat. Add egg yolks, one at a time, beating after each addition. Beat egg whites until stiff. Fold egg whites into potato mixture. Pour batter into a greased and floured 9 inch spring form pan, spreading and smoothing top with spatula. Bake at 350° for 1 hour and 15 minutes or until top is brown and cake tests done. Cool in pan 15 minutes, then remove from pan and let cool on wire rack. Serve cooled cake topped with whipped cream.

CHERRY CORDIAL CHIFFON CAKE

Mary Ponas

2¼ c. sifted flour
1½ c. sugar
3 tsp. baking powder
1 tsp. salt
½ c. salad oil
5 unbeaten egg yolks
¼ c. maraschino cherry juice

½ c. cold water
1 tsp. vanilla
1 c. (7 or 8) egg whites
½ tsp. cream of tartar
½ c. very finely chopped and drained maraschino cherries
½ c. chopped nuts

Combine flour, sugar, baking powder, and salt. Make a well; add salad oil, egg yolks, cherry juice, water, and vanilla. Beat on medium speed until smooth. In a large bowl, beat egg whites and cream of tartar until stiff peaks form. Gradually pour egg yolk mixture over egg whites; fold gently until blended. Sprinkle cherries and nuts over batter; gently fold with a few strokes. Pour into ungreased 10 inch tube pan. Bake at 325° for 65 to 70 minutes.

CHERRY PUDDING CAKE

Julie Sadowitz

¼ c. margarine
1 c. sugar
1 c. milk
2 c. flour
4 tsp. baking powder

1 (1 lb. 5 oz.) can cherry pie filling
1 Tbsp. reconstituted lemon juice
1 c. boiling water

Cream margarine and sugar. Stir in milk, flour, and baking powder; mix well. Spread batter in lightly greased 6½ x 10 x 2 inch baking dish. Cover with pie filling. Combine lemon juice with boiling water; carefully pour over top.

Bake at 350° for 30 to 35 minutes or until a crusty top appears and a toothpick comes out clean. Serves 6 to 8.

Note: Cake reverses itself while baking; cake is on top and pie filling is on the bottom.

CHERRY SHERRY CAKE
Marion Kaspryk

1 (2 layer size) pkg. yellow cake
mix
1 (3¾ oz.) pkg. instant vanilla
pudding
1 tsp. baking powder
4 eggs

½ c. salad oil
½ c. sherry wine
1 c. sour cream
½ c. chopped nuts
½ c. maraschino cherries, cut*

In a large bowl, combine cake mix, instant pudding, and baking powder. Add eggs, oil, wine, and sour cream; beat until thoroughly blended, about 3 minutes. Add nuts and cherries; mix. Pour into well greased and floured 10 inch tube or Bundt pan. Bake at 350° for 1 hour.

* For a festive look at Christmas, use green and red cherries.

CHEESECAKE I
Dorotha Cenesky

Crust:

1 c. graham cracker crumbs
¼ c. sugar

¼ c. butter, melted

Combine ingredients; press into ungreased 8 inch pie plate.

Filling:

1 (8 oz.) pkg. cream cheese
⅓ c. sugar
1 egg, beaten
1 tsp. vanilla
Grated rind of 1 lemon

Juice of 1 lemon
¼ c. melted butter
1 can sweetened condensed
milk

Beat cream cheese to soften. Add sugar; beat. Add egg; beat. Add vanilla, lemon rind, and juice; beat. Add butter and sweetened condensed milk; blend. Pour into prepared pan. Bake at 325° for 15 minutes; reduce temperature to 300°. Bake for 30 minutes.

CHEESECAKE II
Ann Dobransky

1 c. bread crumbs
½ c. sugar

½ tsp. cinnamon
½ c. butter, melted

Mix together all ingredients. Reserve 2 tablespoons of mixture to sprinkle on top of cake; put remaining crumbs on bottom and sides of a 9x13 inch pan.

Filling:

2 lb. cottage cheese	**1 pt. sour cream**
2 c. sugar	**5 eggs**
4 tsp. cornstarch	**1 tsp. vanilla**
½ tsp. salt	

Strain cottage cheese. Add sugar, cornstarch, and salt which have been mixed together. Add sour cream; mix. Add eggs, one at a time, beating after each addition. Add vanilla; mix. Pour into prepared pan; sprinkle with reserved crumbs. Bake at 375° for 1 hour and 15 minutes.

CHEESECAKE III

Eugenia Skarvinko

Crust:

1 c. graham cracker crumbs
2 Tbsp. (100% corn oil)
margarine, melted

Combine graham cracker crumbs and margarine. Pat half the mixture firmly into bottom of a 9 inch spring form pan. Reserve remaining mixture.

Filling:

2 env. unflavored gelatin	**2 c. creamed cottage cheese**
½ c. water	**1 tsp. vanilla**
2 egg whites	**1 (6 oz.) can frozen orange juice**
½ c. sugar	**concentrate, thawed**
1 c. skim milk, chilled	

In a small saucepan, sprinkle gelatin over water. Heat over low heat, stirring constantly, until gelatin is dissolved; set aside. In a small bowl, with mixer at high speed, beat egg whites until soft peaks form; gradually add sugar, beating until stiff peaks form. In a large bowl, beat milk at high speed; slowly add gelatin mixture, beating until soft peaks form. In a small bowl or blender, blend cottage cheese, vanilla, and undiluted orange juice; add to beaten milk along with egg white mixture. Carefully fold all ingredients until combined. Pour into prepared pan; top with reserved graham cracker crumbs. Refrigerate 2 hours. Serves 12.

CHEESECAKE IV (No Crust)

Carol Taylor

1 lb. small curd cottage cheese
1 lb. cream cheese
1½ c. sugar
4 eggs, slightly beaten
Juice of ½ lemon

1 tsp. vanilla
3 Tbsp. flour
3 Tbsp. cornstarch
½ c. butter, melted and cooled
2 c. sour cream

Beat cottage and cream cheese. Add sugar, ½ cup at a time, beating after each addition. Add eggs, lemon juice, and vanilla; beat. Add flour and cornstarch; beat. Add melted butter; beat. Add sour cream; beat. Pour into greased spring form pan. Bake at 325° for 1 hour. Turn oven off; keep cake in oven for 2 hours. Remove pan sides; cool for 2 hours on rack. Refrigerate overnight.

CHEESECAKE V

Josephine Vimislik

Graham cracker crumbs
1 lb. small curd cream style
  cottage cheese
2 (8 oz.) pkg. cream cheese,
  softened
1½ c. sugar
4 eggs, slightly beaten

¼ c. cornstarch
2 Tbsp. lemon juice
1 tsp. vanilla
½ c. butter or margarine,
  melted
1 pt. sour cream

Spread bottom and sides of a 9 inch spring form pan with butter. Dust sides with graham cracker crumbs. Force cottage cheese through a fine mesh sieve into a large mixing bowl; add cream cheese. Beat with electric mixer on high speed until well blended and creamy. Beating at high speed, gradually blend in sugar, then eggs. Reduce speed to low; add cornstarch, lemon juice, and vanilla. Beat until well blended. Add melted butter and sour cream; blend with low speed. Pour into preheated, prepared pan. Bake at 325° until firm around the edge - about 1 hour and 10 minutes. Turn oven off; let cake stand in oven with door closed for 2 hours. Remove from oven; cool completely on wire rack. Chill. Remove sides of pan. Serves 12.

To freeze: Wrap cheesecake with plastic film. Freeze. Defrost, wrapped, in refrigerator overnight. Cake may be frozen up to 1 month.

CHEESECAKE VI

Josephine Vimislik

Crust:

22 crushed graham crackers
3 Tbsp. sugar

½ c. butter or margarine,
  melted

Combine graham cracker crumbs and sugar. Add melted butter; mix with fork. Press mixture into bottom and sides of a 9x13 inch pan.

Filling:

2 c. cottage cheese
1 (8 oz.) pkg. cream cheese
4 egg yolks
1 c. sugar
½ c. flour

Juice and grated rind of 1
  lemon
1 (14 oz.) can condensed milk
1 tsp. vanilla
4 egg whites, stiffly beaten

Beat egg whites until stiff; set aside. In another bowl, combine cottage cheese, cream cheese, egg yolks, sugar, and flour; beat with mixer. Add juice and rind of lemon, condensed milk, and vanilla; mix well. Fold in stiffly beaten egg whites. Pour into prepared pan. Bake at 350° for 40 to 50 minutes.

CHEESECAKE VII

Helen Zellers

Crust:

1 c. margarine
2 c. sifted flour

2 Tbsp. sugar

Blend ingredients with pastry blender. Press mixture in a 9x13 inch Pyrex pan. Bake at 350° for 20 to 25 minutes or until golden brown.

Filling:

1 (8 oz.) pkg. cream cheese
1½ c. confectioners sugar
1 (9 oz.) container whipped
  topping

2 (1 lb. 5 oz.) cans cherry pie
  filling

Beat cheese and sugar until creamy. Add whipped topping; beat on low speed until thoroughly mixed. Pour over crust. Top with cherry pie filling.

APPLE CREAM CHEESE CAKE

Dorothy Skellett

Apples:

5 or 6 apples, sliced
½ c. sugar

½ tsp. cinnamon

Place apples in an 8x12x2 inch pan; sprinkle with sugar-cinnamon mixture. Cover with foil. Bake at 400° for 15 minutes.

Crust:

1½ c. graham cracker crumbs
½ c. melted butter or
  margarine

½ c. brown sugar
1 c. flour

Combine graham cracker crumbs, melted butter, and brown sugar. Add flour; mix well. Pat ½ the mixture in a greased 9x13 inch pan or 9 inch spring form pan. Reserve the rest for topping.

Filling:

4 (8 oz.) pkg. cream cheese	**4 eggs**
1¼ c. sugar	**1 tsp. vanilla**

Beat cheese to soften. Add sugar gradually; beat until smooth and creamy. Add eggs, one at a time, beating well after each addition. Add vanilla; blend. Pour ½ the mixture in prepared pan. Next, add a layer of ½ the apples, then remainder of cream cheese. Top with remaining apples, then sprinkle with remaining graham cracker mixture. Bake at 350° for 70 minutes. Turn oven off, leaving cake in oven for 1 hour with door open slightly.

CRANBERRY CHEESECAKE   Marianne Lawryk

Crust:

¾ c. graham cracker crumbs	**3 Tbsp. butter, melted**

Combine graham cracker crumbs with butter; mix well. Press into bottom of a 9 inch springform pan.

Filling:

2 c. cranberry juice cocktail	**4 (8 oz.) pkg. cream cheese**
2 env. unflavored gelatin	**1 c. sugar**
2 c. heavy cream	**4 tsp. lemon juice**

Pour cranberry juice cocktail into a small saucepan; sprinkle gelatin into the juice. Heat over low heat, stirring until gelatin is dissolved; set aside to cool. In a small mixer bowl, beat heavy cream until soft peaks form. In a large mixer bowl, beat cream cheese and sugar on medium speed until smooth; gradually add cooled gelatin mixture and lemon juice, beating until well mixed. Fold in whipped cream. Pour into prepared pan. Refrigerate until set, about 4 hours.

Glaze:

2 c. fresh or frozen cranberries	**1 c. sugar**
1 c. cranberry juice cocktail	**1 env. unflavored gelatin**

In a 2 quart saucepan, over high heat, heat cranberries, ¾ cup cranberry juice cocktail, and sugar to boiling; reduce heat to medium. Cook 5 minutes, stirring occasionally, until skins of berries pop. In a 1 cup measure, sprinkle gelatin over the remaining ¼ cup cranberry juice cocktail to soften. Stir gelatin mixture into cranberry mixture until gelatin is completely dissolved. Spoon mixture over cream cheese mixture in pan. Refrigerate until cranberry mixture is set, about 4 to 5 minutes.

CRANBERRY-ORANGE CHEESECAKE — Marianne Lawryk

½ c. cranberry-orange relish
2 Tbsp. plus 1 tsp. flour, divided
1 unbaked 9 inch pie shell
2 c. small curd creamed cottage
cheese, put through sieve
2 eggs
½ c. sugar
½ tsp. grated lemon peel
1 Tbsp. lemon juice
¼ tsp. salt
¼ c. half & half or heavy cream
Nutmeg
1 egg yolk, beaten with 1 Tbsp.
water
1 small orange, sliced

Mix relish with 1 teaspoon flour; spread evenly over bottom of pie shell. Set aside. In large mixer bowl, beat cottage cheese until almost smooth; beat in eggs, one at a time, all sugar, remaining 2 tablespoons flour, lemon peel, juice, salt, and half & half. Beat until well blended. Pour into pie shell; sprinkle lightly with nutmeg. Brush edge with egg yolk-water mixture. Bake on bottom rack in a preheated 350° oven 50 to 60 minutes or until filling is firm. Remove from oven; cool on rack. Chill well. Garnish with orange twists prepared from the orange slices.

CREAMY CHEESECAKE — Carol Taylor

Crust:

1½ c. crushed graham crackers
½ tsp. sugar
½ tsp. cinnamon
⅓ c. softened butter

Combine ingredients. Press mixture on bottom of greased 8 inch cake pan.

Filling:

2 (8 oz.) pkg. cream cheese
½ c. sugar
2 eggs (unbeaten)
1 (8 oz.) can crushed pineapple,
well drained

Blend cream cheese, sugar, and eggs with electric mixer. Fold in pineapple. Pour into prepared pan. Bake at 350° for 20 minutes. Cool 30 minutes.

Topping:

½ pt. sour cream
2 Tbsp. sugar
1 tsp. vanilla

Mix ingredients together until smooth. Spread over cooled cake. Bake at 350° for 7 minutes.

CREAM CHEESE CRUMSHUS CAKE   Genevieve Sadowitz

¼ c. butter
½ c. all-purpose flour
½ c. brown sugar, firmly
  packed
2 c. sifted all-purpose flour
2 tsp. baking powder
½ tsp. baking soda
½ tsp. salt

½ c. butter
1 (8 oz.) pkg. cream cheese
1¼ c. sugar
2 eggs (unbeaten)
1 tsp. vanilla
½ c. milk
½ c. chopped nuts (optional)

In a small bowl, cut ¼ cup butter into ½ cup flour and brown sugar. Set aside. Sift together 2 cups flour, baking powder, baking soda, and salt. Cream ½ cup butter with cream cheese. Gradually add sugar; cream well. Add eggs and vanilla; beat well. Add milk alternately with dry ingredients, beginning and ending with dry ingredients; blend well after each addition. Turn into 9x13x2 inch pan, greased on bottom. Sprinkle with crumb mixture and nuts. Bake at 350° for 30 to 40 minutes.

CHEESECAKE DELUXE   Helen Charnetsky

Crust:

1 c. sifted all-purpose flour
¼ c. sugar
1 tsp. grated lemon rind

¼ tsp. vanilla
½ c. butter or margarine
1 egg yolk

Mix first 4 ingredients with pastry blender. Add butter and egg yolk; cut in with pastry blender. Shape into ball. Wrap in plastic wrap; chill 1 hour. Roll about one-third of dough between floured pieces of waxed paper into a 9½ inch circle. Place on bottom of a 9 inch spring form pan; trim to fit. Bake at 400° for 10 minutes or until golden. Cool. Grease sides of spring form pan; fit over filled base. Roll rest of dough into 15x4 inch rectangle; cut in half lengthwise. Line sides of pan, patching if necessary.

Filling:

5 (8 oz.) pkg. soft cream cheese
1¾ c. sugar
3 Tbsp. flour
¼ tsp. salt
½ tsp. grated orange rind
  (optional)

¼ c. heavy cream
½ tsp. grated lemon rind
  (optional)
¼ tsp. vanilla
5 medium eggs (unbeaten)
2 egg yolks

Beat cheese with electric mixer until fluffy. Combine sugar, flour, salt, orange rind, and lemon rind; slowly add to cheese, beating until smooth. Add vanilla; beat. Add eggs and egg yolks, one at a time, beating after each addition. Stir in cream. Turn into lined pan. Bake at 500° for 12 minutes or until crust is golden. Reduce temperature to 200°; bake 1 hour. Cool away from drafts.

Remove spring form ring of pan. Chill. Will serve a large group. Large pieces will serve 12 special guests.

DR. BEAUTY'S CHEESECAKE

Marianne Lawryk

4 (8 oz.) pkg. cream cheese (at
   room temperature)
6 eggs, well beaten

2 c. sour cream
1 Tbsp. vanilla
2 Tbsp. cornstarch

In a large mixing bowl, combine all ingredients; beat well. Pour into a 10 inch spring form pan. Bake at 350° for 1 hour or until done. This cheesecake has no crust.

EASTER CHEESE CAKE

Teklia Farynyk

2 lb. cottage cheese
3 eggs, beaten
1½ c. sugar
1 c. raisins

1 tsp. orange rind
Paska bread dough
1 egg yolk
1 Tbsp. water

Drain cottage cheese in cheesecloth to make it as dry as possible. In a bowl, combine cheese, eggs, sugar, raisins, and orange rind. Grease a 9x13 inch pan. Pat dough (save some for top) thin on bottom and sides of pan. Pour cheese mixture on dough. Roll out remaining dough; cut in ½ inch wide strips. Crisscross dough on top of cheese. Combine egg yolk and water; paint dough. Bake at 350° for 1 hour.

EASY CHEESECAKE

Dorotha Cenesky

Crust:

1 c. fine graham cracker
   crumbs
¼ c. sugar

¼ c. butter or margarine,
   melted

Combine crumbs and sugar; add butter. Press mixture on bottom and sides of ungreased 9 inch layer cake pan building up edge of crust about ¼ inch above rim. Chill until needed.

Filling:

12 oz. cream cheese
½ c. sugar
1 egg, beaten

¼ c. butter, softened
½ tsp. vanilla

Blend cream cheese and sugar; add beaten egg, butter, and vanilla. Blend thoroughly. Pour into prepared pan. Bake at 300° for 45 minutes.

"Secret Crust": Line a greased 8 inch round pan with ¼ inch slices of refrigerated slice and bake sugar cookies. Bake at 375° for 30 minutes or until done.

EGGNOG CHEESECAKE

Pani Julia Lawryk

Crust:

1½ c. vanilla wafer crumbs   ¼ c. butter, melted

Heat oven to 350°. Combine crumbs with butter; mix thoroughly. Press firm and evenly against bottom and sides of a 9 inch spring form pan. Bake 10 minutes. Cool.

Filling:

2 env. unflavored gelatin   ½ c. granulated sugar
1¼ c. dairy eggnog, divided   4 c. creamed cottage cheese
3 large eggs, separated   1 c. heavy cream
    (pasteurized only)*

Dissolve the gelatin in ¼ cup of the eggnog; set aside. In the top of a double boiler, beat egg yolks and sugar; stir in remaining eggnog and cook gently, stirring until mixture thickens slightly. Remove from heat; add gelatin mixture. Blend thoroughly. Press cottage cheese through a sieve into a large mixing bowl; add gelatin mixture. Blend thoroughly. Beat egg whites until soft peaks form; fold into cheese mixture. Whip cream until stiff, but not dry; fold. Pour into pan with prepared crust. Chill 4 hours or until set. Yields 6 to 7 pieces.

* Since the egg whites are used raw in this recipe, there is danger of salmonella. Therefore, it is important to use the pasteurized eggs.

ELLA'S CREAM CHEESE CAKE

Marie Pufky

2 (8 oz.) pkg. cream cheese   3 Tbsp. cornstarch
    (room temperature)   1 tsp. vanilla
1 lb. Ricotta cheese   ½ c. margarine, melted
1¼ c. sugar   1 pt. sour cream
1½ Tbsp. lemon juice   1 (1 lb. 5 oz.) can blueberry pie
4 eggs   filling*
3 Tbsp. flour

In a large bowl, add each ingredient in order as above, keeping beater going constantly. Pour into greased 9 inch spring form pan. Bake at 325° for 1 hour. Turn oven off; leave in oven 2 more hours. Spread pie filling to cover top of cake. Chill. Remove sides of pan. Slice and serve.

* Also good with strawberry or cherry pie filling.

FLUFFY CHEESECAKE

Linda Zapach

Crust:

1½ c. crushed Zwieback
2 Tbsp. sugar

2 Tbsp. butter or margarine,
melted

Combine crumbs, sugar, and melted butter or margarine. Press on bottom of ungreased 9 inch springform pan.

Filling:

2 (8 oz.) pkg. cream cheese
½ c. sugar
1 tsp. grated lemon peel
1 Tbsp. lemon juice
1 tsp. vanilla

Dash of salt
5 egg yolks
2 c. sour cream
5 egg whites
½ c. sugar

Stir cream cheese to soften. Beat in ½ cup sugar, lemon peel, lemon juice, vanilla, and salt. Blend in egg yolks, then sour cream; do not beat. Beat egg whites until soft peaks form. Gradually add ½ cup sugar, beating until stiff peaks form. Fold into cream cheese mixture. Carefully pour into springform pan. Bake at 325° for 1 hour and 20 minutes or until done. Cool in pan 10 minutes. With small spatula, loosen cheesecake from edge of pan about ½ inch down. Cool in pan; chill if desired. Makes 12 to 16 servings.

LEMON CHEESECAKE WITH GLAZED RASPBERRIES

Pani Matka Elizabeth Hutnick

Shell:

2 c. all-purpose flour
½ c. sugar
2 tsp. grated lemon rind
1 c. unsalted butter, cut into
bits

2 large egg yolks
½ tsp. vanilla

Make the shell: In a bowl, combine the flour, sugar, and lemon rind and blend in the butter until the mixture resembles meal. Add the egg yolks and the vanilla and combine the mixture until it forms a dough. Remove the ring from a 10 inch springform pan. Press one-third of the dough onto the bottom of the springform pan; bake the dough in a preheated 400° oven for 8 minutes and let it cool on a rack. Return the ring to the pan and pat the remaining dough onto the sides of the pan, at least 2 inches high.

Filling:

2½ lb. cream cheese, softened
1¾ c. sugar
1 tsp. grated lemon rind
¼ tsp. vanilla
3 Tbsp. all-purpose flour

¼ tsp. salt
4 large whole eggs
2 large egg yolks
¼ c. heavy cream

In the bowl of an electric mixer, beat the cream cheese until it is smooth and beat in the sugar, the lemon rind, and the vanilla. Beat in the flour, the salt, the whole eggs and the egg yolks, 1 at a time, and the cream. Pour the filling into the shell and bake the cheesecake on a baking sheet in a preheated 425° oven for 12 minutes. Reduce heat to 300° and bake the cheesecake for 1 hour more. (It will not be set.) Let the cheesecake cool on a rack.

Topping:

¾ c. sugar
3 Tbsp. cornstarch
3 Tbsp. light corn syrup

3 to 4 drops red food coloring
3 to 4 c. raspberries

In a saucepan, combine ¾ cup water, sugar, and the cornstarch and cook the mixture over moderately high heat, stirring until it is thick and clear. Remove the pan from the heat and stir in the corn syrup and the food coloring. Let the topping cool until it is lukewarm. Arrange the raspberries on the cheesecake and pour the topping over them. Chill the cheesecake for at least 3 hours or overnight.

OLD-FASHIONED CHEESECAKE   Pani Julia Lawryk

2 c. fine Zwieback crumbs
½ c. sugar
1 tsp. cinnamon
½ c. melted butter
4 eggs
1 c. sugar
⅛ tsp. salt

1½ Tbsp. lemon juice
1½ tsp. grated lemon rind
1 c. half & half or evaporated
  milk
1½ lb. dry cottage cheese
¼ c. flour
¼ c. chopped nuts

Mix together Zwieback crumbs, ½ cup sugar, cinnamon, and melted butter. Measure out ¼ cup of the mixture and reserve for sprinkling over the top. Press remaining crumb mixture over the bottom and up the sides of a 9 inch springform pan. Beat the eggs with the 1 cup sugar until light. Stir in salt, lemon juice and rind, half & half or evaporated milk, cottage cheese, and flour. Beat thoroughly; strain through a fine sieve. Pour into prepared springform pan. Sprinkle reserved crumb mixture over the top. Bake in preheated 350° oven, about 1 hour or until center is set. Turn off heat; open oven door and let cheesecake stand in oven 1 hour or until cooled. Yield: 10 to 12 servings.

PINEAPPLE CHEESECAKE

Nancy Tarcha

Crust:

2 c. graham cracker crumbs	**¼ c. butter, melted**
2 tsp. sugar	**2 tsp. chopped nuts (optional)**

Combine all ingredients. Press mixture on bottom of greased 9x13x2 inch pan. Bake at 325° for 12 minutes.

Filling:

4 (8 oz.) pkg. cream cheese	**1 (1 lb. 4 oz.) can crushed**
1 c. sugar	**pineapple***
2 eggs	**2 env. unflavored gelatin**
1 tsp. vanilla	

Cream the cheese (room temperature) with electric mixer. Gradually add sugar; beat. Add eggs, one at a time, beating after each addition. Add vanilla; blend. Drain pineapple. Add gelatin to pineapple juice in small saucepan. Heat until gelatin is dissolved; cool. Add to cheese mixture; beat. Add pineapple; blend. Pour into prepared pan. Bake at 325° for 30 to 35 minutes. Cool cake 20 minutes, then spread with the following.

Sour Cream Topping:

1 pt. sour cream	**1 tsp. vanilla**
4 Tbsp. sugar	

Mix all ingredients together until very smooth. Spread on top of cake. Bake at 475° for 5 minutes. Cool and refrigerate.

* Frozen strawberries or raspberries may be used in place of pineapple.

LOW CALORIE PINEAPPLE CHEESECAKE

Marianne Lawryk

1 (20 oz.) can crushed pineapple	**1 tsp. grated lemon peel**
1 env. unflavored gelatin	**1 tsp. vanilla extract**
½ c. skim milk	**Water**
1 (8 oz.) pkg. imitation cream cheese, softened	**2 egg whites**

In sieve, drain pineapple, pressing with spoon to make ¼ cup juice; set aside pineapple and juice. In a 2 quart saucepan, sprinkle gelatin over milk; let stand 1 minute to soften slightly. Cook over low heat until gelatin is completely dissolved, about 3 minutes, stirring constantly; remove from heat. In a large mixer bowl, with mixer at medium speed, beat cream cheese until smooth; gradually beat in hot gelatin mixture, lemon peel, and vanilla. To reserved pineapple juice, add enough water to make 1 cup. At low speed, gradually beat into cream cheese mixture. Refrigerate until mounds form when dropped from a spoon.

Meanwhile, in small mixer bowl, at high speed, beat egg whites until whites stand in stiff, glossy peaks. Reserve ½ cup crushed pineapple for garnish later. Fold remaining pineapple and gelatin mixture into 9 inch pie dish; refrigerate until set, about 4 hours. Garnish with ½ cup crushed pineapple. Makes 10 servings.

RASPBERRY SWIRL CHEESECAKE   Marianne Lawryk

Crust:

1 c. corn flake crumbs   **3 Tbsp. margarine, melted**
3 Tbsp. sugar

Combine crumbs, sugar, and margarine; press onto bottom of 9 inch spring form pan. Bake at 350° for 10 minutes.

Filling:

2 (8 oz.) pkg. cream cheese,   **2 eggs**
softened   **¼ tsp. almond extract**
¼ c. sugar   **⅓ c. raspberry preserves**

In a large mixing bowl, combine cream cheese and sugar, mixing at medium speed with electric mixer until well blended. Add eggs, one at a time, mixing well after each addition. Add almond extract; blend well. Pour over baked crust. Drop rounded teaspoons of preserves onto cream cheese mixture. Cut through batter with knife once for marble effect. Bake at 350° for 45 minutes. Loosen cake from rim of pan; cool before removing rim. Chill. Makes 10 to 12 servings.

RUM CHEESECAKE   Marianne Lawryk

Crust:

1½ c. vanilla wafer crumbs   **6 Tbsp. butter**
¼ c. sugar

Combine wafer crumbs and sugar. Melt butter in 2 (9 inch) pie plates. Add crumb mixture to butter in pie plates; mix. Press against bottom and sides.

Filling:

3 (8 oz.) pkg. cream cheese   **1 tsp. vanilla**
1½ c. sugar   **1 tsp. pure rum flavoring**
4 eggs   **1 Tbsp. dark rum**
⅛ tsp. salt

Beat cream cheese. Add sugar; beat. Add eggs, one at a time, beating after each addition. Add remaining ingredients; beat. Pour into prepared pans. Bake at 350° for 20 minutes. Cool 15 minutes, then spread with the following.

Topping:

2 c. sour cream
¼ c. sugar
Pinch of salt

1 tsp. vanilla
1 tsp. pure rum flavoring

Mix all ingredients together until smooth. Spread on cooled cakes. Bake at 450° for 5 minutes.

SUNNY'S "NO MIXER" CHEESECAKE   Marianne Lawryk

All ingredients should be at room temperature.

2 (8 oz.) pkg. cream cheese
¾ c. sugar
2 Tbsp. flour
½ tsp. salt
3 eggs, slightly beaten

1 c. sour cream
¼ c. lemon juice
1 tsp. vanilla
1 (21 oz.) can cherry pie filling

In an 8 or 9 inch square pan, mash cream cheese with a fork until very soft. Add sugar, flour, and salt; blend well. Add remaining ingredients except pie filling; mix briskly with fork until thoroughly blended, scraping sides often. Bake at 350° for 45 minutes or until toothpick inserted in center comes out clean. Cool in pan on rack. Spread with pie filling; chill. Serves 9.

Note: If you have a "mixer," you may proceed with above recipe and it's still "easier."

BLACK MIDNIGHT CAKE   Julie Dudik

⅔ c. vegetable oil
1⅔ c. sugar
3 eggs
⅔ c. cocoa
1⅓ c. cold water

2 c. flour
1¼ tsp. baking soda
⅓ tsp. baking powder
1 tsp. salt
1 tsp. vanilla

In a large bowl, beat oil, sugar, and eggs. In a separate bowl, combine cocoa and cold water. Sift together flour, baking soda, baking powder, and salt. Add sifted dry ingredients alternately with cocoa mixture to egg mixture. Mix thoroughly. Add vanilla. Pour into greased 9x13 inch pan or 2 greased 9 inch layer pans. Bake at 350° - 9x13 inch for 35 to 45 minutes, 9 inch layers 25 to 35 minutes. Frost with Ice Cream Frosting.

Ice Cream Frosting:

2 c. sifted confectioners sugar
⅓ c. butter
1 egg white (unbeaten)

1 tsp. warm water
1 tsp. vanilla

Combine all ingredients. Beat thoroughly.

CHOCOLATE CAKE I

Nancy Kanazawich

2 c. flour
2 c. sugar
1 c. cocoa
2 tsp. baking powder
2 tsp. baking soda

Pinch of salt
¾ c. vegetable oil
2 c. boiling water
2 eggs

Combine the first 6 ingredients. Add oil and water; mix thoroughly. Add eggs; beat. Pour into greased 9x13 inch pan. Bake at 350° (do not preheat oven) for 30 minutes. Frost cooled cake with a sour cream frosting; swirl with liquid baking chocolate.

CHOCOLATE CAKE II

Marie Pufky

3 (1 oz.) sq. unsweetened
  chocolate, cut fine
½ c. boiling water
1¾ c. cake flour, sifted
1 c. sugar
¾ tsp. salt
½ tsp. baking powder

¾ tsp. baking soda
½ c. shortening
½ c. dark corn syrup
2 eggs
1 tsp. vanilla
⅓ c. sour milk

Combine chocolate and boiling water in small bowl. Set aside to cool. Combine flour, sugar, salt, baking powder, and baking soda. Set aside. Cream shortening; add corn syrup. Beat. Add eggs, one at a time, beating after each addition. Add vanilla; beat. Combine chocolate mixture with sour milk. Add flour mixture alternately with chocolate-sour milk mixture; blend thoroughly. Pour batter into greased and floured 8x12x2 inch pan. Bake at 350° for 50 to 60 minutes.

CHOCOLATE CHERRY CAKE

Margaret Klish

1 box Duncan Hines dark
  chocolate cake mix
1 (1 lb. 6 oz.) can cherry pie
  filling

3 eggs

Combine all ingredients in large mixer bowl. Beat thoroughly at creaming speed. Pour batter into a 9x13x2 inch pan that has been sprayed with Pam and greased. Bake at 350° for 25 to 30 minutes.

Note: If you wish to bake this rich, moist cake with some cherries left whole, remove some cherries with a teaspoon before mixing, then fold them in at the end.

* Bake 10 inch layers 20 minutes and a 12 inch layer 25 to 30 minutes.

CHOCOLATE CHIP CHIFFON CAKE — Dorothy Skellett

2 c. flour
3 tsp. baking powder
1 tsp. salt
1¾ c. sugar
½ c. salad oil
7 egg yolks

¾ c. cold water
2 tsp. vanilla
1 bar German's chocolate, grated
7 egg whites
½ tsp. cream of tartar

In a large bowl, sift together flour, baking powder, salt, and sugar. In another bowl, beat salad oil, egg yolks, cold water, and vanilla until smooth. Add egg mixture to dry ingredients; fold. Fold in chocolate. Beat egg whites until foamy. Add cream of tartar; beat until stiff, but not dry. Fold the flour and egg mixture gently into egg whites. Pour into an ungreased 10 inch tube pan. Bake at 350° for 50 to 55 minutes. Invert pan to cool.

O'S COCOA CUPLETS — Dorothy Skellett

2 c. flour
1 Tbsp. cocoa
1 tsp. salt
1¼ c. sugar
¾ c. shortening
2 eggs (unbeaten)

1 tsp. vanilla
1 tsp. baking soda
1 c. cold water
1 c. semi-sweet chocolate chips
½ c. chopped nuts

Sift together flour, cocoa, and salt; set aside. Cream sugar and shortening. Add eggs and vanilla; beat. Combine baking soda and cold water; add alternately with dry ingredients to creamed mixture. Fill miniature muffin cups, lined with baking cups, half full. Sprinkle chocolate chips and chopped nuts over cupcake batter. Bake at 375° for 20 to 25 minutes.

CHOCOLATE ECLAIR CAKE

Helen Rucky

1 c. water
8 or 9 oz. chocolate syrup
½ c. margarine
1 c. flour
1 tsp. salt
4 eggs

1 (6 oz.) pkg. vanilla instant
  pudding
Milk
1 (8 oz.) cream cheese
1 pkg. Cool Whip

Boil water and margarine; add chocolate syrup. Add flour and salt and cook until a ball is formed. Remove from heat and add eggs. Spread in greased jelly roll pan. Bake at 400° for 30 to 35 minutes. Press down bubbles; cool. Mix pudding with milk as directed on package. Blend in cream cheese; spread over baked crust. Top with Cool Whip and drizzle with chocolate syrup.

FAST FIXIN' CHOCOLATE CAKE

Olga Gooley
Mary Kostyn

1 (2 layer size) pkg. devil's food
  cake mix
1 (3½ oz.) pkg. instant
  chocolate pudding
¼ c. vegetable oil

2 eggs
1¼ c. water
1 c. chocolate chips
1 c. chopped nuts

Pour oil in 9x13 inch glass pan; coat well. Put all remaining ingredients in pan. Stir with fork 2 minutes. Bake at 325° for 35 to 45 minutes.

CHOCOLATE MINT SQUARES

Jane Ellsworth

Cake Layer:

1 c. sugar
½ c. butter
4 eggs

1 c. sifted flour
½ tsp. salt
16 oz. Hershey's syrup

Cream sugar, butter, and eggs. Add remaining ingredients; mix until smooth. Pour into greased and floured 9x13 inch pan. Bake at 350° for 30 minutes. Cool in pan.

Mint Layer:

2 c. confectioners sugar
½ tsp. peppermint flavoring
½ c. butter

Few drops of green food
  coloring
Few drops of water

Combine all ingredients; beat until smooth. Spread over cooled cake.

Glaze:

1 (6 oz.) pkg. chocolate chips

6 Tbsp. butter

Melt chips and butter, stirring until smooth. Cool. Spread over Mint Layer. Chill until partially set (about 10 minutes). Cut into small squares before Glaze hardens.

CHOCOLATE PEPPERMINT ICE CREAM CAKE
Mary Ponas

Double Chocolate Cake:

½ c. butter or margarine
1¼ c. sugar
1 tsp. vanilla
4 eggs
1¼ c. unsifted all-purpose flour
⅓ c. unsweetened cocoa powder

¾ tsp. baking soda
¼ tsp. salt
1½ c. (1 lb. can) chocolate
    flavor syrup
½ c. water

Cream butter, sugar, and vanilla in large mixing bowl. Add eggs, one at a time, beating well after each addition. Combine flour, cocoa, baking soda, and salt; add alternately with chocolate syrup and water to creamed mixture. Pour batter into 3 greased and floured 9 inch cake pans. Bake at 350° for 27 minutes. Cool in pans 10 minutes; remove and cool completely. Wrap each layer separately in foil; freeze several hours.

Peppermint Filling:

1 qt. vanilla ice cream
⅔ c. crushed peppermint candy
  or 2 tsp. peppermint extract
  plus ⅛ tsp. red food coloring

Line 2 (9 inch) layer cake pans with aluminum foil; chill in freezer. Soften ice cream; quickly stir in crushed peppermint candy or extract and food coloring. Divide evenly between pans; cover. Freeze. Remove ice cream from pans; peel off foil. Alternately layer peppermint and chocolate layers, ending with chocolate. Return to freezer while preparing glaze.

Chocolate Glaze:

3 Tbsp. unsweetened cocoa
3 Tbsp. water
1 Tbsp. light corn syrup

1 Tbsp. butter
1 c. confectioners sugar
½ tsp. vanilla

Combine cocoa, water, corn syrup, and butter in small, heavy saucepan. Cook over low heat, stirring constantly, until mixture boils and becomes somewhat thickened. Remove from heat; add sugar and vanilla, beating until smooth. Spoon on top of cake. Garnish with crushed peppermint candy. Return to freezer until serving time.

EASY CHOCOLATE ROLL-UP

Mary Ponas

¼ c. butter or margarine
1 c. chopped pecans
1⅓ c. flaked coconut
1 c. (15½ oz. can) unsweetened
   condensed milk
3 eggs
1 c. sugar

⅔ c. flour
⅓ c. cocoa
¼ tsp. baking powder
¼ tsp. salt
⅓ c. water
1 tsp. vanilla

Line a 10x15x1 inch jelly roll pan with foil. Melt butter in pan. Sprinkle nuts and coconut evenly in pan; drizzle with milk. Beat eggs at high speed until fluffy. Gradually add sugar; continue beating 2 minutes. Combine flour, cocoa, baking powder, and salt; add to egg mixture alternately with water and vanilla, beating at low speed for 1 minute. Pour evenly into pan. Bake at 375° for 20 to 25 minutes. Sprinkle with confectioners sugar. Cover with towel. Invert pan on towel. Remove pan and foil. Roll up jelly roll fashion, starting with the 10 inch side. Cool.

SMALL CHOCOLATE CAKE

Sophia Malowicky

½ c. cocoa
1½ c. cake flour
1 c. sugar
1 tsp. baking powder
¾ tsp. salt

½ c. buttermilk
1 c. salad oil
1 egg
1 tsp. vanilla
½ c. boiling water

Sift together the first 5 ingredients 3 times. In a medium bowl, beat buttermilk and salad oil; add egg, vanilla, and boiling water. Blend. Add flour mixture to liquids; beat well. Bake at 325° for 15 minutes, then at 350° for 15 minutes.

Icing:

¼ c. butter
2 Tbsp. cocoa
2¼ c. sifted confectioners sugar

3 Tbsp. liquid coffee
1 tsp. vanilla

Combine ingredients. Beat until creamy.

CHOCOLATE YUMMY CAKE

Jane Ellsworth

1 large (21.5 oz.) pkg. brownie
   mix (family size)
½ c. chopped nuts
2 c. graham cracker crumbs

1 (15 oz.) can condensed milk
1 c. chocolate chips
½ c. chopped nuts

Prepare brownie mix according to package directions. Add ½ cup chopped nuts. Spread on greased 11x13 inch pan. Mix together graham cracker crumbs and condensed milk. Spread on brownie batter. Sprinkle with chocolate chips and ½ cup nuts. Bake at 350° for 30 to 35 minutes.

Topping:

1 can vanilla frosting
1 sq. baking chocolate

1 Tbsp. butter

Spread frosting over cooled brownies. Melt chocolate and butter; mix well. Drizzle over frosting. Cut in squares.

CINNAMON PUDDING CAKE

Carol Taylor

1¾ c. brown sugar (light or dark)
1½ c. cold water
2 Tbsp. butter
1 c. sugar
2 Tbsp. butter

2 c. all-purpose flour
2 tsp. baking powder
½ tsp. salt
2½ tsp. cinnamon
1 c. cold milk
½ c. chopped walnuts

In a saucepan, combine brown sugar, water, and 2 tablespoons butter. Bring to a boil, stirring constantly; take pan off heat. Cool. Cream butter; add sugar gradually as you continue beating. Sift together flour, baking powder, salt, and cinnamon; add to creamed mixture alternately with milk, beginning and ending with dry ingredients. Pour into greased 8 or 9 inch square pan. Pour cooled brown sugar mixture over batter; sprinkle with chopped nuts. Bake at 350° for 35 to 40 minutes. (During baking process, the brown sugar mixture seeps through batter and ends up at bottom of pan.) Serve slices "bottom end up." Delicious served with either a dollop of whipped cream or a scoop of vanilla ice cream.

RING OF COCONUT FUDGE CAKE

Pani Julia Lawryk
Mary Ponas

Filling:

1 (8 oz.) pkg. cream cheese
¼ c. sugar
1 tsp. vanilla
1 egg

½ c. flaked coconut
1 c. semi-sweet or milk chocolate chips

In a medium bowl, combine cheese, sugar, coconut, vanilla, egg, and chips; set aside.

Cake:

2 c. sugar	2 tsp. baking powder
1 c. vegetable oil	1½ tsp. salt
2 eggs	1 c. hot coffee or water
3 c. all-purpose flour	1 c. buttermilk
¾ c. unsweetened cocoa powder	1 tsp. vanilla
2 tsp. baking soda	½ c. chopped nuts

Preheat oven to 350°. Generously grease and lightly flour a 10 inch tube or 12 cup Bundt pan. In a large bowl, combine sugar, oil, and eggs; beat one minute at high speed. In another bowl, combine flour, baking soda, baking powder, salt, and cocoa; mix to get all ingredients mixed evenly throughout. With mixer set at medium speed and scraping sides of bowl occasionally, add dry ingredients alternately with liquid, beginning and ending with flour. Stir in nuts. Pour one-half the batter into prepared pan; carefully spoon filling over batter. Top with remaining batter. Bake 70 to 75 minutes or until top springs back when touched lightly in center. Cool upright in pan 15 minutes; remove from pan. Cool completely.

Glaze:

1 c. confectioners sugar	2 Tbsp. margarine or butter
3 Tbsp. unsweetened cocoa powder	2 tsp. vanilla
	1 to 3 Tbsp. hot water

In a medium bowl, combine confectioners sugar, cocoa powder, margarine, vanilla, and enough hot water for glazing consistency. Beat until smooth. Spoon over cake, allowing some to run down the sides.

COCONUTTY LEMON CAKE

Mary Ponas

1 (14.9 oz.) pkg. Pillsbury lemon frosting mix	4 eggs
	1 tsp. lemon extract
1 c. butter or margarine, softened	2 c. all-purpose flour
	2 tsp. baking powder
1 (8 oz.) pkg. cream cheese, softened	1 c. flaked coconut
	½ c. chopped nuts

Measure ½ cup dry frosting mix; reserve for Topping. In large mixer bowl, cream butter, cream cheese, remaining frosting mix, eggs, and lemon extract; beat 3 minutes at high speed. Add flour and baking powder; beat 2 minutes at medium speed, scraping bowl occasionally. By hand, stir in coconut and nuts. Spread in a 9x13 inch pan which has been greased only on the bottom. Bake at 350° for 30 to 35 minutes or until toothpick comes out clean. *Do not overbake.* Cool completely. Spread Topping over cake.

Topping:

½ c. reserved frosting mix
½ c. flaked coconut
¼ c. milk

¼ tsp. lemon extract
2 Tbsp. butter or margarine,
softened

In small mixing bowl, combine all ingredients; mix well.

ANY FRUIT COFFEE CAKE

3 c. flour
1 c. sugar
1 Tbsp. baking powder
1 tsp. salt
1 tsp. cinnamon

¼ tsp. mace
1 c. butter or margarine
2 eggs, beaten
1 c. milk
1 tsp. vanilla

In a large mixing bowl, stir together flour, sugar, baking powder, salt, cinnamon, and mace. Cut in butter until mixture resembles fine crumbs. Combine eggs, milk, and vanilla; add to flour mixture, mixing until blended. Spread half the batter in a greased 9x13x2 inch pan. Spread cooled Fruit Filling over batter. Spoon remaining batter over fruit, spreading out as much as possible. Sprinkle Topping over batter. Bake at 350° for 50 minutes.

Fruit Filling:

4 c. chopped apples, apricots,
peaches, pineapple,
blueberries, or rhubarb
1 c. water

2 Tbsp. lemon juice
1¼ c. sugar
⅓ c. cornstarch

In a saucepan, combine fruit and water. Simmer, covered, 5 minutes or until fruit is tender. Stir in lemon juice. Combine sugar and cornstarch; stir into fruit mixture. Cook and stir until thickened and bubbly.

Topping:

½ c. sugar
½ c. flour

¼ c. butter or margarine
½ c. chopped nuts

Combine sugar and flour. Cut in butter until mixture resembles coarse crumbs. Stir in nuts.

IRENE'S COFFEE CAKE

Evelyn Kanazawich

1 c. sugar
½ c. margarine
2 eggs
½ pt. (1 c.) sour cream
2 c. flour

1 tsp. baking powder
1 tsp. baking soda
Pinch of salt
1 pt. frozen blueberries

Cream sugar, margarine, and eggs. Add sour cream. Combine flour, baking powder, baking soda, and salt. Add to creamed mixture; blend thoroughly. Fold in frozen blueberries. Pour into 2 greased 8 inch round pans. Sprinkle topping on batter; cut through and swirl. Bake at 350° for 30 minutes.

Topping:

½ c. sugar
2 tsp. cinnamon

½ c. chopped nuts

Combine ingredients. Sprinkle on cake batter in pans.

SOUR CREAM COFFEE CAKE I
Mary Kostyun

Cake:

1 Duncan Hines butter recipe
   golden cake mix
½ c. sugar

½ c. oil
8 oz. sour cream
4 eggs

Combine cake mix and sugar; add oil and sour cream. Blend. Add eggs, one at a time, beating well after each using medium speed. Turn into well greased Bundt pan. Sprinkle with Topping. Bake at 350° for 30 to 50 minutes or until cake tester or toothpick comes out clean when poked in highest part of cake. Cool in pan 10 minutes before removing from pan.

Topping:

3 Tbsp. light brown sugar
2 tsp. cinnamon

½ c. finely chopped nuts

Combine all ingredients; sprinkle on top of cake before baking.

Frosting:

1 c. confectioners sugar
1 Tbsp. melted butter

1 Tbsp. milk
1 tsp. vanilla

Combine all ingredients; beat well. Drizzle on top and down sides of cooled cake.

SOUR CREAM CAKE II
Sophia Malowicky

1 c. butter
1 c. sugar
2 eggs
1 c. sour cream

2½ c. flour
1 tsp. baking powder
1 tsp. baking soda

Cream butter and sugar; add eggs. Beat thoroughly. Add sour cream; blend well. Sift together flour, baking powder, and baking soda; add to batter. Mix.

Spread ⅔ batter in greased 9x13 inch pan. Spread Filling over batter. Top with remaining batter. Bake at 350° for 45 minutes.

Filling:

1 (1 lb. 14 oz.) can crushed
   pineapple
½ c. sugar

2 Tbsp. cornstarch
Juice of 1 lemon

Combine ingredients in saucepan; boil until thickened. Cool.

SYRIAN NUTMEG COFFEE CAKE   Helen Rucky

2 c. brown sugar
2 c. sifted flour
½ c. shortening
1 c. sour cream

1 tsp. baking soda
1 egg
1 tsp. nutmeg
½ c. chopped nuts

Cut shortening into flour and sugar with a pastry blender to form crumbs. Pat half the crumb mixture in a very well greased 9 inch square pan. Combine sour cream and baking soda; set aside. Add egg, nutmeg, and sour cream to remaining crumbs; mix. Pour batter over first layer in pan. Sprinkle with nuts. Bake at 350° for 35 to 40 minutes.

CRANBERRY RIPPLE CAKE   Jane Ellsworth

2 c. all-purpose flour
1 tsp. baking powder
1 tsp. baking soda
¼ tsp. salt
½ c. butter or margarine
1 c. sugar

½ tsp. almond extract
2 eggs
1 c. sour cream
1 (8 oz.) can whole cranberry
   sauce
½ c. chopped pecans

Stir together flour, baking powder, baking soda, and salt. In large mixer bowl, beat butter 30 seconds. Add sugar and almond extract; beat until fluffy. Add eggs; beat well. Add flour mixture and sour cream alternately to creamed mixture, beating after each addition until smooth. Spread half the batter in greased and floured 10 inch tube pan. Spoon ½ cup cranberry sauce over batter. Spoon remaining batter over sauce, spreading as much as possible. Top with remaining cranberry sauce. Sprinkle pecans on top. Bake at 350° for 40 to 50 minutes. Cool 10 minutes; remove from pan. Cool on wire rack.

CRUMB CAKE

Linda Zapach

1 c. margarine
3 c. flour
1 c. light brown sugar
1 c. sugar
2 eggs

1 tsp. baking soda
1 c. buttermilk
½ c. chopped nuts
1 (6 oz.) pkg. semi-sweet
    chocolate chips

In a large bowl, blend margarine, flour, and sugars with pastry blender to form a crumbly mixture. Save ½ cup for topping. Add eggs alternately with buttermilk to which baking soda has been added and dissolved; beat thoroughly. Add nuts and chocolate chips; blend. Pour batter into greased 10 inch tube or Bundt pan. Sprinkle with reserved crumb mixture. Bake at 350° for 50 to 60 minutes.

SWEDISH CRUMB CAKE

Ann Dobransky

2 c. flour
1 c. rolled oats
1 tsp. baking soda

¼ tsp. salt
1 c. brown sugar
¾ c. shortening

In a large bowl, mix flour, oats, baking soda, salt, and sugar. Cut in shortening. Press half the mixture in a well greased 9x13 inch pan. Cover with Date Filling. Sprinkle with remaining crumb mixture. Bake at 325° for 40 minutes or until nicely browned. Cool. Cut in squares.

Date Filling:

1 c. chopped dates
1 c. brown sugar

1 c. water

Combine ingredients in a saucepan. Cook over medium heat until slightly thickened. Cool.

CUSTARD CAKE

Nell Boser

1 c. cornmeal
½ c. flour
1 tsp. baking soda
1 tsp. salt

2 Tbsp. sugar
1 c. buttermilk
2 eggs, well beaten
1 c. sweet milk

Sift together cornmeal, flour, baking soda, salt, and sugar. Add buttermilk; beat. Stir in eggs. Add sweet milk; blend. Pour into greased 9x13x2 inch pan. Bake at 350° for 35 minutes. Serve immediately. The custard will rise to the top in baking.

DIRT CAKE

Dorothy Skellett
Carol Williams

2 (1 lb.) pkg. Oreo cookies
8 oz. cream cheese
¼ c. butter or margarine
¼ c. confectioners sugar

2 (3 oz.) pkg. instant vanilla
pudding
3½ c. milk
12 oz. whipped topping

Crush cookies in blender; set aside. Combine cream cheese, butter, and confectioners sugar; beat until smooth. Combine pudding and milk; beat. Add Cool Whip; fold into pudding. Combine cream cheese mixture with pudding mixture; beat until creamy. Put 2 inches of cookie crumbs on bottom of bowl or decorative container. Next, add a layer of filling (pudding mixture). Alternate layers, ending with 2 inches cookie crumbs on top. Place in freezer.

I put this recipe in plastic containers (resembling flower pots) for parties. A few hours before serving, place in refrigerator. Decorate with artificial flowers, wrapping stems in plastic wrap before inserting in cake.

DUMP CAKE

Dorotha Cenesky
Jane Ellsworth

1 (1 lb. 5 oz.) can fruit pie
filling
1 (20 oz.) can crushed pineapple
(undrained)
1 (2 layer size) yellow or white
cake mix

½ c. margarine, melted
Chopped nuts (desired amount)
Coconut (desired amount)

Grease a 9x13 inch baking pan. Spread pie filling evenly on bottom of pan. Empty can of crushed pineapple over pie filling. Sprinkle dry cake mix over contents of pan. Drizzle melted margarine over cake mix. Sprinkle with chopped nuts and coconut. Bake at 350° for 45 minutes. Cool. Spread with whipped topping.

DUNDEE CAKE

Mary Kasprowitz

1 lb. butter
2 c. sugar
6 eggs
½ tsp. mace
4 c. cake flour

1 (1 lb.) jar maraschino
cherries, drained
½ lb. walnut meats
(unchopped)

Cream butter and sugar. Add eggs, one at a time; beat after each addition. Sift together cake flour and mace; add to egg mixture. Beat until creamy. Put batter in alternating layers with whole cherries and nuts in a greased and floured 10 inch angel food pan,* ending with batter. Bake on lower rack in oven at 325° about 2 hours. When cool, sprinkle with confectioners sugar.

Note: No baking powder or soda is used in this cake.

* Two bread pans may be used in place of a 10 inch angel food pan.

FRUITCAKE

Mary Ponas

1 c. butter or margarine	1 tsp. baking powder
1½ c. sugar	3 c. prunes, chopped
6 eggs	3 c. figs, chopped
Grated rind of 1 large orange	3 c. apricots, chopped
1 tsp. vanilla	3 c. raisins
2½ c. flour	3 c. nuts

Cream butter until fluffy. Add sugar gradually, beating until very creamy. Add eggs, one at a time, beating after each addition. Stir in orange rind and vanilla. Add flour and baking powder, beating until smooth and well blended. Fold in fruits and nuts. Grease 2 (9x5 inch) loaf pans; line with foil or brown paper. Grease again. Spoon mixture into pans, pressing to eliminate air spaces. Smooth top. Cover pans with greased foil. Bake at 275° for 1½ hours. Remove foil; raise temperature to 300°. Bake 1 hour longer.

CANDIED FRUIT CAKE

Eloise Maliwacki

1½ lb. pitted dates	½ tsp. salt
1 lb. candied pineapple	4 eggs
1 lb. whole candied cherries	1 c. sugar
2 c. sifted flour	2 lb. pecan halves
2 tsp. baking powder	Light corn syrup

Cut dates and pineapple in coarse pieces. Reserve a few cherries for decorating tops of cakes; add remainder to dates and pineapple. Sift flour, baking powder, and salt into bowl with fruit; mix, separating pieces of fruit, coating them with flour. Beat eggs until frothy; add sugar gradually, beating thoroughly. Add to fruit mixture; mix thoroughly. Add pecan halves, reserving some for decorating tops of cakes.

Pack into 2 (9x5x3 inch) loaf pans or 2 spring form pans that have been greased, lined with brown paper on bottom and sides and greased again. Decorate with reserved cherries and pecans. Bake at 275°, loaves 1½ hours, spring form 1¼ hours. Remove cake from pans; peel off paper. Brush with corn syrup. When thoroughly cooled, wrap tightly in plastic wrap and foil. Store in a cool place or for longer storage freeze.

UNBAKED FRUIT CAKE

Eloise Maliwacki

1 c. candied cherries
1 c. candied pineapple
4 c. nuts (walnuts, pecans,
   Brazil nuts)

¾ c. milk
1 lb. marshmallows
1 lb. graham cracker crumbs
1 (15 oz.) box raisins

Line two 9x5x3 inch pans with waxed paper, leaving enough paper hanging over edge of pans to fold over cake. Grease waxed paper. Cut cherries in halves; cut pineapple in small pieces. Leave nuts whole. Heat milk in double boiler until film forms on top; add marshmallows. Heat until marshmallows melt. In a large bowl, combine cracker crumbs with cherries, pineapple, nuts, and raisins; add milk mixture and mix, mix, mix. Mixture will be very heavy. Turn into pans; fold waxed paper over cake. Wrap in foil; refrigerate. If you prefer to age them, drizzle sherry or cognac over cakes about twice a week.

GINGERBREAD

Marie Brink

¼ c. butter
¼ c. shortening
½ c. sugar
1 egg
1 c. molasses
2½ c. flour

½ tsp. salt
1 tsp. cloves
1 tsp. ginger
1 tsp. cinnamon
1½ tsp. baking soda
1 c. boiling water

Cream butter and shortening; add sugar. Beat until light. Add egg; beat. Add molasses; beat. Sift together flour, salt, cloves, ginger, and cinnamon. Add baking soda to boiling water. Add sifted dry ingredients to creamed mixture alternately with water. Pour into greased 9x13 inch pan. Bake at 350° for 40 to 50 minutes. Serve with applesauce or whipped cream.

GRAHAM CRACKER CAKE

Josephine Baranyk

1 c. sugar
½ c. butter
3 eggs, separated
1 c. milk
½ c. flour

2 tsp. baking powder
23 graham crackers, ground
   fine
1 c. chopped nuts

Cream sugar and butter. Add egg yolks; beat. Sift together flour and baking powder; add alternately with milk to egg mixture. Add graham cracker crumbs; mix. Add nuts. Fold in stiffly beaten egg whites. Pour into 2 greased 9 inch layer pans. Bake at 350° for 35 minutes.

HAWAIIAN CAKE

Anna Chyl

1 (18½ oz.) pkg. yellow cake mix
1 large (5½ oz.) pkg. instant
  vanilla pudding
1 c. cold milk
1 (8 oz.) pkg. cream cheese,
  softened
1 (9 oz.) container non-dairy
  whipped topping

1 (20 oz.) can crushed
  pineapple, drained
½ c. chopped pecans
½ c. flaked coconut
½ c. chopped maraschino
  cherries, drained

Prepare cake mix according to package directions. Pour batter into greased 10x15 inch jelly roll pan. Bake at 350° for 15 to 20 minutes or until cake tests done. Cool in pan. Blend pudding with milk. Add cream cheese; beat until smooth. Fold whipped topping into the mixture. Spread on cooled cake. Sprinkle pineapple, nuts, coconut, and cherries over pudding. Refrigerate until ready to serve. Serves 15 to 18.

HONEY CAKE

3 c. all-purpose flour
1 tsp. baking powder
1 Tbsp. baking soda
1 Tbsp. cinnamon
¼ c. raisins
1 c. triple strength coffee

½ c. shortening
1 c. sugar
3 large eggs
¾ c. honey
¼ c. chocolate chips
Grated rind of 1 orange

Sift together flour, baking powder, baking soda, and cinnamon. Set aside. Soak raisins in coffee 10 to 15 minutes. Beat shortening and sugar until light and fluffy. Add eggs, one at a time, alternately with honey. Drain raisins; save coffee. Add sifted dry ingredients alternately with coffee, beginning and ending with flour mixture. *Do not overbeat.* Fold in chocolate chips, raisins, and orange rind. Turn into greased 10 inch tube pan. Bake at 325° for 1 hour or until cake tests done. Cool in pan about 30 minutes. Remove from pan to complete cooling.

JELLY ROLL

Sophia Malowicky

3 eggs
1 c. sugar
5 Tbsp. water
1 c. flour

1 tsp. vanilla
1 tsp. baking powder
¼ tsp. salt

Beat eggs until foamy. Add sugar gradually; continue beating. Add water. Add remaining ingredients gradually; beat well. Pour into a 10½ x 15½ x 1 inch jelly roll pan which has been greased and then lined with waxed paper. Bake at 350° for 16 minutes or until no impression is left when touched with finger lightly. Reverse pan onto clean towel dusted with sifted confectioners sugar. Remove waxed paper immediately. Roll cake in towel while hot; unroll when cool. Spread with Filling; roll again. Frost with whipped topping or sweetened whipped cream.

Filling:

1 lb. frozen raspberries   **3 Tbsp. tapioca**

Combine raspberries and tapioca in saucepan. Cook, stirring constantly, until it comes to a boil. Cool.

LADYFINGERS

Mary Ponas

3 egg yolks   **½ tsp. vanilla**
⅜ c. sugar   **3 egg whites**
⅜ c. flour   **1 Tbsp. confectioners sugar**
Dash of salt   **½ Tbsp. granulated sugar**

Beat egg yolks and sugar together until light yellow and foamy. Add flour and salt; mix until smooth. Add vanilla. Beat egg whites firm; fold into egg yolk mixture. Grease a baking sheet; sprinkle with flour. Drop batter by tablespoons on baking sheet. Shape into fingers 3 inches in length. Combine confectioners sugar and ½ tablespoon granulated sugar; sprinkle half the mixture over fingers. Let stand 10 minutes. Sprinkle with remaining sugar; let stand 5 minutes. Bake at 375° for 10 minutes or until golden. Remove from pan; cool.

LEKVAR CAKE

Evelyn Kanazawich
Marion Kaspryk

1½ c. confectioners sugar   **1 tsp. baking powder**
1 c. butter   **Dash of salt**
2 eggs   **½ lb. ground walnuts**
1 tsp. vanilla   **1 to 1½ lb. lekvar**
2 c. flour

Cream butter and sugar well. Add eggs; beat. Add vanilla; blend. Add flour, baking powder, and salt; mix thoroughly. Add nuts. Spread half the dough in a greased 9x13 inch pan; spread layer of lekvar.* Form dough in strips; make lattice over lekvar layer. Bake at 350° for 30 minutes.

* Add jelly to lekvar if lekvar is too thick to spread easily.

LEMON-ORANGE RAINBOW POKE CAKE

Anne Petras

1 (2 layer size) pkg. lemon cake
  mix
1 (3¾ oz.) pkg. vanilla instant
  pudding
½ c. vegetable oil
1 c. water

4 eggs
1 (3 oz.) pkg. orange flavored
  Jell-O
1 c. boiling water
½ c. orange juice

Blend first 5 ingredients in large bowl; beat at medium speed for 2 minutes. Pour batter into greased and floured 9x13 inch pan. Bake at 350° for 35 to 40 minutes. Cool cake in pan 15 minutes; prick with utility fork at ½ inch intervals. Dissolve gelatin in boiling water. Add orange juice; stir. Pour carefully over warm cake. Chill at least 2 hours before serving. If desired, frost with a whipped cream frosting using orange extract instead of vanilla.

MY AUNT'S QUICK LUNCH BOX CAKE

Mary Ann Klish

2¼ c. flour
2 tsp. baking soda
1 c. brown sugar
1 tsp. vanilla
2 eggs

¼ c. margarine
1 (1 lb.) can fruit cocktail
  (undrained)
½ c. chopped nuts
½ c. chocolate chips

Combine all ingredients except nuts and chocolate chips. Beat 2 minutes at medium speed. Pour into greased 9x13 inch pan. Sprinkle with nuts and chocolate chips. Bake at 350° for 35 to 40 minutes.

MILLION DOLLAR MACADAMIA OR PECAN FUDGE TORTE

Marianne Lawryk

Filling:

⅓ c. low fat sweetened
  condensed milk

½ c. semi-sweet chocolate chips

In a small saucepan, combine sweetened condensed milk and chocolate chips; place over medium-low heat, stirring occasionally until chocolate is melted. Set aside to use in cake.

Cake:

1 pkg. devils food cake mix (pudding included)	2 eggs
½ tsp. cinnamon	2 tsp. water
⅓ c. oil	⅓ c. chopped macadamia nuts
1 (16 oz.) can pears in light syrup, drained	or pecans

Preheat oven to 350°. Spray a 9 or 10 inch springform pan with nonstick cooking spray. In a large bowl, combine cake mix with cinnamon and oil; blend at low speed 20 to 30 seconds or until mixture is crumbly (it will be dry). Place pears in a blender or food processor bowl; use metal blade to puree pears. Combine 2½ cups of the cake mixture with the pureed pears and eggs in a medium bowl; beat 2 minutes at low speed until moistened, then at medium speed for 2 minutes. Spread batter evenly in prepared pan. Drop filling by spoonfuls over batter. Add nuts and water to remaining cake mix mixture; mix until combined. Sprinkle over the filling. Bake 45 to 50 minutes or until top springs back when touched lightly in the center. Cool 10 minutes; remove sides of pan. Cool 1½ hours or until thoroughly cooled.

Sauce:

1 (17 oz.) jar butterscotch caramel fudge ice cream topping	⅓ c. milk

In a small saucepan, combine ice cream topping and milk. Heat over medium-low heat 3 to 4 minutes or until well blended, stirring occasionally. To serve, spoon 2 tablespoons of warm sauce onto each serving plate; top with wedge of torte. If desired, serve with vanilla ice cream or frozen yogurt and garnish with chocolate curls.

MOCHA NUT MARBLE CAKE
Linda Zapach

White Batter:

1½ c. sifted flour	⅓ c. shortening
1 c. sugar	½ c. water
2 tsp. baking powder	1 tsp. almond or vanilla extract
½ tsp. salt	4 egg whites (unbeaten)

Sift together flour, sugar, baking powder, and salt. Add shortening, water, and extract. Beat 1½ minutes at low speed. Add egg whites; beat another 1½ minutes.

Mocha Nut Batter:

1½ c. sifted flour
1 c. brown sugar, packed
2 tsp. baking powder
½ tsp. salt

⅓ c. shortening
½ c. cold strong coffee
4 egg yolks (unbeaten)
½ c. chopped nuts

Sift together flour, brown sugar, baking powder, and salt. Add shortening and coffee; beat 1½ minutes. Add egg yolks; beat 1½ minutes. Stir in nuts. Spoon light and dark batters alternately in a well greased 9x13 inch pan. Cut through batter with knife, but do not stir.

PRIZE WINNER ORANGE CHIFFON CAKE

Marianne Lawryk

2¼ c. cake flour
1½ c. sugar
4 tsp. baking powder
1 tsp. salt
⅓ c. vegetable oil

6 eggs, separated
¾ c. freshly squeezed orange
 juice
2 Tbsp. grated orange rind
½ tsp. cream of tartar

In a large mixer bowl, combine flour, sugar, baking powder, and salt; make a well in the mixture into which add the following in the order given: Oil, egg yolks, orange juice, and grated orange rind. Beat 5 minutes or until smooth. In another bowl, beat egg whites with cream of tartar until stiff, but not dry. Gently fold first mixture into the egg whites. Gently pour into a 10 inch ungreased tube pan. Bake at 350° for 45 to 50 minutes or until cake springs back when lightly touched. Immediately invert pan. Cool. Remove from pan.

ORANGE KISS-ME CAKE

Carol Taylor

2 oranges
2 c. sifted all-purpose flour
1 c. sugar
1 tsp. baking powder
1 tsp. baking soda
1 tsp. salt

½ c. shortening
2 eggs
1 c. milk
⅓ c. finely chopped walnuts
1 c. raisins

Grind oranges including peel; drain. Reserve juice. Sift together in large bowl flour, sugar, baking powder, baking soda, and salt. Add shortening, eggs, and milk; beat until well blended. Add ground orange, walnuts, and raisins; mix. Pour into greased 9x13 inch pan. Bake at 350° for 40 to 45 minutes. Pour reserved orange juice over hot cake. Sprinkle with a mixture of cinnamon and sugar according to your taste. Sprinkle with chopped nuts.

GRANDMA'S PAN CAKE

Carol Williams

1 yellow cake mix plus
  ingredients listed on box to
  prepare the mix
1 (20 oz.) can crushed pineapple
1 (8 oz.) pkg. cream cheese
1 (3.4 oz.) pkg. instant vanilla
  pudding

¼ c. milk
¼ c. chopped nuts
¼ c. flaked coconut
Cool Whip

Prepare cake according to package directions; pour into a well-greased and floured jellyroll pan (a cookie sheet with sides). Bake at 350° for 20 minutes or until cake tester or toothpick comes out with no batter clinging to it. Do not overbake.

Topping: Drain pineapple. In a bowl, beat cream cheese, instant pudding, and milk until thick and creamy. Spread drained pineapple over pudding, then spread one large container of Cool Whip over pineapple. Sprinkle coconut and chopped nuts over top. Store in refrigerator until ready to use.

PINEAPPLE CAKE

Mary Gulachok

2 c. flour
1 to 1½ c. sugar
2 tsp. baking soda

2 eggs, beaten
1 (20 oz.) can crushed pineapple
  (undrained)

Combine all ingredients; mix well. Pour into a greased 9x13x2 inch pan. Bake at 350° for 35 to 40 minutes.

Frosting:

8 oz. cream cheese
2 c. confectioners sugar

1 stick margarine, melted
1 tsp. vanilla

In a bowl, combine all ingredients; beat until smooth. Spread on cooled cake.

PINEAPPLE CARROT CAKE

Jane Ellsworth

2 c. flour
2 tsp. baking soda
1 tsp. salt
2 c. sugar
1 tsp. cinnamon

1¼ c. vegetable oil
4 eggs
2 c. grated carrots
1 (8 oz.) can crushed pineapple
  (undrained)

Sift dry ingredients into large bowl. Add oil; beat. Add eggs, one at a time, beating after each. Add carrots and pineapple; blend well. Pour into greased 9x13 inch pan. Bake at 350° for 30 to 35 minutes. Spread Cream Cheese Frosting on cooled cake.

Cream Cheese Frosting:

3 oz. cream cheese
¼ c. butter or margarine
2 c. confectioners sugar

1 tsp. vanilla
1 (4 oz.) can shredded coconut
Chopped nuts (optional)

Blend cream cheese, butter, sugar, and vanilla until smooth and creamy. Add coconut and nuts; blend.

PINEAPPLE CHIFFON CAKE

Mary Ponas

1 c. egg whites
2¼ c. sifted flour
1½ c. sugar
3 tsp. baking powder
1 tsp. salt

½ c. salad oil
7 egg yolks (unbeaten)
1 Tbsp. grated lemon rind
¾ c. pineapple juice
½ tsp. cream of tartar

Place egg whites in large bowl. Let stand at room temperature 1 hour. Sift together flour, sugar, baking powder, and salt into a mixing bowl. Make a well in dry ingredients; add oil. Combine egg yolks, rind, and juice; pour over oil. Add cream of tartar to egg whites; beat until very stiff - 3 to 4 minutes. Beat egg yolk mixture until smooth. Add egg yolk mixture to egg whites very slowly; keep folding until well blended. Pour into ungreased 10 inch tube pan. Bake at 325° for 50 minutes, then at 350° for 10 to 15 minutes or until done.

PINEAPPLE UPSIDE-DOWN CAKE

Sophia Malowicky

½ c. butter
1 c. brown sugar
1 (No. 2) can sliced pineapple, drained
Maraschino cherries
1 c. sifted cake flour

1 tsp. baking powder
⅛ tsp. salt
3 eggs, separated
1 c. granulated sugar
5 Tbsp. pineapple juice (saved from drained pineapple)

Melt butter in 9 inch square pan. Sprinkle brown sugar evenly over butter. Arrange pineapple slices on sugar; place cherry in hole of each pineapple ring. Sift together cake flour, baking powder, and salt. Beat egg yolks until light, adding granulated sugar gradually; beat. Add pineapple juice alternately with sifted dry ingredients. Fold in stiffly beaten egg whites. Pour batter over pineapple. Bake at 350° for 30 to 35 minutes. Turn upside-down on cake plate immediately. Serve with whipped topping or whipped cream.

PISTACHIO CAKE

Helen Kaspryk
Celia Matias

1 pkg. yellow cake mix
1 c. sour cream
4 eggs, beaten

1 (3.4 oz.) pkg. pistachio instant
    pudding
½ c. oil

In a large bowl, combine all ingredients; beat until well blended. Turn one-half the batter into a greased and floured 9x13 inch pan; sprinkle with one-half the crumb mixture. Spread remaining half of batter over crumb mixture layer. Sprinkle remaining half of crumb mixture over last batter layer. Bake at 350° for 45 minutes or until toothpick comes out clean.

Crumb Mixture:

¼ c. brown sugar
1 tsp. cinnamon

2 Tbsp. butter
1 c. chopped nuts

In a small bowl, combine all ingredients to form a crumb mixture. Sprinkle one-half on the first layer of batter in the pan. Sprinkle last half over second layer of batter. Bake at 350° for 45 minutes or until toothpick comes out clean.

PISTACHIO DESSERT

Helen Rucky

Crust:

1 stick margarine
½ c. walnuts, chopped fine

1¼ c. flour

Mix and put in greased 9x13 inch pan. Bake at 350° for 25 minutes. Cool.

Filling:

1 (8 oz.) cream cheese
1 c. confectioners sugar
1 (8 or 9 oz.) Cool Whip

2 boxes instant pistachio
    pudding
3 c. milk

Mix cream cheese and confectioners sugar. Add Cool Whip. Mix and spread on cooled crust. Whip instant pudding with milk and spread on cream cheese mixture. Spread 1 container Cool Whip on top and sprinkle with chopped walnuts.

May substitute any other flavor instant pudding.

POPPY SEED CAKE I

Margaret Klish

¾ c. ground poppy seed
¾ c. milk
1½ c. sugar
¾ c. Crisco

1 tsp. vanilla
2 c. sifted flour
2 tsp. baking powder
4 egg whites, stiffly beaten

Soak poppy seed in milk for 3 hours. Cream together sugar and Crisco; add poppy seed mixture and vanilla. Sift together flour and baking powder; add to previous mixture. Fold in stiffly beaten egg whites. Pour into greased 9x13x2 inch pan. Bake at 350° for 30 minutes or until cake tests done.

POPPY SEED CAKE II   Julie Sadowitz

1 c. poppy seed	1 tsp. vanilla
⅓ c. honey	1 c. sour cream
¼ c. water	2½ c. sifted all-purpose flour
1 c. butter	1 tsp. baking soda
1½ c. sugar	1 tsp. salt
4 eggs, separated	

Cook poppy seed with honey and water in small saucepan for 5 to 7 minutes. Cool. Cream butter and sugar until light and fluffy. Add poppy seed mixture; blend. Add egg yolks, one at a time, beating well after each addition. Blend in vanilla and sour cream. Sift together flour, baking soda, and salt; add gradually to poppy seed mixture, beating well. Beat egg whites until stiff; fold into batter. Pour into greased and lightly floured 9 inch tube pan. Bake at 350° about 1 hour and 15 minutes or until done. Cool in pan 5 minutes. Remove from pan; cool on wire rack. Frost with Vanilla Frosting.

Vanilla Frosting:

2 Tbsp. butter or margarine	Pinch of salt
1¾ c. sifted confectioners sugar	¾ tsp. pure vanilla
2 Tbsp. milk	

Cream butter until soft and fluffy. Add confectioners sugar alternately with milk until mixture is of spreading consistency. Blend in salt and vanilla. Spread over top of cake; let frosting dribble down sides of cake. Sprinkle poppy seed over frosting.

POPPY SEED CAKE III   Jane Ellsworth

2 c. sugar	1½ tsp. baking soda
1½ c. vegetable oil	1 tsp. salt
4 eggs	1 (13 oz.) can evaporated milk
1 tsp. vanilla	1½ c. poppy seed
3 c. flour	1 c. chopped nuts

In a large bowl, combine sugar and oil. Add eggs and vanilla; beat 1 minute on low speed. Combine flour, baking soda, and salt; add to egg mixture alternately with milk. Stir in poppy seed and nuts. Beat 1 minute. Pour into ungreased 10 inch tube pan. Bake at 325° for 1 hour and 15 minutes.

POPPY SEED CREAM SHERRY CAKE

Carol Williams

1 yellow cake mix
4 eggs
1½ pkg. instant butterscotch
  pudding

1 c. oil
1 c. cream sherry wine
½ c. ground dry poppy seed

Blend all ingredients together; pour into a greased Bundt pan. Bake at 350° for 55 to 60 minutes. Cool on rack. Turn onto plate. Sprinkle top (bottom) with confectioners sugar.

LEMON POPPY SEED CAKE

Margaret Klish

1 Duncan Hines Lemon
  Supreme cake mix
1 (3.4 oz.) pkg. lemon instant
  pudding

4 eggs
1 c. water
½ c. melted Crisco or Crisco oil
4 Tbsp. ground poppy seed

Combine cake mix and instant pudding in a large bowl. Add eggs, water, and oil; beat on creaming speed approximately 3 minutes. Fold in ground poppy seed. Pour into pan sprayed with Pam and greased. Bake at 350° - 9x13x2 inch for 25 to 30 minutes, 2 (10 inch) layers 20 minutes, 1 (12 inch) round 25 to 30 minutes, and 10 inch Bundt pan 25 to 30 minutes. Cool 15 minutes before removing from pan.

PORK CAKE I

Marie Brink

1 lb. pork
1 c. hot water
1 lb. raisins
½ lb. currants
1 pt. molasses
½ c. butter

1 tsp. baking soda
1 tsp. cloves
¼ tsp. cinnamon
¼ tsp. nutmeg
2 c. flour

Fry pork; chop fine. Pour hot water over pork. Combine remaining ingredients. Add pork with water; mix thoroughly. Pour into greased 9x5 inch loaf pan. Bake at 350° for 1½ to 1¾ hours. Pour brandy over cake before serving.

PORK CAKE II

Dorothy Skellett

1 lb. ground pork sausage
1 lb. seedless raisins
1 lb. dates, chopped
1 c. chopped walnuts
4 c. brown sugar

3 c. boiling water
6 c. all-purpose flour
2 Tbsp. cinnamon
1 Tbsp. cloves
1 Tbsp. baking soda

Combine sausage, raisins, dates, nuts, brown sugar, and boiling water; mix thoroughly. Sift dry ingredients together; add to sausage mixture. Blend well. Grease and line bottoms of three 9x5x3 inch loaf pans with waxed paper; grease paper. Pour batter into prepared pans. Bake at 350° for 1½ hours. Frost with Cream Cheese Frosting. Decorate with red and green candied cherries for Christmas.

Cream Cheese Frosting:

2 (3 oz.) pkg. cream cheese
2 Tbsp. milk
4½ c. confectioners sugar

⅛ tsp. salt
1 tsp. vanilla

Blend cheese and milk. Add sugar, salt, and vanilla. Beat until smooth.

POUND CAKE

Linda Zapach

1 c. butter, softened
2 (3 oz.) pkg. cream cheese, softened
2 c. sugar

6 eggs
2 tsp. vanilla
2 c. flour

Combine butter, cream cheese, and sugar; cream well. Add eggs, one at a time, beating well after each. Add vanilla; blend. Add flour; mix well. Pour into greased 10 inch tube or Bundt pan. Bake at 350° for 1 hour. Sprinkle with confectioners sugar when cool.

Note: For added flavor, add 1 cup chopped nuts, raisins, or chocolate chips.

SUE'S POUND CAKE

Olga Gooley

1 c. butter
1 c. margarine
1 lb. confectioners sugar
6 eggs

2 Tbsp. vanilla or 1 Tbsp. vanilla and 1 Tbsp. lemon extract
3 c. cake flour, sifted

Cream butter and margarine. Add sugar; cream thoroughly. Add eggs, one at a time, beating 1 minute after each addition. Add flavoring; beat. Add flour gradually; beat well. Pour into well-greased and floured 10 inch tube pan. Bake at 350° for 1 hour and 20 minutes. Cool 5 minutes in pan.

Variation 1: Add chopped raisins, nuts, or candied cherries to batter.

Variation 2 - Marble Cake: Reserve 1 cup batter. Add 1½ squares melted chocolate; mix. Pour half the white batter in prepared pan; pour chocolate batter over first layer. Top with remaining white batter. Cut through and swirl to form marble effect.

PUDDIN' CAKE

Mary Kostyun

1 (3.4 oz.) pkg. dark chocolate
  pudding and pie filling
2 c. milk
1 pkg. devils food or chocolate
  cake mix

½ c. semi-sweet chocolate
  morsels
½ c. chopped nuts

Grease and flour a 9½ x 13 x 2 inch pan. Cook pudding with milk as directed on package. In a large bowl, blend cake mix with hot pudding. Pour into prepared pan; sprinkle chocolate morsels and nuts on top. Bake at 350° for 30 to 35 minutes. Serve warm or cold with whipped cream or ice cream if desired.

PUMPKIN CHIFFON CAKE

Anna Smyk

2 c. sifted cake flour
1½ c. sugar
3 tsp. baking powder
1 tsp. salt
1 tsp. cinnamon
½ tsp. cloves
½ tsp. nutmeg

½ c. salad oil
8 egg yolks
½ c. water
¾ c. pumpkin
½ tsp. cream of tartar
8 egg whites

Sift dry ingredients into mixing bowl. Make well in center. Add in order oil, egg yolks, water, and pumpkin; beat until satin smooth. Add cream of tartar to egg whites; beat to very stiff peaks. Pour egg yolk batter, in a thin stream, gradually over entire surface of whites; fold. Pour into ungreased 10 inch tube pan. Bake at 325° for 55 minutes, then at 350° for 10 minutes. Invert pan to cool.

PUMPKIN CREAM CHEESE ROLL

Jane Ellsworth
Josephine Vimislik

3 eggs
1 c. sugar
⅔ c. pumpkin
1 tsp. lemon juice
¾ c. sifted flour
1 tsp. baking powder

½ tsp. salt
2 tsp. cinnamon
1 tsp. ginger
½ tsp. nutmeg
½ c. chopped nuts

Beat eggs at high speed for 5 minutes. Gradually beat in sugar. Fold in pumpkin and lemon juice. Combine dry ingredients; add to pumpkin mixture, beating at low speed. Spread in greased 10x15x1 inch pan. Sprinkle with nuts. Bake at 350° for 15 minutes. Cool 5 minutes. Invert pan on towel sprinkled with confectioners sugar. Roll as for jelly roll. Cool 15 minutes. Unroll cake;

cut in half crosswise. Spread each half with Filling; roll. Wrap in foil; refrigerate until ready to serve.

Filling:

1 c. confectioners sugar	4 tsp. butter
1 (8 oz.) pkg. cream cheese	½ tsp. vanilla

Combine all ingredients; beat until fluffy.

RHUBARB CAKE I

Ann Dobransky

1½ c. brown sugar	1 tsp. baking soda
½ c. margarine	2 c. flour
1 egg	1½ c. rhubarb, cut fine
1 c. buttermilk	1 tsp. vanilla

Cream margarine and brown sugar. Add egg, buttermilk, baking soda, and flour; mix. Fold in rhubarb and vanilla. Pour batter into a well greased 8x10 inch pan. Sprinkle with Topping. Bake at 350° for 40 to 45 minutes.

Topping:

¾ c. brown sugar	1 tsp. cinnamon

Combine sugar and cinnamon. Sprinkle on unbaked cake.

RHUBARB CAKE II

Marion Kaspryk

2 c. flour	1 egg
1 tsp. baking soda	1 c. sour cream
¼ tsp. salt	1 tsp. vanilla
1½ c. light brown sugar	2½ c. rhubarb, thinly sliced
½ c. margarine	

Mix flour, baking soda, and salt; set aside. In large bowl of mixer, cream brown sugar and shortening until fluffy; beat in egg. At low speed, beat in flour mixture alternately with sour cream until well blended. Stir in vanilla and rhubarb. Turn into greased and floured 9x13x2 inch pan. Sprinkle Topping over top of cake. Bake at 350° for 40 minutes.

Topping:

½ c. sugar	½ c. chopped nuts
1 tsp. cinnamon	

Mix together sugar and cinnamon. Add nuts.

RHUBARB CAKE III

Julieanne Marra

½ c. shortening
2 c. flour
2½ tsp. baking powder
¼ tsp. salt
¼ c. sugar

1 egg
¾ c. milk
6 c. rhubarb
1 (3 oz.) pkg. strawberry or
   raspberry jello

Mix first 5 ingredients as you would for pie crust; add egg and milk. Spread in greased 9x13 inch pan. Sprinkle with rhubarb, then jello evenly over crust.

Topping:

1½ c. sugar
½ c. flour

6 Tbsp. margarine

Mix topping ingredients until crumbly; sprinkle over cake. Bake at 350° for 50 minutes.

RHUBARB UPSIDE-DOWN CAKE

Helen Rucky

Topping:

4 c. sliced rhubarb
1 c. sugar

2 Tbsp. melted margarine
1 tsp. cinnamon

Batter:

1½ c. flour
¼ tsp. salt
1½ tsp. baking powder
2 eggs, well beaten

1 c. sugar
½ c. hot water
1 tsp. vanilla

Mix topping and place in greased 9 inch pan. Cream eggs and sugar. Stir in water and vanilla. Add dry ingredients. Pour into pan over rhubarb. Bake at 350° for 50 to 60 minutes or until toothpick comes out clean. Let stand a few minutes; turn upside-down.

OLGA'S RUM CAKE DeMAISON

Anna Chyl

2 c. sifted cake flour
2 tsp. baking powder
¼ tsp. baking soda
¼ tsp. salt
½ c. butter
¾ c. sugar
2 eggs, separated
1 tsp. grated orange rind
½ c. orange juice

3 Tbsp. white rum
¼ tsp. vanilla
¼ tsp. almond extract
¼ c. sugar
Whipped Cream Filling
Chocolate Frosting
8 Tbsp. white rum
1½ c. walnuts, coarsely chopped

Sift together flour, baking powder, baking soda, and salt; set aside. Beat butter at medium speed until very soft and creamy. Gradually beat in ¾ cup sugar; continue beating until light and fluffy. Beat in egg yolks, one at a time. Add orange rind; beat. Combine orange juice, rum, vanilla, and almond extract. Add alternately with flour mixture to creamed mixture, beating at low speed.

In medium bowl, beat egg whites to soft peaks. Gradually beat in ¼ cup sugar; continue beating stiff peaks. Fold whites into batter. Pour batter into 2 (9 x 1½ inch) layer cake pans that have been greased and bottom lined with waxed paper. Bake at 350° for 25 minutes or until top springs back when gently pressed with fingers. Cool in pan on rack 10 minutes; remove from pans to finish cooling.

Split cooled layers horizontally to make 4 layers. Sprinkle each layer with 2 tablespoons rum. Put layers together, on a serving plate, using 1½ cups Whipped Cream Filling between layers. Spread Chocolate Frosting on top and sides of cake. Press walnuts into frosting all around sides of cake. Refrigerate until serving time.

Whipped Cream Filling:

2 tsp. unflavored gelatin	½ c. confectioners sugar
2 Tbsp. cold water	⅓ c. white rum
2 c. heavy cream	

Chill a medium bowl. Sprinkle unflavored gelatin over cold water; heat over hot water until gelatin is dissolved. Cool slightly. In cold bowl, beat heavy cream with confectioners sugar until thick. Add rum gradually while beating. Add gelatin, gradually, beating until just stiff enough to hold its shape.

Chocolate Frosting:

4 (1 oz.) sq. unsweetened chocolate	2 Tbsp. hot water
	2 eggs
1 c. confectioners sugar	6 Tbsp. soft butter

In top of double boiler (over *hot water, not boiling*), melt chocolate; remove from heat. Gradually add sugar and water, beating constantly. Add eggs, one at a time, beating after each addition. Add butter, 2 tablespoons at a time; continue beating until smooth and light in color.

MOCHA RUM CAKE

Pani Matka Elizabeth Hutnick

Unsweetened cocoa powder for
   dusting
3 c. all-purpose flour
1½ tsp. baking soda
¾ tsp. salt
¾ lb. bittersweet chocolate,
   chopped
3 sticks unsalted butter, cut
   into pieces

⅓ c. dark rum
2 c. strong brewed coffee
2¼ c. granulated sugar
3 large eggs, beaten lightly
1½ tsp. vanilla
Confectioners sugar

Preheat oven to 300°. Butter 4½ inch deep Bundt pan and dust with cocoa powder; remove excess. In a bowl, whisk together flour, baking soda, and salt. In large metal bowl set over saucepan of simmering water (double boiler), melt chocolate and butter, stirring until smooth. Remove from heat. Stir in rum, coffee, and granulated sugar. With mixer, beat in flour mixture, ½ cup at a time. Beat in eggs and vanilla until batter is combined. Pour into pan. Bake in middle of oven about 1 hour and 50 minutes or until tester is cleaned. Let cool completely in pan on rack; turn onto rack. Dust with confectioners sugar.

SAND CAKE

Helen Chubinsky

1⅓ c. butter or margarine
2¾ c. flour

¾ c. confectioners sugar

Beat butter with electric mixer until it looks like thick cream. Sift flour and sugar together; add to creamed butter gradually, beating continuously. The more you beat, the better the cake will be. Spoon into 2 greased round 9 inch cake pans. Bake at 400° for 15 minutes or until cake pulls away from sides of pan. Cool. Cut into wedges.

TWO EGG CAKE

Carol Taylor

2¼ c. sifted cake flour
1½ c. sugar
3 tsp. baking powder
1 tsp. salt
½ c. shortening

2 eggs (unbeaten)
½ c. cold milk
1½ tsp. flavoring (almond,
   maple, coconut)

Sift together flour, sugar, baking powder, and salt. Add shortening, eggs, milk, and flavoring. Beat with electric mixer on medium speed for 2 minutes. Pour into greased 9x13x2 inch pan or 2 (8 inch) layer pans. Bake at 350° for 25 to 30 minutes.

VANILLA WAFER CAKE

Sophie Cox

1 c. margarine
2 c. sugar
6 eggs
1 (12 oz.) pkg. vanilla wafers,
  crushed

½ c. milk
1 (7 oz.) pkg. coconut
1 c. chopped pecans

Cream margarine and sugar until light. Add eggs, one at a time, beating well after each addition. Add crushed wafers alternately with milk. Add coconut and pecans. Pour into well greased and floured 10 inch tube pan. Bake at 350° for 1¼ to 1½ hours.

WALNUT CAKE

Helen Chubinsky

½ c. butter
1½ c. sugar
Grated rind of ½ lemon
2 c. flour
2½ tsp. baking powder

¾ c. milk
1 tsp. vanilla
1 c. chopped walnuts
4 egg whites, stiffly beaten

Cream butter; gradually add sugar, beating until light. Add lemon rind. Sift together flour and baking powder; add alternately with milk to creamed mixture. Beat well. Add vanilla and walnuts; blend. Fold in stiffly beaten egg whites. Pour into 2 well greased 9 inch layer pans or a 9x13 inch pan. Bake at 350°, layers 30 to 35 minutes, oblong 40 to 45 minutes. When cool, frost with Brown Sugar Frosting.

Brown Sugar Frosting:

2 c. brown sugar
½ c. water

2 egg whites, beaten

Combine brown sugar and water in a saucepan; boil until mixture reaches 230° or a fine thread forms poured from a spoon. Pour over beaten egg whites, beating until mixture is thick and spreading consistency. Cool. Spread on cake; sprinkle walnuts on top.

BLACK WALNUT CAKE

Linda Zapach

⅓ c. ground walnuts
¼ c. chopped walnuts
1 c. flaked coconut
½ c. shortening
1½ c. sugar
2 c. sifted flour
1 tsp. baking powder

1 tsp. baking soda
½ tsp. salt
2 eggs (unbeaten)
½ tsp. vanilla
½ tsp. black walnut extract
1 c. buttermilk or soured milk
⅓ c. hot strong coffee

Combine walnuts and coconut. Reserve about 2 tablespoons to sprinkle on top of cake after it is frosted. Cream shortening; add sugar gradually. Beat until very creamy. Sift together flour, baking powder, baking soda, and salt; set aside. Add eggs to creamed mixture, one at a time, beating well after each addition; add vanilla and black walnut extract. Blend. Add dry ingredients to egg mixture alternately with liquid ingredients, blending well after each addition; begin with flour and end with flour. Add remaining walnut-coconut mixture.

Pour into 2 (8 inch) greased and floured cake pans. Bake at 375° for 30 to 35 minutes or until cake tests done. Cool. Frost with your favorite frosting; sprinkle with the reserved 2 tablespoons of walnut-coconut mixture after cake is frosted.

WHIPPED CREAM ROLL
Linda Zapach

4 egg whites	4 egg yolks
½ tsp. salt	¼ c. flour
1 tsp. vanilla	½ c. chopped nuts
½ c. sugar	

Beat egg whites with salt and vanilla until soft peaks form. Gradually beat in sugar. Beat yolks until thick and lemon color. Fold yolks into whites. Carefully fold in flour and nuts. Line bottom and sides of a 15x10x1 inch jelly roll pan with waxed paper. Spread batter in pan. Bake at 350° for 12 minutes or until cake springs back when touched lightly. (Will be a little brown on top.) Cool 5 minutes.

Loosen sides; turn onto towel which has been sprinkled with confectioners sugar. Peel off paper; cool to lukewarm. Roll with towel from narrow end. Cool ½ hour. Unroll. Spread with Whipped Cream Filling; roll. Put in waxed paper. Keep in freezer until ready to serve.

Whipped Cream Filling:

1 c. heavy cream	½ tsp. vanilla
1 to 3 Tbsp. sifted confectioners sugar	

Whip cream until stiff. Fold in sugar (for desired sweetness) and vanilla.

WHITE CAKE
Josephine Baranyk

3 c. flour	1 c. shortening
4 tsp. baking powder	1 c. milk
½ tsp. salt	1 tsp. vanilla
2 c. sugar	4 eggs

Combine all ingredients in large mixer bowl. Beat for 2 minutes at full speed. Scrape down sides of bowl; beat at full speed 4 minutes. Again, scrape sides of bowl; beat 2 more minutes. Pour into greased 9x13 inch pan. Bake at 325° for 45 minutes.

NEVER FAIL YOGURT CAKE

Mary Kostyun

1½ c. sugar
2½ c. water
1 c. butter
2½ c. sugar
5 eggs, well beaten
1 c. yogurt

½ tsp. baking soda
½ c. milk
3 c. sifted cake flour
3 tsp. baking powder
1 c. walnuts, chopped medium
fine

Combine 1½ cups sugar and water in heavy saucepan; stir to dissolve. Bring to boil; boil 25 minutes. Cool. Melt butter; cool. Add 2½ cups sugar gradually, creaming thoroughly. Add eggs; beat. Stir in yogurt. Combine soda and milk; add to mixture. Combine flour and baking powder; add one cup at a time to egg mixture. Beat until thoroughly blended. If using an electric mixer, be careful not to overbeat. Pour batter in a greased 9x13x2 inch pan. Bake at 325° for 1 hour or until cake springs back when touched and is medium brown on top. While cake is hot, cut into serving size pieces; sprinkle with nuts and spoon cooled syrup slowly over hot cake. Yield: 20 servings.

ORANGE YOGURT CAKE

Mary Kostyun

1 c. butter
1 c. sugar
4 eggs
Grated rind of 1 orange
1 tsp. vanilla
1 c. yogurt
2½ c. flour

1 tsp. baking powder
1 tsp. baking soda
⅛ tsp. salt
1 c. chopped nuts
Juice of 1 orange
½ c. sugar

Cream butter and sugar. Add eggs, orange rind, vanilla, and yogurt; beat. Sift together flour, baking powder, baking soda, and salt; add to egg mixture. Beat until thoroughly blended. Add nuts. Pour into well greased 10 inch tube pan. Bake at 350° for 1 hour or until done. Combine juice and sugar. Pour over cake while hot.

CHOCOLATE ZUCCHINI CAKE I
Helen Rucky

1 pkg. devil's food cake mix
1 tsp. cinnamon
¼ tsp. cloves
2 c. shredded, unpeeled
   zucchini

½ c. buttermilk
⅓ c. oil
½ c. chopped nuts
½ c. chocolate chips

In large bowl, blend cake mix, cinnamon, cloves, zucchini, buttermilk, oil, and eggs until moistened. Beat 2 minutes; pour into greased 9x13 inch pan. Sprinkle with nuts and chips. Bake at 350° for 35 to 45 minutes.

CHOCOLATE ZUCCHINI CAKE II
Helen Rucky

½ c. margarine
½ c. oil
1 tsp. vanilla
2½ c. flour
4 Tbsp. cocoa
1 tsp. baking soda
1¾ c. sugar

2 eggs
½ c. sour milk
½ tsp. baking powder
¼ tsp. salt
1 c. chocolate chips
½ c. chopped walnuts
2 c. grated zucchini

Cream margarine, oil, and sugar. Add eggs, vanilla, and sour milk; mix in dry ingredients. Add zucchini, chips, and nuts. Pour into greased and floured 9x13 inch pan. Bake at 350° for 55 minutes.

ZUCCHINI CAKE WITH ORANGE ICING
Pani Julia Lawryk

2 c. all-purpose flour
½ c. whole wheat flour
2 tsp. baking powder
½ tsp. salt
2¼ tsp. cinnamon
½ tsp. ground cloves
3 eggs

½ c. vegetable oil
1⅓ c. granulated sugar
½ c. orange juice
1 tsp. vanilla
1½ c. shredded zucchini,
   packed

In a large mixing bowl, mix together flours, baking powder, salt, and spices. In a smaller bowl, beat eggs well; stir in oil, granulated sugar, orange juice, vanilla, and zucchini. Add zucchini mixture to flour mixture, mixing just until flour is moistened. Pour batter into prepared pan; bake in preheated oven for 35 to 40 minutes. Cool cake on a rack.

Orange Icing:

2 tsp. soft butter
3 c. confectioners sugar

¼ c. orange juice
2 tsp. lemon juice

120

Combine butter and sugar; add juices gradually, beating while adding. Beat until smooth. Drizzle over cooled cake.

Notes

Candies

Frostings

Fillings

CANDIES, FROSTINGS, FILLINGS

CHRISTMAS FUDGE BALLS
Mary Ponas

1 (12 oz.) pkg. semi-sweet
  chocolate chips
½ c. butter
2 c. chopped walnuts
2 c. miniature marshmallows

1 c. confectioners sugar
1 whiskey glass water
2 eggs
Coconut

In a saucepan, melt chocolate chips and butter. Cool. Add walnuts, marshmallows, sugar, water, and eggs; mix until thoroughly combined. Refrigerate to harden slightly. Form balls; roll in coconut. Place on cookie sheet. Refrigerate.

FRUIT BALLS
Eloise Maliwacki

½ c. pitted dates
½ c. dried apricots
½ c. golden raisins

½ c. walnuts
½ tsp. lemon rind
½ tsp. orange rind

Put dates, apricots, raisins, and walnuts through food chopper, using medium-coarse blade. Add lemon and orange rind to chopped fruits; blend thoroughly. Shape into small balls. Roll in confectioners sugar if desired.

PEANUT BUTTER BALLS
Mary Mihalko

1½ c. graham cracker crumbs
1 lb. confectioners sugar
1 c. butter
1 (18 oz.) jar crunchy peanut
  butter

¾ block paraffin
1½ c. ground walnuts
1 (12 oz.) pkg. semi-sweet
  chocolate chips
1 (7 oz.) milk chocolate bar

Combine crumbs, sugar, butter, peanut butter, and walnuts; refrigerate. Form into small balls; refrigerate. In top of double boiler, melt chocolate chips, milk chocolate, and paraffin. Dip balls in hot chocolate mixture. Put on wax paper lined cookie sheet to harden.

JEAN'S PEANUT BUTTER BALLS
Zenna Mihovan
Dorothy Skellett, Jody Klym

2 c. crunchy peanut butter
1 lb. confectioners sugar
½ c. margarine
2 c. Rice Krispies

1 (8 oz.) Hershey's bar
1 (6 oz.) pkg. semi-sweet
  chocolate chips
½ bar paraffin wax

Combine peanut butter, confectioners sugar, margarine, and Rice Krispies. Form into balls. Melt Hershey's bar, chocolate chips, and wax in the top of a double boiler. Dip balls in melted chocolate; put on waxed paper to cool. Makes 80 to 100 balls.

CARAMEL CORN

Millie Finch
Dorothy Skellett

1 c. margarine
2 c. light brown sugar
½ c. corn syrup
1 tsp. salt
½ tsp. baking soda
1 tsp. vanilla
6 qt. popped corn
2 c. nuts (optional)

In a 4 quart heavy saucepan, melt margarine. Add sugar, corn syrup, and salt; stir. Bring to a boil, stirring constantly. Boil, *without stirring*, for 5 minutes. Remove from heat; stir in baking soda and vanilla. Gradually pour over corn in a medium size roasting pan. Bake at 250° for 1 hour, stirring every 15 minutes. Remove from oven; cool completely. Break apart; store in airtight container.

CRAZY CRUNCH

Olga Tarcha

2 qt. popped corn
1 c. pecans
⅔ c. almonds
½ c. light Karo syrup
1⅓ c. sugar
1 c. margarine
1 tsp. vanilla

Mix popcorn and nuts; spread on cookie sheet. Combine syrup, sugar, and margarine; bring to a boil over medium heat, stirring constantly. Cook until light brown, about 10 to 15 minutes. Remove from heat; stir in vanilla. Pour over popcorn and nuts; mix to coat. Spread out to dry. When dry, break apart; store in tightly covered container. Makes about 2 pounds.

EASTER EGGS

Evelyn Kanazawich

2 egg whites, slightly beaten
2 Tbsp. cold, firm mashed
  potatoes or 2 Tbsp. firm
  instant mashed potatoes
2 lb. confectioners sugar
2 Tbsp. butter
¼ tsp. salt
½ bar paraffin wax
2 tsp. vanilla
1 c. coconut
2 (8 oz.) bars bitter or semi-
  sweet baking chocolate or 2
  (12 oz.) pkg. semi-sweet
  chocolate chips

Mix whites with potatoes. Add sugar, butter, salt, and vanilla. Mixture must be firm, similar to consistency of dough for refrigerator cookies. Add more potatoes if dough isn't firm enough to roll into egg shapes. If dough is too firm, add a few drops evaporated milk. Add coconut; shape as desired or divide dough into portions and add any of the following: Chopped nuts, candied fruit, peanut butter, liquor, or extracts.

Powder hands with confectioners sugar; shape as desired. Refrigerate on waxed paper lined trays. Combine baking chocolate or chocolate chips and paraffin in top of double boiler. When melted and hot, dip candy; place on waxed paper. Candy may be dipped again for thicker coating.

Note: Instant potatoes make a smoother candy.

FUDGE I
Ann Dobransky

1 c. sugar
1 c. brown sugar
1 c. milk
2 Tbsp. light Karo syrup
Pinch of salt

¼ c. cocoa
3 Tbsp. butter or margarine
¼ c. peanut butter
2 c. miniature marshmallows
½ tsp. vanilla

Combine sugars, milk, Karo, salt, cocoa, and butter in saucepan; mix. Cook over medium heat until a soft ball forms when a small quantity is dropped in ice water. Add remaining ingredients; beat until thick. Pour into buttered 9 inch square pan. Cut into small squares after thoroughly cooled.

FUDGE II
Marie Richardson

1 (12 oz.) pkg. chocolate chips
1 tsp. butter
1 (14 oz.) can condensed milk

1 tsp. vanilla
½ c. chopped nuts

Melt chocolate chips in double boiler. Add butter; stir. Stir in milk and vanilla. Add nuts;* mix. Pour into buttered 8 inch square pan. Let stand 12 hours or more before cutting into squares.

* If desired, sprinkle nuts on top rather than putting them in the fudge.

FUDGE III
Colleen Rucky

1 c. graham cracker crumbs
1 (12 oz.) pkg. chocolate chips
¾ c. flour
¾ c. chopped nuts

1 tsp. vanilla
1 stick margarine, melted
1 c. evaporated milk
2 c. sugar

Melt margarine and evaporated milk; add sugar and rest of ingredients. Pour in greased 9x13 inch pan. Chill completely.

BROWN SUGAR FUDGE

Dorothy Skellett

1 c. brown sugar
1 c. granulated sugar
⅓ c. milk
⅓ c. light cream

2 sq. chocolate, broken
2 Tbsp. butter
1 tsp. vanilla
½ c. chopped nuts (optional)

Combine sugars, milk, cream, and chocolate in saucepan. Cook slowly, stirring constantly, until it reaches the soft-ball stage or 236° on candy thermometer. Remove from heat at once. Add butter without stirring. Set pan aside to cool at room temperature. When candy has cooled to lukewarm, add vanilla and nuts; begin beating. Continue beating until fudge has lost its shiny look and a small amount dropped from spoon onto a plate holds its shape. Pour into 2 greased, shallow square pans. Cool. Cut into squares. Makes 1¼ pounds.

CANAVAN FUDGE

Julieanne Marra

⅓ c. margarine
4½ c. sugar
1 large can evaporated milk

2 (12 oz.) pkg. chocolate chips
2 tsp. vanilla
2 c. chopped nuts (optional)

Combine margarine, sugar, and milk in a large saucepan. Bring to boil and continue boiling 5½ minutes. Remove from heat; add remaining ingredients. Pour into buttered 15x10 inch jelly roll pan. Cool until firm before cutting.

SIMPLE CHOCOLATE FUDGE

Evelyn Kanazawich
Dorothy Skellett

½ c. butter
1 (6 oz.) pkg. chocolate pudding
  mix
½ c. milk

4¾ c. sifted confectioners sugar
½ tsp. vanilla
½ c. chopped walnuts

Melt butter in saucepan. Stir in pudding mix and milk; bring to a boil. Boil 1 minute. Remove from heat; beat in confectioners sugar. Stir in vanilla and nuts. Pour into buttered 10 x 6 x 1¾ inch pan. Chill.

SODA CRACKER CHOCOLATE CANDY

Marianne Lawryk

35 to 40 soda crackers
1 c. margarine
1 c. packed brown sugar

1½ c. semi-sweet chocolate
  chips
1½ c. coarsely chopped walnuts

Line a 10x15x1 inch baking pan with foil. Spray with nonstick cooking spray. Place crackers in rows on foil. In saucepan, melt margarine; add brown sugar. Bring to a boil. Boil 3 minutes. Pour over crackers and spread until crackers are completely covered. Bake at 350° for 5 minutes (crackers will float). Remove from oven.

Sprinkle chocolate chips and walnuts over crackers. Return to oven until chocolate is melted, about 3 to 5 minutes. Remove from oven; using a greased spatula, press walnuts into chocolate. Cut into 1 inch squares while warm. Cool completely. Remove candy from foil. Makes 5 dozen.

SODA CRACKER PEANUT BUTTER CANDY
Marianne Lawryk

2 c. sugar
½ c. evaporated milk
1 stick butter
1 stack (¼ of regular box) saltine crackers, coarsely crumbled

½ c. crunchy peanut butter
Pecan or walnut halves or almonds (optional)

Combine sugar, milk, and butter in saucepan. Stir over low heat until sugar is dissolved and butter melted, then bring to a full boil. Boil hard for 1 minute. Remove from heat and stir in crackers and peanut butter until mixed well. Drop by teaspoonfuls onto waxed paper. Press nuts into centers if desired. Cool until firm and remove from paper.

SODA CRACKER TOFFEE CANDY
Marianne Lawryk

1¼ c. butter, divided
35 to 40 soda crackers
1 c. packed dark brown sugar
1¼ c. (14 oz. can) Carnation sweetened condensed milk

1½ c. semi-sweet chocolate chips
¾ c. finely chopped walnuts

In a medium saucepan, melt ¼ cup of the butter. Pour into foil-lined 15x10 inch jelly roll pan. Arrange crackers over butter. In same saucepan, melt remaining butter and add sugar. Bring to a boil over medium heat. Reduce heat and cook for 2 minutes, stirring occasionally. Remove from heat. Add sweetened condensed milk. Spread over crackers. Bake at 425° for 10 to 12 minutes, until mixture is bubbly and slightly darkened. Remove from oven. Cool 1 minute. Sprinkle with chocolate chips. Let stand 5 minutes, until melted. Spread chocolate. Sprinkle with nuts and press them into chocolate. Cool; refrigerate until chocolate is set. Remove foil and cut candy into 2 x 1½ inch pieces. Makes 50 pieces.

BUTTER CREAM FROSTING (Basic Recipe)

Marion Kaspryk

½ c. milk
½ c. butter, softened
½ c. shortening
1 c. sugar

⅛ tsp. salt
2 egg whites, stiffly beaten
1 tsp. vanilla

Bring milk to a boil; cool. Put butter, shortening, sugar, and salt in bowl of electric mixer; beat 8 to 10 minutes, or until very creamy. Beat in egg whites, then milk and flavoring. Makes about 2 cups frosting or enough for top and sides of two 9 inch layers.

Orange Frosting: Add 1 tablespoon grated orange rind to Basic Recipe.

Coffee Frosting: Blend 1 tablespoon instant coffee powder with 1 tablespoon water. Beat into Basic Recipe.

Chocolate Frosting: Melt and cool 2 or 3 squares unsweetened chocolate; beat into Basic Recipe.

Rum Frosting: Add 2 teaspoons light rum or 1 teaspoon rum extract to Basic Recipe.

EASY CHOCOLATE FROSTING

Miranda Klish

¼ c. melted shortening
½ c. cocoa
¼ tsp. salt

⅓ c. milk
1½ tsp. vanilla
3½ c. sifted confectioners sugar

Combine melted shortening, cocoa, and salt; add milk and vanilla. Mix in sugar, a little at a time. Mix until smooth and creamy.

CREAMY LEMON FROSTING

Olga Tarcha

½ c. butter, softened
1 egg
1 (1 lb.) box confectioners sugar

1 tsp. grated lemon rind
1 Tbsp. lemon juice
¼ tsp. lemon extract

Place all ingredients in large mixing bowl. Beat at high speed with electric mixer until creamy and of good spreading consistency.

NO-COOK MARSHMALLOW FROSTING

Celia Matias

2 egg whites
¼ tsp. salt
¼ c. sugar

¾ c. Karo light corn syrup
1¼ tsp. vanilla

Beat egg whites and salt with electric beater until soft peaks form. Add sugar, about 1 teaspoon at a time, beating until smooth and glossy. Add Karo syrup, a little at a time, beating after each addition until frosting peaks. Fold in vanilla. Makes enough to frost two 9 inch layers.

ORNAMENTAL FROSTING
Miranda Klish

2½ c. sifted confectioners sugar
¼ tsp. cream of tartar

2 egg whites
½ tsp. vanilla

Sift together confectioners sugar and cream of tartar into bowl. Add egg whites and vanilla. Beat until frosting holds its shape. Cover with damp cloth until ready to use.

BLUEBERRY GLAZE
Dorothy Skellett

½ c. sugar
½ c. water
2 c. blueberries

2 tsp. cornstarch
1 Tbsp. lemon juice
¼ tsp. salt

Combine all ingredients in a saucepan. Cook over medium heat until thick. Serve over cake, ice cream, pudding, pancakes, even cheesecake.

MOCHA GLAZE
Eloise Maliwacki

2 Tbsp. butter
2 sq. baking chocolate
1 tsp. instant coffee

⅛ tsp. cinnamon
1 c. confectioners sugar
2 Tbsp. hot water

Melt butter with chocolate. Remove from heat; stir in coffee, cinnamon, sugar, and hot water.

Notes

CANNING

CANNING

MARINATED BEETS

Josephine Baranyk
Anna Lewkowicz

24 medium beets
3 medium onions, sliced
2 c. beet liquid
2 c. vinegar

1¼ c. sugar
2 tsp. salt
6 whole cloves
1 tsp. cinnamon

Cook beets in boiling water. Reserve 2 cups liquid from beets. Cool beets; peel. Slice with ripple cutter. Combine beets and onions. In a large pot, combine beet liquid, vinegar, sugar, salt, cloves wrapped in a cheesecloth bag, and cinnamon. Cover pot; bring to a full boil. Add beets and onions; bring to a boil again. Remove cloves. Fill hot, sterilized pint jars with hot beet mixture. Be sure to cover beets with liquid. Seal immediately with sterilized caps.

BRINE FOR PICKLING

Chuck Sarnoski

2½ c. water
1½ c. cider vinegar
½ tsp. oregano
1 tsp. salt

2 cloves garlic, cut small
Pinch of red crushed pepper
1 tsp. dill seed

Combine ingredients. Do not cook. Pour over quartered green tomatoes, cauliflower, eggs, celery, peppers (red or green), kielbasi, or any other food adaptable to pickling. Refrigerate 3 to 4 days before serving.

PICKLED BEETS

Julie Sadowitz

2 (1 lb. size) cans whole beets
1 c. white wine vinegar
½ c. sugar
1 tsp. salt
3 whole cloves

4 whole black peppercorns
1 small bay leaf
2 medium onions, peeled and
   sliced

Drain beets, reserving ¼ cup liquid. Place beets in 1½ to 2 quart jar or bowl. In medium saucepan, combine vinegar, sugar, salt, cloves, peppercorns, bay leaf, and reserved liquid; bring to boiling. Reduce heat and simmer, uncovered, 5 minutes. Add onion slices to jar. Pour hot liquid over beets and onions. Refrigerate, covered, several hours. Makes 6 cups.

PICKLED CARROTS

Eloise Maliwacki

10 medium carrots
1 c. vinegar
1 c. water
1 c. sugar

2 Tbsp. mustard seed
1 stick cinnamon
3 whole cloves

Pare or scrape carrots; cut in 1 inch sticks. Cook in boiling, salted water just until tender. Combine remaining ingredients; heat to boiling. Simmer 20 minutes. Pack carrots in hot sterilized jars; pour vinegar mixture over carrots. Seal. Makes 2 pints.

PICKLED CAULIFLOWER

Julia Dudik

4 large heads cauliflower
2 qt. vinegar
4 c. sugar
2 Tbsp. salt
1 Tbsp. celery seed
1 Tbsp. mustard seed

12 whole cloves
1 Tbsp. turmeric
1 Tbsp. dry mustard
4 sweet red peppers
1 sweet green pepper
4 onions

Wash and divide cauliflower into small pieces. Cover with hot water; cook 5 minutes. Drain. Combine vinegar, sugar, salt, and spices; bring to a boil. Add cauliflower, peppers, and onions to hot brine. Pack in pint jars; seal. Makes 6 pints.

PICKLED EGGS

1 doz. eggs
1½ c. white vinegar
½ c. water
1 c. sugar
½ tsp. salt

12 whole cloves
2 bay leaves
1 large onion, sliced
2 Tbsp. salad oil

In a saucepan, cover eggs with cold water; bring to a boil. Reduce heat; simmer 15 to 20 minutes. Drain; immediately cover eggs with cold water for several minutes. Peel eggs; place in a narrow deep jar. In a saucepan, combine vinegar, water, sugar, salt, cloves, and bay leaves; bring to a boil. Reduce heat; simmer 5 minutes. Pour over eggs to cover completely. Place onion slices on top of eggs; top with oil. Cover tightly; refrigerate. Let stand several days before serving whole, halved, or sliced plain, in salads or in sandwiches.

PICKLED PEPPERS

Dorothy Skellett

2 qt. vinegar
1 qt. water
½ c. pure salt (not iodized or free flowing)

½ c. sugar
Garlic
Peppers

Combine vinegar, water, salt, and sugar; bring to a boil. Put a clove of garlic in each jar. Fill jars with peppers which have been washed, seeded, and cut. Pour boiling hot brine into jars; seal. Makes about 8 pints.

CHOW CHOW

Ann Dobransky

1 peck green tomatoes
2 qt. onions
8 red peppers
4 qt. chopped cabbage
2 qt. vinegar
1 tsp. mustard seed

1 tsp. celery seed
1 tsp. allspice
1 Tbsp. cinnamon
4 c. sugar
3 Tbsp. salt
1 Tbsp. pepper

Put tomatoes, onions, and peppers through food chopper. Drain each vegetable in a separate bag for 2 to 3 hours. Combine tomatoes, onions, peppers, and cabbage. Combine remaining ingredients; add to vegetables. Heat to boiling point. Pack in jars; seal.

AUNT JULIE'S CHOW CHOW

Julie Sadowitz

6 lb. green tomatoes, chopped
3 c. boiling water
1 c. salt
5 large onions, chopped
3 sweet red peppers, chopped
3 green peppers, chopped
1 head cabbage, coarsely chopped

3 medium cucumbers, chopped
3 medium carrots, chopped
1 qt. vinegar
2 c. sugar
½ c. dry mustard
1 Tbsp. turmeric
1 bunch celery, chopped

Put chopped tomatoes in a large bowl. Add salt to boiling water; stir until dissolved. Pour over tomatoes. Let stand 3 hours. Drain. Add remaining vegetables, except celery, to the tomatoes. Heat vinegar, sugar, mustard, and turmeric to boiling in a large kettle. Add vegetables except celery; simmer 10 minutes. Add celery; stir. Fill clean, hot pint jars to ½ inch of top. Wipe off tops and threads of jars; seal. Process in boiling water bath 15 minutes. Makes about 11 pints.

NECTARINE CHUTNEY

Millie Finch

Delicious with meats.

2½ lb. nectarines or peaches,
  peeled and cut in chunks
1½ c. brown sugar
1 c. cider vinegar
½ c. diced crystallized ginger
1 tsp. salt

¼ c. instant minced onion
1 tsp. dry mustard
1 tsp. cinnamon
¼ tsp. cloves
½ c. slivered almonds

Simmer all ingredients, except almonds, covered, for 30 minutes. Uncover; cook another 30 minutes or until thick. Add almonds last 3 minutes of cooking. Immediately pour into hot ½ pint jars; seal. Makes 6 (½ pint) jars. Store in a cool place.

GREEN TOMATO JELLY

Mary Mihalko

2 c. green tomato puree
2 c. sugar

1 (3 oz.) pkg. raspberry or
  strawberry gelatin

Combine puree and sugar in large saucepan; boil 20 minutes, skimming off foam as it's cooking. Add gelatin; cook 20 minutes. Pour into jelly glasses; seal with melted paraffin.

PICKLES

Helen Charnetsky

8 c. water
1 c. white vinegar
½ c. sugar
¼ c. canning salt

Hot peppers
Garlic
Dill
Cucumbers

Combine water, vinegar, sugar, and salt; bring to a boil. Cool to lukewarm. In each quart jar, place a hot pepper, 2 cloves cut up garlic, and a head of dill. Pack cucumbers in jars; fill with cooled brine to cover cucumbers. Seal. Let stand in refrigerator 2 weeks before serving. Pickles will last indefinitely if you can keep your family from eating them. Makes 4 quarts.

PICKLES
(No-cooking)

Marie Pufky

Cucumbers
Onions
4 c. sugar
4 c. vinegar

¼ c. canning salt
1½ tsp. turmeric
1½ tsp. celery seed
1½ tsp. mustard seed

Slice cucumbers and onions; pack in jars. Combine sugar, vinegar, and salt; stir until dissolved. Add turmeric, celery seed, and mustard seed; stir. Pour brine over cucumbers and onions. Refrigerate. Ready to eat in 5 days.

ANNE'S PICKLES
Mary Kostyun

3 lb. cucumbers, sliced
1 lb. onions, sliced
3 c. sugar

2 c. vinegar
¼ c. salt

Combine cucumbers and onions in a large bowl. In a saucepan, combine sugar, vinegar, and salt. Heat until mixture comes to a boil, stirring until sugar dissolves. Cool. Pour over cucumbers and onions. Store in glass jars in refrigerator. Will keep for months.

BREAD AND BUTTER PICKLES
Anna Chyl

6 qt. sliced cucumbers
9 medium onions
2 green peppers
2 sweet red peppers
3 cloves garlic
½ c. canning salt

4½ c. white vinegar
7½ c. sugar
2 tsp. turmeric
2 tsp. celery seed
3 Tbsp. mustard seed

Wash cucumbers; slice thinly. Slice onions thinly. Wash peppers; remove stem ends and seeds. Cut in thin strips. Combine cucumbers, onions, peppers, and garlic in large pan, sprinkling each layer with salt. Mix a tray of ice cubes throughout the cucumbers and cover top with another tray of ice. Let stand 3 hours. The ice and salt make for especially crisp pickles. Drain cucumbers; divide in half for cooking so that pickles retain their crispness and color.

Combine vinegar, sugar, turmeric, and celery seed and mustard seed which have been tied in a cheesecloth bag. Pour half the mixture over half the drained pickles. Heat only to boiling; pack into hot jars. Seal. Repeat with second half of cucumbers. Store at least 1 month before serving.

COMPANY BEST PICKLES
Nancy Tarcha

10 medium cucumbers
8 c. sugar
2 Tbsp. pickling spices

5 tsp. salt
4 c. cider vinegar
Green food coloring

Cover whole cucumbers with boiling water; let stand overnight. Drain. Repeat procedure the next 3 mornings. On the fifth day, drain and slice in ½ inch slices. Combine sugar, spices, salt, vinegar, and a few drops green food coloring; bring to a boil. Pour over cucumbers. Let stand 2 days. On the third day, bring to a boil; seal in hot, sterilized jars. Makes 7 pints.

CRISP SQUASH PICKLES

Chuck Sarnoski

5 lb. zucchini and/or yellow
 squash, sliced thin
3 medium onions, sliced thin
Ice cubes
3 c. cider vinegar
3 c. sugar

2 tsp. celery seed
2 tsp. mustard seed
1½ tsp. turmeric
1 tsp. ginger
½ tsp. pepper

Combine squash and onions in a large bowl. Top with ice cubes; let stand 3 hours. Drain. Rinse with cold water. Combine remaining ingredients in large pot; add squash and onions. Bring to a boil; reduce heat to a slow boil. Cook 8 minutes. Fill canning jars; seal.

ICICLE PICKLES

Mary Kostyun

2 gal. cucumber sticks
 (cucumbers sliced
 lengthwise)
2 c. salt
1 gal. boiling water
1 gal. boiling water

2½ Tbsp. alum
1 gal. boiling water
2½ qt. white vinegar
15 c. sugar
1 box mixed pickling spices

Put cucumbers in a crock. Combine salt and 1 gallon boiling water; pour over cucumbers. Let stand 6 days. On the seventh day, drain off liquid; add 1 gallon boiling water. Let stand 24 hours. Drain. Add alum to 1 gallon boiling water; pour over pickles. Let stand 24 hours. Drain. Combine vinegar, sugar, and spices; bring to a boil. Pour over pickles. Let stand 24 hours. Drain; reheat the drained liquid to boiling. Pour over pickles. On the fifth day, seal pickles in jars or you may leave them in the crock.

24 HOUR PICKLES

Mike Charnetsky

12 cucumbers
Garlic
Dill
2 qt. water

1¼ c. vinegar
½ c. sugar
⅓ c. salt

Wash cucumbers. Pack gallon jar with cucumbers, garlic, and dill. Combine water, vinegar, sugar, and salt; bring to a boil. Cool. Pour over cucumbers in jar; put top on jar. Refrigerate 24 hours.

136

24 HOUR CUKES

Anna Chyl
Josephine Vimislik

Cucumbers
6 c. water
1 c. vinegar
¼ c. salt
½ c. sugar

2 tsp. turmeric
1 tsp. dry mustard
Dill
5 garlic cloves

Wash cucumbers; cut lengthwise. Put in cold water. Combine water, vinegar, salt, sugar, turmeric, and dry mustard; bring to a boil. Cool. Put dill and garlic in gallon jar. Drain cucumbers; pack in gallon jar. Pour cooled brine over cucumbers. Cucumbers should be completely covered with brine. Refrigerate. Ready to eat in 24 hours.

24 HOUR QUICK DILLS

Genevieve Sadowitz

2 cloves garlic
Dill
Sliced cucumbers
½ c. vinegar

¼ c. sugar
1 Tbsp. canning salt
3 c. water

Put a clove of garlic and some dill in each jar. Fill jars with sliced cucumbers. In a saucepan, combine vinegar, sugar, salt, and water; bring to a boil. Pour boiling brine over cucumbers in jars; seal. Refrigerate immediately. Pickles will keep for 4 to 6 months in refrigerator. Makes 2 quarts.

SALT WATER PICKLES

Shirley Buchma

12 to 15 cucumbers
2 qt. cold water
Canning salt

6 cloves garlic
4 large heads fresh dill
2 Tbsp. pickling spice

Wash cucumbers. Put water in gallon jar. Add salt gradually, mixing with wooden spoon. Taste water periodically. Enough salt has been added when water is so salty that you want to spit it out. Add 4 cloves garlic, 2 heads dill, and pickling spices to the jar. Now, pack cucumbers in jar; put in as many as will fit, leaving room for 2 cloves garlic and 2 heads dill on top. Salt water should cover cucumbers; if it doesn't, add plain cold water. Screw lid on jar. Keep at room temperature 4 to 5 days; the warmer the temperature, the faster the pickles ferment. When pickles are ready, refrigerate. Pickles should be firm and crunchy.

SWEET SLICED PICKLES

Josephine Vimislik

2 gal. cucumbers, sliced
1 gal. boiling water
2 c. salt
1 gal. boiling water
1 gal. boiling water
2 Tbsp. alum

2¼ qt. vinegar
8 pt. white and brown sugar
1 Tbsp. mustard seed
1 Tbsp. cloves
1 Tbsp. celery seed

Put cucumbers in a crock. Combine 1 gallon boiling water and salt; pour over cucumbers. Let stand 1 week. Drain. Pour 1 gallon boiling water over cucumbers. Let stand 24 hours. Drain. Combine 1 gallon boiling water with alum; pour over cucumbers. Let stand 24 hours. Drain. Combine vinegar and sugars; add mustard seed, cloves, and celery seed which you've tied in a cloth. Stir and heat until sugar is dissolved. Add cucumbers to syrup; heat to almost boiling. Pack in jars; seal. Process for 10 minutes.

TERRY'S REFRIGERATOR PICKLES

Dorothy Skellett

4 qt. sliced cucumbers
2 c. sliced onion
3 Tbsp. salt
2 c. white vinegar

4 c. sugar
1 tsp. celery seed
½ tsp. alum

Combine cucumbers, onion, and salt; let stand 3 hours. Do not drain. Mix together remaining ingredients; do not heat. Pour over cucumber mixture. Cover; refrigerate. Ready to eat in 3 to 7 days.

ZUCCHINI PICKLES

Shirley Buchma

1 gal. sliced small zucchini
8 medium onions, sliced
2 large green peppers, cut into
    strips
½ c. canning salt

5 c. vinegar
5 c. sugar
2 Tbsp. mustard seed
1 tsp. turmeric
1 tsp. whole cloves

Dissolve salt in ice water; pour over vegetables. Let stand 3 hours. Drain. Combine vinegar, sugar, and spices in a large pot; bring to a boil. Add vegetables; heat again to boiling point. Do not boil. Pack in sterilized jars; seal. Do not process.

BEET RELISH

Katherine Baranyk

1 qt. chopped cooked beets
1 qt. chopped cabbage
1 c. chopped onions
1 c. chopped sweet red peppers

1 Tbsp. salt
1 Tbsp. prepared horseradish
1½ c. sugar
3 c. vinegar

Combine all ingredients; simmer 10 minutes. Bring to boiling. Pack (boiling hot) into sterilized jars, leaving ⅛ inch head space. Seal. Yield: 4 pints.

CRANBERRY RELISH

Mary Ponas

1 lb. cranberries
2 apples
1 peeled orange

1 orange with rind
1 c. sugar
1 (3 oz.) pkg. cherry gelatin

Grind cranberries, apples, and oranges; add sugar. Let stand. Prepare gelatin according to package directions; refrigerate until partially set. Add ground fruit; refrigerate until completely set.

OLGA'S MANHATTAN CRANBERRY RELISH

Marion Sarnoski

1 (16 oz.) can whole cranberry
  sauce
1 (20 oz.) can crushed
  pineapple, drained
½ c. diced orange peel
2 inch cinnamon stick or ½ tsp.
  ground cinnamon

½ tsp. ground ginger
3 oz. bourbon or blended
  whiskey
1 oz. sweet vermouth

Combine all ingredients. Refrigerate at least 24 hours before serving. Makes 4 cups.

CUCUMBER RELISH

Ann Dobransky

12 cucumbers
4 large onions
2 green peppers
3 red peppers
½ c. canning salt

Ice water
2½ c. vinegar
3 c. sugar
2 tsp. turmeric
2 tsp. celery seed

Grind cucumbers, onions, and peppers with coarse blade. Dissolve salt in enough ice water to cover vegetables. Let stand 1 hour. Drain. Rinse. Drain; squeeze out all water. Set aside. Combine vinegar, sugar, turmeric, and celery seed; bring to a boil. Add vegetables; cook slowly for 15 minutes. Pack in pint jar; seal.

GREEN TOMATO RELISH
Anne Girnis

4 qt. ground green tomatoes
1 qt. ground red and green
  peppers
1 qt. ground onions
½ c. salt

1 qt. sugar
1 qt. vinegar
1 qt. mayonnaise
1 (8 oz.) jar mustard

Combine tomatoes, peppers, onions, and salt; let stand overnight. Drain. Add sugar and vinegar; boil 20 minutes. *Drain well.* Add mayonnaise and mustard; mix well. Pack in jars; refrigerate. Keep in refrigerator until ready to use.

UNCLE BILL'S HOT TOMATO RELISH
Bill Sadowitz

6 lb. green tomatoes, chopped
4 large onions, chopped
4 sweet red peppers, chopped
2 c. (or less) chopped hot
  peppers

1 qt. vinegar
4 c. sugar
¼ c. canning salt
1 Tbsp. whole cloves

Combine all ingredients in a large kettle. Heat to boiling; continue cooking at a very low boil for 3 hours or until thick, stirring occasionally. Fill hot pint jars to within ½ inch from top. Wipe off tops and threads of jars; seal. Process in boiling water bath 15 minutes.

ONION RELISH
Millie Finch

Delicious with all foods.

7 c. finely chopped white
  onions
½ c. chopped green pepper
1 (4 oz.) can pimientos

¼ c. sugar
2 tsp. dry mustard
1 tsp. prepared horseradish
1½ c. white vinegar

Combine all ingredients; boil 10 minutes, stirring often. Mixture should be moist, but not soupy - if too dry after cooking first 5 minutes, add some vinegar. Heat to boiling. Fill ½ pint jars to ⅛ inch of top; seal. Store in a cold, dark, dry place. Makes 6 (½ pint) jars.

Note: Great mixed with mustard or ketchup and served with hot dogs and hamburgers.

140

SAUERKRAUT I

Anna Chyl

Cabbage
1 tsp. salt
1 tsp. sugar

1 tsp. vinegar
Boiling water

Shred cabbage. Put salt in quart jar. Pack full with cabbage, all sugar, and vinegar. Fill jar with boiling water. Seal. (Sauerkraut will stay white.) Let stand 2 weeks before eating.

SAUERKRAUT II

Anna Grech

10 heads cabbage
Cold water

½ c. canning salt

Clean cabbage by removing outer leaves and core; place in cold water. Let stand 15 minutes. Drain. Shred cabbage; add salt. Place in crock; mix. Place a plate on cabbage, then a 10 pound weight on plate. Cover crock with clean towel. Crock should be kept in a room where temperature is 60° to 70° for 2 to 3 weeks. Amount of time depends on temperature of room.

The plate should always be covered with juice - if there is too much, remove some; if there isn't enough, add 1 quart warm water with 1 tablespoon salt. After 2 weeks sauerkraut is ready to be placed in canning jars. (If you wish your sauerkraut to be more sour, let stand another week.) Process 20 minutes. If you wish to freeze sauerkraut rather than canning, place in freezer bags.

TOMATO JUICE

Anna Grech

Wash ripe tomatoes; cut into pieces. Cook for 10 minutes. Put cooked tomatoes through food strainer. Cook juice for 1 hour. Add salt to taste. Fill canning jars; seal. Process 10 minutes.

DELICIOUS DILL TOMATOES

Josephine Baranyk

Piece of celery (2 inches long)
½ small onion
1 large clove garlic, cut in small
  pieces
1 hot pepper (optional)
1 Tbsp. (heaping) pure salt (not
  iodized or free flowing)

1 tsp. sugar
Dill
Small green tomatoes
1 c. white vinegar
2 Tbsp. pickling spices
4 c. water

In a washed and sterilized quart jar, put celery, onion, garlic, pepper, salt, sugar, and dill. Pack tomatoes in jar. In a saucepan, combine vinegar, pickling spices, and water; bring to boiling. Pour over tomatoes in jar; seal. Steam (do not boil) for 20 minutes. Tomatoes will be ready to eat in 4 weeks.

Notes

CASSEROLES

AND

MAIN

DISHES

CASSEROLES, MAIN DISHES

BARLEY CASSEROLE

Olga Gooley

Great with Chicken Kiev.

1 c. barley
½ c. butter
6 bouillon cubes (chicken or beef)
4 c. hot water
½ lb. mushrooms, sliced
2 medium onions, sliced

Saute barley in ¼ cup butter until browned. Add bouillon and water; simmer until tender, about 45 to 55 minutes. Saute mushrooms and onions in remaining butter; add to barley. Mix. Put in casserole. Bake at 350° about 45 minutes.

BEEF AND BREW CASSEROLE PIE

Patricia Hoover

½ lb. stewing beef
¼ c. flour
Cooking oil
1 (12 oz.) can beer
2½ tsp. salt
¼ tsp. pepper
2 cloves garlic, crushed
1 bay leaf
1½ c. lima beans
1 large potato, cubed
1 small onion, chopped
1 (9 inch) pie crust

Cut beef into cubes; coat with flour. Brown in hot oil. Add beer and spices; cover. Simmer 2 hours. Remove bay leaf. Stir in vegetables; simmer 5 to 10 minutes. Spoon into casserole dish; place pie crust on top. Bake at 400° for 40 minutes.

BEEF AND VEGETABLE CASSEROLE

Genevieve Sadowitz

3 slices bacon
1½ lb. lean round steak (½ inch thick)
½ c. flour
1 tsp. salt
1 c. dry burgundy red wine
2 Tbsp. parsley
½ clove garlic
½ tsp. thyme
1 (10½ oz.) can condensed beef broth
6 medium potatoes, peeled and halved
6 small white onions, peeled
3 carrots, sliced lengthwise
1 (4 oz.) can mushroom stems and pieces, finely chopped

Cook bacon until crisp; drain on paper towels. Cut beef into cubes. Shake a few cubes at a time in paper bag containing flour and salt. Brown cubes on all sides in bacon drippings; place in 2 quart casserole. Pour wine into blender.

Add parsley, garlic, thyme, and beef broth; blend until solid ingredients are pureed. Pour over meat in casserole; cover. Bake at 350° for 1 hour. Add potatoes, onions, and carrots to casserole; cover. Bake 1 hour longer or until vegetables are tender. Add mushrooms; mix. Crumble bacon on top and sprinkle with additional chopped parsley. Serves 4 or 5.

ROZ'S "DILLY" DALLY BEEF CASSEROLE
Linda Kocich

1½ lb. ground beef
1 medium onion, chopped
1½ tsp. salt
⅛ tsp. pepper
½ tsp. paprika
¼ tsp. dill weed or fresh dill to your taste

¼ c. flour
1 beef bouillon cube
1 c. hot water
1 (10 oz.) pkg. frozen mixed vegetables
2 medium tomatoes, peeled

Brown ground beef with onion; pour off drippings. Add salt, pepper, paprika, dill, and flour; mix well. Dissolve bouillon cube in hot water; add to meat mixture. Cook 5 minutes. Cook mixed vegetables in 1 cup unsalted water for 10 minutes; drain, saving liquid. Add water to make 1 cup. Add cooked vegetables and liquid to meat mixture; stir. Place half the meat mixture in a 1½ quart casserole. Add layer of tomatoes which have been sliced ½ inch thick. Pour remaining meat mixture over tomatoes; top with another layer of tomato slices. Sprinkle with additional dill weed or fresh dill. Bake at 375° for 25 to 30 minutes or microwave on HIGH for 20 minutes.

DOWN HOME CASSOULET

Cooked ham bone with meat (about 2 lb.)
¼ c. water
2 medium carrots, sliced
3 stalks celery, sliced
3 bay leaves
3 tsp. thyme
1 lb. navy or northern beans
1½ lb. kielbasa, cut in small pieces

2 c. chopped onions
2 cloves garlic, minced
2 Tbsp. flour
1 (3 oz.) can green chilies (optional)
1 tsp. salt
1 c. dry white wine
Salt and pepper

In a Dutch oven, heat ham bone, water, carrots, celery, bay leaves, and 1½ teaspoons thyme to boiling. Reduce heat; simmer 1½ hours. Strain broth, reserving ham and vegetables. Skim off fat; discard. Cut ham off bone. Add ham and beans to broth. Heat to boiling; simmer 5 minutes. Remove from heat; cover. Let stand 45 minutes. Again, heat bean mixture to boiling over high heat. Reduce heat; simmer, uncovered, for 1 hour or until beans are tender, stirring occasionally.

Meanwhile, cook kielbasa in large skillet over low heat until golden brown. Add onions and garlic; cook until tender, about 3 to 5 minutes. Stir in flour until smooth. Add green chilies, salt, wine, and 1½ teaspoons thyme. Simmer 20 minutes, uncovered. Add kielbasa mixture and reserved vegetables to bean mixture. Carefully season to taste with salt and pepper. Makes 8 servings.

HAMBURG VARIETY CASSEROLES   Patricia Hoover

1 medium onion, chopped
1 clove garlic, chopped
1 Tbsp. cooking oil

1 lb. ground chuck
1 tsp. salt

In a skillet, saute onion and garlic in oil. Add ground chuck and salt; cook until brown. Drain fat from meat. Add one of the *varieties* from below to this mixture.

Variety No. 1: Add diced carrots, potatoes, and beans. Cook with the meat until tender. Add gravy.

Variety No. 2: Add sliced, cooked potatoes and ½ cup sour cream.

Variety No. 3: Add mushrooms and sour cream; serve over rice or noodles.

Variety No. 4: Add macaroni and a 1 pound can stewed tomatoes. Garnish with cheese.

Variety No. 5: Add mushrooms and chopped green peppers.

Variety No. 6: Add sliced potatoes, mushrooms, and a 10½ ounce can tomato soup.

BROCCOLI AND RICE CASSEROLE   Rose Klodowski

1 (10 oz.) pkg. frozen broccoli
1 tsp. salad oil
¼ c. chopped onion
1 (10½ oz.) can cream of
  mushroom soup

1 tsp. salt
1¼ c. shredded American
  cheese
1½ c. cooked rice

Thaw broccoli; chop into small pieces. Put oil in saucepan; add broccoli and onions. Cook 5 minutes. Add soup; mix well. Heat to boiling, stirring constantly. Remove from heat. Stir in salt, 1 cup cheese, and rice. Pour into greased 1½ quart casserole. Top with remaining cheese. Bake at 350° about 40 minutes or until bubbly. Serves 6.

BROCCOLI CASSEROLE I

Mary Mihalko

2 (10 oz.) pkg. frozen chopped
   broccoli
4 Tbsp. butter or margarine
¼ c. chopped onion
2 tsp. flour

½ c. water
8 oz. Velveeta or Cheddar
   cheese, grated
3 eggs, beaten
13 Ritz crackers, crushed

Thaw broccoli. Melt butter in medium saucepan; add onion. Saute until a light golden color. Add flour; cook 1 minute. Add water; mix well. Add cheese; stir constantly until cheese is melted. Add broccoli and eggs; mix well. Pour into greased 2 quart casserole. Top with cracker crumbs. Bake at 350° for 45 to 50 minutes.

BROCCOLI CASSEROLE II

Jeanne Sankowski

2 (10 oz.) pkg. frozen chopped
   broccoli
½ c. butter
4 Tbsp. flour
4 chicken bouillon cubes,
   crushed

2 c. milk
⅔ c. water
6 Tbsp. butter
⅔ pkg. (8 oz. size) herb stuffing
   mix
⅔ c. coarsely chopped walnuts

Cook broccoli according to package directions. Drain; turn into 1½ quart casserole. In saucepan, melt ½ cup butter; add flour and crushed bouillon, mixing to form a smooth paste. Gradually add milk, stirring until smooth (using a whisk for this step makes it easy). Cook until thick and smooth, stirring constantly. Pour sauce over broccoli. Heat water and 6 tablespoons butter until butter is melted. Add stuffing mix and walnuts; toss lightly. Top broccoli with stuffing mixture. Bake at 350° for 30 minutes.

CABBAGE CASSEROLE

Mary Ponas

1 medium head cabbage
4 green peppers
5 stalks celery
2 large onions
Salt and pepper

2 (8 oz.) cans tomato sauce
1 (8 oz.) can water
1 (1 lb.) can tomatoes
Cut up cooked chicken or
   meatballs

Shred cabbage; cut green peppers and celery. Slice onions; mix. Place half the vegetable mixture in a casserole; sprinkle with salt and pepper to taste. Pour one can tomato sauce, one-half can water, and half can tomatoes over cabbage mixture. Top with remaining cabbage mixture, tomato sauce, water, and tomatoes. Cover. Bake at 350° for about 2 hours or until cabbage is done. Add more water and tomatoes if necessary.

CASHEW NUT CASSEROLE

Olga Gooley

1 c. cashew nuts, chopped
1 c. onion, chopped
1 can mushrooms, drained
1 c. celery, chopped
2 Tbsp. oil
Pinch of salt

1 c. fine, dry egg noodles
1 tsp. Accent
1 c. dry Chinese noodles
1 c. liquid from mushrooms
   (add water to make 1 c.)

Mix all ingredients together and bake in greased casserole at 350° for 1 hour.

CHICKEN CASSEROLE

Mary Kostyun

1 (10½ oz.) can mushroom soup
1 c. uncooked rice
2 soup cans water

Melted butter
1 frying chicken

Combine soup, rice, and water; set aside. Place chicken in roasting pan; brush with butter. Add soup mixture to roasting pan. Cover with aluminum foil. Bake at 400° for 30 minutes; remove foil. Bake another 30 minutes.

MAKE-AHEAD CHICKEN CASSEROLE

Mary Mihalko

¼ c. butter, melted
5 slices white bread, cubed
1 (10¾ oz.) can cream of
   mushroom soup
1 (10¾ oz.) can cream of celery
   soup
1 (10¾ oz.) can cream of
   chicken soup

2 c. milk
1 (4 oz.) can mushrooms
½ lb. Cheddar cheese, grated
¼ c. chopped onion
¾ c. diced cooked chicken
⅔ to 1 c. canned or frozen peas
⅔ to 1 c. canned or frozen corn
2 c. uncooked macaroni

Melt butter; add bread cubes. Toss to coat. In a large bowl, blend soups and milk with electric mixer. Add mushrooms, cheese, onion, chicken, peas, corn, and uncooked macaroni; mix well. Pour into a lasagna pan; sprinkle with buttered bread cubes. Cover; refrigerate overnight. Next day, let casserole come to room temperature. Bake, uncovered, at 350° for 1 hour. Serves 12.

WHITE MEAT CHICKEN AND VEGETABLE CASSEROLE
Carol Taylor

2 (10 oz.) pkg. cooked broccoli, drained
4 chicken breasts, cooked and sliced thin
2 (10½ oz.) cream of chicken soup
¾ c. mayonnaise
1 tsp. lemon juice
½ tsp. curry (optional)
½ c. shredded Cheddar cheese
3 Tbsp. melted butter
1 (8 oz.) pkg. dressing mix

Arrange broccoli in bottom of a deep casserole. Layer chicken over vegetable. Combine remaining ingredients except butter and dressing mix; pour over chicken. Toss melted butter with dressing mix; sprinkle on top of chicken. Bake, uncovered, at 350° for 30 minutes or until bubbly. Serves 6 to 8. Excellent served with a tossed salad and garlic bread.

CHICKEN RICE CASSEROLE
Dorothy Skellett

3 c. diced cooked chicken
4 hard-boiled eggs, diced
2 c. cooked rice
1 small onion, chopped fine
1½ c. chopped celery
1 c. mayonnaise
2 Tbsp. lemon juice
2 (10 oz.) cans cream of mushroom soup
Stuffing mix or crushed corn flakes

In a large bowl, combine chicken, eggs, rice, onion, and celery. In another bowl, combine mayonnaise, lemon juice, and mushroom soup; add to chicken mixture. Mix well. Pour into a 2½ quart casserole. Top with stuffing mix or crushed corn flakes. Bake at 350°, covered, for 30 minutes and uncovered for 15 minutes.

BAVARIAN FRANKFURTER CASSEROLE
Patricia Hoover

3 medium potatoes, sliced into rounds
4 to 6 hot dogs, sliced into penny rounds
1 c. green beans
½ c. sharp cheese
1 c. flour
½ tsp. salt
2 eggs
¼ tsp. baking powder

Cook potatoes and hot dogs in enough water to keep from sticking. Add green beans and cheese. While cheese is melting, make spaetzle. Combine flour, salt, eggs, and baking powder; mix to a soft dough. Roll out on floured surface; cut into strips ¼ inch wide x 2 inches long. Add to frankfurters. Salt and pepper to taste. Stir occasionally until spaetzle is cooked (about 10 minutes), adding small amounts of water to keep from sticking.

MUSHROOM-ASPARAGUS CASSEROLE   Marianne Lawryk

2 (8 oz.) pkg. frozen asparagus
4 Tbsp. margarine
4 c. fresh mushrooms
1 c. chopped onion
2 Tbsp. all-purpose flour
1 tsp. instant chicken bouillon
   granules
½ tsp. salt

Dash of pepper
½ tsp. nutmeg
1 c. milk
¼ c. chopped pimiento
1½ tsp. lemon juice
¾ c. soft bread crumbs
1 Tbsp. butter or margarine,
   melted

Cook asparagus according to package directions; drain. Set aside. Melt margarine in skillet. Add mushrooms and onion; cook 10 minutes. Remove vegetables. Add flour, chicken bouillon granules, salt, pepper, and nutmeg to remaining margarine in skillet; blend thoroughly, cooking on low heat until bubbles form. Add milk gradually, stirring constantly to prevent lumps. Cook, stirring constantly, until it comes to a boil; boil 1 minute. Add asparagus, mushrooms, onion, pimiento, and lemon juice; stir. Turn into a 1½ quart casserole. Combine bread crumbs with melted butter; sprinkle on top of casserole contents. Bake at 350° for 35 to 40 minutes.

EASY POTATO CASSEROLE   Julie Sadowitz

2 bags O'Brien potatoes (frozen
   Ore-Ida)
½ c. melted butter
1 can cream of chicken soup

1 large ctn. sour cream
2 c. shredded sharp cheese
1 c. corn flakes
¼ c. butter

Thaw potatoes; butter baking pan or casserole. Melt butter in a fry pan. Add corn flakes; keep on heat until brown. Combine potatoes, soup, sour cream, and cheese in casserole; spread corn flake mixture over potatoes. Bake in 350° oven for 40 minutes.

HASH BROWN BAKE   Colleen Rucky

2 lb. frozen hash browns,
   thawed
1 tsp. salt
½ tsp. pepper

½ c. chopped onion
1 can cream of chicken soup
1 pt. sour cream
8 oz. shredded Cheddar cheese

Topping:

1 c. corn flake crumbs

½ stick margarine, melted

Combine all potato ingredients and place in greased 3 quart casserole. Top with corn flake/margarine mix. Bake at 350° for 1 hour.

RICE CASSEROLE

Chuck Sarnoski

1 pkg. Spanish rice (uncooked)
1 (10½ oz.) can onion soup
1 (10½ oz.) can beef broth
1 (2 oz.) jar pimientos, drained

1 (4 oz.) can mushrooms, drained
1 stick margarine, melted

Combine all ingredients in a 2 quart casserole. Bake at 325° for 1 hour and 15 minutes. Stir once halfway through cooking time.

SAUERKRAUT CASSEROLE

Melodye Onysko

1 lb. spiral noodles
¼ lb. butter
2 large onions, chopped fine
1 large can sauerkraut
(undrained)

2 large cans mushrooms, drained
2 cans Cheddar cheese soup
Shredded Cheddar cheese
(optional)

Cook spirals 1 minute only; drain. Set aside. Saute onions in butter; add undrained sauerkraut, mushrooms, and Cheddar cheese soup. Simmer a few minutes; blend well. Add to noodles. Top with shredded cheese if desired. Bake in a 9x13x2 inch pan at 325° for 40 minutes.

SUMMER SQUASH CASSEROLE

Sophia Malowicky

6 c. sliced summer yellow
squash
¼ c. chopped onion
1 (10½ oz.) can cream of
chicken soup

1 c. sour cream
1 c. shredded carrots
½ c. melted butter
1 (8 oz.) pkg. herb seasoned
stuffing mix

Cook squash and onion in boiling water for 5 minutes. Drain. Combine soup and sour cream; add carrots. Pour soup mixture over squash; stir. Combine butter and stuffing mix. Spread half the stuffing mix on bottom of a 12 x 7½ inch pan. Spoon squash on stuffing mix; sprinkle remaining stuffing over squash. Bake at 350° for 35 to 45 minutes.

TEXAS HASH

2 c. canned tomatoes
2 large onions, sliced
2 green peppers, cut fine
3 Tbsp. salad oil

1 lb. ground beef
½ c. rice
1 tsp. salt
¼ tsp. pepper

Drain tomatoes; save juice. Saute onions and peppers in oil until tender. Add beef, cooking until brown. Add remaining ingredients; stir. Place mixture in a casserole; cover. Bake at 350° for 45 minutes. Add tomato juice; bake 15 minutes longer.

TUNA NOODLE CASSEROLE — Mary Ann Klish

1 (16 oz.) pkg. egg noodles
2 (6 oz.) cans tuna, drained and
  flaked
2 (10¾ oz.) cans cream of
  mushroom soup
1 soup can milk

1 tsp. salt
¼ tsp. pepper
1 (16 oz.) can peas or green
  beans, drained*
6 slices American cheese

Cook noodles according to package directions; drain. In a 5 quart casserole, combine tuna, soup, milk, salt, pepper, and peas; add drained noodles. Mix well. Top with cheese slices. Cover. Bake at 350° for 20 to 25 minutes.

* Frozen vegetables may be substituted for the canned.

TURKEY GREEN BEAN CASSEROLE — Olga Tarcha Drost

Good way to use leftover turkey.

2 c. fresh or frozen green beans
1¼ c. boiling water
2½ c. diced turkey
1½ c. mushroom sauce or 1½
  (10 oz.) cans mushroom soup

⅛ tsp. pepper
1 c. precooked rice
1 (3½ oz.) can French fried
  onion rings
6 tomato slices

Cook green beans in boiling water 5 minutes. Add turkey, mushroom sauce, and pepper; simmer 2 minutes. Stir in rice and half the onion rings. Pour into 2 quart casserole; top with remaining onion rings and tomato slices. Bake at 400° for 20 to 25 minutes.

CHEESY ZUCCHINI CASSEROLE — Dorothy Skellett

6 to 10 medium zucchini
½ c. butter or margarine
¾ c. grated Cheddar cheese
¼ c. grated Swiss cheese
1 c. sour cream

½ tsp. salt
¼ tsp. paprika
¼ c. green onion, chopped
1 c. bread crumbs
¼ c. Parmesan cheese

Boil whole zucchini for 10 minutes. Cut off ends; slice lengthwise. Arrange in buttered casserole or 8x12x2 inch pan. Melt butter; add Cheddar cheese, Swiss cheese, and sour cream. Mix. Add salt, paprika, and onions; mix. Pour over zucchini. Sprinkle with bread crumbs and Parmesan cheese; dot with butter. Bake, uncovered, at 350° for 45 minutes. Serves 6 to 8.

DENISE'S ZUCCHINI CASSEROLE   Helen Charnetsky

1 lb. fettuccini
1½ lb. zucchini
1 lb. mushrooms
¼ c. butter
1 pt. heavy cream

½ c. butter
Parsley, chopped
Salt and pepper
1 c. Parmesan cheese

Cook fettuccini according to package directions. Cut zucchini in julienne strips. Saute mushrooms in ¼ cup butter; add zucchini and heavy cream. Cut butter in slices; add to zucchini mixture. Heat to boil; simmer 3 minutes. *Do not overcook.* Add fettuccini; mix. Add parsley, salt and pepper, and cheese; mix. Serves 4.

ZUCCHINI CASSEROLE IMPERIAL   Carol Wasylko

4 c. sliced zucchini
2 c. boiling water
2 eggs
1 c. mayonnaise
1 onion, chopped

¼ c. chopped green pepper
1 c. grated Parmesan cheese
Salt and pepper to taste
1 Tbsp. butter or margarine
2 Tbsp. buttered bread crumbs

Cook zucchini in water until just tender. Drain. In a large bowl, beat eggs; add mayonnaise, onion, green pepper, cheese, salt, and pepper; stir until combined. Add zucchini. Turn into a greased 1½ quart casserole. Dot with butter; sprinkle with bread crumbs. Bake, uncovered, at 350° for 30 minutes. Serves 6.

OLGA'S ZUCCHINI CASSEROLE

1 pkg. Stove Top stuffing
1 medium zucchini
1 (10¾ oz.) can cream of
  chicken soup

1 c. sour cream

Prepare stuffing according to package directions. Slice unpeeled zucchini; cook 10 minutes. Drain. Combine soup and sour cream. In a casserole, layer stuffing, zucchini, and soup-sour cream mixture until all is used. Bake at 350° until heated through and bubbly.

BAKED BEANS I

Marie Brink

A good way to use up the end of a ham or a small daisy ham.

1 lb. navy or Northern beans	¼ c. brown sugar
1 tsp. baking soda	¼ c. molasses
Ham	1 tsp. dry mustard
1 large onion, diced	1 tsp. vinegar
1 Tbsp. salad oil	Salt and pepper

Soak beans overnight. Add baking soda; parboil. Rinse in very hot water. Place beans and ham in large saucepan with just enough hot water to cover; cook about 30 minutes or until done. Saute onion in oil until soft. Add brown sugar, molasses, dry mustard, vinegar, and salt and pepper to taste. Place half the cut-up ham in bottom of baking dish; pour in beans and dressing. Top with remaining ham. Use as much water as necessary from the beans to make the casserole moist. Bake at 400° for 1 hour.

BAKED BEANS II

Carol Wasylko

1 lb. northern or marrow beans	1 c. sugar
Water	⅓ lb. salt pork, sliced

Place beans in saucepan; add water to about 1 inch above beans. Cook until tender. Transfer beans to casserole, adding sugar and salt pork. Bake, uncovered, at 350° for 2 hours.

FRIJOLES (REFRIED BEANS)

Patricia Hoover

¼ c. chopped onion	¼ c. bacon crumbs
1 clove garlic, crushed	1 tsp. salt
¼ c. green pepper (optional)	1 tsp. chili powder
Cooking oil	Sharp cheese strips
1 (15 oz.) can pinto beans	

Saute onion, garlic, and pepper in cooking oil. In a bowl, mash undrained pinto beans. Add to pan containing sauteed vegetables; add salt and chili powder. Mix well over medium heat until creamy. Turn into serving dish; garnish with sharp cheese strips.

BAR-B-Q BEEF

Shirley Buchma

1 lb. chuck beef cubes	1 tsp. chili powder
½ c. hot water	½ c. chopped green pepper
1 medium onion, chopped	1 c. catsup
½ c. diced celery	2 Tbsp. vinegar
1 tsp. salt	2 Tbsp. Worcestershire sauce

Brown beef cubes in hot fat; drain. Add hot water; simmer for several hours or until beef shreds into pieces. Add remaining ingredients; simmer 30 to 40 minutes. Freezes well.

OLGA'S BRAISED BEEF IN MACARONI RING
Anna Chyl

2 lb. beef stew meat, cubed
Flour
2 Tbsp. salad oil
1 medium onion, minced
1 clove garlic, minced
1 (4 oz.) can mushrooms (stems and pieces, undrained)

½ c. water
2 (8 oz.) cans tomato sauce
½ c. dry wine or water
½ tsp. oregano
Salt and pepper

Dredge meat with flour; saute in hot oil until brown. Add onion and garlic; cook until soft. Add mushrooms and water; bring to boiling. Reduce heat. Add tomato sauce, wine, oregano, salt, and pepper. Cover; simmer about 2 hours (or until tender), stirring occasionally. Add wine or water if necessary. Serve in center of Macaroni Ring.

Macaroni Ring:

¾ lb. elbow macaroni
¼ c. melted butter or margarine

½ c. grated Parmesan cheese
2 Tbsp. chopped parsley
Salt and pepper

Cook macaroni according to package directions; drain. Combine macaroni with melted butter, cheese, chopped parsley, and salt and pepper to taste. Pack mixture into well-oiled 1¼ quart ring mold. Place in shallow pan of hot water. Bake at 350° for 15 minutes. Unmold on heated serving plate. Fill center with meat mixture.

EASY CALZONES
Emily Klish

1 (15 oz.) pkg. frozen pizza dough
Spaghetti sauce
Pepperoni
Fresh tomato slices
Thinly sliced deli ham
Shredded cheese (your choice)
Anything else you would normally put on pizza

Oregano
Garlic powder
Onion powder
Basil
Pepper
Red pepper flakes
Olive oil

Thaw pizza dough overnight. Preheat oven to 350°. Place a piece of aluminum foil on a cookie sheet; spray with cooking spray. Remove dough from package; spread into a large flat circle with your hands or roll out with a rolling pin.

If you want a thinner, smaller calzone, use only a portion of the dough from the package. Once dough is stretched out evenly, carefully lay it on the foil. Spread a generous amount of sauce on one-half the circle to 1 inch from the edge. Layer pepperoni, tomato slices, ham, and cheese, then sprinkle a small amount of desired seasonings on filling. Spread a thin layer of sauce to 1 inch from edge on the opposite half of circle. Fold this half over the half with the fillings.

Pinch edges together to seal, then roll edge over once and pinch so that none of the filling will come out during baking. Brush olive oil on top with pastry brush or fingers. Bake about 20 minutes or until golden brown, but not dark. Remove from oven; let rest 5 to 10 minutes before eating. Serve with heated spaghetti sauce on the side for dipping.

BEEF ENCHILADAS

Patricia Hoover

Meat Filling:

1 lb. ground chuck	1 Tbsp. tequila or water
1 clove garlic, chopped	2 tsp. chili powder
2 tsp. salt	1 (1 lb.) can kidney beans
1 Tbsp. wine vinegar	(undrained)

Saute chuck; add garlic, salt, wine, vinegar, tequila, and chili powder. Add kidney beans; stir. Set aside.

Sauce:

¼ c. chopped onion	1 beef bouillon cube
1 clove garlic, chopped	1 c. boiling water
3 Tbsp. oil	2 Tbsp. chopped green pepper
2 Tbsp. flour	½ tsp. salt
2 (10½ oz.) cans tomato puree	1 tsp. chili powder
1 Tbsp. wine vinegar	½ tsp. cumin

Saute onion and garlic in oil; remove from heat. Stir in flour until smooth. Add puree, vinegar, and bouillon, which has been dissolved in boiling water; heat to boiling. Reduce heat to simmer. Add remaining ingredients; simmer, uncovered, about 5 minutes. Set aside.

Enchiladas - Prepare tortillas:

1½ c. yellow corn meal	3 Tbsp. shortening
1½ c. unsifted flour	¾ c. warm water
¾ tsp. salt	

Combine corn meal, flour, and salt; cut in shortening. Add water to moisten; form ball. Knead until no longer sticky, about 5 minutes. Allow to set 20 minutes at room temperature. Roll out on floured surface. Cut tortillas using a 5 to 6 inch bowl as a guide. Bake tortillas on a heated, ungreased griddle for one minute on each side.

If desired, purchase tortillas frozen or in a can.

Assembling enchiladas: Place about ⅓ cup filling into each tortilla; roll up. Place in 13x9x2 inch baking dish, seam side down. Pour tomato sauce over all; sprinkle with cheese. Bake at 350° for 25 minutes. Makes 10 enchiladas or 5 servings.

Note: All may be prepared in advance and refrigerated.

MILANO'S FAGOCCIA (FAGOTCH)
Olga Gooley

Bread dough for 2 loaves
1 lb. ground chuck
2 eggs
1 tsp. fennel seed
1 tsp. oregano
1 tsp. salt

1 tsp. parsley
1 clove garlic, minced, or ¼ tsp. garlic powder
1 (6 oz.) can tomato paste
Romano cheese or Parmesan cheese

Combine ground chuck with eggs, all seasonings, and tomato paste. Divide dough in 2 parts; roll out as thin as possible. Spread with meat mixture; sprinkle with grated Romano or Parmesan cheese. Roll like a jelly roll; place on greased baking sheet. Bake at 375° about 45 to 55 minutes.

FRENCH PIZZA
Chuck Sarnoski

1 (8 or 9 inch) unbaked pie shell
1 lb. ground beef
½ c. mayonnaise
½ c. milk

2 eggs, beaten
1 Tbsp. cornstarch
1½ c. Cheddar cheese
⅓ c. sliced green onion
Dash of pepper

Brown meat in skillet over medium heat; drain fat. Blend mayonnaise, milk, and eggs. Mix cornstarch in small amount of water until smooth; add to milk mixture. Add meat, cheese, onion, and pepper; mix. Pour into unbaked pie shell. Bake at 350° for 35 to 40 minutes or until golden brown and knife inserted in center comes out clean. Serves 6 to 8.

MEAL IN A BUNDLE

Mary Ponas

2 lb. chuck
6 medium potatoes
6 carrots
6 Tbsp. chopped onion
½ c. chopped parsley

2 (10½ oz.) cans golden
mushroom soup
Salt and pepper
Tabasco sauce

Cut chuck into 1 inch cubes. Peel potatoes; dice. Peel carrots; cut into ¼ inch slices. Divide ingredients into 6 equal portions onto 6 pieces of aluminum foil. Season with salt and pepper and a dash of Tabasco sauce. Add 1 tablespoon water to each portion. Wrap in the foil. Place on grill for 1 to 2 hours.

Note: All ingredients may be mixed together and baked in a covered casserole at 350° for 1½ to 2 hours or until meat is tender. Add more water as needed.

SLOPPY JOES

Marie Richardson

2 lb. ground beef
2 small onions, chopped
½ c. chopped celery
¼ c. brown sugar
1 Tbsp. lemon juice

2 tsp. Worcestershire sauce
1 (8 oz.) can tomato sauce
1 (8 oz.) can water
½ tsp. salt
¼ c. catsup

Cook ground beef, onions, and celery until meat is brown. Drain fat. Add remaining ingredients; cover. Cook 30 minutes.

BEEF STEW

Martha Maliwacki

1½ lb. boneless beef (chuck,
rump, or round)
3 Tbsp. shortening
2 c. water
½ c. red wine
1 bouillon cube
1 clove garlic, minced
Few sprigs of parsley, chopped
1 bay leaf

Dash of thyme
8 potatoes
5 carrots
2 small white onions
3 stalks celery
2 leeks or 4 scallions
2 tsp. salt
Dash of pepper

Cut beef into 1½ inch cubes. Heat shortening in heavy skillet. Add meat; cook on high heat until brown on all sides. Add water, wine, bouillon cube, garlic, parsley, bay leaf, and thyme. Bring to boiling point; reduce heat. Cover and cook slowly for about 1½ hours. Peel potatoes; cut into chunks. Scrape carrots; cut into 2 or 3 pieces, depending on size. Peel onions; leave whole. Cut celery in 3 inch pieces. Cut leeks in slices. Add vegetables and salt and pepper to meat; simmer for another hour or until tender. Serves 4. Delicious when served with French bread.

A MS'S BEEF STEW FOR MEN

1½ to 2 lb. stew beef
½ c. sliced onions
4 small potatoes, sliced
3 carrots, sliced
1 green pepper, chopped
¼ c. oil

1 c. sliced mushrooms
1 (10¾ oz.) can beef broth
½ c. water
½ c. ketchup
2 Tbsp. prepared mustard
Seasonings to taste

In a Dutch oven, brown meat and onion in oil until tender for about 45 minutes. Pour off fat. Add broth, water, ketchup, mustard, potatoes, carrots, and peppers. Cover; simmer over low heat until done - about 30 minutes. Fifteen minutes before serving, add mushrooms. Serves 3 to 4 people.

BEEF STEW - HUNT'S STYLE   Julia Dudik

2 lb. lean cubed beef
2 Tbsp. flour
2 Tbsp. shortening
2 c. water
1 can Hunt's tomato sauce
6 carrots, cut up
6 small onions, cut up

6 potatoes, cut up
1 c. green peas
1½ tsp. salt
¼ tsp. pepper
½ tsp. thyme
½ bay leaf (optional)

Roll beef in flour. In saucepan, brown meat in fat. Add water, Hunt's tomato sauce, and seasonings. Cover tightly and cook over low heat until meat is almost tender, about 1½ hours, then add prepared carrots, onions, and potatoes. Cook about 30 to 45 minutes or until vegetables are just tender; add green peas. Serves 6.

OLD-FASHIONED BEEF STEW   Mary Charnetsky

3 lb. chuck, round, or rump
½ c. flour
Salt and pepper
1 small onion, sliced
1 qt. tomato juice

2 c. boiling water
6 to 8 carrots, cut in chunks
10 to 12 small onions (whole)
10 to 12 small potatoes (whole)

Cut meat into 1½ inch cubes, trimming fat. In a heavy pan, melt down some of the fat cut from meat. Combine flour, salt, and pepper in plastic bag. Place a few cubes of meat at a time in the flour; shake to coat. Brown meat in melted fat to a deep brown color. Add sliced onion to meat while browning for added flavor. Add tomato juice and water to cover meat; bring to boiling point.

Reduce heat; cook very slowly for 1½ hours. Add carrots and onions; cook ½ hour. Add potatoes and any other vegetables such as peas and beans.

Cook another ½ hour or until meat and vegetables are tender. If gravy is too thin, mix 2 tablespoons flour with ¼ cup water until smooth. Add to stew, stirring and cooking for 1 minute after it comes to a boil. Season to taste with salt and pepper and any other seasoning such as thyme or Worcestershire sauce.

NO PEEK STEW   Carol Walling

2 to 3 lb. stew meat
1 c. chopped celery
2 c. sliced carrots
1 Tbsp. salt
1 Tbsp. sugar

½ c. water
1 c. chopped onion
4 to 6 potatoes, cubed
2 Tbsp. tapioca
1 (10¾ oz.) can tomato soup

Mix water, soup, and tapioca together; combine with the rest of ingredients and bake, covered, at 250° for 5 hours. Don't peek.

CABBAGE AND HAM   Anna Smyk

1 large onion, chopped
2 Tbsp. butter or margarine
1 (28 oz.) can tomatoes
1 medium head cabbage,
    chopped

4 c. cubed ham
2 tsp. sugar
⅛ tsp. pepper
2 Tbsp. vinegar

Saute onion in butter. Add tomatoes; cook for 10 minutes. Add cabbage, ham, sugar, and pepper; cover. Cook for 1 hour over low heat. Add vinegar; mix well. Cook, uncovered, 5 minutes.

CABBAGE WITH SAUSAGE   Mary Ponas

1 lb. hot or sweet sausage
1 medium head cabbage,
    shredded
1 medium onion, diced

1 to 2 hot peppers, cut small
Salt and pepper
1 (1 lb. 13 oz.) can tomatoes

In a large fry pan, brown sausage; remove from pan. Add cabbage, onion, peppers, salt, and pepper; partly cook. Cut sausage into slices; add to cabbage along with tomatoes. Cover; cook until done.

Excellent served with fresh bread and butter!

ITALIAN CHEESE BALLS

Olga Gooley

1 c. fine seasoned bread crumbs
½ c. shredded Cheddar cheese
½ c. finely chopped walnuts
6 eggs, slightly beaten
½ c. finely chopped onions
½ clove garlic, minced
½ tsp. salt
1 (8 oz.) can tomato soup

1 (8 oz.) can tomato sauce
1 c. water
1 packet vegetable broth
 granules
Sprinkle of basil
Sprinkle of oregano
¼ c. shredded Cheddar cheese
¼ c. shredded Romano cheese

Combine first seven ingredients. Drop by teaspoonful into hot deep fat; brown. Place in casserole. Combine tomato soup, tomato sauce, water, vegetable broth, basil, and oregano; pour over casserole contents. Top with shredded Cheddar and Romano cheese. Bake at 375° for 30 minutes.

CHICKEN A LA NANCY

Linda Zapach

4 skinless, boneless chicken
 breast halves
¼ c. vegetable oil
1 clove garlic, finely chopped
½ lemon, thinly sliced
½ lb. mushrooms, sliced
1 Tbsp. flour

¼ tsp. freshly ground pepper
¼ tsp. dried oregano
½ c. dry white wine
1 (14 oz.) can whole artichoke
 hearts, drained and
 quartered

Pound chicken breasts to ¼ inch thickness between sheets of plastic wrap or wax paper. Cut chicken into 2 inch squares. In a large fry pan, heat oil over medium heat; add chicken. Cook 2 to 3 minutes on each side, until tender and opaque. Remove chicken; keep warm. To the pan, add garlic, lemon, and mushrooms; cook until tender, 3 to 5 minutes. Sprinkle with flour, salt, pepper, and oregano. Cook, stirring 1 minute; add wine. Bring to a boil, stirring until mixture thickens; add artichokes and return chicken to pan. Simmer 2 minutes or until heated through.

ARROZ CON POLLO

Anna Smyk

2 medium stalks celery, sliced
 thin
1 medium onion, sliced thin
1 medium green pepper, diced
6 Tbsp. oil
6 Tbsp. butter
½ tsp. garlic powder
1 bay leaf
1 Tbsp. parsley

1 c. crushed tomatoes
1 to 2 bouillon cubes
1 c. hot water
1½ c. rice
Chicken (1 to 2 pieces per
 serving)
A.1. Sauce
Salt and pepper

Saute celery, onion, and green pepper in oil and butter; do not brown. Add garlic powder, bay leaf, and parsley; cook on low heat for 10 minutes. Add tomatoes and bouillon which has been dissolved in hot water. Add rice; cover. When almost done, about 10 minutes, add precooked chicken. Cover; cook 10 to 15 minutes. Stir with a fork. Season with A.1. Sauce, salt, and pepper.

CHICKEN BAKE
Colleen Rucky

1 (6 oz.) pkg. Stove Top stuffing
   mix for chicken
4 boneless, skinless chicken
   breast halves
1 (10¾ oz.) can cream of
   mushroom soup

⅓ c. sour cream
1⅔ c. water
1 (8 oz.) can mushrooms,
   drained

Combine contents of vegetable seasoning packet, stuffing mix, and water; set aside. Place chicken in 9x13 inch baking dish. Mix soup and sour cream; spoon over chicken. Spoon stuffing mixture over top. Bake at 375° for 35 minutes.

CHICKENY BEAN PILAF
Mary Ann Klish

2 lb. chicken parts
2 Tbsp. margarine, melted
Paprika
1½ c. tomato juice*
½ c. water
1 tsp. oregano leaves, crushed

½ tsp. salt
⅛ tsp. hot pepper sauce
1 (1 lb.) can pork and beans
¾ c. uncooked rice
½ c. sliced stuffed olives
   (optional)

In a 1½ quart shallow baking dish, arrange chicken, skin side down. Pour margarine over chicken; sprinkle with paprika. Bake at 400° for 15 minutes. Remove chicken from baking dish. Blend remaining ingredients in drippings. Top with chicken, skin side up. Sprinkle with paprika. Bake 45 minutes more or until chicken and rice are done and liquid is absorbed.

* Tomato soup can be used in place of tomato juice.

CHICKEN CHOW MEIN
Mary Ponas

1 c. cooked chicken
3 Tbsp. salad oil
¼ tsp. garlic salt
2 c. sliced celery
1 onion, sliced
½ tsp. Accent

2 c. chicken broth
1 (1 lb.) can Chinese vegetables,
   drained
2 Tbsp. cornstarch
2 Tbsp. soy sauce
1 (5 oz.) can Chinese noodles

Brown chicken in oil, stirring gently. Add garlic salt, celery, onion, and Accent; mix gently. Add chicken broth; cover. Cook until celery is tender. Add vegetables and more broth if needed. Thicken with cornstarch; add soy sauce. Serve with Chinese noodles over rice.

CURRIED CHICKEN AND BROCCOLI

4 whole chicken breasts
2 (10 oz.) pkg. frozen broccoli
2 (10½ oz.) cans cream of chicken soup
⅔ c. mayonnaise

⅓ c. milk
¾ c. grated Cheddar cheese
1 tsp. lemon juice
½ tsp. curry powder
1 c. buttered bread crumbs

Cook and season chicken to your taste. Skin and bone cooked chicken. Place broccoli in casserole; top with slices of chicken. Combine undiluted soup with mayonnaise, milk, ½ cup cheese, lemon juice, and curry; pour over chicken. Sprinkle with remaining ¼ cup cheese and buttered bread crumbs. Bake at 350° about 30 minutes or until bubbly. Serves 6.

CHILI CON CARNE
Julia Dudik

1½ lb. ground beef
1 Tbsp. salad oil
1 small onion
½ green pepper
1 clove garlic
1 (1 lb.) can chili with beans

1 (1 lb.) can kidney beans (undrained)
1 (1 lb.) can water
1 tsp. salt
3 Tbsp. catsup

Cook meat in oil until there is no pink. Add onion, green pepper, and garlic which have been finely chopped. Cook until browned. Add chili with beans, kidney beans, and water; stir. Add salt and catsup; mix well. Cover; simmer 45 minutes.

"JEFF'S" CHILI
Evelyn Kanazawich

3 lb. ground beef
1 (10½ oz.) can El Paso chili beans
3 cloves garlic, chopped fine
2 small onions, chopped
1 green pepper, chopped

2 (8 oz.) cans tomato sauce
2 c. crushed tomatoes
1 c. spaghetti sauce
1 to 3 tsp. chili powder
Salt and pepper to taste

Brown meat in large saucepan over medium heat until brown. Add remaining ingredients. Cook over low heat 1 to 2 hours.

MY SISTER'S CHOW MEIN HOT DISH

Pani Lawryk

1 lb. ground beef
1 small onion, chopped
1 (10½ oz.) can mushroom soup
1 can hot water
½ c. celery

1 c. bean sprouts
1 to 2 Tbsp. soy sauce
1½ c. chow mein noodles
½ c. uncooked Minute rice

In a fry pan, brown ground beef and onion. Add remaining ingredients; mix. Transfer to 2 quart casserole; cover. Bake at 350° for 1½ hours.

POTATO STUFFED FRANKS

Marie Richardson

1 lb. frankfurters
3 c. mashed potatoes
1½ tsp. imitation bacon bits

¼ c. shredded Cheddar cheese
¼ tsp. mustard
Salt and pepper

Combine potatoes, bacon bits, cheese, and mustard. Add salt and pepper to taste. Split franks lengthwise; stuff with potato mixture. Bake at 350° for 15 to 20 minutes.

Variation: Saute a chopped, small onion in ¼ cup butter or margarine; add to potatoes. Add ¼ cup Cheddar cheese. Mix; stuff franks. Bake as above.

UKRAINIAN GOULASH

Dorothy Skellett

¼ c. salad oil
3 lb. beef chuck
4 medium onions, chopped
¼ c. tomato paste
¼ c. chopped parsley

1 tsp. dried thyme
1 small bay leaf
2 tsp. salt
¼ tsp. pepper
1½ c. water

Preheat oven to 300°. Heat oil in a Dutch oven or heavy kettle. Cut beef into 1½ inch cubes; add to heated oil, ⅓ at a time, and brown on all sides. Remove meat from pan. Add onion to drippings in pan and saute until golden, about ten minutes. Return browned meat to pan. Stir in 1½ cups water, tomato paste, parsley, salt, thyme, pepper, and bay leaf; bring to boiling. Bake, covered, 2 hours or until beef is tender. Serve with buttered noodles. Yields 5 servings.

HALUSHKI

Helen Rucky

Dough:

1½ c. flour
Pinch of salt

Water

Mix flour, salt, and enough water to make a sticky dough. Drop by heaping tablespoons on a dinner plate. Dip a spoon in boiling water and rub over top of dough. Dip spoon in boiling water again. Using edge of spoon, cut dough into several smaller pieces. Drop pieces in boiling water. Continue until all dough is used up.

Topping:

½ medium cabbage, shredded
    fine
1 medium onion, chopped fine

Oil
Salt to taste

Saute cabbage and onion in oil. Add cabbage and saute until transparent. Season to taste with salt; pour over dough and mix well.

AMERICAN HOLUPKI
Colleen Rucky

1½ lb. chopped cabbage
1½ lb. lean ground chuck
1 medium onion, diced
½ c. uncooked rice

1 can tomato soup
2 cans water
Salt and pepper to taste
Garlic powder to taste

Saute chopped cabbage in a little oil until soft. Place in bottom of greased 3 quart casserole. Brown meat and onion; stir in rice and seasonings. Pour over cabbage; mix soup and water and pour over mixture. Bake, covered, at 350° for 1 to 1½ hours or until cabbage is done.

PLAIN CABBAGE ROLLS
Julia Dudik

1 large head cabbage or 2 small
    heads
1 c. rice
2 medium onions
2 to 3 Tbsp. butter
¾ lb. ground beef

¼ lb. ground pork
1 egg
1 tsp. salt
¼ tsp. pepper
¼ tsp. garlic powder
1 (6 oz.) can tomato sauce

Cut out core from cabbage; parboil. Let cool; take off leaves, making sure not to puncture them. Cook rice ½ the usual time. Chop onions fine; fry in butter until golden brown. In a large mixing bowl, combine remaining ingredients except tomato sauce; mix thoroughly. Fill cabbage leaves with mixture by placing a spoonful of mixture on leaf and rolling leaf, tucking in sides.

Line bottom of a large saucepot with cabbage leaves. Put cabbage rolls in layers on top of leaves. Combine tomato sauce with 2 cans of water; pour over rolls. Cook on high until liquid comes to a boil; lower heat. Simmer with lid on for about 1½ hours or until done.

JAMBALAYA
Marie Richardson

3 cloves garlic, chopped
1 large onion, chopped
½ green pepper, chopped
2 stalks celery, chopped
2 to 3 Tbsp. vegetable oil
1 (16 oz.) can tomatoes

¾ lb. sliced turkey kielbasa
1 c. cubed ham
1 Tbsp. Worcestershire sauce
¼ c. chopped fresh parsley
Dash of cayenne pepper
2 c. instant rice

Saute garlic, onion, pepper, and celery in oil until wilted. Add tomatoes, kielbasa, ham, and Worcestershire sauce. Cover; cook 30 minutes. Add parsley, cayenne, and rice; simmer until rice is done.

LOUISIANA JAMBALAYA
Anna Smyk

2 medium stalks celery, sliced
  thin
1 medium onion, sliced thin
1 medium green pepper, diced
6 Tbsp. oil
6 Tbsp. butter
½ tsp. garlic powder
1 bay leaf
1 Tbsp. parsley
1 c. crushed tomatoes
1 to 2 bouillon cubes

1 c. hot water
1½ c. rice
Shrimp (2 per serving)
Scallops (2 per serving)
Clams (2 per serving)
Lobster (2 bite-size pieces per
  serving)
Halibut (2 bite-size pieces per
  serving)
A.1. Sauce
Salt and pepper

Saute celery, onion, and green pepper in oil and butter; do not brown. Add garlic powder, bay leaf, and parsley; cook on low heat for 10 minutes. Add tomatoes and bouillon which has been dissolved in hot water. Add rice; cover. When almost done, about 10 minutes, add all seafood raw; cover. Cook 10 to 15 minutes. Stir with a fork. Season with A.1. Sauce, salt, and pepper.

KOLBASSI SKILLET SUPPER
Linda Zapach

1 lb. kolbassi
¾ c. converted rice
1 (10¾ oz.) can golden
  mushroom, cream of
  mushroom, or cream of celery
  soup

¾ c. water
1 Tbsp. butter
1 (10 oz.) pkg. frozen peas
1 (2½ oz.) can mushrooms,
  drained
1 c. grated Swiss cheese

Cut kolbassi into 1 inch chunks; combine with rice, soup, water, and butter in a large skillet over medium heat. Bring to a boil; reduce heat. Simmer 5 minutes. Stir in frozen peas and mushrooms; sprinkle with Swiss cheese if desired. Cover; simmer 10 minutes or until rice is cooked. Serve with salad and bread.

KUGAL-BAKED POTATO LOAF

Anne Girnis

Potatoes
¼ lb. bacon
2 large onions, diced

1 egg
3 Tbsp. flour

Peel and grate potatoes, enough to fill a 9x5x3 inch bread pan to ½ inch from top. Dice and fry bacon. Add diced onions; fry until brown. Add to grated potatoes; stir. Add egg and flour; mix thoroughly. Pour into greased pan. Bake at 375° for 2 hours or until brown. Serve with roast pork and milk gravy.

OLGA'S LASAGNA

Marion Sarnoski

1 lb. ground beef
1 lb. sweet sausage, crumbled
1 (1 lb.) can tomatoes
2 (6 oz.) cans tomato paste
Garlic powder
Grated Romano cheese
2 pinches of sugar

3 c. Ricotta cheese
½ c. grated Romano cheese
2 Tbsp. parsley flakes
2 eggs, beaten
Salt and pepper
Cooked lasagna noodles
Grated Mozzarella cheese

Fry ground beef and sausage until lightly browned; drain. Add tomatoes, tomato paste, and ½ tomato paste can of water; sprinkle with garlic powder, Romano cheese, and sugar. Simmer 2 to 3 hours. In a bowl, blend Ricotta cheese, ½ cup Romano cheese, parsley flakes, eggs, salt, and pepper. Assemble layers in lasagna pan in the following order: Lasagna noodles, Ricotta mixture, meat sauce, and Mozzarella cheese. Repeat layers until pan is filled. Bake at 375° for 1 hour. May be frozen after assembling. Thaw before baking.

OLGA'S SPINACH LASAGNA

1 (10 oz.) pkg. frozen chopped
   spinach
1 egg
1 tsp. salt
¾ tsp. oregano
⅛ tsp. pepper

2 c. cottage cheese
1 (32 oz.) jar spaghetti sauce
1 (1 lb.) pkg. lasagna noodles
2 c. grated Mozzarella cheese
1 c. water

Thaw and drain spinach. Combine egg, salt, oregano, pepper, cottage cheese, and spinach. Grease a 13x9x2 inch pan. Pour ½ cup spaghetti sauce to cover bottom of pan. Layer uncooked lasagna noodles, spaghetti sauce, Mozzarella cheese, and spinach mixture; repeat layers, ending with Mozzarella cheese on top. Carefully pour water around edge of pan. Cover tightly. Bake at 350° for 1 hour and 15 minutes. Let stand 20 minutes before serving.

VEGETABLE LASAGNA

Julieanne Marra

1 pkg. lasagna noodles, cooked
  as package directs, drained
3 lb. Ricotta cheese
1 (8 oz.) pkg. cream cheese,
  softened
½ c. onion, minced
2 tsp. dried basil

1 tsp. garlic powder
4 to 5 c. combined broccoli,
  carrots, mushrooms,
  cauliflower, shredded
4 c. Mozzarella cheese,
  shredded
¾ c. Parmesan cheese

Mix Ricotta, cream cheese, onion, basil, and garlic powder. Combine Mozzarella and Parmesan cheese. In buttered 9x13 inch pan, layer ⅓ noodles, ⅓ Ricotta mixture, ⅓ vegetables, and ⅓ Mozzarella. Repeat until all ingredients are used. Bake at 375° for 45 minutes. Let stand 15 minutes before serving.

ZUCCHINI LASAGNA

Chuck Sarnoski

Spaghetti sauce
Meatballs
1 medium zucchini, sliced thin

Ricotta cheese
Mozzarella cheese
Parmesan cheese

Prepare spaghetti sauce and meatballs using your favorite recipe. Cover bottom of 9x13 inch pan with sauce, then make layers in the following order: Zucchini, sliced meatballs, Ricotta cheese, Mozzarella cheese, and sauce. Repeat layers. Sprinkle with Parmesan cheese. Bake at 350° for 1 to 1½ hours or until zucchini is tender.

BAKED MACARONI WITH MEAT SAUCE (PASTITSIO)

Mary Kostyun

½ lb. elbow macaroni
1 lb. ground beef
1 large onion, chopped
¼ lb. butter
1 tsp. cinnamon
Salt and pepper

½ (6 oz.) can tomato paste
¾ c. water
3 eggs, beaten
2 c. hot milk
½ c. grated cheese

Cook macaroni according to package directions; drain. Saute meat and onion in butter until lightly browned. Sprinkle with cinnamon, salt, and pepper. Add tomato paste and water; simmer slowly until thick. Add hot milk to beaten eggs; add to meat. Add macaroni to meat mixture; mix. Pour half the mixture in a greased 7x11 inch pan. Sprinkle with half the cheese. Top with remaining macaroni mixture; sprinkle with remaining cheese. Bake at 325° for 30 minutes. To serve, cut into squares.

MACARONI - DOUBLE DECKER

1½ Tbsp. salt
4½ qt. boiling water
3 c. elbow macaroni
¼ c. chopped onion
¼ c. chopped green pepper
¼ c. butter or margarine
¼ c. flour
¾ tsp. salt
⅛ tsp. black pepper
1¼ c. milk

1 c. heavy cream
3 c. shredded Cheddar cheese
1 egg
1½ c. soft bread crumbs
¼ c. catsup
1½ tsp. salt
¼ tsp. black pepper
½ tsp. thyme
1½ lb. ground beef
6 thick slices tomatoes

Add 1½ tablespoons salt to rapidly boiling water. Add macaroni. Cook, uncovered, stirring occasionally until tender. Drain; set aside. Saute onion and green pepper in butter until tender. Blend in flour, ¾ teaspoon salt, and ⅛ teaspoon pepper. Slowly add milk and cream. Cook over low heat, stirring constantly, until thickened. Add cheese; stir until melted. Add macaroni to cheese sauce.

Combine egg, bread crumbs, catsup, 1½ teaspoons salt, ¼ teaspoon pepper, and thyme; add beef. Mix lightly. Spread on bottom of 13x9x2 inch baking pan. Cover with macaroni mixture. Bake at 400° for 15 minutes. Top with tomato slices; bake 15 minutes.

FETTUCCINE ALFREDO   Julieanne Marra

12 oz. fettuccine
¾ c. margarine
1 c. heavy cream
¼ tsp. pepper

1¼ c. grated Parmesan cheese
2 tsp. chopped fresh parsley
1 (8 oz.) can mushrooms

Cook fettuccine as directed; drain. Rinse with hot water. In pot, melt margarine; stir in cream and pepper. Cook over low heat until mixture thickens (about 5 minutes), stirring frequently. Stir in cheese and cook until melted. Immediately stir in cooked fettuccine and mushrooms; toss to coat with sauce. Stir in parsley. If sauce begins to separate, stir in a little more cream and cook until smooth.

GREEK MOUSSAKA

Carol Wasylko

3 medium eggplants
Salt
3 medium ripe tomatoes
2 c. finely minced onion
¾ c. butter or margarine
2 lb. ground lean lamb
1 clove garlic, finely minced
1 (8 oz.) can tomato sauce
¼ c. chopped parsley

1 Tbsp. salt
½ tsp. cinnamon
¼ c. flour
2 c. milk
1⅛ tsp. salt
Dash of nutmeg
1 c. Ricotta or cottage cheese
3 eggs, beaten

Pare eggplant; cut in ½ inch slices. Sprinkle with salt; set aside to draw out excess liquid and bitterness. Plunge tomatoes into boiling water for 15 to 20 seconds. Cool in cold water. Skins should slip off. Halve tomatoes; squeeze each half gently to remove seeds and some juice. Dice tomatoes. Cook onion in 2 tablespoons butter or margarine over medium heat until soft. Add lamb and garlic; stir to crumble meat. Add tomatoes, tomato sauce, parsley, 1 tablespoon salt, and cinnamon; cook, stirring until most of the moisture disappears.

Dry eggplant; brown on both sides in butter or margarine, using 2 tablespoons per batch. Blend flour into 2 tablespoons melted butter in saucepan; cook 1 minute, stirring constantly. Add milk, salt, and nutmeg. Bring to a boil, stirring; boil 1 minute. Cool slightly. Stir in cheese and eggs. Layer half the eggplant in a 9x13 inch baking dish. Spoon half the meat mixture over eggplant. Repeat layers. Spoon on cheese sauce. Bake at 375° for 30 minutes; brown under broiler. Let stand 15 minutes before serving. Serves 8.

Serve with a green salad, Greek style with olives and Feta cheese, hard rolls, and dry red wine.

OMELET ESPANOL

Patricia Hoover

6 eggs
¼ tsp. chili powder
1 tsp. salt
2 Tbsp. cold water
2 Tbsp. chopped green pepper
1 small onion, chopped

1 clove garlic, chopped fine
¼ c. sliced ripe olives*
2 Tbsp. chopped pimientos*
½ c. sliced mushrooms
Grated Parmesan cheese
Sliced sharp cheese

Beat eggs; add chili powder, salt, and cold water. Beat to mix, but not frothy. Add remaining ingredients; mix well. Melt enough margarine to cover bottom of skillet using medium heat. Heat until a drop of water skips across pan. Turn mixture into skillet. As eggs set, run spatula under eggs to loosen, tilting pan to allow uncooked portion to run underneath. Continue procedure until bottom is golden and top is set.

Place in 350° oven for 15 minutes to "puff" or under broiler for about 2 minutes. Slide omelet onto platter. Sprinkle with more cheese, if desired, or serve with tomato sauce. Serves 3.

* One-fourth cup sliced, stuffed olives may be substituted for the ¼ cup ripe olives and 2 tablespoons chopped pimientos.

SHREDDED ZUCCHINI FRITTATA (OMELET)
Marie Pufky

3 Tbsp. cooking oil
¼ c. chopped onion
1 medium clove garlic, crushed
4 small zucchini (¾ lb.), shredded

4 eggs
¼ c. grated Parmesan cheese
Salt and pepper to taste

In heavy 6 or 7 inch skillet, heat 2 tablespoons oil. Saute onion and garlic until tender; add zucchini. Continue to saute, stirring frequently. In medium size bowl, beat eggs slightly. Stir in cheese, salt, and pepper; add to zucchini mixture. Reduce heat; cover. Cook until eggs are set on bottom. Loosen sides and bottom; invert onto warm plate. Add remaining 1 tablespoon oil to skillet. Slide frittata back into skillet; cover. Cook until set. Cut into wedges. Serves 4.

BACON AND CHEESE PUFF PIE
Nancy Kanazawich

10 slices bacon, cut in 1 inch pieces
1 can crescent rolls
2 medium tomatoes, sliced
½ tsp. salt
Pepper
5 slices American cheese

3 eggs, separated
¾ c. sour cream
½ c. flour
½ tsp. salt
Dash of pepper
Paprika

Fry bacon until crisp; drain. Unroll crescent rolls, placing triangles in ungreased 9 inch pie pan, pressing to form crust. Place bacon on crust; top with tomato slices. Sprinkle with salt and pepper. Top with cheese. Beat egg whites until stiff; set aside. Combine egg yolks, sour cream, flour, salt, and pepper; blend well. Fold in egg whites until very few lumps remain. Do not overblend. Pour over cheese layer; sprinkle with paprika. Bake at 350° for 35 to 40 minutes or until crust and top brown and knife comes out clean.

CHEESE LUNCHEON PIE

Chuck Sarnoski

2 eggs
2 c. cream style cottage cheese
2 c. hot mashed potatoes
¾ c. thick sour cream
¼ c. finely chopped onion

2 Tbsp. chopped pimiento
1 tsp. salt
½ tsp. white or black pepper
Unbaked pie shell
2 Tbsp. butter

Beat eggs until thick. Add cottage cheese, potatoes, sour cream, onion, pimiento, salt, and pepper; blend thoroughly. Pour into unbaked pie shell, spreading evenly; dot with butter. Bake at 350° for 1½ hours or until lightly browned. Serve hot or cold.

MEAT-ZA PIE

1 lb. ground round
⅔ c. condensed milk
½ c. bread crumbs
½ tsp. garlic salt
1 (6 oz.) can tomato paste

1 (6 oz.) can sliced mushrooms, drained
1 c. grated sharp cheese
3 Tbsp. Parmesan cheese
1 Tbsp. oregano

Combine ground beef, condensed milk, bread crumbs, and garlic salt; mix thoroughly. With this mixture, form a pie shell in a 9 inch pie pan. Cover pie shell with tomato paste, mushrooms, grated sharp cheese, Parmesan cheese, and oregano. Bake at 350° for 30 minutes. Cut and serve like a pie.

DEEP DISH TURKEY PIE

Marie Richardson

6 medium potatoes, chunked
6 medium carrots, sliced
¼ c. chopped onion
¼ c. chopped green pepper
2 Tbsp. butter or margarine

1 (10½ oz.) can cream of chicken soup
1 c. cooked frozen peas
3 c. cooked turkey
Biscuits

In a large saucepan, cook potatoes and carrots in salted, boiling water or turkey broth for 15 to 20 minutes or until tender. Drain, reserving 1 cup liquid. In a medium saucepan, saute onion and green pepper in butter or margarine until soft. Add chicken soup and reserved liquid; heat to boiling. Put turkey, potatoes, carrots, and peas in a 2 quart casserole. Pour sauce over all. Bake at 425° for 30 minutes. Serve with your favorite biscuits.

ANNETTE'S POTATO STUFFING

Chuck Sarnoski

2 Tbsp. chopped onion
4 Tbsp. margarine, melted
2 c. hot, mashed potatoes
1 c. bread crumbs

½ tsp. salt
½ tsp. pepper
1 tsp. sage
Pinch of parsley

Saute onion in margarine. Combine remaining ingredients in order given; add sauteed onions. Turn into an 8 inch square pan. Bake, uncovered, at 350° for 1 hour or may be used to stuff a chicken.

PORK CHOP AND RICE BAKE

Mary Ford
Dorothy Skellett

6 pork chops (½ to 1 inch thick)
2 Tbsp. shortening
1 c. uncooked rice

1 (1.5 oz.) pkg. onion soup mix
1 (4 oz.) can sliced mushrooms
Hot water

Brown pork chops in shortening in fry pan. Grease a 9x13x2 inch baking dish. Sprinkle rice on bottom of baking dish. Sprinkle onion soup mix over rice; mix. Drain mushrooms, reserving liquid; sprinkle mushrooms over rice. Add enough hot water to reserved liquid to make 3 cups; pour over rice. Arrange browned chops on rice; cover tightly with foil. Bake at 350° for 1 hour; remove foil. Bake 10 to 15 minutes more or until excess liquid evaporates.

PORK CHOP SKILLET

Mary Kostyun

4 pork chops
2 Tbsp. flour
⅓ c. grated Parmesan cheese
½ tsp. salt
¼ tsp. pepper

4 medium potatoes, sliced
2 medium onions, sliced
3 beef bouillon cubes
¾ c. hot water

Trim excess fat from pork chops. Cook fat in skillet until there are 2 tablespoons drippings. Coat chops with flour; brown in fat. Combine cheese, salt, and pepper; sprinkle 2 tablespoons over chops. Cover with potato slices; sprinkle with 2 tablespoons more cheese mixture. Add onion slices. Dissolve bouillon cubes in water; pour over all. Sprinkle with remaining cheese. Cover. Simmer about 30 minutes or until meat and vegetables are done. Serves 4.

PORK MEDALLIONS OVER EGG NOODLES

Marianne Lawryk

1 Tbsp. flour
1 Tbsp. thyme
½ tsp. salt
2 lb. peeled pork tenderloins,
   cut into 1 oz. medallions
   (silver skin removed)
2 lb. homestyle cooked egg
   noodles

4 Tbsp. butter
1 Tbsp. basil leaves
½ tsp. Kitchen Bouquet
½ tsp. minced garlic
1 pt. heavy cream

Precook pork tenderloin medallions in a large saucepan and remove; add butter and garlic to pork drippings. Simmer 1 minute. Add flour and blend well. Add all remaining ingredients and cook until reduced by ¼ volume. Place 6 ounces precooked egg noodles on a large plate; top noodles with 5 precooked medallions, slightly overlapping each other. Top all with ¼ cup herb sauce. Makes 5 servings.

OVEN PORCUPINES

Anna Smyk

1 lb. ground beef
½ c. uncooked rice
½ c. water
⅓ c. chopped onion
1 tsp. salt
½ tsp. celery salt

⅛ tsp. garlic powder
⅛ tsp. pepper
1 (15 oz.) can tomato sauce
1 c. water
2 tsp. Worcestershire sauce

Heat oven to 350°. Combine meat, rice, ½ cup water, onion, salt, garlic powder, and pepper. Shape mixture by rounded tablespoonfuls into balls. Place meatballs in ungreased 8x8x2 inch baking dish. Stir together tomato sauce, 1 cup water, and Worcestershire sauce; pour over meatballs. Cover with foil. Bake 45 minutes; uncover. Bake 15 minutes longer.

IMPOSSIBLE CAULIFLOWER QUICHE

Marie Pufky

2 c. thinly sliced cauliflorets
1 small onion, chopped
1 small pepper, chopped
1 c. (4 oz.) shredded Colby
   cheese

Salt and pepper
1 c. milk
½ c. biscuit mix
3 eggs

Boil cauliflorets 10 minutes; drain. Place in greased 9 inch pie plate. Sprinkle with onion, pepper, cheese, salt, and pepper. Place remaining ingredients in a blender or food processor; cover. Whirl 15 seconds or in a bowl, beat with rotary beater 1 minute. Pour into pie plate. Bake at 375° for 25 minutes or until knife inserted in center comes out clean. Let stand 5 minutes before serving.

CHEESE QUICHE

Marianne Lawryk

Good with green salad and red wine.

1 unbaked 10 inch pie shell	1 c. heavy cream*
¾ c. American cheese, grated	½ c. milk*
¾ c. Swiss cheese, grated	½ tsp. salt
1½ c. prepared mushrooms	¼ tsp. pepper
4 eggs	½ tsp. dry mustard

Sprinkle bottom of pastry lined pan with cheese and mushrooms. Combine remaining ingredients; beat thoroughly. Pour over cheese and mushrooms. Bake at 375° for 45 minutes or until firm and browned.

* One and one-half cups half & half may be substituted for the heavy cream and milk to "halve" the calories.

Variation 1: Substitute bacon for mushrooms, 5 slices cooked bacon, cut into 1 inch pieces, 3 slices cooked bacon, cut in halves.

Prepare quiche as described, substituting the 1 inch pieces of bacon for mushrooms. Bake 10 minutes; place bacon strips on top. Bake 35 more minutes.

Variation 2: Use only American cheese with the bacon version if you find it too salty when using American and Swiss cheese.

CRUSTLESS QUICHE

Shirley Buchma

1 (10 oz.) pkg. frozen chopped spinach or broccoli	6 slightly beaten eggs
8 oz. grated Swiss cheese	4 tsp. grated onion
2 slices day old bread, cubed	Salt and pepper

Place frozen vegetables in colander to thaw; press out all moisture. Combine spinach, cheese, bread, eggs, onion, salt, and pepper. Turn into buttered 8 inch pie plate. Bake at 350° for 30 minutes or until knife comes out clean when placed in center. Serve hot or cold. Garnish with sour cream, mixed with dill weed. Serves 8.

QUICHE LORRAINE

1 unbaked 9 inch pie shell	1 c. milk
¼ lb. slivered Swiss cheese	1 c. heavy cream
¼ lb. slivered ham slices	1 Tbsp. butter
4 eggs	

Line bottom of pie shell with cheese and ham. Combine eggs, milk, and heavy cream; beat thoroughly. Pour into pie shell. Dot with butter. Bake at 400° for 35 minutes. Cool. Serves 6 to 8.

SPINACH QUICHE

Marie Pufky

9 inch baked pie shell
1 (10 oz.) pkg. frozen chopped
  spinach, thawed and drained
1 c. (4 oz.) shredded Swiss
  cheese

4 eggs, beaten
1 c. milk
¾ tsp. salt
¼ tsp. pepper
¼ tsp. nutmeg

Layer spinach and one-half the cheese in baked pie shell. Combine eggs, milk, and seasonings. Pour over spinach and cheese. Sprinkle with remaining cheese. Bake at 425° for 10 minutes. Reduce oven temperature to 325°; bake 25 minutes more or until set. Let stand 5 minutes before serving.

PEAS AND MUSHROOM BAKE

Sophie Smyk

½ lb. mushrooms
1 Tbsp. butter
1 tsp. lemon juice

1 (14½ oz.) can consomme
1 (16 oz.) pkg. frozen peas
Sour cream

Brown mushrooms in butter; add lemon juice. Add consomme; bring to a boil. Add peas; cook 5 minutes or until peas are tender. Add enough sour cream to your liking. Serve.

ROSA MARINA

Helen Rucky

1 box Rosa Marina macaroni,
  cooked as pkg. directs,
  drained, and let cool
1 pkg. onion soup mix
½ c. water
1 stick margarine

1 (8 oz.) can sliced mushrooms,
  drained
1 (16 oz.) pkg. frozen peas,
  cooked, drained
½ c. slivered almonds

In greased 9x13 inch dish, layer cooked Rosa Marina. Add ingredients in layers as listed above. Bake at 350° for 15 to 20 minutes.

SAUERKRAUT WITH SPARERIBS

Anna Chyl

1 (1 lb. 11 oz.) can sauerkraut
1 tart apple, peeled and
  chopped
1 small onion, chopped
1 bay leaf

½ tsp. caraway seed
2 Tbsp. brown sugar
1½ c. water
Spareribs

Drain sauerkraut. In a roasting pan, combine all ingredients except spareribs. Cut spareribs in serving size pieces; place on top of sauerkraut. Cover. Bake at 350° for 2 hours; uncover. Bake 30 minutes or until tender.

SPAGHETTI SAUCE

Anna Chyl
Dorothy Skellett

4 qt. pureed tomatoes
2 green peppers
1½ onions
2 cloves garlic
5 tsp. salt
1 tsp. pepper

1 tsp. oregano
1½ tsp. basil
Parsley to taste
¾ c. oil
½ c. sugar
2 (6 oz.) cans tomato paste

Place pureed tomatoes in a 12 quart pan. Place green peppers, onions, and garlic in a blender; blend thoroughly. Add to pan of pureed tomatoes; add salt, pepper, oregano, basil, and parsley; mix well. Add oil and sugar; mix. Cook 2 hours. Add tomato paste; mix thoroughly. Cook 1 more hour. Total cooking time: 3 hours.

Sauce may be canned or frozen for use later.

BAKA'S SPAGHETTI SAUCE

Linda Zapach

2 (29 oz.) cans tomato puree
1 (28 oz.) jar Prego spaghetti
  sauce with mushrooms
3 heaping tsp. garlic powder
2 tsp. salt

¼ to ½ tsp. hot pepper
4 Tbsp. sugar
1 (4½ oz.) can mushrooms
1 lb. ground beef

In a saucepan, combine puree, spaghetti sauce, garlic powder, salt, hot pepper, and sugar; cover. Simmer 2 hours. Brown ground beef; add to sauce together with mushrooms. Simmer 1 hour. Serve over pasta.

SPINACH SOUFFLE

Pan Scannell

1 (10½ oz.) can cream of
  mushroom soup
1 small onion, chopped
2 (10 oz.) pkg. chopped spinach,
  thawed
1 c. grated Cheddar cheese

1 egg, beaten
Pepper
Bread crumbs
Parmesan cheese
2 Tbsp. butter

Combine mushroom soup, onion, thawed spinach, cheese, egg, and pepper to taste; pour into buttered casserole. Sprinkle with bread crumbs and Parmesan cheese; dot with butter. Bake at 350° for 30 minutes.

STEAK KABOBS

Evelyn Kanazawich

1 lb. round steak, cut 1 inch
   thick
2 large onions
2 Tbsp. catsup
2 Tbsp. cider vinegar
1 Tbsp. water
1 clove garlic, crushed
1 tsp. salt

½ tsp. dry mustard
⅛ tsp. chili powder
12 cherry tomatoes
1 medium zucchini, cut in ½
   inch thick slices
1 medium green pepper, cut in
   pieces

Cut steak into 1 inch cubes. Cut onions in wedges; mince enough onion to make ¼ cup. In a bowl, combine minced onion, catsup, vinegar, water, garlic, salt, dry mustard, and chili powder for marinade. Add meat; toss to coat all pieces. Cover. Refrigerate at least 3 hours or overnight, turning occasionally. About 20 minutes before serving, preheat broiler. On long metal skewers, alternate marinated meat with onion wedges, tomatoes, zucchini, and green pepper. Broil 10 minutes, turning once.

STIR-FRIED BEEF AND PEPPERS

Ann Bycz

Long grain rice for 4 servings
1 lb. frozen flank steak, partly
   thawed
3 Tbsp. soy sauce
2 Tbsp. dry sherry
4 tsp. cornstarch
¼ tsp. sugar

⅛ tsp. ground ginger
½ c. salad oil
½ lb. mushrooms, sliced thick
2 medium onions, sliced
2 small green or red peppers,
   cut in chunks
½ tsp. salt

Begin preparation about 30 minutes before serving. Prepare rice according to package directions. Cut flank steak in half lengthwise; cut each piece diagonally against the grain into paper-thin slices. In medium bowl, mix soy sauce, dry sherry, cornstarch, sugar, and ginger. Add meat; toss lightly to coat. Set aside. In a 5 quart Dutch oven or Chinese wok, heat salad oil over high heat. Add mushrooms, onions, peppers, and salt, stirring quickly and frequently (stir-frying) until vegetables are tender-crisp, about 5 minutes. Spoon vegetables into a bowl. Add meat to oil; stir-fry until meat loses its pink color, about 2 minutes. Add vegetables; stir-fry until hot. Serve over rice. Serves 4.

ARMENIAN COMBINATION DOLMA - "STUFFED VEGETABLES"

Carol Wasylko

2 cabbage leaves
2 green peppers
2 tomatoes
1 zucchini
1 eggplant
1½ lb. ground lamb
½ c. uncooked rice

2 medium onions, chopped
3 to 4 Tbsp. snipped parsley
1 (1 lb.) can tomatoes
2½ tsp. salt
¾ tsp. pepper
Mint leaves, crushed (optional)

Prepare vegetables to be stuffed.

Cabbage: Separate leaves; cook a few minutes in boiling, salted water to soften. Drain; cut off hard rib.

Green peppers: Slice ½ inch off top; remove seeds.

Tomatoes: Cut out stem; scoop out pulp.

Zucchini: Cut in half lengthwise or crosswise; hollow out center.

Eggplant: Slice in half crosswise; hollow out center. Slice a bit off bottom of each half so it will stand up.

In a bowl, combine remaining ingredients except crushed mint leaves; mix lightly. Fill vegetables loosely. Place filling near stem end of cabbage leaf; fold over sides. Roll up and secure with toothpicks. Arrange filled vegetables in baking dish. Pour a little diluted tomato juice or water in bottom of dish. Cover. Bake at 350° for 30 minutes. Sprinkle vegetables with crushed mint leaves if desired. Continue baking 30 minutes more or until vegetables are tender.

STULNIKI

Mary Gormish

12 large cabbage leaves,
  washed
Potatoes
Butter
Onions

Salt and pepper
Sweet cabbage, diced
1 c. flour
1 tsp. baking powder

Peel enough potatoes to make a medium size bowl after mashed. Cook; mash. Season with salt and pepper and fried butter and onions. Cook enough diced sweet cabbage to make a medium size bowl after cooked. After cooking, squeeze out water; season with fried butter and onions and salt and pepper. Grate a large bowl of raw potatoes; drain. Season with salt and pepper. Add flour and baking powder.

Place cabbage leaves on table; spread with a ¼ inch thick layer of grated potatoes to ½ inch from edge of cabbage leaves. Place a mound of mashed potato mixture or sweet cabbage mixture in center of cabbage leaf on grated potatoes. Carefully fold cabbage leaf over mound in center. Line oven with foil; place each one carefully on rack. Bake at 450° until cabbage almost burns off and grated potato filling is brown and set, about 1 hour. Peel off burned cabbage; toss with browned butter and onions.

TACOS
Patricia Hoover

1 lb. ground chuck
1 clove garlic, crushed
1 Tbsp. Worcestershire sauce
1 tsp. salt
½ tsp. cumin
12 tortillas
Oil for deep-frying

1 medium onion, chopped
1 c. shredded lettuce
1 medium onion, coarsely
chopped
1 c. grated sharp Cheddar
cheese

Cook ground chuck and garlic in hot skillet until meat is brown. Add Worcestershire sauce, salt, and cumin; mix thoroughly. Keep warm. In another skillet, slowly heat oil to 420°. Gently drop a tortilla in hot oil; when it rises to top, hold one edge with tongs and bend into U-shape. Hold in oil until crisp - about 2 minutes. Remove; drain on paper towels. Continue until all tortillas are done. In each tortilla, arrange in order: A mound of meat filling, a sprinkle of raw onion, some shredded lettuce, chopped tomato, and grated cheese. Serve warm.

TATER-TOT HOT DISH
Pani Lawryk

2 lb. ground beef
1 small onion, chopped
2 (10½ oz.) cans cream of
chicken soup

1 (2 lb.) pkg. tater tots

In a large fry pan, cook ground beef and onion until brown. Add soup. Pour into a 2 quart casserole; top with tater tots. Bake, uncovered, at 350° for 30 minutes. Cover; bake another 30 minutes.

CALIFORNIA TUNA BAKE
Mary Kostyun

8 oz. elbow macaroni, cooked
1 (7 oz.) tuna, drained and
flaked
1 (10 oz.) pkg. frozen peas,
cooked and drained
¼ c. sliced pimiento-stuffed
olives

2 Tbsp. minced onion
½ tsp. salt
¼ tsp. pepper
1 can cream of mushroom soup
1 (3 or 4 oz.) pkg. cream cheese,
cubed

Combine macaroni, tuna, peas, olives, and onion in a large bowl; toss lightly. Add salt and pepper and toss lightly. Stir in soup until evenly coated; fold in cream cheese cubes. Spoon mixture into an 8 cup baking dish. Cover. Bake at 350° for 30 minutes or until bubbly hot.

Rotini macaroni, small shells, or ditalini can be substituted for elbow macaroni.

JIFFY TUNA NOODLE SKILLET
Linda Zapach

2 c. water
1 env. chicken noodle soup mix
1 (7 oz.) can tuna, drained and flaked

1 (10 oz.) pkg. frozen mixed vegetables
¼ c. flour
1 c. light cream or half & half

In a large skillet, bring water to a boil; stir in soup mix, tuna, and vegetables. Simmer, covered, 5 minutes. Combine flour with cream; add to skillet mixture, stirring constantly until sauce is thickened, about 5 minutes. If desired, top with buttered bread crumbs and Parmesan cheese. Makes about 4 servings.

UPSIDE-DOWN PINEAPPLE BAKE
Jody Dimitriou

½ c. brown sugar
1 (8 oz.) can pineapple slices, drained and halved
3 c. ground cooked ham
1 c. oats
⅓ c. milk

¼ c. chopped onion
1 egg
2 Tbsp. brown mustard
⅛ tsp. ginger
⅛ tsp. cloves
½ tsp. salt

Press brown sugar into a greased 9x5 inch pan; place pineapple halves over brown sugar. Combine remaining ingredients; mix well. Press in pan over pineapple and brown sugar. Bake at 350° for 1 hour. Invert onto serving plate.

OLGA'S BAKED ZITI

2 lb. ziti
3 lb. Ricotta cheese
2 egg yolks

3 lb. Ragu meat sauce
3 lb. Mozzarella cheese, cubed

Cook ziti according to package directions. Combine Ricotta with egg yolks; mix well. Heat meat sauce to boiling. Combine drained ziti with remaining ingredients, reserving some Mozzarella for topping. Fill a glass 9x13 inch baking dish with ziti mixture; top with reserved Mozzarella. Bake at 450° for 35 minutes or until bubbly. Serve piping hot with a tossed salad and crusty bread.

SKILLET ZITI

Carol Williams

1 lb. ground beef
2 c. uncooked ziti
1 (32 oz.) jar Prego spaghetti
  sauce

1½ c. water
Salt and pepper
4 oz. shredded Mozzarella
  cheese

Brown meat. Add ziti (or spirals), spaghetti sauce, water, salt, and pepper; stir. Bring to a boil. Simmer 30 minutes, stirring every 10 minutes. Remove from heat; sprinkle with cheese. Cover until cheese is melted. Serve.

BAKED ZUCCHINI

Anna Chyl

Zucchini
Ground beef
Basil
Oregano

Salt and pepper
Spaghetti sauce
Parmesan cheese
Mozzarella cheese

Cut zucchini in half lengthwise; scoop out seeds. Chop. Brown meat with seeds; add basil, oregano, salt, and pepper. Drain fat from meat; fill zucchini. Spoon spaghetti sauce over filled zucchini; sprinkle with grated Parmesan cheese. Bake, uncovered, at 350° for 1 hour or until done. Turn oven off. Sprinkle with Mozzarella cheese; leave in oven until cheese melts.

ZUCCHINI RISOTTO

Sophie Smyk

2 lb. ground round
1 medium onion, chopped
1 green pepper, diced
1 c. raw rice
¼ c. cooking oil

1 (28 oz.) can tomatoes
Salt and pepper
Oregano
8 medium zucchini

In fry pan, brown meat, onion, pepper, and rice in oil. Add tomatoes, salt, pepper, and oregano to taste. Bring to a boil. Slice unpeeled zucchini; place in casserole. Pour tomato mixture over zucchini. Cover. Bake at 350° for 45 minutes.

TUNA ZUCCHINI SUISSE

Ann Dobransky

2 c. shredded, unpared zucchini
  (about 3 large zucchini)
¾ tsp. salt, divided
4 eggs
1½ c. milk
2 (6½ oz.) cans tuna, drained
  and flaked

1 c. shredded Swiss cheese
½ c. finely chopped onion
1 Tbsp. lemon juice
¼ tsp. pepper
¼ tsp. dried dill weed
2 Tbsp. fine dry bread crumbs

Mix zucchini with ½ teaspoon salt. Let stand 15 minutes. Drain; pat dry. Combine zucchini with remaining ¼ teaspoon salt and all other ingredients except bread crumbs. Mix thoroughly. Sprinkle greased 10 inch quiche dish or 9 inch pie pan with bread crumbs; turn mixture into dish. Bake at 350° for 40 minutes or until knife inserted in center comes out clean. Let stand 5 minutes. Garnish with green pepper rings if desired. Makes 6 servings.

Cookies

COOKIES

APPLE BETTY BARS

Josephine Vimislik

2¼ c. quick cooking oats
2¼ c. sifted all-purpose flour
1½ c. brown sugar
¾ tsp. baking soda
1 c. plus 2 Tbsp. softened butter
  or margarine

2½ c. thinly sliced cooking
  apples
2 Tbsp. butter or margarine
½ c. granulated sugar

Mix together oats, flour, brown sugar, and baking soda. With pastry blender, cut in butter. Press ⅔ (about 4⅔ cups) of crumb mixture in greased 8x12x2 inch baking pan. Place apples on crumb mixture; dot with 2 tablespoons butter. Sprinkle with sugar. Cover with remaining crumb mixture. Bake at 350° for 30 to 35 minutes.

APRICOT NESTS

Anna Grech

6 c. flour
½ tsp. salt
¾ lb. (1½ c.) butter
2 cakes compressed yeast
¼ c. lukewarm milk

1 tsp. sugar
4 egg yolks
½ pt. heavy cream
Apricot preserves
1 egg

Combine flour and salt. Add butter; blend as for pie crust with pastry blender. Dissolve yeast and sugar in ¼ cup lukewarm milk. Cover. Set aside until foamy, about 10 minutes. Combine egg yolks and cream; beat. Add yeast to egg yolk mixture; stir. Add liquids to flour mixture; blend thoroughly. Refrigerate overnight.

Cut dough into 2 inch squares. Roll 1 square at a time; refrigerate the rest. Cut with 2 size cutters or glasses - 1 large and 1 smaller. Cut a hole in center of smaller round. Place ½ teaspoon preserves on larger round; place smaller one on top. Put on greased cookie sheet. Let stand 30 minutes. Beat egg; brush on cookies. Bake at 350° for 15 minutes.

APRICOT-NUT BARS

Helen Rucky

4 eggs, well beaten
2½ c. light brown sugar
1⅔ c. evaporated milk
2 Tbsp. lemon juice
2½ c. sifted flour
1½ tsp. baking soda

1 tsp. cinnamon
½ tsp. salt
1 c. chopped, dried apricots
1 c. chopped walnuts
1 c. flaked coconut
Confectioners sugar

Combine first 4 ingredients in large mixing bowl. Sift together flour, baking soda, cinnamon, and salt; add to egg mixture. Stir just until blended. Fold in apricots, walnuts, and coconut; do not overmix. Pour into 2 well greased 15½ x 10½ x 1 inch jelly roll pans. Bake at 350° for 20 minutes. Cool in pans; sprinkle with confectioners sugar. Cut into bars. Store in airtight container.

BACHELOR BUTTONS
Helen Rucky

1½ c. sugar
¼ c. margarine, softened
3 oz. (3 sq.) unsweetened
  chocolate, melted
1 tsp. vanilla
3 eggs

2 c. flour
2 tsp. baking powder
½ tsp. salt
Confectioners sugar
1 (9 oz.) pkg. nonpareils topped
  chocolate wafers

In large bowl, combine sugar, margarine, chocolate, and vanilla; blend. Beat in eggs. Stir in flour, baking powder, and salt. Chill dough 30 minutes. Shape dough into 1 inch balls; roll in confectioners sugar. Place 2 inches apart on ungreased cookie sheet. Bake at 350° for 12 to 15 minutes or until edges are set. Remove from oven; immediately press chocolate wafer firmly in center of each cookie. Cool 1 minute; remove from cookie sheet.

BROWN SUGAR BROWNIES
Marie Pufky

1 c. brown sugar
¼ c. butter
1 egg, beaten
¾ c. flour

1 tsp. baking powder
¼ tsp. salt
1 tsp. vanilla
½ c. chopped nuts

Combine sugar and butter in saucepan; melt over low heat. Cool. Add egg; beat. Sift together flour, baking powder, and salt; add to egg mixture. Mix thoroughly. Add vanilla. Stir in chopped nuts. Pour into greased 8x8x2 inch square pan. Bake at 350° for 30 minutes. When cool, drizzle top with melted sweet chocolate.

BUTTERSCOTCH BROWNIES
Ann Dobransky

¼ c. shortening
1 c. light brown sugar, firmly
  packed
1 egg (unbeaten)
½ c. sifted all-purpose flour

1 tsp. baking powder
½ tsp. salt
½ tsp. vanilla
½ c. coarsely chopped nuts

Melt shortening. Remove from heat; stir in sugar. Cool. Add egg; beat well. Sift together flour, baking powder, and salt; add to shortening mixture. Mix. Stir in vanilla and nuts. Spread in well-greased 8 inch square pan. Bake at

350° for 20 to 25 minutes. Cut into bars while warm. Makes 18 bars 1 x 2½ inches.

CAROB BROWNIES

Genevieve Sadowitz

½ c. margarine
½ c. honey
2 eggs
1 tsp. vanilla

⅓ c. carob powder*
1 c. flour
1 tsp. baking powder
⅔ c. chopped nuts

Combine margarine, honey, eggs, and vanilla; mix well. Combine carob powder, flour, and baking powder; add to previous mixture. Mix well. Add nuts. Pour into greased 8 inch square pan. Bake at 325° for 20 to 25 minutes. Cool; cut in squares.

Substituting carob for cocoa: Use an equal amount of carob powder for cocoa. Use 1 tablespoon water and 3 tablespoons carob powder for 1 square chocolate. Use less sugar in the recipe when substituting carob powder for chocolate or cocoa.

* Carob powder or flour is a chocolate flavored powder, milled from the carob tree pod, which is also known as St. John's bread. It is a nutritious substitute for chocolate for those who are allergic to chocolate. It is low in fat and delicious in its own right.

CHOCOLATE CHIP BROWNIES

Patricia Hoover

2 c. flour
½ tsp. salt
1 c. chopped nuts
1 c. chocolate chips
1 c. margarine or cooking oil
¾ c. granulated sugar

¾ c. brown sugar
2 eggs, beaten
1 Tbsp. vanilla
¾ tsp. baking soda
2 Tbsp. hot water

Combine flour, salt, nuts, and chocolate chips; set aside. Combine margarine, sugars, eggs, and vanilla; beat thoroughly. Add flour mixture; blend well. Add baking soda and hot water; mix. Spread in greased 15½ x 10½ x 1 inch pan. Bake at 350° for 15 to 20 minutes. Cut into squares while warm. Store in airtight container.

NO BAKE CONFETTI BROWNIES
Mary Ponas

1 c. chopped walnuts or pecans
2 c. colored miniature
  marshmallows
3 c. graham cracker crumbs
  (about 42 crackers)
1 c. confectioners sugar

1 (12 oz.) pkg. semi-sweet
  chocolate chips
1 c. evaporated milk
½ tsp. peppermint or vanilla
  extract

In a large bowl, combine nuts, marshmallows, crumbs, and sugar. In saucepan, melt chocolate chips in evaporated milk over low heat, stirring until thick and smooth. Remove from heat; add flavoring. Reserve ½ cup chocolate mixture for frosting; add remainder to crumb mixture. Mix until all crumbs are moistened. Turn into greased 8 inch square pan; press down into pan. Spread reserved chocolate mixture over top. Chill until ready to serve. If desired, garnish with walnuts, pecans, or candied cherries.

FAMOUS BROWNIES
Mary Charnetsky

½ c. (scant) salted butter
1½ c. sugar
⅜ c. milk
3 eggs, beaten
1 c. sifted pastry flour

3 env. premelted chocolate
5 tsp. cocoa
1½ c. chopped walnuts
1 tsp. vanilla

Cream butter and sugar until fluffy. Add remaining ingredients in the order given, beating well after each addition. Spread in well greased 9x9 inch pan; sprinkle with sugar. Bake at 350° for 45 minutes. Cool 30 minutes; cut in squares.

BUCHMA SISTERS' FUDGE BROWNIES
Karen Buchma
Cathy Teinert, Bonnie Whiting

1 c. margarine
8 Tbsp. cocoa
2 c. sugar
3 eggs

2 tsp. vanilla
¼ tsp. salt
1½ c. flour
¾ c. chopped nuts

In a 2 quart saucepan, melt margarine over medium heat. Add next six ingredients; mix thoroughly. Remove from heat. Add nuts; mix. Pour into well greased 9x13 inch pan. Bake at 350° for only 20 minutes.

This baking time gives you a moist brownie with a fudge texture.

GIRDLE BUSTER BROWNIES

Helen Rucky

1 pkg. German chocolate cake
  mix
⅓ c. evaporated milk
¾ c. melted margarine
¾ c. chopped nuts

1 tsp. vanilla
1 c. chocolate chips
1 (16 oz.) pkg. caramels
½ c. evaporated milk

Mix first five ingredients and put half of mixture in a 9x13 inch pan. Bake at 350° for 6 minutes. Remove from oven and sprinkle 1 cup chocolate chips evenly over baked mixture. Melt caramels and add ½ cup evaporated milk. Pour over chocolate chip layer. Crumble rest of brownie mixture evenly over caramel and bake an additional 15 to 20 minutes.

MARBLED BROWNIES

Jayne Maliwacki

1 (8 oz.) pkg. cream cheese
5 Tbsp. butter
⅓ c. sugar
2 eggs

2 Tbsp. flour
¾ tsp. vanilla
1 pkg. (family size) Duncan
  Hines brownies

Beat together cream cheese and butter. Add sugar, eggs, flour, and vanilla; beat until smooth. Set aside. Prepare brownie mix following package directions. Pour half the brownie mix into greased 9x13 inch pan. Pour cream cheese mixture over brownie layer. Spoon brownie mix in spots over the top; swirl with a knife. Bake at 350° for 30 to 40 minutes. Cool. Frost with chocolate frosting.

ZUCCHINI BROWNIES

Melodye Onysko

2 c. flour
1½ tsp. baking soda
1 tsp. salt
1¼ c. sugar
¼ c. cocoa

½ c. chopped nuts
½ c. salad oil
2 tsp. vanilla
2 c. grated zucchini

In a large bowl, combine flour, baking soda, salt, sugar, cocoa, and chopped nuts; mix. Add remaining ingredients; mix until well blended and moistened. Pour into well greased 9x13x2 inch pan. Bake at 350° for 25 minutes. Cool before cutting.

BUTTER COOKIES

Dorothy Skellett

12 egg yolks
2¼ c. sugar
8 c. sifted flour

1 lb. butter
1 Tbsp. water
Colored sugar (optional)

Beat 10 egg yolks until light and lemon colored. Stir in sugar until mixture is very creamy. Put flour in a mound on pastry board or in large bowl; work in butter with pastry blender. Add egg yolk mixture; knead well. Allow dough to rest in refrigerator about an hour. Roll to slightly more than ⅛ inch thick; cut with cookie cutters. Brush with remaining 2 egg yolks which have been mixed with water or sprinkle with colored sugar. Place on ungreased cookie sheet. Bake at 375° for 8 to 10 minutes or until edges are golden. Makes 16 dozen small cookies.

ARMENIAN BUTTER COOKIES

Evelyn Kanazawich

1 c. sweet butter
1 c. superfine sugar

2 c. flour
Confectioners sugar

Melt butter over low heat. Pour off yellow liquid into a mixing bowl; put in a cool place to solidify. Discard milky residue. Cream butter until very light and creamy. Add sugar gradually, beating until very creamy. Add flour gradually; knead until dough is medium soft. Make balls the size of walnuts; place on ungreased cookie sheet. Flatten and shape into bars. Bake at 325° for 10 to 12 minutes. Do not overbake or cookies will become very hard. Sprinkle lightly with confectioners sugar. Store in airtight container. Makes about 3 dozen.

DANISH BUTTER COOKIES

1 c. butter (room temperature)
1 c. sugar
1 egg

2 c. flour
30 whole red or green candied
cherries, cut in halves

In medium bowl, beat together butter, sugar, and egg until light and fluffy. Add flour; beat until blended. Place dough in large pastry bag fitted with a large open star ¾ inch diameter decorating tip, filling bag half full. (Cookie press may be used in place of pastry bag.) Pipe dough into 1½ inch diameter cookies, 2 inches apart, on ungreased baking sheets. Top center of each cookie with cherry half, pressing in lightly. Bake at 375° for 8 to 10 minutes or until edges are golden. Cookies should not brown on top. Remove cookies from baking sheets; cool on racks. Makes about 60 cookies.

BUTTERMILK COOKIES

Marie Pufky

1 c. shortening
2 c. sugar
2 eggs
1 tsp. vanilla or lemon extract
3½ c. flour

2 tsp. baking powder
1 tsp. baking soda
Pinch of salt
Dash of nutmeg
1 c. buttermilk

Cream shortening and sugar. Add eggs and flavoring; beat well. Sift together flour, baking powder, baking soda, salt, and nutmeg; add alternately with buttermilk to creamed mixture. Drop by teaspoonfuls on greased cookie sheet; sprinkle with sugar. Bake at 400° for 13 minutes.

BUTTERSCOTCH COOKIES
Dorothy Skellett

1 c. evaporated milk
1 Tbsp. vinegar
½ c. butter
1½ c. firmly packed brown
   sugar
2 eggs
1 tsp. vanilla

2½ c. sifted flour
1 tsp. baking soda
½ tsp. baking powder
½ tsp. salt
⅔ c. chopped walnuts or pecans
Walnut or pecan halves

Add vinegar to evaporated milk; set aside. Beat butter until light; add brown sugar, beating until mixture is light and fluffy. Add eggs and vanilla; blend thoroughly. Sift together flour, baking soda, baking powder, and salt; add to creamed mixture alternately with milk. Stir in nuts. Drop by rounded tablespoon, 2½ inches apart, on lightly greased baking sheet. Bake at 350° for 10 to 12 minutes or until lightly browned and barely firm to touch. Cool. Spread with Brown Butter Frosting; press walnut or pecan half in each cookie. Makes 5 dozen cookies.

Brown Butter Frosting:

½ c. butter
2 c. confectioners sugar

2 to 4 Tbsp. boiling water

Melt butter in small saucepan; cook over medium heat, stirring constantly until butter stops bubbling and is a nut-brown color. Add confectioners sugar and boiling water; beat until smooth and of spreading consistency.

CARAMEL LAYER CHOCO-SQUARES
Marion Kaspryk

1 (2 layer size) pkg. German
   chocolate cake mix
¾ c. butter or margarine,
   melted
⅓ c. evaporated milk

1 c. chopped nuts
1 (14 oz.) pkg. (about 50) light
   caramels
⅓ c. evaporated milk
1 c. semi-sweet chocolate chips

In large mixing bowl, combine dry cake mix, melted butter, ⅓ cup evaporated milk, and nuts; mix until dough holds together. Press half the dough into a greased and floured 9x13 inch pan. Reserve remaining dough for topping. Bake at 350° for 6 minutes.

In heavy saucepan, combine caramels and ⅓ cup evaporated milk. Cook over low heat, stirring constantly, until caramels are melted. Sprinkle chocolate chips on hot baked crust; spread caramel mixture over chocolate chips. Crumble reserved dough over caramel mixture. Return to oven; bake at 350° for 15 to 18 minutes. Cool slightly; refrigerate about 30 minutes to set caramel layer.

O'S GLAZED CHEESECAKE PUFFS   Dorothy Skellett

2 (8 oz.) pkg. cream cheese
¾ c. sugar
2 eggs
1 tsp. vanilla

24 vanilla wafers
2 (1 lb. 5 oz.) cans pie filling
   (cherry, blueberry, pineapple)

With electric mixer, whip cream cheese, sugar, eggs, and vanilla together. Line cupcake tins with double paper liners; put vanilla wafer in each one. If foil baking cups are used, no muffin pans are needed. Fill ¾ full with cream cheese mixture. Bake at 375° for 10 minutes. Cool; dab with pie filling. Chill. Makes 2 dozen. These keep well for several days.

CHERRY WHIMSIES (CHRISTMAS COOKIES)   Genevieve Sadowitz

3 eggs
¾ c. sugar
½ tsp. vanilla
⅔ c. sifted flour
½ tsp. baking powder

½ tsp. salt
½ c. chopped pecans
¾ c. chopped dates
10 red maraschino cherries
10 green maraschino cherries

Beat eggs until light. Gradually add sugar; beat until thick. Add vanilla. Sift together flour, baking powder, and salt; fold into egg mixture. Add pecans and dates. Spread in 10½ x 15½ inch pan lined with greased waxed paper. Arrange cherries across each narrow end about ½ inch from edge of pan. Bake at 325° for 30 to 35 minutes.

To decorate: Immediately upon removing from oven, turn out on waxed paper which has been sprinkled lightly with confectioners sugar. Remove greased waxed paper; trim edges and cut across to form 2 equal rectangles. Roll each tightly, beginning with cherry end. Wrap in waxed paper; chill. Spread rolls with Butter Frosting; roll in chopped pecans. Chill. To serve, cut in ½ inch slices. Makes 3 dozen cookies.

Butter Frosting:

2 Tbsp. butter
1¼ c. sifted confectioners sugar

3 to 4 tsp. milk
¼ tsp. vanilla

Cream butter. Add sugar, milk, and vanilla; beat until smooth.

* These cookies freeze well.

190

CHERRY WINKS

Mary Ponas

2¼ c. sifted flour
1 tsp. baking powder
½ tsp. baking soda
½ tsp. salt
¾ c. butter
1 c. sugar
2 eggs

2 Tbsp. milk
1 tsp. vanilla
1 c. chopped nuts
1 c. chopped dates
⅓ c. maraschino cherries
Corn flakes, crushed fine

Sift together flour, baking powder, baking soda, and salt; set aside. Cream butter and sugar; add eggs. Beat well. Add milk and vanilla; blend. Add sifted dry ingredients with nuts, dates, and cherries; mix well. Shape level teaspoonfuls of dough into a ball; roll in corn flake crumbs. Place on greased cookie sheets; top each with a piece of cherry. Bake at 375° for 12 minutes or until lightly browned.

CHINESE ALMOND COOKIES I

Mary Charnetsky

⅓ c. butter
½ c. shortening
½ c. sugar
1½ c. sifted all-purpose flour
1½ tsp. baking powder
¼ tsp. salt

1 Tbsp. milk
½ tsp. almond extract
2 egg whites, stiffly beaten
Colored sugar*
Slivered almonds

Blend butter and shortening; add sugar. Cream well. Sift together flour, baking powder, and salt; add to creamed mixture alternately with milk and almond extract. Fold in stiffly beaten egg whites. Form teaspoonfuls of dough into balls; roll in colored sugar. Place on very lightly greased cookie sheet. Press almond in center of each. Bake at 325° for 12 to 15 minutes. Makes 3½ to 4 dozen.

* Color sugar by putting some in a jar with a drop or 2 of food coloring. Shake covered jar until sugar is evenly colored.

CHINESE ALMOND COOKIES II

Sophie Smyk

2¾ c. sifted flour
1 c. granulated sugar
½ tsp. baking soda
½ tsp. salt

1 c. butter, margarine, or lard
1 egg, slightly beaten
2 tsp. almond extract
⅓ c. whole almonds

Sift flour, sugar, baking soda, and salt together into mixing bowl. Add butter; cut in with pastry blender until mixture resembles cornmeal. Add egg and almond extract; mix well. Shape dough into 1 inch balls and place 2 inches apart on ungreased cookie sheet. Place an almond on each cookie; press down to flatten slightly. Bake at 325° for 15 to 18 minutes. Makes 4½ dozen cookies.

OLGA'S CHOCOLATE BALLS I

Anna Chyl
Marion Sarnoski

1½ c. shortening
2½ c. sugar
2 c. milk
2 to 3 oz. brandy or whiskey
5 eggs
8 c. flour
9 tsp. baking powder
1 tsp. cinnamon

1 tsp. vanilla
1 c. cocoa
1 c. chopped nuts
1 tsp. nutmeg
1 tsp. cloves
2 tsp. black pepper
½ tsp. salt

Mix all ingredients by hand in order given. Roll into walnut size balls. Bake on lightly greased cookie sheet at 400° for 12 to 15 minutes. Frost when cool.

Frosting:

2 tsp. butter
1 lb. confectioners sugar

3 Tbsp. cocoa
Boiling water

Combine butter and sugar; blend. Add cocoa; blend. Add enough water to moisten and make spreading consistency; beat until smooth.

OLGA'S CHOCOLATE BALLS II

Anna Chyl
Marion Sarnoski

8 c. flour
2 tsp. baking powder
1 tsp. baking soda
½ tsp. salt
2 c. sugar
¾ c. cocoa
1 tsp. cinnamon

1 tsp. cloves
½ tsp. black pepper
1 c. shortening
4 oz. whiskey
2 c. milk
1 c. chopped nuts

In a large bowl, sift together flour, baking powder, baking soda, and salt. Add sugar, cocoa, cinnamon, cloves, and pepper; mix. Add shortening and liquids; mix thoroughly. Add nuts; mix with hands. Shape into balls; place on greased cookie sheet. Bake at 350° for 15 minutes. Cool; frost with glaze.

192

CHOCOLATE BARS
Ann Uhrinec

First Layer:

½ c. butter
¼ c. sugar
¼ c. cocoa
¼ c. milk
1 egg, slightly beaten

1 tsp. vanilla
1⅔ c. fine graham cracker
crumbs
1 (3½ oz.) can flaked coconut
¾ c. finely chopped nuts

In a 2 quart saucepan, melt butter; add sugar and cocoa. Stir until smooth. Add milk; heat to boiling. Blend small amount into egg; return to saucepan with remaining hot mixture. Stir until slightly thickened. Add vanilla. Stir in crumbs, coconut, and nuts. Press mixture on bottom of greased 8x8x2 inch pan.

Second Layer:

6 Tbsp. butter
1½ c. confectioners sugar

1 Tbsp. milk
1 tsp. vanilla

In a small mixing bowl, cream butter. Add sugar gradually; beat until light and fluffy. Add milk and vanilla; blend. Spread over first layer. Chill 15 minutes.

Third Layer:

1 c. milk chocolate chips
2 Tbsp. butter

1½ Tbsp. milk
Coarsely chopped nuts

In small saucepan, combine chocolate chips, butter, and milk. Heat over low heat, stirring until smooth. Spread over second layer; garnish with chopped nuts. Chill. When firm, cut into 1½ x 1 inch pieces. Makes 30 bars.

CHOCOLATE CHIP COOKIES
Patricia Hoover

½ c. margarine
½ c. granulated sugar
¼ c. brown sugar
1 egg, beaten
1 c. plus 2 Tbsp. flour

½ tsp. baking soda
½ tsp. salt
¼ tsp. hot water
½ tsp. vanilla
1 c. chocolate chips

Cream margarine and sugars until light; add egg. Beat well. Sift together flour, baking soda, and salt; add to creamed mixture alternately with hot water and vanilla. Add chocolate chips. Drop by teaspoonfuls on greased cookie sheet. Bake at 375° for 10 to 12 minutes. Cool slightly before removing from pan. Makes 3½ dozen.

BANANA CHOCOLATE CHIP COOKIES
Nancy Tarcha

¾ c. shortening
1 c. sugar
1 c. mashed bananas
1 egg
1½ c. flour
½ tsp. baking soda

¾ tsp. cinnamon
¼ tsp. nutmeg
1¾ c. uncooked oats
1 (6 oz.) pkg. semi-sweet
  chocolate chips

Cream shortening and sugar. Add bananas; mix well. Add egg; beat. Combine flour, baking soda, cinnamon, nutmeg, and oats; add to banana mixture. Mix well. Add chocolate chips. Drop by teaspoonfuls on greased baking sheet. Bake at 350° for 10 to 12 minutes.

HONEY CHOCOLATE CHIP COOKIES
Olga Tarcha Drost

⅓ c. butter or margarine
½ c. honey
1 egg, well beaten
1¼ c. sifted flour
½ tsp. baking soda

½ tsp. salt
1 (6 oz.) pkg. semi-sweet
  chocolate chips
½ c. chopped nuts
1 tsp. vanilla

Cream butter. Add honey; beat until light and fluffy. Add egg; blend thoroughly. Sift together flour, baking soda, and salt; add gradually to egg mixture. Add chocolate chips, nuts, and vanilla; blend thoroughly. Drop by teaspoonfuls, 2 inches apart, on ungreased baking sheets. Bake at 350° for 10 minutes or until golden brown. Makes about 3½ dozen.

CHOCOLATE CHIP MERINGUE BARS
Jane Ellsworth

¾ c. margarine
1½ c. brown sugar
½ c. granulated sugar
3 eggs, separated
1 tsp. vanilla
3 c. flour

1 tsp. baking powder
¼ tsp. baking soda
¼ tsp. salt
1 (6 oz.) pkg. chocolate chips
¾ c. chopped nuts

Combine margarine, ½ cup brown sugar, granulated sugar, egg yolks, and vanilla; beat until smooth. Sift together dry ingredients; add to previous mixture. Mix thoroughly. Pat into greased 9x13 inch pan. Sprinkle with chocolate chips and nuts. Beat egg whites, adding remaining 1 cup brown sugar until peaks form. Spread over chocolate chips and nuts. Bake at 350° for 25 minutes. Cut into bars when cool.

MOTHER'S OATS CHOCOLATE CHIP COOKIES

Edie Chebiniak

¾ c. shortening
½ c. brown sugar
½ c. granulated sugar
3 eggs
1 c. plus 2 Tbsp. flour
1 tsp. baking powder
¼ tsp. salt

⅓ c. milk
1 tsp. vanilla
⅔ c. chopped nuts
3 c. oatmeal
1 (6 oz.) pkg. semi-sweet
    chocolate chips

Cream shortening with sugars. Add eggs, one at a time, beating until light. Sift together flour, baking powder, and salt; add to egg mixture alternately with milk. Add vanilla; mix. Add nuts and oatmeal; blend. Add chocolate chips. Drop by teaspoonfuls on greased baking sheet. Bake at 375° for 15 minutes.

CHOCOLATE COOKIES

Mary Ponas

½ c. sugar
2 eggs
½ c. oil
½ c. milk
½ tsp. vanilla
3 c. flour

⅓ c. cocoa
2 Tbsp. baking powder
Pinch of salt
1 c. chocolate chips
½ c. chopped nuts

Combine sugar and eggs; beat. Add oil, milk, and vanilla; beat well. Sift together flour, cocoa, baking powder, and salt; add gradually to egg mixture, beating well. Add chocolate chips and nuts. Form into 1 inch balls. Bake on ungreased cookie sheet at 325° for 12 to 15 minutes. Cool. Frost with a very thin frosting.

Variation: Substitute coconut or dates for chocolate chips.

O'S DOUBLE CHOCOLATE DROPS

Dorothy Skellett

1 c. semi-sweet chocolate chips
½ c. soft butter
½ c. sugar
1 egg
¼ c. water

1 c. flour
½ tsp. baking soda
½ tsp. salt
½ c. chopped nuts

Melt ½ cup chocolate chips in top of double boiler placed over hot water. In large bowl of electric mixer, beat butter, sugar, and egg at medium speed until light and fluffy. At low speed of mixer, beat in melted chocolate and water. Sift together flour, baking soda, and salt; add to chocolate mixture using low speed on mixer. Stir in remaining ½ cup chocolate chips and nuts. Refrigerate

30 minutes. Drop teaspoonfuls on greased cookie sheet. Bake at 375° for 10 to 12 minutes.

CHOCOLATE MACAROONS
Mary Ponas

1 c. semi-sweet chocolate chips
2 egg whites
⅛ tsp. cream of tartar
½ c. sugar

½ tsp. vanilla
⅛ tsp. salt
1 c. flaked coconut
1 c. bran flakes

Melt chocolate chips in top of double boiler. Cool slightly. Combine egg whites and cream of tartar; beat until foamy. Add sugar gradually, beating until very stiff. Fold in vanilla and cooled chocolate. Add salt, coconut, and bran flakes. Drop by rounded teaspoonfuls on lightly greased baking sheets. Bake at 300° for 20 minutes. Remove from cookie sheets immediately; cool on racks.

CHOCOLATE MARSHMALLOW CRISPS
Ann Dobransky

1 c. semi-sweet chocolate chips
¼ c. peanut butter

3 c. Rice Krispies
1 c. mini marshmallows

In a large saucepan, melt chocolate and peanut butter over low heat, stirring constantly until smooth. Remove from heat. Stir in Rice Krispies and marshmallows. Press mixture evenly in a buttered 8x8x2 inch pan. Chill until firm. Cut in squares. Yield: 16 (2x2 inch) squares.

CHOCOLATE MINT SQUARES
Jane Ellsworth

Cake Layer:

1 c. sugar
4 eggs
½ c. butter
1 c. flour

½ tsp. salt
16 oz. Hershey's chocolate
 syrup

Combine all ingredients; beat until smooth. Pour into greased and floured 9x13 inch pan. Bake at 350° for 30 minutes. Cool in pan.

Mint Layer:

2 c. confectioners sugar
½ tsp. peppermint flavoring

½ c. butter
Green food coloring

Combine all ingredients; beat until smooth. Spread over cooled cake.

Glaze:

1 c. chocolate chips

6 Tbsp. butter

Melt chips and butter in saucepan over low heat, stirring until smooth. Cool. Spread over Mint Layer. Chill 10 minutes; cut into squares.

O'S CHOCOLATE REVEL BARS   Dorothy Skellett

1 c. butter or margarine
2 c. brown sugar
2 eggs
2 tsp. vanilla
2½ c. sifted flour
1 tsp. baking soda
1 tsp. salt
3 c. quick cook oats

1 (15 oz.) can sweetened
  condensed milk
1 (12 oz.) pkg. chocolate chips
2 Tbsp. butter or margarine
½ tsp. salt
1 c. chopped nuts
2 tsp. vanilla

In a large bowl, cream together 1 cup butter and brown sugar. Beat in eggs and 2 teaspoons vanilla. In another bowl, sift together flour, baking soda, and 1 teaspoon salt; add oats. Mix. Add dry ingredients to creamed mixture; blend. Set aside. In a heavy saucepan, combine condensed milk, chocolate chips, 2 tablespoons butter, and salt. Place over low heat, stirring until chocolate is melted and mixture is smooth. Stir in nuts and 2 teaspoons vanilla. Pat ⅔ of dough into bottom of greased 15½ x 10½ x 1 inch pan. Spread with chocolate mixture. Dot with remaining dough. Bake at 350° for 20 to 25 minutes. Cool; cut in bars.

KAY'S CHOCOLATE SPONGE COOKIES   Sophie Smyk

4 oz. melted baking chocolate
½ c. salad oil
2 c. sugar
4 eggs
2 tsp. vanilla

2 c. sifted flour
2 tsp. baking powder
½ tsp. salt
Confectioners sugar

In a large bowl, mix melted chocolate, salad oil, and sugar. Add eggs, one at a time, beating after each addition. Add vanilla; blend. Sift together flour, baking powder, and salt; add to chocolate mixture. Mix thoroughly. Refrigerate overnight. Form in balls; roll in confectioners sugar. Bake on lightly greased cookie sheet at 350° for 8 minutes. Makes 4 dozen.

BETTY'S CHRISTMAS COOKIES   Marion Kaspryk

1 c. butter
1 c. confectioners sugar
1 egg (unbeaten)
1 tsp. vanilla
2¼ c. sifted flour

1 c. pecan halves
1 c. candied red cherries, cut in
  halves
1 c. candied green cherries, cut
  in halves

Combine butter, sugar, egg, and vanilla; blend thoroughly. Add remaining ingredients; mix. Chill dough one hour; divide into thirds. Form into 3 rolls. Chill 3 hours. Cut in ⅛ inch slices; place on ungreased cookie sheet. Bake at 325° for 12 to 15 minutes or until lightly browned. Makes about 10 dozen.

CHRISTMAS HOLLY COOKIES
Marion Kaspryk

½ c. margarine
30 marshmallows
1½ tsp. green food coloring

1½ tsp. vanilla
4 c. corn flakes
Red cinnamon candies

In large saucepan, melt margarine and marshmallows over medium heat. Remove from heat; add food coloring and vanilla. Stir in corn flakes. Drop by teaspoonfuls onto waxed paper. Place 6 red cinnamon candies as holly berries on each cookie. Cool 30 minutes. Refrigerate or freeze.

CHRISTMAS ROCKS
Marion Kaspryk

1 c. butter or margarine
3 c. brown sugar
6 eggs
6 c. flour
1 tsp. baking powder
1 tsp. baking soda
Pinch of salt

1 tsp. cinnamon
⅔ c. whiskey or brandy
½ lb. raisins
1 lb. maraschino cherries, cut
1 lb. dates, chopped
1 lb. walnuts, chopped

Cream butter and sugar; add eggs. Beat thoroughly. Sift together flour, baking powder, baking soda, salt, and cinnamon; add alternately with whiskey to egg mixture. Add raisins, cherries, dates, and nuts. Drop by teaspoonfuls on greased baking sheets. Bake at 350° for 15 minutes. Makes 28 dozen.

OLGA'S COCONUT BUTTERBALLS
Anna Chyl

½ c. butter
2 Tbsp. sugar
½ tsp. vanilla
1 c. flour

¾ c. flaked coconut, chopped
 slightly
Confectioners sugar

Cream butter with 2 tablespoons sugar until very creamy. Add vanilla; blend. Add flour; mix thoroughly. Add coconut; mix well. Shape into small balls; place on ungreased cookie sheet. Chill 15 minutes. Bake at 350° for 15 minutes or until lightly browned. Roll at once in confectioners sugar.

OLGA'S COCONUT COOKIES

Anna Chyl

2 c. sifted flour
½ c. sugar
½ tsp. baking powder
¼ tsp. salt
¾ c. butter or margarine
1 egg yolk

1 egg
2 tsp. grated orange rind
2 Tbsp. orange juice
Raisins
2 c. coconut

Sift together flour, sugar, baking powder, and salt; cut in butter. Combine egg yolk, egg, and orange rind and juice; blend. Sprinkle egg mixture over flour mixture, stirring with fork until mixture forms a dough. Chill. Shape by rounded teaspoonfuls into balls. Place on ungreased cookie sheets. Flatten to slightly less than ½ inch thickness with floured fork. Place a raisin in center of each cookie. Bake at 375° for 12 to 15 minutes. Cool. Spread with Apricot Glaze on top of cookies, then dip into coconut.

Apricot Glaze:

½ c. sugar
⅓ c. apricot preserves

1 Tbsp. orange juice
3 Tbsp. water

Combine all ingredients in saucepan; boil 3 minutes. Cool.

COCONUT-DATE DROPS

Miranda Klish

2 c. walnuts
1 c. pitted dates
1 c. brown sugar

2½ c. coconut
2 eggs, slightly beaten

Grind or chop fine walnuts and dates. Add sugar, 1 cup coconut, and eggs; mix thoroughly. Drop by teaspoon into remaining coconut; shape into balls. Place on lightly greased cookie sheet. Bake at 350° for 15 minutes.

CRUNCHY CHEWS

Ann Dobransky

4½ c. corn flakes
½ c. chopped nuts
¾ c. sugar

¾ c. dark corn syrup
¾ c. peanut butter

Combine corn flakes and nuts in large bowl. Combine sugar and corn syrup in small saucepan; cook over low heat, stirring until sugar is dissolved. Bring to a rolling boil. Add peanut butter; stir. Pour over corn flakes; mix to coat evenly. Pat mixture in greased 9x13 inch pan. Cut into squares.

DATE AND NUT BALLS I

Rose Klodowski
Martha Maliwacki

2 c. chopped, pitted dates
2 eggs, beaten
¾ c. sugar
¾ c. butter (no substitutes)

2 c. chopped nuts
2 c. Rice Krispies
Flaked coconut

In a saucepan, combine dates, eggs, sugar, butter, and nuts; cook 10 minutes. Remove from heat; add Rice Krispies. Cool. Grease hands with butter; make 1 inch balls. Roll in coconut.

DATE AND NUT BALLS II

Ann Dobransky

½ c. butter or margarine
1½ c. chopped, pitted dates
⅓ c. chopped maraschino
   cherries

¾ c. sugar
3 c. Rice Krispies
1 c. chopped nuts
Confectioners sugar

In a saucepan, combine margarine, dates, cherries, and sugar; cook over medium heat, stirring constantly, until mixture is smooth. Remove from heat; stir in Rice Krispies and nuts. Form into balls; roll in confectioners sugar. Makes 3½ dozen.

DATE AND NUT BARS

Evelyn Kanazawich

¾ c. flour
1 c. sugar
¼ tsp. baking powder
⅛ tsp. salt
½ c. corn oil

2 eggs
½ tsp. vanilla
1 c. chopped dates
1 c. chopped nuts

Sift flour, sugar, baking powder, and salt into bowl; make well in center. Add corn oil, eggs, and vanilla; beat until smooth. Add dates and nuts; mix well. Bake at 350° in a greased 8 inch square pan 30 to 35 minutes. Cut into bars while warm. May be sprinkled with confectioners sugar.

O'S DATE BOW TIES

Dorothy Skellett

1 c. chopped dates
¼ c. finely chopped walnuts
1 tsp. grated orange rind
½ c. orange juice
2¼ c. flour
1¼ tsp. salt

¾ c. shortening
¼ c. orange juice
¼ c. water
Milk
Sugar

In a saucepan, combine dates, nuts, orange rind, and ½ cup orange juice; cook until dates are soft. Cool. Sift together, in large bowl, flour and salt. Cut in shortening until particles are fine. Combine ¼ cup orange juice and water; sprinkle over flour mixture. Stir with fork until dough holds together. Form into a ball. Roll out on floured surface to a 16x18 inch rectangle. Spread date mixture over half the rectangle along 16 inch side; fold over other half. Cut into 1½ x 4 inch strips; twist in center to form bow tie. Brush with milk; sprinkle with sugar. Bake on ungreased baking sheets at 400° for 12 to 15 minutes.

OLGA'S FROSTY FRUIT BARS
Marion Sarnoski

½ c. margarine
1 c. sugar
1 egg
1 Tbsp. grated orange rind
½ c. pineapple or orange juice
2½ c. sifted flour
1 tsp. baking soda
½ tsp. salt
½ tsp. cinnamon
½ tsp. nutmeg
1 c. light, seedless raisins
1 c. mixed candied fruit
½ c. chopped nuts

Cream margarine and sugar; add egg and rind. Beat. Stir in juice. Sift together flour, baking soda, salt, cinnamon, and nutmeg; add to egg mixture. Add remaining ingredients; mix. Divide dough in half. Roll each half on lightly floured surface into a 7x12 inch rectangle. Cut into 6 (2x7 inch) strips. Bake on lightly greased cookie sheet at 400° for 10 to 12 minutes. While warm, spread with confectioners sugar icing. Decorate with bits of candied fruit. Cut baked strips into bars of desired length.

FRUIT CAKE MINIATURES
Mary Charnetsky

½ c. butter
1½ c. brown sugar
3 eggs, separated
2½ c. flour
½ tsp. baking powder
½ tsp. baking soda
½ tsp. salt
1 tsp. cinnamon
1 tsp. allspice
½ tsp. nutmeg
½ c. sour cream
1 tsp. brandy or vanilla
1½ c. white seedless raisins
1½ c. currants
1 lb. mixed candied fruits
1½ c. broken nuts

Cream butter; add sugar gradually, creaming until light and fluffy. Add egg yolks; beat. Sift together flour, baking powder, baking soda, salt, cinnamon, allspice, and nutmeg; add alternately with sour cream and flavoring to egg mixture. Stir in remaining ingredients. Beat egg whites until stiff; fold into dough. Drop by teaspoonfuls on greased baking sheet. Bake at 325° for 20 to 25 minutes.

DRECHTERKUCHE (FUNNEL CAKES) Evelyn Kanazawich

4 eggs	¼ tsp. salt
1 qt. milk	4 c. (approx.) flour
2 Tbsp. sugar	Confectioners sugar
½ tsp. baking soda	Cooking oil

Beat eggs; add milk. Stir in sugar, baking soda, and salt. Add flour, a cup at a time, until 3 cups have been mixed in. Add as much of the remaining flour as is necessary to form a medium batter that will run through a funnel. Heat cooking oil in large pot to 365°. Hold finger over hole of funnel; fill with batter. Release finger to begin flow of batter into hot oil, moving and turning funnel to form various shapes, i.e. balls, circles, sticks. Drain on paper towels; sprinkle with confectioners sugar. Serve hot.

GERMAN COOKIES Mary Ponas

1 c. shortening	4 c. flour
1¼ c. brown sugar	4 tsp. baking powder
1 c. granulated sugar	2½ Tbsp. cocoa
5 eggs	1 tsp. cloves
8 oz. mixed candied fruit	2 tsp. cinnamon
1 c. coarsely chopped walnuts	

Cream shortening and sugars. Add eggs, reserving one yolk for top; beat. Add fruit and nuts; mix. Sift together remaining ingredients; add to fruit nut mixture working to form a smooth dough. Form dough into rolls approximately 3 inches in diameter and 8 to 10 inches in length. Place on lightly greased cookie sheet; glaze top with egg yolk, mixed with a few drops of water. Bake at 350° for 55 minutes. Cut into diagonal 1 inch slices when slightly cooled.

GINGER SNAPS Sophie Smyk

1 c. sugar	2 tsp. baking soda
¾ c. shortening	1 tsp. salt
4 Tbsp. molasses	1 tsp. ginger
1 egg	1 tsp. cloves
2 c. sifted flour	1 tsp. cinnamon

Cream sugar and shortening. Add molasses and egg; blend. Sift together remaining ingredients; add to creamed mixture. Blend. Form dough into ¾ inch balls; roll in granulated sugar. Flatten on greased cookie sheet. Bake at 375° for 10 to 12 minutes. Makes 5 dozen.

GINGERBREAD MEN

Miranda Klish

1 c. shortening
1 c. sugar
1 c. unsulphured molasses
2 egg yolks
4 c. sifted flour
1 tsp. salt
1 tsp. baking soda

2 tsp. baking powder
2 tsp. ground cloves
2 tsp. ground ginger
3 tsp. ground cinnamon
1 tsp. ground nutmeg
Raisins or nuts

Cream together shortening, sugar, and molasses. Add egg yolks; blend. In a separate bowl, combine sifted flour, salt, baking soda, baking powder, and spices; add gradually to molasses mixture. Mix well. Chill. On lightly floured surface, roll dough to ¼ inch thickness. Cut with 5 inch gingerbread man cookie cutter. Place on ungreased cookie sheet; decorate with raisins or nuts. Bake at 350° for 8 to 10 minutes. Decorate with ornamental frosting.

GRAHAM COOKIES

Dorothy Skellett

12 graham crackers
¾ c. margarine

½ c. sugar
½ c. chopped nuts

Grease a 10x15x1 inch jelly roll pan. Lay out graham crackers to cover bottom of entire pan. Melt margarine. Add sugar; bring to a boil. Boil 2 minutes. Pour syrup over crackers; sprinkle with chopped nuts. Bake at 350° for 5 to 10 minutes (I bake mine 6 minutes). Cut along perforations immediately; remove from pan to cool. Makes 4 dozen.

HAWAIIAN DELIGHTS

Mary Ponas

1 (9 oz.) can crushed pineapple
½ c. sugar
½ c. butter
½ c. shortening
1 c. sugar
1 tsp. vanilla
½ tsp. lemon extract

3 eggs, well beaten
½ tsp. baking soda
3 c. flour
1½ tsp. baking powder
1 lb. chopped dates
1 c. chopped nuts
Coconut

Cook pineapple and ½ cup sugar in uncovered saucepan until thick, stirring often to prevent scorching. Cool. Cream butter, shortening, 1 cup sugar, flavorings, and eggs until creamy smooth. Add baking soda to cooled pineapple. Combine flour and baking powder; add half to creamed mixture. Blend. Add pineapple; mix. Add remaining flour; mix thoroughly. Stir in dates and nuts. Chill dough 20 minutes. Drop by teaspoonfuls on greased cookie sheet; sprinkle with coconut. Bake at 375° for 12 minutes.

HOLIDAY DELIGHTS
Mary Charnetsky

½ c. butter
2 eggs, beaten
1 c. sugar
¼ c. coconut
1 tsp. vanilla

2¼ c. fine graham cracker
   crumbs
½ c. chopped walnuts
3 c. miniature marshmallows

Melt butter in top of double boiler; add eggs, sugar, and coconut. Put over simmering water; cook, stirring often, until thick, about 10 minutes. Stir in vanilla. Cool to lukewarm. Add crumbs and nuts; blend. Add marshmallows. Put into greased 8x12x2 inch pan. Bake at 350° for 30 minutes. Frost with a butter icing if desired.

HOLIDAY SPICE BARS
Mary Ponas

½ c. butter or margarine
1½ c. brown sugar
1 tsp. vanilla
1 egg
3 c. sifted flour
1½ tsp. baking powder
½ tsp. baking soda
1 tsp. salt

1 tsp. cinnamon
½ tsp. nutmeg
½ tsp. cloves
½ tsp. allspice
1 (8 oz.) can tomato sauce
¾ c. candied cherries
¾ c. candied pineapple
1 c. chopped walnuts

Cream butter and sugar; add vanilla and egg. Beat until smooth. Sift together flour, baking powder, baking soda, salt, cinnamon, nutmeg, cloves, and allspice; add alternately with tomato sauce to creamed mixture. Mix thoroughly. Fold in candied fruit and nuts. Spread in greased 10x15x1 inch jelly roll pan. Bake at 350° for 30 to 35 minutes. Cool. Cut into bars. Decorate with white frosting if desired.

HONEY DAINTIES (MELOMACARONA)
Mary Kostyun

1 c. butter
1 c. sugar
Juice of 1 orange
1 shot glass cognac
1 tsp. vanilla

4 c. flour
1 tsp. baking powder
½ tsp. baking soda
1 c. chopped almonds or
   walnuts

Cream butter and sugar. Add orange juice, cognac, and vanilla; blend. Sift together flour, baking powder, and baking soda; add gradually to creamed mixture. Form into oval shapes; place on greased pans. Bake at 350° for 20 minutes. Cool. Dip in syrup; sprinkle immediately with chopped nuts. Dry on rack.

Syrup:

2 c. sugar	**1 c. honey**
1½ c. water	

Combine ingredients in saucepan; boil 5 minutes.

HONEY SPONGE COOKIES Edie Chebiniak

½ c. margarine	**2 c. flour**
½ c. sugar	**3 tsp. baking powder**
2 eggs, separated	**½ tsp. salt**
Grated rind of ½ orange	**1 tsp. cloves**
½ c. milk	**½ c. finely chopped nuts**
½ c. honey	**(optional)**

Cream margarine, sugar, and egg yolks until light and fluffy. In small bowl, combine orange rind, milk, and honey; stir until well blended. Sift together flour, baking powder, salt, and cloves; add to creamed mixture alternately with milk mixture. Add nuts. Beat egg whites until stiff peaks form; fold into batter. Drop by teaspoonfuls 2 inches apart on greased cookie sheet. If desired, decorate with raisins, nuts, dates, or coconut. Bake at 375° about 12 minutes. Remove from cookie sheet while warm. Makes 3 dozen.

KHRUSTY Josephine Baranyk

¼ c. butter	**1 jigger rum**
½ c. confectioners sugar	**2 c. flour**
4 egg yolks	**½ tsp. salt**
2 eggs	

Cream butter and sugar; beat until light. Add egg yolks and whole eggs, one at a time, beating after each addition. Add rum; blend. Combine flour and salt; add to egg mixture. Mix thoroughly until smooth. Cover dough; refrigerate 1 to 2 hours. On a floured surface, roll a small amount of dough at a time to ⅛ inch thickness. Cut into strips 1¼ x 3 inches; slit in center. Pull one end through slit to form a loose loop. Fry in deep fat until delicately browned. Drain on absorbent paper. Sprinkle with confectioners sugar.

KOLACHKI I Mary Buckingham

Dough:

½ lb. butter	**1 lb. cream cheese**
½ lb. shortening	**4 c. flour**

In a large bowl, combine all ingredients; mix until well blended. Refrigerate overnight. Roll out dough to ⅛ inch thickness; cut into 2 inch squares. Place a teaspoon of nut filling or any desired filling on center of each square; bring 2 opposite corners to center, lapping one over the other. Pinch to seal. Place on cookie sheet lined with parchment paper. Bake at 350° for 10 to 15 minutes or until very delicately browned.

Filling:

1 lb. ground walnuts
1 c. sugar
1 slightly beaten egg white

1 tsp. vanilla
Milk (enough to moisten)

In a large bowl, combine ground walnuts and sugar; mix until well blended. In a separate small bowl, combine egg white and vanilla; add to nut mixture. Mix thoroughly, adding milk, if needed, to moisten nuts enough to hold together. Refrigerate until ready to use.

KOLACHKI II
Dorothy Skellett

½ c. butter
1 c. shortening
2 Tbsp. sugar
2 egg yolks

1 cake compressed yeast
½ pt. light cream
5 c. flour

Combine butter, shortening, and sugar; beat well. Add egg yolks; beat. Blend yeast with a small amount of cream; add to previous mixture. Beat until creamy. Add flour and cream alternately; blend. Form dough into 4 balls. Refrigerate overnight. Roll a small portion of dough at a time to ⅛ inch thickness on pastry cloth sprinkled with confectioners sugar. Cut with diamond cookie cutter; put filling in center. Overlap opposite long corners to close cookies. Place on ungreased cookie sheet. Bake at 400° for 15 minutes.

Filling:

½ lb. walnuts, ground
Sugar to taste

1 tsp. vanilla
Water

Combine walnuts, sugar, vanilla, and enough water to hold mixture together.

COTTAGE CHEESE KOLACHKI
Mary Kostyun

½ c. margarine
½ c. cottage cheese

1 tsp. vanilla
1 c. sifted flour

Blend margarine with cheese. Add vanilla; blend. Add flour; mix well. Chill dough. Roll out on floured surface; cut with diamond cookie cutter. Fill with your favorite filling. Brush top with mixture of egg yolk with a few drops of water. Sprinkle with sugar; place on lightly greased cookie sheet. Bake at 375° for 12 to 15 minutes.

ICE CREAM KOLACHKI

Anna Chyl

4 c. flour
2 Tbsp. sugar

1 lb. butter
1 pt. vanilla ice cream, softened

Combine flour and sugar. Cut in butter until mixture resembles fine meal. Add ice cream; blend. Wrap in plastic wrap; chill overnight. Roll out ¼ inch thick on lightly floured surface. Cut into rounds or squares; fill center with any filling. Pinch corners together. Bake at 350° on ungreased cookie sheet 20 to 25 minutes. Makes about 5 dozen.

KOLACHKI STARS

Anna Lewkowicz

1 lb. sweet butter, softened
1 lb. cream cheese, softened
4 egg yolks

4 c. flour
Apricot filling
Confectioners sugar

Cream butter and cream cheese. Add egg yolks; beat well. Add flour; mix thoroughly. Make 4 or 5 balls; cover. Refrigerate overnight. Roll ball of dough on surface dusted with confectioners sugar. Fold dough over and over making a square, then roll out again. (By doing this, the dough fans out when it bakes, giving it a layered effect.) Cut in 2 inch squares; slit each corner. Place ½ teaspoon apricot filling in center of square. Take the right side of each split; bring to center and lightly press together, then press lightly into filling. Place on ungreased cookie sheets. Bake at 350° for 10 to 15 minutes or until lightly browned on bottom.

Hints: (1) Dough becomes very sticky and difficult to work with on a very warm day. (2) The star may come apart while baking. Remedy this by pushing the points back down into filling while cookie is still hot.

KOULOURAKIA (GREEK COOKIE)

Mary Kostyun

1 lb. butter, softened
2 c. sugar
8 egg yolks
4 egg whites
1 c. half & half or milk
½ tsp. baking soda

6 tsp. baking powder
4 tsp. vanilla
12 c. flour
2 egg yolks
½ tsp. sugar

Cream butter and 2 cups sugar. Add 8 egg yolks and the egg whites; beat well. Add half & half, baking soda, baking powder, and vanilla; beat 10 minutes. Add flour gradually; mix. If dough is too soft, add more flour, mixing until it leaves sides of bowl. Take a tablespoon of dough; roll in a 7 or 8 inch rope. Make a figure 8 leaving bottom end open, then twist top part over. Combine 2 egg yolks and ½ teaspoon sugar; brush on cookies. Bake at 350° on greased cookie sheet 20 to 30 minutes.

KOURABIETKES (BUTTER TEA COOKIES)

Mary Kostyun

1 lb. sweet butter
½ c. confectioners sugar
2 egg yolks
6 c. cake flour
1 tsp. baking powder

1 c. chopped almonds or
  walnuts
1 oz. whiskey
Whole cloves
Confectioners sugar

Let butter stand at room temperature until very soft; beat well with electric mixer. Add sugar; beat until fluffy and light colored. Add egg yolks; beat thoroughly. Sift together flour and baking powder; add to creamed mixture. Mix. Add nuts. Sprinkle dough with whiskey; knead thoroughly. Roll dough on floured surface; cut into diamond shapes or roll into balls. Center with a clove. Bake on lightly greased cookie sheet at 350° for 20 minutes. Sprinkle liberally with confectioners sugar.

EASY LAYER BARS

Margaret Klish
Marie Pufky

½ c. melted butter
1½ c. graham cracker crumbs
1 c. flaked coconut
1 c. semi-sweet chocolate chips

1 c. butterscotch chips
1 c. chopped nuts
1 (14 oz.) can sweetened
  condensed milk

Melt butter in 9x13x2 inch pan; sprinkle with graham cracker crumbs. Sprinkle crumbs with coconut; top with chocolate chips, butterscotch chips, and nuts. Pour milk over entire mixture. Bake at 350° for 30 minutes or until lightly browned.

LEKVAR CAKE AND WALNUT PRESS COOKIES

Mary Charnetsky

2 c. butter
3½ c. confectioners sugar
4 eggs

4 c. ground walnuts
4 c. flour
1 lb. lekvar

Cream butter; add sugar gradually, beating until light. Add eggs; beat thoroughly. Add nuts. Add flour gradually; mix thoroughly. Pat a ¼ inch layer of dough on bottom and sides of a greased 10x15 inch pan. Spread lekvar on dough. With a pastry tube, make lattice on top. Bake at 350° for 30 minutes. Make press cookies with remaining dough on lightly greased baking sheet. Bake at 350° for 10 minutes or until lightly browned around edges.

LEMON BARS

Cheryl Lewkowicz
Dorothy Skellett

1 c. flour
½ c. margarine
¼ c. confectioners sugar
1 c. sugar
2 eggs, beaten

2 Tbsp. flour
½ tsp. baking powder
3 Tbsp. lemon juice
Grated rind of 1 lemon
Confectioners sugar

In large bowl, mix 1 cup flour, margarine, and ¼ cup confectioners sugar. Press mixture into greased 8x8x2 inch pan. Bake at 350° for 20 minutes. In medium bowl, mix sugar, eggs, 2 tablespoons flour, baking powder, lemon juice and rind. Pour over baked crust. Bake 25 minutes. While warm, sprinkle with confectioners sugar; cut into bars and remove from pan.

LEMON COCONUT SQUARES

Jane Ellsworth

1½ c. plus 2 Tbsp. sifted flour
1½ c. brown sugar
½ c. margarine
2 eggs, beaten
1 c. coconut

1 c. chopped nuts
½ tsp. baking powder
¼ tsp. salt
½ tsp. vanilla

In mixing bowl, combine 1½ cups flour, ½ cup brown sugar, and margarine. Pat into greased 9x13 inch pan. Bake at 275° for 10 minutes. Combine eggs, 1 cup brown sugar, coconut, nuts, 2 tablespoons flour, baking powder, salt, and vanilla. Spread on baked crust. Bake at 350° for 20 minutes. Frost while still warm. Cool; cut into squares.

Frosting:

1 c. confectioners sugar
1 Tbsp. margarine

2 Tbsp. lemon juice

In a bowl, combine confectioners sugar and margarine. Add lemon juice gradually, using only enough to make spreading consistency.

LEMON WHIPPERSNAPS

Evelyn Kanazawich

1 pkg. lemon cake mix
2 c. frozen whipped topping, thawed

1 egg
½ c. confectioners sugar

Combine cake mix, whipped topping, and egg in large bowl; mix thoroughly. Drop by teaspoonfuls into confectioners sugar; roll to coat. Place 1½ inches apart on greased cookie sheet. Bake at 350° for 10 to 15 minutes or until light golden brown. Remove from cookie sheet; cool. Yield: About 4 dozen.

TERRY'S MELTING MOMENTS
Dorothy Skellett

1 c. unsifted flour
½ c. cornstarch
½ c. confectioners sugar

¾ c. butter or margarine
1 tsp. vanilla

In medium bowl, stir together flour, cornstarch, and confectioners sugar. In large bowl, on medium speed, beat butter until smooth. Add flour mixture and vanilla; beat until blended. If necessary, refrigerate dough 1 hour for easier handling. Shape into 1 inch balls; place 1½ inches apart on ungreased cookie sheet. Flatten with lightly floured fork. Bake at 300° for 20 to 25 minutes or until edges are lightly browned. Cool. Store in tightly covered container. Makes about 3 dozen.

MY SISTER'S MILLION DOLLAR COOKIES
Pani Lawryk

½ c. margarine
½ c. shortening
½ c. granulated sugar*
½ c. brown sugar*
1 egg

1 tsp. vanilla
2 c. flour
¼ tsp. baking soda
½ tsp. salt

Cream together margarine, shortening, and sugars. Add egg and vanilla; beat well. Sift together flour, baking soda, and salt; add to creamed mixture. Mix well. Make 1 inch balls; roll in sugar. Place on lightly greased cookie sheet and press with glass. Bake at 350° for 8 to 10 minutes. Makes 4 dozen.

* One cup granulated sugar may be substituted for ½ cup granulated and ½ cup brown sugar.

MINT SURPRISES
Helen Rucky

3 c. flour
1 tsp. baking soda
½ tsp. salt
1 c. sugar
1 c. oleo

½ c. firmly packed brown sugar
2 eggs
2 (6½ oz.) chocolate mint candy
  wafers
Walnut halves

Combine all ingredients, except candy wafers and walnuts, in large bowl. Mix until dough forms. Drop by scant teaspoonfuls on ungreased cookie sheets. Press candy wafers on top. Cover with scant teaspoonful of dough. Top with walnut half - smooth edges. Bake at 375° for 9 to 12 minutes. Makes 92 cookies.

SNACK TIME MOLASSES COOKIES
Ann Dobransky

½ c. shortening
¾ c. sugar
1 egg
¼ c. molasses
1½ c. sifted flour

¾ tsp. baking soda
½ tsp. salt
½ c. moist coconut
½ c. chopped nuts

Cream shortening and sugar. Add egg and molasses; beat well. Sift together flour, baking soda, and salt; add gradually to creamed mixture. Add coconut and nuts; mix. Drop by teaspoonfuls 2 inches apart on greased cookie sheet. Bake at 375° for 10 minutes.

NO BAKE COOKIES

2 c. sugar
½ c. milk
2 Tbsp. butter

½ c. peanut butter
3 c. rolled oats
1 tsp. vanilla

Place sugar, milk, and butter in saucepan; bring to boiling. Boil 3 minutes. Add remaining ingredients. Drop by teaspoon onto waxed paper; cool.

NO BAKE APRICOT BOWLING BALLS
Jane Ellsworth

¾ c. Grape-Nuts cereal
¾ c. finely crushed graham
   crackers
¾ c. finely diced dried apricots
½ c. finely chopped pecans or
   walnuts

¾ c. sifted confectioners sugar
¼ c. light corn syrup
1 Tbsp. orange juice or water

Combine cereal, graham crackers, apricots, nuts, and ½ cup confectioners sugar. Stir in corn syrup and juice. With buttered hands, shape into ¾ inch balls; roll in remaining confectioners sugar. Makes 36 balls.

CATHEDRAL WINDOW COOKIES ("NO-BAKE")
Eloise Maliwacki

1 egg
1 c. sugar
1 (4 oz.) pkg. German's
   chocolate
2 Tbsp. butter

1 (10 oz.) pkg. colored
   miniature marshmallows
½ c. chopped nuts
Flaked coconut

In a bowl, beat egg and sugar until smooth. Melt chocolate and butter; add to egg mixture, mixing until combined. Fold in marshmallows and nuts. Divide mixture into 2 parts. Form into a log; roll in coconut to coat. Wrap rolls in plastic wrap, then put in a freezer bag. Freeze. Keep frozen until ready to use, then just slice ¼ to ⅜ inch.

NO BAKE CHERRY COOKIES
Sophia Malowicky

½ c. butter
1½ c. confectioners sugar
1 tsp. vanilla or almond extract

1½ c. coconut
Maraschino cherries
Graham cracker crumbs

Cream butter and sugar. Add flavoring; blend. Add coconut; mix. Refrigerate at least 30 minutes. Drain cherries; if large, cut in half. Wrap dough around cherries, using enough to cover cherry. Roll in graham cracker crumbs. Store in a cool place.

NO-ONE-CAN-EAT-JUST-ONE COOKIES
Genevieve Sadowitz
Josephine Vimislik

1 c. soft butter or margarine
½ c. sugar
1 tsp. vanilla
1 Tbsp. water

2 c. sifted all-purpose flour
1 c. ground walnuts
Walnut pieces

Cream butter and sugar until light. Add vanilla and water; beat. Add flour and ground nuts; mix thoroughly. Chill until firm. Shape into ¾ inch balls. Arrange on ungreased cookie sheets; top each with a walnut piece. Bake at 325° for 20 minutes. Makes 6 to 8 dozen.

NUT BALLS
Genevieve Sadowitz

½ c. butter
¼ c. sugar
1 egg, separated
2 tsp. grated orange rind
2 tsp. fresh lemon juice

½ tsp. vanilla
1 c. unsifted flour
½ c. (about) finely chopped
 walnuts

In medium mixing bowl, cream butter and sugar; add egg yolk, orange rind, lemon juice, and vanilla. Beat. Gradually mix in flour; chill. Shape into small balls using ½ tablespoon for each. Dip in slightly beaten egg white; roll in nuts. Place a few inches apart on greased cookie sheet. Bake at 350° for 16 to 18 minutes or until lightly browned. Cool. Store in tightly covered container. Makes about 3 dozen.

OATMEAL COOKIES I

Miranda Klish

1 c. shortening
1½ c. brown sugar
2 eggs
½ c. sour milk
1¾ c. sifted flour
1 tsp. baking soda
1 tsp. baking powder

1 tsp. salt
1 tsp. cinnamon
1 tsp. nutmeg
¼ tsp. cloves
3 c. quick cooking rolled oats
1 c. raisins
½ c. chopped nuts

Cream together shortening, brown sugar, and eggs. Stir in sour milk. Sift together flour, baking soda, baking powder, salt, cinnamon, nutmeg, and cloves; mix into creamed mixture. Add rolled oats, raisins, and nuts. Drop by teaspoonfuls on greased cookie sheet. Bake at 400° for about 8 minutes.

OATMEAL COOKIES II

Sophie Smyk

1 c. shortening
1½ c. sugar
2 eggs
2 c. sifted flour
1 tsp. baking soda
½ tsp. salt

½ tsp. nutmeg
¼ tsp. cinnamon
2 c. oatmeal
½ c. raisins
½ c. chopped nuts

Cream shortening and sugar; add eggs. Beat. Combine flour, baking soda, salt, nutmeg, cinnamon, and oatmeal; add to egg mixture. Mix thoroughly. Add raisins and nuts; mix. Shape into small balls; place on greased baking sheets. Bake at 375° for 8 to 10 minutes or until done. Makes about 6 dozen cookies.

OATMEAL COOKIES III

Eugenia Skarvinko

1 c. corn oil
2 c. brown sugar
½ c. flour
4 c. rolled oats
⅛ tsp. salt

1 tsp. cinnamon
1 tsp. baking soda
½ c. boiling water
1 tsp. vanilla

Combine oil and brown sugar; beat. Combine flour, rolled oats, salt, and cinnamon. Combine baking soda and water; add alternately with dry ingredients to oil-sugar mixture. Add vanilla; blend well. Drop dough by teaspoonfuls on greased baking sheet. Bake at 450° for 10 to 12 minutes.

BANANA OATMEAL COOKIES

Ann Dobransky

1 c. soft shortening
1 c. sugar
2 eggs
1 c. mashed bananas
2 c. flour
1 tsp. baking powder

¼ tsp. baking soda
1½ tsp. salt
1 tsp. cinnamon
¼ tsp. nutmeg
2 c. uncooked oats
½ c. chopped nuts

Cream shortening and sugar; add eggs. Beat well. Mix in mashed bananas. Sift together flour, baking powder, baking soda, salt, cinnamon, and nutmeg; add gradually to banana mixture. Stir in oats and nuts. Drop by teaspoonfuls onto greased baking sheet. Bake at 400° for 10 minutes. Makes about 5 dozen cookies.

OATMEAL CARMELITES

Sophie Smyk

1 c. all-purpose flour
1 c. quick-cooking rolled oats
¾ c. firmly packed brown sugar
½ tsp. baking soda
¼ tsp. salt
¾ c. butter or margarine, melted

1 c. semi-sweet chocolate chips
½ c. chopped pecans
¾ c. caramel ice cream topping
3 Tbsp. flour

In large mixer bowl, combine flour, rolled oats, brown sugar, baking soda, salt, and melted butter. Blend well on low speed to form crumbs. Press half the crumbs in bottom of a greased 11x7 inch or 9 inch square pan. Bake at 350° for 10 minutes. Remove from oven; sprinkle with chocolate chips and pecans. Combine caramel topping and 3 tablespoons flour; drizzle over chocolate pieces and pecans. Sprinkle with remaining crumb mixture. Bake 15 to 20 minutes longer or until golden brown. Chill 1 to 2 hours. Cut into bars.

FILLED OATMEAL COOKIES

Edie Chebiniak

1 c. butter
1 c. brown sugar
2 c. ground oatmeal
2 c. flour

1 tsp. baking soda
½ c. hot water
1 tsp. vanilla

Cream butter and sugar. Combine ground oatmeal and flour. Combine baking soda and hot water; add to creamed mixture alternately with dry ingredients. Add vanilla. Roll dough to ⅛ inch thickness on floured surface; cut with round cookie cutters. Bake on lightly greased baking sheet at 350° for 8 minutes or until lightly browned. Cool. Spread cooled filling on one cookie and top with another to form a sandwich.

Filling:

1 c. chopped dates
1 c. sugar
1 c. cold water

1 tsp. grated lemon rind
½ tsp. vanilla

Combine all ingredients; cook over low heat until thick. Cool.

ORANGE COOKIES

Mary Charnetsky

1 c. butter
1 c. sugar
2 egg yolks
1 Tbsp. grated orange rind

1 Tbsp. orange juice
2½ c. sifted all-purpose flour
½ tsp. baking powder
Candied cherries

Cream butter and sugar, beating until light. Add egg yolks, orange rind, and juice; beat. Sift together flour and baking powder; add gradually to creamed mixture. Blend well. Fill cookie press; form cookies on ungreased cookie sheet. Decorate with pieces of candied cherries. Bake at 375° for 10 minutes or until very lightly browned. Makes 5 dozen.

Note: Do not overbake or flavor will be impaired.

ORANGE CARROT COOKIES

Dorothy Skellett

1 c. shortening
¾ c. sugar
1 c. cooked, mashed carrots
1 egg (unbeaten)

1 tsp. vanilla
2 c. sifted flour
2 tsp. baking powder
½ tsp. salt

Cream shortening and sugar until fluffy. Add carrots, egg, and vanilla; mix well. Sift together flour, baking powder, and salt; add to carrot mixture. Mix well. Drop by teaspoonfuls on greased baking sheet. Bake at 350° for 20 minutes. Frost with Golden Glow Frosting while warm. Makes 5 dozen.

Golden Glow Frosting:

1 c. sifted confectioners sugar
1 Tbsp. butter

Grated rind of 1 orange
Juice of ½ orange

Combine all ingredients; beat until smooth.

ORANGE DATE BARS

Anna Chyl
Marion Sarnoski

½ c. butter or margarine
½ c. sugar
1 tsp. grated orange peel
2 Tbsp. orange juice
1 egg

1 c. sifted flour
½ tsp. baking soda
½ c. chopped nuts
1½ c. pitted dates, chopped

Melt butter in saucepan; remove from heat. Add sugar, orange peel, and juice; blend. Add egg; blend. Sift together flour and baking soda; add to butter mixture. Blend well. Add nuts and dates; stir lightly to combine. Pour into greased 9 inch square pan. Bake at 350° for 25 to 30 minutes. Frost with Orange Frosting. Cut in squares after frosting has set.

Orange Frosting:

1 Tbsp. margarine
1 c. sifted confectioners sugar

1 Tbsp. plus 1 tsp. orange juice

Cream margarine. Add confectioners sugar; blend. Add orange juice; beat until smooth.

ORANGE OATMEAL COOKIES

Julia Malewiacki

1 c. margarine, softened
1 c. brown sugar
1 egg
½ tsp. grated orange rind
¼ c. orange juice
1 c. flour

½ tsp. baking powder
½ tsp. baking soda
¼ tsp. salt
¼ tsp. nutmeg
2 c. quick rolled oats

In a large bowl, combine margarine and sugar until light and fluffy. Add egg; beat. Add orange rind and juice; blend. Combine flour, baking powder, baking soda, salt, and nutmeg; add gradually to orange mixture. Add rolled oats; mix. Drop by teaspoonfuls 2 inches apart on greased baking sheet. Bake at 350° for 10 minutes.

PEACH SEED NUT COOKIES

Dorothy Skellett

½ c. shortening
1½ c. sugar
2 eggs
½ tsp. baking soda
3 Tbsp. flour
3 c. flour

⅛ tsp. salt
Dash of nutmeg
½ c. sour milk or buttermilk
¼ to ½ c. peach seed nuts,
chopped fine

Cream shortening and sugar. Add eggs; beat. Combine all dry ingredients; add alternately with milk to creamed mixture. Add nuts. Drop by teaspoon on greased cookie sheet. Bake at 350° for 12 to 15 minutes until light in color. Cool. Pack in airtight container; let mellow for 1 week.

PEANUT CHIP THUMBPRINTS
Marion Kaspryk

1 c. shortening
1 c. brown sugar
1 egg, separated
2 c. sifted flour
1 tsp. baking powder

1 tsp. salt
1½ c. chopped, salted peanuts
½ c. creamy peanut butter
1 (12 oz.) pkg. milk chocolate
chips or miniature kisses

Cream shortening and brown sugar. Add egg yolk; blend. Sift together flour and baking powder; gradually add to creamed mixture, blending after each addition. Combine egg white and water; mix well. Shape dough into 1 inch balls; dip in egg white mixture, then roll in chopped peanuts. Place 1 inch apart on lightly greased baking sheet; make indentation in center of each ball by pressing down with thumb. Place about ¼ teaspoon peanut butter in each indentation; top with milk chocolate chips. Bake at 375° for 12 minutes or until golden brown. Makes 4 dozen.

PEANUT OATMEAL BUTTER BRITTLE COOKIES
Marianne Lawryk

2 c. quick or old-fashioned oats
(uncooked)
1¼ c. flour
½ tsp. baking powder
2 sticks (1 c.) margarine, chilled
1 c. confectioners sugar
⅔ c. firmly packed brown sugar

1½ tsp. water
1 tsp. vanilla
1 c. chopped, dry roasted or
lightly salted peanuts
1 (12 oz.) pkg. semi-sweet
chocolate chips

Heat oven to 350°. Line 2 cookie sheets with foil. Combine oats, flour, and baking powder; mix to evenly disperse ingredients. Add margarine; blend with electric mixer on low to medium speed until mixture is crumbly. Add sugars, water, and vanilla. Mix until dough starts to form. Stir in peanuts. Divide dough in half. Pat one-half into a 9x13 inch rectangle on one of the foil lined cookie sheets. Repeat with second half of dough on second cookie sheet. Bake 22 to 25 minutes or until golden brown, rotating cookie sheets after 12 minutes.

When baked, place cookie sheets on cooling racks. Sprinkle 1 cup chocolate chips evenly over each large cookie. Cool completely. Chill 15 minutes to set chocolate. Remove from cookie sheets; peel off foil. Break into pieces; store in a tightly covered container. Makes 4 to 5 dozen cookies.

PEANUT BUTTER COOKIES I   Ann Dobransky

½ c. butter
½ c. granulated sugar
½ c. brown sugar
1 c. peanut butter
1 egg

½ tsp. vanilla
1½ c. flour
½ tsp. baking soda
½ tsp. salt

Cream butter; add sugar. Cream well. Add peanut butter; beat. Add egg and vanilla; beat well. Sift together flour, baking soda, and salt; add to peanut butter mixture gradually. Mix thoroughly. Shape teaspoonfuls into balls; place on greased cookie sheets. Crisscross with fork. Bake at 375° for 15 minutes.

PEANUT BUTTER COOKIES II   Mary Kostyun

1 (2 layer size) pkg. yellow cake
    mix
1 c. peanut butter

½ c. cooking oil
2 Tbsp. water
2 eggs

Combine all ingredients; mix thoroughly. Drop by teaspoonfuls on ungreased cookie sheet. Press a crisscross on each cookie with tines of fork which have been dipped in water. Bake at 350° for 10 to 12 minutes.

PEANUT BUTTER COOKIES III   Jeanne Sankowski

2 c. raisins
Water
1 c. shortening
1 c. peanut butter
1 c. granulated sugar
1 c. brown sugar

2 eggs, beaten
3 c. flour
1½ tsp. baking soda
2 tsp. vanilla
1 c. oatmeal

In a saucepan, combine raisins with enough water to cover; simmer 5 minutes. Set aside. In mixing bowl, cream shortening, peanut butter, and sugars. Add eggs; beat well. Add flour and baking soda, which have been combined, to the creamed mixture gradually. Add vanilla. Add oatmeal; blend well. Drain raisins; add to cookie dough. Shape dough into walnut size balls. Press with fork on greased cookie sheet. Bake at 375° for 12 to 15 minutes.

PEANUT BUTTER BALLS I   Mary Buckingham

1 c. margarine
1 (12 oz.) jar crunchy peanut
    butter
1 lb. confectioners sugar

1 tsp. vanilla
⅓ c. graham cracker crumbs
¼ stick paraffin
1 (12 oz.) pkg. chocolate chips

Melt margarine; add peanut butter, confectioners sugar, vanilla, and graham cracker crumbs. Mix. Form into balls. In a double boiler, melt paraffin and chocolate chips; mix to evenly distribute paraffin throughout chocolate. Dip balls in chocolate mixture. Place balls on wax paper in refrigerator to set.

PEANUT BUTTER BALLS II
Marion Kaspryk

½ c. peanut butter
1 c. confectioners sugar
1 c. chopped nuts
1 c. finely chopped dates
1 c. graham cracker crumbs

3 Tbsp. orange juice
¼ piece paraffin wax
1 (12 oz.) pkg. milk chocolate
   chips

Mix first 6 ingredients together. Shape into small balls the size of small walnuts or bonbons; refrigerate a few hours. Melt wax and chocolate together. Dip each ball in chocolate to coat; cool on waxed paper. Store in refrigerator or can be frozen.

PEANUT BUTTER BALLS III
Colleen Rucky

1¼ c. peanut butter
1 c. graham cracker crumbs
½ lb. melted butter
1 lb. confectioners sugar

1 tsp. vanilla
1 c. milk chocolate, melted
1 Tbsp. Crisco

Melt butter; add peanut butter and blend. Add graham cracker crumbs, vanilla, and sugar. Roll in 1 inch balls or desired rounds. Dip balls in melted chocolate, mixed with Crisco.

Optional: Sprinkle with nonpareils.

PEANUT BUTTER TEMPTATIONS
Mary Mihalko

½ c. butter
½ c. peanut butter
½ c. sugar
½ c. brown sugar
1 egg
½ tsp. vanilla

1¼ c. flour
¾ tsp. baking soda
½ tsp. salt
10 oz. miniature chocolate
   covered peanut butter cups

Cream butter, peanut butter, and sugars together. Add egg and vanilla; beat. Sift together flour, baking soda, and salt; add to creamed mixture. Blend. Shape dough into 1 inch balls; place in ungreased or paper cup lined mini-muffin pans. Bake at 375° for 8 to 10 minutes or until lightly browned. Immediately after removing from oven, press peanut butter cup (paper removed) into center of each cookie until only the top of peanut butter cup shows. Let cool

10 minutes, then remove from tins. Store in airtight container. Makes 40 cookies.

PECAN DAINTIES

Genevieve Sadowitz
Josephine Vimislik

1 c. soft butter
½ c. sugar
2 c. sifted flour
1 tsp. vanilla

1 Tbsp. water
2 c. pecans, ground
Pecan halves

Cream butter and sugar until light. Add remaining ingredients; mix well. Chill until firm. Shape into ¾ inch balls; place on ungreased cookie sheet. Top each cookie with a pecan half. Bake at 325° about 20 minutes. Store in airtight containers. Makes 6 to 8 dozen cookies.

Note: Walnuts may be substituted for pecans.

PECAN MELTS

Carol Taylor

½ c. butter
⅓ c. sugar
1 c. sifted all-purpose flour
½ tsp. salt

½ tsp. orange rind
2 Tbsp. orange juice
1 egg (unbeaten)
¾ c. chopped pecans

Cream together butter and sugar. Sift together flour and salt; gradually add to creamed mixture. Add orange rind, orange juice, and egg; blend well. Stir in pecans. Drop onto ungreased cookie sheet by teaspoonful. Bake at 350° for 9 to 12 minutes. Sprinkle with confectioners sugar while hot.

PECAN PIE SQUARES

Dorothy Skellett

3 c. flour
¼ c. plus 2 Tbsp. sugar

¾ c. margarine
¾ tsp. salt

Beat all ingredients in a large bowl, on medium speed, until crumbly. Press firmly in a greased 10½ x 15½ x 1 inch jelly roll pan. Bake at 350° for 20 minutes or until golden brown. Prepare filling; pour over baked crust, spreading evenly. Bake 25 minutes. Cool. Cut into squares.

Filling:

4 eggs, slightly beaten
1½ c. sugar
1½ c. light corn syrup

3 Tbsp. margarine
1½ tsp. vanilla
2½ c. chopped pecans

Mix all ingredients, except pecans, until well blended. Stir in pecans.

PECAN TURTLES

Dorothy Skellett

2 c. flour
1 c. brown sugar
½ c. butter
1 c. pecan halves

⅔ c. butter
½ c. brown sugar
1 c. chocolate chips

Blend flour, 1 cup brown sugar, and ½ cup butter with mixer 2 to 3 minutes. Pat firmly in ungreased 9x13 inch pan. Cover crust with pecan halves. In saucepan, combine ⅔ cup butter and ½ cup brown sugar; cook over medium heat until mixture boils. Pour evenly over pecans. Bake at 350° for 18 to 20 minutes or until light brown and bubbly. Sprinkle with chocolate chips; return to oven 2 to 3 minutes. Smooth chocolate over all. Cool completely. Cut into squares, about 56.

PLUM POCKETS

Helen Rucky

2 c. flour
2 Tbsp. sugar
1 tsp. salt
½ c. shortening
6 Tbsp. oleo

3 to 4 Tbsp. water
1 c. chopped purple plums
¼ c. chopped walnuts
½ c. sugar
Confectioners sugar

In mixing bowl, stir together flour, sugar, and salt; cut in shortening and oleo until mixture resembles coarse crumbs. Add enough water to hold dough together. On floured surface, roll to ½ inch thickness and cut in about 48 rounds. Combine plums, nuts, and sugar. Cover half of the rounds with plum mixture; top with the other half. Seal. Make small cut in tops. Bake at 425° for 12 to 15 minutes. Dust with confectioners sugar.

PINEAPPLE SQUARES

Anna Chyl

1 (No. 2) can crushed pineapple
½ c. sugar
3 heaping Tbsp. tapioca
1 c. butter or margarine
1 c. sugar
3 egg yolks
2 c. flour

1 tsp. baking powder
1 tsp. vanilla
3 hamburger rolls
3 egg whites
½ c. ground nuts
½ c. sugar

In a saucepan, combine pineapple, sugar, and tapioca; cook until thick, stirring constantly. Cool. Cream butter and sugar; add egg yolks. Beat. Sift together flour and baking powder; add to creamed mixture gradually. Add vanilla; mix. Add rolls which have been broken into pieces; mix with hand. Pat half the dough in a greased 9x13 inch pan. Spread filling on dough. Cover with other half of dough. Beat egg whites until stiff; spread on top. Sprinkle with nuts and sugar. Bake at 350° for 1 hour or until done.

PRUNE NUT SQUARES

Helen Chubinsky

1 c. butter
1¾ c. confectioners sugar
2 eggs
1 tsp. vanilla
1 tsp. grated lemon rind

2 c. flour
1 tsp. baking powder
1½ c. ground walnuts
¾ lb. prune butter
3 Tbsp. apricot jam

Cream butter and sugar. Add eggs; beat well. Add vanilla and lemon rind. Sift together flour and baking powder; add to creamed mixture. Mix thoroughly. Add walnuts; blend. Reserve 4 to 5 tablespoons dough for topping. Spread remaining dough in greased 9x13 inch pan. Combine prune butter and jam; spread over dough in pan. Crumble reserved dough over prune butter. Bake at 350° for 40 minutes.

PUDDING COOKIES

Mary Kostyun

1 pkg. yellow cake mix
1 (3.4 oz.) pkg. instant vanilla
   pudding and pie filling

1 c. sour cream
2 tsp. vanilla
2 eggs

In a large bowl, combine all ingredients; mix until well moistened. Drop dough by teaspoonful about 2 inches apart onto a greased baking sheet. Bake at 350° for 10 to 12 minutes or until edges are light brown. Yield: About 4 dozen cookies.

PUMPKIN COOKIES I

Miranda Klish

2 c. shortening
2 c. sugar
1 (16 oz.) can pumpkin
2 eggs
2 tsp. vanilla
4 c. flour
2 tsp. baking powder

1 tsp. baking soda
1 tsp. salt
2 tsp. cinnamon
1 tsp. nutmeg
½ tsp. allspice
2 c. raisins
1 c. chopped nuts

Cream together shortening and sugar. Add pumpkin, eggs, and vanilla; beat well. Sift together dry ingredients; add to pumpkin mixture. Stir in raisins and nuts. Drop by teaspoon onto greased cookie sheet. Bake at 350° for 12 to 15 minutes.

PUMPKIN COOKIES II

Carol Walling

1 c. shortening
1 c. sugar
1½ c. mashed pumpkin
1 egg
2 c. flour
1 tsp. baking soda

1 tsp. cinnamon
½ tsp. salt
½ c. butterscotch chips
  (optional)
½ c. chopped nuts (optional)
½ c. raisins (optional)

Cream shortening and sugar. Add pumpkin and egg; mix thoroughly. Combine flour, baking soda, cinnamon, and salt; add to creamed mixture. Add any or all of remaining ingredients if desired. Drop dough by teaspoon onto ungreased cookie sheet. Bake at 375° for 10 to 12 minutes. Frost cookies while hot. Makes 3 dozen.

Frosting:

3 Tbsp. butter
4 tsp. milk
½ c. brown sugar

1 c. confectioners sugar
¾ tsp. vanilla

Combine butter, milk, and brown sugar in saucepan; cook until sugar is dissolved. Cool. Add confectioners sugar and vanilla; mix thoroughly.

EASY RAISIN BARS

Miranda Klish

1 c. raisins
1 c. water
½ c. shortening
1 c. sugar
1 egg, slightly beaten
1¾ c. sifted flour
¼ tsp. salt

1 tsp. baking soda
1 tsp. cinnamon
½ tsp. nutmeg
½ tsp. allspice
¼ tsp. cloves
½ c. chopped walnuts

Combine raisins and water in saucepan; bring to a boil. Remove from heat; stir in shortening. Cool to lukewarm. Add sugar and egg; blend. Sift together dry ingredients; add to raisin mixture. Mix thoroughly. Stir in nuts. Pour into greased 10½ x 15½ x 1 inch pan. Bake at 375° for 15 minutes or until done. Cool. Cut into bars.

JUMBO RAISIN COOKIES

Mary Ford

1 c. water
2 c. raisins
1 c. shortening
2 c. sugar
3 eggs
1 tsp. vanilla
4 c. flour

2 tsp. baking powder
1 tsp. baking soda
½ tsp. salt
1½ tsp. cinnamon
½ tsp. nutmeg
¼ tsp. allspice
1 c. chopped nuts

In a saucepan, bring water and raisins to a boil; boil 5 minutes. Cool. Cream shortening and sugar. Add eggs; beat well. Add vanilla. Sift together flour, baking powder, baking soda, salt, and spices; add to creamed mixture. Blend well. Dough will be stiff. Add raisin mixture and nuts; mix well. Drop by rounded teaspoonfuls on greased cookie sheet. Bake at 350° for 10 to 15 minutes.

PEANUT RAISIN JUMBOS

Edie Chebiniak

¾ c. margarine
1 c. chunk style peanut butter
1½ c. brown sugar
2 eggs
1 tsp. vanilla
2¼ c. oat flour*

1½ tsp. baking soda
¼ tsp. salt
1 tsp. cinnamon
1 c. raisins
½ c. chocolate chips (optional)

Cream together margarine, peanut butter, and brown sugar. Add eggs and vanilla; blend. Combine oat flour, baking soda, salt, and cinnamon; add to creamed mixture. Mix well. Add raisins and chocolate chips. Drop by tablespoonfuls on lightly greased cookie sheet. Bake at 350° for 12 to 14 minutes. Makes 3 dozen.

* To make oat flour, process Mother's Oats in a blender or food processor.

ROCKY ROAD BARS

Colleen Rucky

1 (6 oz.) pkg. semi-sweet
  chocolate chips
2 Tbsp. margarine or butter
2 c. Bisquick baking mix
1 c. sugar

½ tsp. vanilla
2 eggs
1 c. miniature marshmallows
¼ c. chopped nuts

Heat ½ cup chocolate chips in margarine in 1 quart saucepan over low heat, stirring until melted. Mix baking mix, sugar, vanilla, and eggs. Stir in chocolate mixture; spread in greased 9x13 inch pan. Bake at 350° for 15 minutes. Remove from oven; sprinkle with marshmallows and remaining chips. Bake 10 to 15 minutes or until marshmallows are light brown.

RUGLACH
Sue Blue

2 c. sifted flour
1 c. unsalted butter
1 (8 oz.) pkg. cream cheese
⅓ c. sugar

1 Tbsp. cinnamon
½ c. chopped walnuts
¼ to ½ c. raisins

Combine flour, butter, and cream cheese; mix thoroughly. Divide into 4 balls. Wrap each in plastic wrap. Refrigerate at least 2 hours. On floured surface, roll dough into a 10 to 12 inch circle of ¼ inch thickness. Combine sugar, cinnamon, walnuts, and raisins; sprinkle on rolled circle. Cut into 12 wedges. Starting at wide end, roll each wedge to form a crescent. Place on greased cookie sheet. Bake at 375° for 15 to 20 minutes.

RUM BALLS I
Helen Kaspryk

1 (6 oz.) pkg. semi-sweet
  chocolate chips
3 Tbsp. white corn syrup
½ c. liquor (rum, brandy, or
  Southern Comfort)

½ c. confectioners sugar
2½ c. crushed vanilla wafers
1 c. finely chopped walnuts

Melt chocolate over hot water. Remove from heat. Add corn syrup and liquor. In a mixing bowl, combine sugar, crushed wafers, and chopped walnuts. Add chocolate mixture to dry ingredients; mix thoroughly. Let stand ½ hour. Form into balls; roll in confectioners sugar. Store in airtight container for 3 to 4 days.

RUM BALLS II
Helen Rucky

1¾ c. fine vanilla wafer crumbs
1 c. finely chopped pecans or
  walnuts
1 c. confectioners sugar
⅛ tsp. salt

2 Tbsp. cocoa
⅓ c. rum
2 Tbsp. dark corn syrup,
  confectioners sugar, or
  granulated sugar

In large mixing bowl, combine crumbs, nuts, 1 cup confectioners sugar, salt, and cocoa. Mix together rum and corn syrup; slowly stir into crumb mixture. Form into 1 inch balls and roll in either confectioners sugar or granulated sugar. Store overnight in covered container to enhance flavors.

SHERRY BALLS III
Genevieve Sadowitz

2½ c. finely crushed vanilla
  wafers
½ c. honey

¾ c. sherry wine
4 c. finely ground walnuts
Granulated sugar

Combine crushed wafers, honey, wine, and walnuts; mix well. Form into 1 inch balls; roll in sugar. Store in tightly covered container for a few days before serving.

OLGA'S SESAME COOKIES
Anna Chyl

½ c. margarine, softened
¾ c. sugar
1 egg
1 tsp. vanilla

1⅓ c. flour
1½ tsp. baking powder
⅛ tsp. salt
3 Tbsp. sesame seeds

Cream margarine and sugar. Add egg and vanilla; beat well. Sift together flour, baking powder, and salt; add to creamed mixture. Mix well. Roll dough into balls the size of small walnuts; dip tops in sesame seeds, flattening slightly. Place 2 inches apart (important, they do spread) on greased cookie sheet. Bake at 375° for 8 to 10 minutes.

SHORTBREAD COOKIES
Mary Kostyun

4 c. flour
¾ c. rice flour
¾ c. sugar

1 lb. butter or 1 c. butter and 1
  c. margarine
Confectioners sugar

Sift dry ingredients into softened butter. Use pastry blender to blend ingredients, then work with hand until smooth. Roll out dough on floured surface; cut with cookie cutters. Prick with fork; place on ungreased cookie sheets. Bake at 350° for 15 to 20 minutes. Sprinkle with confectioners sugar.

MY FRIEND'S YEAST SHORTBREAD, UKRAINIAN STYLE
Pani Lawryk

1 lb. butter
1 c. sugar
2 egg yolks
1 cake compressed yeast

4 c. sifted bread flour
2 egg whites
Finely chopped nuts

Cream butter and sugar; add egg yolks. Beat well. Crumble yeast into egg mixture; mix until smooth. Add flour gradually, kneading after each addition. Chill several hours. Shape a walnut size piece of dough into a ball; dip in beaten egg whites. Roll in nuts. Place on lightly greased cookie sheet; flatten slightly. Bake at 350° for 20 minutes.

226

SLEEP TIGHT COOKIES

Genevieve Sadowitz
Dorothy Skellett

4 egg whites
1½ c. sugar
1 tsp. vanilla
1 Tbsp. vinegar

Large pinch of salt
1 (12 oz.) pkg. (2 c.) chocolate
chips

Set oven at 325°. Beat egg whites until stiff. Gradually stir in sugar, vanilla, vinegar, and salt. Fold in chocolate chips. Drop by teaspoonfuls on greased baking sheet. Preheat oven to 325°. Place cookies in oven; turn oven off at once. Leave cookies in oven 5 hours or overnight. *Do not* open door to peek. Say "sleep tight" and go to bed.

SOUR CREAM BARS

Nancy Kanazawich

1 c. shortening
1 c. sugar
2 eggs
2½ c. flour
1 tsp. baking powder

1 tsp. baking soda
1 c. sour cream
1 tsp. vanilla
1 (1 lb. 5 oz.) can pie filling

Cream shortening and sugar. Add eggs; beat thoroughly. Sift together flour, baking powder, and baking soda; add to creamed mixture alternately with sour cream. Add vanilla; blend. Spread in a greased and floured 9x13 inch pan, reserving approximately a fist full. Spread pie filling over dough; dot with reserved dough. Bake at 350° for 30 to 40 minutes.

SQUARE COOKIES

Josephine Baranyk

2½ c. flour
2 Tbsp. sugar
2 tsp. baking powder
1 c. butter
4 egg yolks

½ c. cream or milk
Jam or preserves
4 egg whites, stiffly beaten
1½ c. ground walnuts
1 c. confectioners sugar

Combine flour, sugar, and baking powder. Add butter; cut in with pastry blender. Combine egg yolks and cream; add to flour mixture. Mix thoroughly. Roll out dough on floured surface into a rectangle to fit a 12x18 inch lightly greased pan. Spread with jam. Combine stiffly beaten egg whites, walnuts, and confectioners sugar; spread over jam. Bake at 350° for 45 minutes. Cool. Cut in squares.

SUGAR COOKIES

Josephine Merena

1 c. shortening
2 c. sugar
2 eggs
1 tsp. vanilla

4 c. flour
3 tsp. baking powder
½ tsp. salt
1 c. milk

Cream shortening and sugar. Add eggs and vanilla; beat. Sift together flour, baking powder, and salt; add alternately with milk to egg mixture. Drop by teaspoonfuls on greased baking sheets; sprinkle with sugar. Bake at 375° for 7 to 10 minutes.

SUGAR CRISPS

Sophie Smyk

1 cake compressed yeast
¼ c. lukewarm water
3¾ c. sifted all-purpose flour
1½ tsp. salt
1 c. butter

2 eggs, beaten
½ c. sour cream
1 tsp. vanilla
1½ c. sugar
1 tsp. cinnamon or 2 tsp. vanilla

Soften yeast in lukewarm water. In a large bowl, sift flour and salt. Add butter; cut in until particles are the size of small peas. Add eggs, sour cream, 1 teaspoon vanilla, and softened yeast; mix thoroughly. Cover. Chill at least 2 hours, but may be refrigerated up to four days. Combine sugar and cinnamon or vanilla. Roll out half the dough on a pastry cloth which has been sprinkled with ½ cup sugar mixture. Roll out to a 16x8 inch rectangle. Sprinkle with about 1 tablespoon sugar mixture; fold one end of dough over to the center. Fold other end on center line to make 3 layers.

Turn ¼ turn; repeat rolling and folding twice, sprinkling cloth and dough with additional sugar mixture as needed. Roll out to a 16x8 inch rectangle about ¼ inch thick. Cut into 4x1 inch strips. Twist each strip 2 or 3 times. Place on ungreased baking sheets. Repeat the process with remaining dough. Bake at 375° for 15 to 20 minutes or until light golden brown.

SWEDISH SANDWICH CREMES

Helen Rucky

1 c. oleo
½ c. heavy cream

2¾ c. flour
Granulated sugar

Creme Filling:

¼ c. oleo
¾ c. confectioners sugar
1 egg yolk

1 tsp. vanilla
Food coloring

Mix with pastry blender. Chill 2 hours. Roll thin in desired circle. Dip both sides in granulated sugar. Bake in greased pan at 375° for 7 to 9 minutes.

Cool. Frost 1 cookie and layer with another to make sandwich. Combine frosting ingredients; beat until smooth. Add couple drops of food coloring of desired color.

TOFFEE SQUARES
Marie Richardson

1 c. margarine
1 c. brown sugar
¼ c. confectioners sugar
1 egg
1 tsp. vanilla
2 c. flour

¼ tsp. salt
2 Tbsp. chopped walnuts
3 to 4 (⅞ oz. each) milk
   chocolate bars
½ c. chopped walnuts

Cream margarine, sugars, egg, and vanilla. Sift together flour and salt; add to creamed mixture. Mix thoroughly. Add 2 tablespoons chopped walnuts; mix. Spread dough on greased cookie sheet in a 10x13 inch rectangle. Bake at 350° for 20 to 25 minutes. It will be soft. Immediately place separated squares of chocolate on top. Let stand until soft; spread evenly. Sprinkle with chopped walnuts. Cut into small squares while warm.

WALNUT COOKIES
Sophie Pufky

1 lb. butter or margarine
1 c. confectioners sugar
1 c. granulated sugar
3 eggs
4 c. flour

1 tsp. baking powder
½ tsp. salt
1 c. cracker (soda) crumbs
1 lb. ground walnuts

Cream butter and sugar. Add eggs; beat thoroughly. Sift together flour, baking powder, and salt; add to creamed mixture. Blend in cracker crumbs and walnuts. Let dough stand overnight. Roll out dough on confectioners sugar to ¼ inch thickness. Cut with cookie cutters; place on ungreased cookie sheet. Bake at 350° for 10 to 15 minutes.

WATERMELON SLICES
Colleen Rucky

1 pkg. sugar cookie mix
1 egg
½ c. oil
4½ tsp. water

Red food coloring
Green food coloring
Miniature semi-sweet chocolate
   pieces

Combine cookie mix, egg, oil, and water. Stir until thoroughly blended. Reserve ⅓ dough.

For red cookie dough, combine remaining dough with red food coloring (about 10 to 12 drops). Stir until evenly tinted. On waxed paper, shape dough into long roll with one side flattened. Refrigerate, flat side down, until firm.

For green cookie dough, combine reserved dough with 4 to 5 drops green food coloring; stir until evenly tinted. Roll in rectangle. Refrigerate 15 minutes.

To assemble, place red dough, long flat side up, along center of green dough. Mold green dough up to edge of flattened side of red dough. Trim excess green dough if necessary. Cut ¼ inch thick slices, placing about 2 inches apart on lightly greased cookie sheet pans. Insert a few chocolate chip pieces at random to resemble seeds. Bake at 375° for about 7 minutes or until set. Cool completely. Makes 3 to 4 dozen cookies.

FRAN'S YUM YUMS

Sophie Smyk

1 c. flour	2 Tbsp. flour
1 Tbsp. dark brown sugar	¼ tsp. baking powder
½ c. butter	1 tsp. vanilla
2 eggs	½ c. coconut
1½ c. dark brown sugar	1 c. chopped walnuts

Combine 1 cup flour and 1 tablespoon brown sugar; add butter. Cut in with pastry blender until crumbly. Pat in bottom of greased 8 inch square pan. Beat eggs; add remaining ingredients. Mix thoroughly. Spread on mixture in pan. Bake at 350° for 40 minutes. Cut into squares.

SCRUMPTIOUS ZUCCHINI BARS

¾ c. butter, softened	1½ tsp. baking powder
½ c. brown sugar	2 c. shredded, unpared zucchini
½ c. granulated sugar	1 c. shredded coconut
2 eggs	¾ c. finely chopped walnuts
1 tsp. vanilla	Cinnamon Frosting
1¾ c. flour	

Cream butter until fluffy. Add sugars gradually; beat. Add eggs, one at a time, beating after each addition. Add vanilla. Sift together flour and baking powder; add to creamed mixture gradually, mixing thoroughly. Stir in zucchini, coconut, and walnuts. Spread in greased 10 x 15 x 1½ inch pan. Bake at 350° for 40 minutes. While slightly warm, top with Cinnamon Frosting. Makes 36 bars.

Cinnamon Frosting:

1 c. confectioners sugar	1½ Tbsp. melted butter
½ tsp. cinnamon	1 tsp. vanilla
2½ Tbsp. milk	

Combine sugar and cinnamon. Add remaining ingredients; beat until smooth.

ZUCCHINI COOKIES I

Eloise Maliwacki

1 c. shortening
⅔ c. brown sugar
2 eggs
1 tsp. vanilla
⅔ c. shredded zucchini
2 c. flour
1 tsp. baking soda
½ tsp. baking powder
½ tsp. salt
½ tsp. cinnamon
½ tsp. ginger
½ tsp. nutmeg
⅔ c. uncooked oatmeal
⅔ c. uncooked wheat cereal
1 c. chopped nuts

Cream shortening and sugar; add eggs and vanilla. Beat until light and fluffy. Stir in zucchini. Sift together flour, baking soda, baking powder, salt, cinnamon, ginger, and nutmeg; add to zucchini mixture. Mix thoroughly. Add cereals and nuts; mix. Drop by teaspoonfuls onto greased cookie sheet. Bake at 375° for 10 to 12 minutes.

ZUCCHINI COOKIES II

Genevieve Sadowitz

1 c. peeled, shredded zucchini
½ c. margarine
1 egg
1 c. sugar
2 c. flour
1 tsp. baking soda
½ tsp. salt
1 tsp. cinnamon
½ tsp. cloves
1 c. chopped nuts
1 c. raisins or chopped dates

Combine zucchini, margarine, egg, and sugar. Sift together flour, baking soda, salt, cinnamon, and cloves; add to zucchini mixture. Add nuts and raisins. Chill dough at least 2 hours. Drop by teaspoon onto greased cookie sheet. Bake at 375° for 12 to 15 minutes. Makes 4 to 5 dozen. Freezes well.

Notes

Desserts

DESSERTS

COCONUT FILLED BAKED APPLES
Eloise Maliwacki

6 tart apples
½ c. heavy cream, whipped
½ c. shredded coconut

½ c. milk
¼ c. sugar
½ tsp. orange extract

Peel and core apples. Cover bottom of casserole with water; put apples in casserole. Cover. Bake at 350° until tender. Simmer coconut in milk until all milk is absorbed; cool. Add sugar and orange extract to whipped cream; stir gently. Add cooled coconut. Place cooled apples on serving platter; fill centers with coconut mixture. Chill.

APPLE BROWN BETTY
Mary Ponas

4 c. small soft bread cubes
½ c. margarine, melted
¾ tsp. cinnamon
⅛ tsp. salt

¾ c. brown sugar
4 c. chopped apples
Milk

Combine bread cubes, margarine, cinnamon, salt, and brown sugar. Arrange alternate layers of bread mixture and apples in buttered, shallow 1 quart covered baking dish; sprinkle top layer of bread with milk. Bake at 375° for 1 hour or until apples are tender.

APPLE CRISP I
Natalia Boser

5 c. sliced, pared tart apples
1 c. brown sugar
¾ c. flour

¾ c. quick cooking rolled oats
1 tsp. cinnamon
½ c. butter or margarine

Arrange apples in buttered 9 inch pie plate. Combine brown sugar, flour, oats, and cinnamon; cut in butter until crumbly. Sprinkle mixture over apples. Bake at 350° for 45 to 50 minutes or until lightly browned.

APPLE CRISP II
Natalia Boser

6 c. pared, thinly sliced apples
⅓ c. sugar
1 tsp. cinnamon
½ tsp. salt
2 Tbsp. butter or margarine, melted

½ tsp. lemon juice
¾ c. sugar
½ c. flour
⅓ c. butter or margarine

Mix together apples, ⅓ cup sugar, cinnamon, salt, melted butter, and lemon juice; put in greased 13x9x2 inch pan. Combine ¾ cup sugar and flour. Cut in butter until crumbly; sprinkle over apples. Bake at 375° about 45 minutes. Serve warm with whipped cream topping.

APPLE CRISP III
Sophia Malowicky

5 or 6 tart apples
1 c. flour
1 c. sugar
1 tsp. baking powder
½ tsp. salt
1 egg
⅓ c. melted butter
½ tsp. cinnamon

Pare and slice apples into greased 7½ x 11¾ inch baking dish. Combine flour, sugar, baking powder, and salt; add egg. Mix with fork until crumbly. Sprinkle over apples. Drizzle with melted butter. Sprinkle with cinnamon. Bake at 350° for 30 to 40 minutes. Serve warm with whipped topping.

APPLE CRISP IV
Eugenia Skarvinko

5 to 6 apples, pared, sliced*
½ c. water
Cinnamon
½ c. sugar
¾ c. flour
6 Tbsp. margarine

Fill greased 9 inch square pan three-quarters full with sliced apples. Pour water over apples; sprinkle with cinnamon. Combine sugar and flour; cut in margarine until crumbly. Sprinkle over apples. Bake, uncovered, at 400° for 50 minutes.

* Rhubarb may be substituted for apples. Cut rhubarb into small pieces, filling greased 9 inch square Pyrex pan three-quarters full. Sprinkle each layer of rhubarb with sugar, then proceed as for apples.

PEGGY'S APPLE CRISP
Dorothy Skellett

4 c. thinly sliced Granny Smith
   apples
½ c. brown sugar
2 Tbsp. lemon juice
1 c. flour
½ c. sugar
1 tsp. baking powder
1 egg, beaten
1 tsp. salt (optional)
⅓ c. butter, melted and cooled
½ tsp. cinnamon

Combine apples, brown sugar, and lemon juice; put in lightly greased 8 inch square pan. Combine flour, sugar, baking powder, and salt; add egg. Mix until crumbly. Sprinkle over apples. Combine melted butter and cinnamon; drizzle over topping. Bake at 350° for 35 minutes.

APPLE CRUNCH

Josephine Vimislik

6 apples
6 to 8 Tbsp. sugar
1 tsp. cinnamon
1 Tbsp. lemon juice (if apples aren't tart)
1 c. sugar

1 c. sifted flour
1 tsp. baking powder
¼ tsp. salt
1 egg, beaten
1 Tbsp. sugar
2 tsp. cinnamon

Pare, core, and slice apples into greased 8 inch square pan. Sprinkle with 6 to 8 tablespoons sugar, cinnamon, and lemon juice. Mix 1 cup sugar, flour, baking powder, salt, and egg together with fork, until crumbly. Spread crumbs over sliced apples. Sprinkle combined sugar and cinnamon on top. Bake at 375° for 45 minutes. Serve warm with cream.

ERICA'S APPLE DESSERT

Sophie Smyk

6 to 8 c. pared, sliced Northern Spy apples
¼ c. water
¼ c. sugar

Lemon juice
Cinnamon
½ c. slivered almonds
½ pt. heavy cream, whipped

Cook apples with water until soft and mushy. Add sugar; stir. Add lemon juice and cinnamon to taste. Cool in refrigerator. Add slivered almonds. Fold in whipped cream. Garnish with chocolate curls.

APPLE NUT TORTE

Ann Dobransky

1 egg
¾ c. sugar
½ c. flour
1 tsp. baking powder

½ tsp. salt
1 c. chopped tart apples
½ c. chopped walnuts
1 tsp. vanilla

Beat egg with electric mixer until light and lemon colored. Gradually beat in sugar. Sift together flour, baking powder, and salt; fold into egg mixture. Stir in apples, walnuts, and vanilla. Turn into buttered 8 inch square pan. Bake at 350° for 35 to 40 minutes. Serve warm with whipped cream. Serves 6.

MOM'S APPLE ROLLS

Linda Zapach

Dough:

2 c. sifted flour
3 tsp. baking powder
1 tsp. salt

⅓ c. shortening
⅔ c. milk
1 egg, slightly beaten

Sift flour, baking powder, and salt into a bowl; cut in shortening with 2 knives or pastry blender. Remove one cup of flour-shortening mixture; set aside in another bowl. Combine milk and egg; add to the one-cup portion of the flour-shortening mixture. Mix to form a paste; add to original flour-shortening mixture. Mix just enough to hold dough together. Roll dough on a floured cloth or board to form a 10x18 inch rectangle. Sprinkle filling over dough; roll lengthwise like a jellyroll. Seal edges lightly. Cut in one-inch slices. Place on greased cookie sheet. Bake at 400° for 20 to 25 minutes.

Filling:

3 c. diced tart apples	**½ tsp. cinnamon**
⅓ c. sugar	**1 Tbsp. lemon juice**

Sprinkle lemon juice over apples; combine sugar and cinnamon. Add to apples; mix to coat apples. Sprinkle on the rolled 10x18 inch rectangle of dough.

APPLE STRUDEL I

Mary Charnetsky

Dough:

½ c. margarine or butter	**1 c. dairy sour cream**
2 c. flour	**3 Tbsp. butter or margarine,**
½ tsp. salt	**melted**

Combine flour and salt and cut in butter or margarine with 2 knives or pastry blender. Stir in sour cream until a soft dough forms. Wrap dough and refrigerate at least two hours. Divide dough into 3 parts. Roll one part into a 15x10 inch rectangle on a lightly floured pastry cloth or board. Brush melted butter or margarine over ⅔ of dough. Sprinkle, if you wish, with corn flake crumbs.

Filling:

5 Cortland or Rome apples,	**¼ c. raisins**
peeled and sliced thin	**¼ c. walnuts or pecans,**
½ tsp. cinnamon	**chopped**
½ c. sugar	**Melted butter or margarine**

Spread apples over ⅔ of dough. Combine cinnamon, sugar, raisins, and nuts and sprinkle over apples. Roll gently and wet edges so they stick when pressed together; have fold on the bottom. Brush some melted butter or margarine on top of strudel. Place strudel gently on a greased cookie sheet, shaping strudel like a horseshoe and bake at 350° for about 1 hour or until top is quite brown.

APPLE STRUDEL II

Jane Ellsworth

Dough:

½ lb. margarine (2 sticks)
3 c. flour
½ c. water

1 Tbsp. vinegar
3 egg yolks

Combine margarine and flour and blend with pastry blender as for pie crust, until fine particles are formed. Blend together water, vinegar, and egg yolks and add to flour mixture. Knead into a soft dough, adding more flour if needed. Divide dough into 6 rolls. Refrigerate. This dough rolls out paper thin on a floured cloth. Brush dough with melted butter. Spread ½ cup of bread crumbs and sliced apples over ¾ of dough; sprinkle ½ cup sugar mixed with ½ teaspoon cinnamon on top of apples. Roll up jelly roll style and place on a greased baking pan. Bake at 350° for about 25 to 45 minutes, depending on the hardness of the apples.

LAZY STRUDEL

Mary Charnetsky

2 c. flour
Pinch of salt
1 c. margarine
¼ c. cold water
1 Tbsp. vinegar
3 egg yolks, beaten
Melted butter or margarine
7 apples, sliced thin

½ c. bread crumbs, corn flake
   crumbs, or finely chopped
   nuts
1½ tsp. sugar
1½ tsp. cinnamon
1½ tsp. nutmeg
Handful of raisins

Combine flour and salt. Cut in margarine with pastry blender until crumbly. Combine water, vinegar, and egg yolks; add to previous mixture. Mix with fork; form a ball by pressing mixture together. Divide dough into 3 equal balls; refrigerate overnight. Roll out one ball of dough into a circle as thin as possible; brush with melted butter. Near the edge of the dough, using ⅓ of the apples, place apples in a row. Sprinkle with ⅓ mixture of crumbs, nuts, sugar, cinnamon, and nutmeg. Sprinkle with raisins; roll up. Repeat with remaining dough, apples, and crumb mixture. Place on ungreased baking sheet. Bake at 375° for 40 to 50 minutes.

BAKLAVA

Mary Kostyun

1 lb. chopped walnuts
3 tsp. cinnamon
½ tsp. cloves

1 c. sugar
¾ lb. butter
1 lb. pastry sheets (phyllo)

Combine walnuts, cinnamon, cloves, and 1 cup sugar. Melt butter and clarify. Brush bottom of pan 14x20 inches with melted butter. Place 1 strip of pastry sheet over buttered pan. Brush with melted butter. Repeat 3 times. Sprinkle fourth pastry layer with nut mixture. Repeat process until nut mixture is all used, ending with 4 layers of pastry brushed with butter. Cut into diamond shapes. Bake at 300° until golden brown.

Topping:

1½ c. honey	3 c. water
¼ tsp. lemon extract	3 c. sugar

Boil honey, lemon extract, water, and sugar to make a syrup. Cool. Using a large spoon, pour syrup very slowly over baked Baklava.

BAKED BANANAS Eugenia Skarvinko

2 medium green-tipped bananas	2 Tbsp. honey
2 Tbsp. lemon or lime juice	

Peel bananas; halve lengthwise. Combine lemon juice and honey; spread over bananas, coating all surfaces. Bake at 400° for 10 to 15 minutes or until golden. Makes 4 servings.

Variation 1: Add ½ cup fresh or unsweetened pineapple tidbits to coated bananas.

Variation 2: Dust coated bananas with nutmeg, cinnamon, curry, or ginger to taste.

Variation 3: Sprinkle coated bananas with 1 tablespoon minced almonds.

Variation 4: Sprinkle bananas with 4 teaspoons crushed Grape-Nuts.

Variation 5: Add brandy, rum, orange, almond, or vanilla extract to taste to lemon-honey mixture.

ISLANDS BANANA CAKE Patricia Hoover

2 c. Bisquick	3 Tbsp. margarine
½ c. sugar	¼ c. brown sugar
½ tsp. ground mace	3 Tbsp. margarine
2 eggs	½ c. flaked coconut
½ c. milk	½ c. chopped nuts
1 tsp. vanilla	3 medium ripe bananas

Combine Bisquick, sugar, mace, eggs, milk, vanilla, and 3 tablespoons margarine in a large bowl; beat at low speed ½ minute to blend, then at medium-high speed. Spread evenly in buttered 9x9x2 inch pan. Bake at 350° for 30 minutes. Cool a few minutes.

238

Combine brown sugar and 3 tablespoons margarine in a small bowl. Stir in coconut and nuts. Peel bananas; slice diagonally. Arrange petal fashion, overlapping on top of cake, from corner to corner to cross in middle, then rest of "petals" to fill in spaces. Sprinkle with brown sugar mixture. Broil, with top about 3 inches from heat, just until bubbly and lightly browned, about 2 minutes. Watch carefully. Cut while warm.

BANANA SPLIT CAKE

Marion Kaspryk

½ c. margarine
2 c. graham cracker crumbs
2 eggs
1 c. margarine
2 c. confectioners sugar
4 to 5 medium ripe bananas
1 (20 oz.) can crushed
    pineapple, drained

2 (10 oz.) pkg. frozen
    strawberries, drained
1 (8 oz.) container whipped
    topping
½ c. ground nuts
¼ c. maraschino cherries,
    quartered

Melt ½ cup margarine; add graham cracker crumbs. Press mixture into 9x13 inch pan. Beat eggs, 1 cup margarine, and confectioners sugar for 15 minutes. Pour onto graham cracker crust; smooth out to edges. Slice bananas; arrange on previous layer. Sprinkle pineapple over bananas. Arrange strawberries over pineapple. Spread whipped topping over strawberries; sprinkle with nuts. Place cherries on top last. Refrigerate several hours before serving.

BERRY SHORTCAKE

Martha Maliwacki

1 can cherry or strawberry pie
    filling

½ c. margarine
½ box white cake mix

Pour pie filling into greased 9 inch square pan. Cut margarine into cake mix until crumbly; sprinkle over pie filling. Bake at 350° for 30 minutes or until golden brown. Serve with whipped cream.

BLUEBERRY DELIGHT

Dorothy Skellett

1 c. margarine
2 c. flour
1 c. chopped nuts
1 (8 oz.) pkg. cream cheese,
    softened

1 (8 oz.) Cool Whip
2 c. (scant) confectioners sugar

Melt margarine; add flour and nuts. Mix. Turn into 9x13 inch pan; pat evenly. Bake at 350° for 30 minutes. Cool. Mix cream cheese, Cool Whip, and confectioners sugar; spread over cooled crust. Spread with cooled Glaze.

Glaze:

1 c. sugar	1 Tbsp. lemon juice
2 Tbsp. cornstarch	2 c. fresh or frozen blueberries
1 c. water	

Combine sugar and cornstarch in saucepan. Add water and lemon juice; mix until smooth. Add blueberries; cook until thick. Cool.

BOURBON WALNUT SAUCE
Julie Sadowitz

½ c. bourbon	½ c. cream
½ c. corn syrup	1 c. broken walnuts or pecans

Combine all ingredients in a saucepan; mix well. Simmer gently 20 minutes. Serve warm over ice cream. Refrigerate remainder in a covered container. Yield: About 2 cups sauce.

BRANDIED CARAMEL FLAN (MEXICAN EGG CUSTARD)
Carol Wasylko

¾ c. sugar	½ tsp. salt
2 c. milk	2 tsp. vanilla
2 c. light cream	⅓ c. brandy
6 eggs	Boiling water
½ c. sugar	1 Tbsp. brandy

Place ¾ cup sugar in large, heavy skillet. Cook over medium heat until sugar melts and forms a light brown syrup, stirring occasionally. Immediately pour syrup into a heated 8¼ inch round, shallow baking dish.* Hold dish with pot holder; cover bottom and sides completely. Set aside.

In medium saucepan, heat milk and cream just until bubbles form around edge of pan. In large bowl, beat eggs slightly; add ½ cup sugar, salt, and vanilla. Gradually stir in hot milk mixture and ⅓ cup brandy. Pour through very fine strainer to remove any egg membrane. Pour into prepared dish. Set dish in shallow pan; pour boiling water to ½ inch level around dish. Bake at 325° for 35 to 40 minutes or until silver knife inserted in center comes out clean. Cool. Refrigerate 4 hours or overnight.

To serve, run small spatula around edge of dish to loosen. Invert on shallow serving dish, shaking gently to release. The caramel acts as sauce. Warm 1 tablespoon brandy slightly; ignite and quickly pour over flan. Serves 8.

* Individual custard cups may be used instead of the 8¼ inch round baking dish.

OLGA'S CASSATA NAPOLITANA

Anna Chyl

1 (30 oz.) can fruit cocktail
1 yellow Bundt, pound, or other
  cake
1 pt. cottage cheese
¼ c. sugar
⅓ c. cream

1 tsp. vanilla
¼ tsp. almond extract
¼ c. semi-sweet chocolate chips
¼ c. toasted almonds, chopped
2 Tbsp. rum or 1 tsp. rum
  extract

Drain fruit cocktail, reserving syrup. Cut cake to form 2 layers; refrigerate. Sieve the cottage cheese; blend with sugar, cream, vanilla, and almond extract. Add chocolate chips, almonds, and drained fruit (reserve ¼ to ½ cup to decorate cake). Place bottom layer of chilled cake on serving dish; top with filling. Top with second layer. Sprinkle with rum or rum extract combined with fruit syrup to make 2 tablespoons. Drizzle glaze over cake. Decorate with reserved fruit. Refrigerate until ready to serve. Serves 10 to 12.

Glaze:

1 c. confectioners sugar
2 Tbsp. fruit cocktail syrup

1 tsp. almond extract
1 tsp. lemon rind

Combine all ingredients; beat until smooth.

CHERRY COBBLER

Vera Cibulsky

3 c. flour
¾ c. sugar
2½ tsp. baking powder
½ tsp. salt
½ tsp. baking soda
½ c. margarine
¼ c. Crisco

2 eggs
¼ c. milk
1 tsp. vanilla
2 (1 lb. 5 oz.) cans cherry pie
  filling
2 tsp. lemon juice
Cinnamon

Sift together flour, sugar, baking powder, salt, and baking soda in a large bowl. Cut in margarine and Crisco with pastry blender until crumbly. In a separate bowl, beat eggs, milk, and vanilla; add to dry ingredients. Mix. Spread all but a fistful of dough in a greased 15 x 10½ x 1 inch pan. Combine cherry pie filling, lemon juice, and a few dashes of cinnamon. Spread filling on dough in pan. Top with dots of reserved dough. Bake at 350° for 25 to 30 minutes.

CHIFFON DESSERT

Eugenia Skarvinko

1 (3 oz.) pkg. gelatin (any
  flavor)
1 c. boiling water

½ c. cold water
¾ c. dry milk powder

Dissolve gelatin in boiling water; add cold water. Refrigerate for 35 minutes. Add dry milk powder; beat with electric mixer until well blended. Refrigerate until firm; do not put in freezer.

CHOCOLATE BLANCMANGE
Julia Dudik

2 c. milk
3 Tbsp. cornstarch
3 Tbsp. cocoa
⅜ c. sugar
½ tsp. vanilla
⅛ tsp. salt

Scald milk in double boiler. In a bowl, mix cornstarch, cocoa, and sugar; add scalded milk, stirring constantly. Pour mixture back into top of double boiler. Cook until thickened, stirring constantly. Cover; cook for 20 minutes. Add vanilla and salt. Pour in dessert bowls. Refrigerate when cool. Serve plain, with nuts or whipped topping.

CHOCOLATE-COCONUT DESSERT
Martha Maliwacki

1 c. semi-sweet chocolate chips
1 (13 oz.) can evaporated milk
1 (10½ oz.) pkg. (5 c.) miniature
   marshmallows
1⅓ c. flaked coconut
6 Tbsp. butter or margarine
2 c. rice cereal, crushed
1 c. chopped walnuts
½ gal. brick vanilla ice cream

In saucepan, melt chocolate in milk. Bring to boiling; boil gently, uncovered, 4 minutes or until thickened, stirring constantly. Add marshmallows; heat and stir until melted. Chill. In skillet, cook and stir coconut in butter until lightly browned. Stir in cereal and nuts. Spread 3 cups of cereal mixture in bottom of a 13x9x2 inch pan. Cut ice cream in half lengthwise and then horizontally into 12 slices, making a total of 24 pieces. Arrange half the ice cream over cereal. Spread with half the chocolate mixture. Repeat layers. Top with remaining cereal. Cover; freeze firm. Let stand at room temperature 5 to 10 minutes before serving. Makes 16 servings.

CHOCOLATE MOUSSE
Patricia Hoover

2½ c. sweet butter
2 c. sugar
6 egg yolks
16 oz. sweet cooking chocolate,
   melted
¼ c. cognac
1½ c. chopped walnuts or
   pecans
6 egg whites
1 c. heavy cream, whipped

Beat butter and sugar at high speed until very fluffy, about 20 minutes. Add egg yolks, one at a time, beating thoroughly after each. Gradually beat in melted chocolate; beat 3 minutes more. Add cognac; beat 3 minutes. Mix in nuts. In another bowl, beat egg whites until peaks form. Fold into chocolate mixture; pour into 2 quart ring mold. Refrigerate about 3 hours. Unmold onto serving plate. Fill center with whipped cream.

NO-BAKE CHOCOLATE CHIP TORTE
Nancy Tarcha

30 chocolate chip cookies
1 pt. heavy cream
2 Tbsp. granulated sugar
1 tsp. vanilla
1 (1 lb.) can sliced peaches

Place 12 cookies on bottom of 9 inch springform pan. Crumble a few cookies to fill in spaces. Beat heavy cream with sugar and vanilla until peaks stand up. Spread half over cookies in pan. Repeat with remaining cookies and cream mixture. Cover. Refrigerate overnight. Before serving, drain and dry peaches. Top with rows of peaches. Slide a metal spatula around sides; remove rim. Slice and serve.

CHOCOLATE-PEANUT DESSERT
Linda Zapach

⅔ c. dry roasted peanuts, crushed
1 c. flour
½ c. margarine, melted
⅓ c. peanut butter
1 c. confectioners sugar
1 (8 oz.) pkg. cream cheese, softened
2 (9 oz.) Cool Whip
1 (3.4 oz.) pkg. vanilla instant pudding
1 (3.4 oz.) pkg. chocolate instant pudding
2¾ c. milk
Crushed peanuts

Combine ⅔ cup crushed peanuts, flour, and melted margarine; spread in greased 13x9 inch pan. Bake at 350° for 10 minutes. Cool. In a bowl, beat peanut butter, confectioners sugar, and cream cheese until smooth. Add 9 ounces Cool Whip; mix. Spread on cooled crust. Combine puddings and milk; beat until slightly thickened. Spread on top of peanut butter mixture. Top with 9 ounces Cool Whip; sprinkle with crushed peanuts. Refrigerate.

CHOCOLATE-PEANUT SQUARES
Martha Maliwacki

¼ c. butter or margarine
1 c. semi-sweet chocolate chips
1½ c. rolled oats
½ c. peanut butter
1 (8 oz.) pkg. cream cheese, softened
¼ c. sugar
1 tsp. vanilla
½ c. milk
1 c. whipping cream
¼ c. chopped peanuts

In saucepan, heat together butter and ¼ cup of the chocolate chips over low heat just until melted. Stir in oats until coated. Press into the bottom of an 8x8x2 inch pan; chill. In small saucepan, heat and stir peanut butter and remaining chocolate together over low heat until melted. Cool slightly. In mixer bowl, beat cream cheese, sugar, and vanilla until fluffy. Beat in peanut butter mixture. (Mixture will be quite stiff.) Blend in milk. Whip cream just to soft peaks. Fold into peanut butter mixture. Turn into pan. Sprinkle nuts atop. Cover; chill well. Makes 9 to 12 servings.

CHOCOLATE PEPPERMINT ICE CREAM CAKE
Mary Ponas

Double Chocolate Cake:

½ c. butter or margarine
1¼ c. sugar
1 tsp. vanilla
4 eggs
1¼ c. unsifted all-purpose flour
⅓ c. unsweetened cocoa powder

¾ tsp. baking soda
¼ tsp. salt
1½ c. (1 lb. can) chocolate
  flavor syrup
½ c. water

Cream butter, sugar, and vanilla in large mixing bowl. Add eggs, one at a time, beating well after each addition. Combine flour, cocoa, baking soda, and salt; add alternately with chocolate syrup and water to creamed mixture. Pour batter into 3 greased and floured 9 inch cake pans. Bake at 350° for 27 minutes. Cool in pans 10 minutes; remove and cool completely. Wrap each layer separately in foil; freeze several hours.

Peppermint Filling:

1 qt. vanilla ice cream
⅔ c. crushed peppermint candy
  or 2 tsp. peppermint extract
  plus ⅛ tsp. red food coloring

Line 2 (9 inch) layer cake pans with aluminum foil; chill in freezer. Soften ice cream; quickly stir in crushed peppermint candy or extract and food coloring. Divide evenly between pans; cover. Freeze. Remove ice cream from pans; peel off foil. Alternately layer peppermint and chocolate layers, ending with chocolate. Return to freezer while preparing glaze.

Chocolate Glaze:

3 Tbsp. unsweetened cocoa
3 Tbsp. water
1 Tbsp. light corn syrup

1 Tbsp. butter
1 c. confectioners sugar
½ tsp. vanilla

Combine cocoa, water, corn syrup, and butter in small, heavy saucepan. Cook over low heat, stirring constantly, until mixture boils and becomes somewhat thickened. Remove from heat; add sugar and vanilla, beating until smooth. Spoon on top of cake. Garnish with crushed peppermint candy. Return to freezer until serving time.

LEMON CREAM CHEESE DESSERT

Doris Okrepkie
Mary Buckingham

½ c. butter, melted
1 c. flour
¾ c. chopped nuts
8 oz. cream cheese

12 oz. Cool Whip
1 c. confectioners sugar
3 oz. instant lemon pudding
3½ c. milk

Mix together ½ cup nuts, flour, and butter and spread in a 9x13 inch pan. Bake at 350° for 20 to 25 minutes. Cream together cream cheese, confectioners sugar, and 1 cup Cool Whip. Spread over the baked layer. Mix instant pudding and cold milk. Spread it over the top and top with the remaining Cool Whip and nuts.

Note: The instant pudding may also be chocolate or vanilla.

MARCIE'S BAKED DEVILS FLOAT

Olga Gooley

1 c. flour
½ tsp. salt
¾ c. sugar
2 tsp. baking powder
3½ Tbsp. cocoa
½ c. milk
1 tsp. vanilla

2½ Tbsp. melted butter or
  shortening
½ c. sugar
½ c. brown sugar
2 Tbsp. cocoa
1 c. boiling water

In a bowl, combine the first 8 ingredients; mix by hand. Pour into a greased 9x9 inch square pan. Combine ½ cup sugar, brown sugar, and 2 tablespoons cocoa; sprinkle over mixture in pan. Pour boiling water over contents of pan. Bake at 350° for 45 to 60 minutes or until crust has formed on top. Serve with vanilla ice cream or whipped cream.

Variation: Substitute 1 cup cold coffee for 1 cup boiling water.

DREAM WHIP JELLO

Ann Dobransky

1 (8 oz.) pkg. cream cheese
1 (1 lb.) can fruit cocktail
1 pkg. Dream Whip

1 (3 oz.) pkg. raspberry or black
  cherry gelatin

Bring cheese to room temperature. Chill fruit cocktail. Whip Dream Whip; set in refrigerator. Drain juice from fruit cocktail; heat juice to a boil. Remove from heat; add gelatin. Beat. Add cream cheese; whip until creamy. Fold in fruit and Dream Whip. Chill.

Can be served as a dessert as is or by putting it in a pie shell and topping with whipped cream.

FRUIT AND ANGEL DESSERT

Anna Chyl

1 (10 oz.) angel food cake
1 (15 oz.) can crushed pineapple
1 (12 oz.) container whipped
   topping
1 (3½ oz.) can flaked coconut,
   toasted

1 (6 oz.) jar maraschino
   cherries, drained and
   chopped

Break cake into bite-size pieces (should have about 8 cups). Arrange half the cake pieces on bottom of 13x9x2 inch pan. Top with half the undrained pineapple and cherries. Spread half the dessert topping over all; top with half the coconut. Repeat layers. Cover; refrigerate overnight. Makes 12 servings.

FRUIT AND DUMPLINGS

Millie Finch

Preparation time: 15 minutes.

1 (1 lb. 5 oz.) can apple or
   cherry pie filling
1 c. Bisquick

1 Tbsp. sugar
½ tsp. cinnamon
½ to ¾ c. milk

Slowly heat pie filling in saucepan. Combine Bisquick, sugar, and cinnamon; mix. Add milk; mix thoroughly. (Dough should be wet.) Drop dough by tablespoonfuls on simmering pie filling; cook 3 to 4 minutes uncovered. Place lid on saucepan; cook 5 to 8 minutes. (Test with toothpick.) Serve warm with cream or whipped topping.

PARTY FRUIT COMBINATION

Natalia Boser

2 (13½ oz.) cans pineapple
   chunks
5 medium oranges
2 ripe bananas

2 c. white seedless grapes
1 (3½ oz.) can flaked coconut
7 oz. ginger ale (optional)
Whole maraschino cherries

Drain pineapple, reserving syrup. Cut peel from oranges with sharp knife; remove sections by cutting close to membrane, reserving juice. Peel bananas; slice diagonally. Put in orange juice. For a lovely arrangement, use a crystal bowl; keep pineapple, oranges, bananas, and grapes separate, allotting ¼ of the bowl to each. Following this plan, place half of each fruit in bowl; sprinkle with half the coconut. Top with remaining fruit. Pour reserved pineapple syrup over all; chill thoroughly. At serving time, pour ginger ale over fruit if desired. Sprinkle with remaining coconut; garnish with whole maraschino cherries. Makes 8 to 12 servings.

HARVEST TORTE

Natalia Boser

4 c. diced, unpared tart apples
1 c. sugar
½ c. sifted flour
2 tsp. baking powder
1 egg, beaten
1 Tbsp. melted butter or
    margarine

1 tsp. vanilla
½ c. broken or chopped
    walnuts
½ c. pitted dates, chopped

Combine all ingredients in large bowl; mix thoroughly, but do not beat. Turn into greased 8x8x2 inch pan. Bake at 400° for 40 minutes or until apples are tender. Cut in 6 to 8 squares. Serve with whipped cream.

LEMON LUSH

Tammy Chebiniak
Jane Ellsworth, Dorothy Skellett

½ c. margarine
1 c. flour
½ c. ground pecans (optional)
1 c. confectioners sugar
1 (8 oz.) pkg. cream cheese,
    softened

10 to 12 oz. Cool Whip
2 (3½ oz.) lemon instant
    pudding
3 c. milk
3 Tbsp. ground pecans

Cut margarine into flour and ½ cup pecans; spread and press on bottom of greased 13x9 inch pan. Bake at 350° for 12 minutes. Cool. Beat sugar and cream cheese until smooth. Add 1 cup Cool Whip; blend. Spread over cooled crust. Combine pudding with milk. Follow directions on pudding box for beating. Spread on cream cheese layer. Spread remaining Cool Whip on pudding. Sprinkle with 3 tablespoons pecans. Refrigerate until ready to serve.

PEACH BETTY

Eugenia Skarvinko

3 Tbsp. brown sugar
½ tsp. cinnamon
½ tsp. nutmeg
Dash of salt
¼ c. dry bread crumbs

1 Tbsp. corn oil margarine,
    melted
3 c. fresh, unsweetened, sliced
    peaches

Combine brown sugar, cinnamon, nutmeg, and salt. Toss crumbs with melted margarine; combine with sugar mixture. Sprinkle one-fourth of crumb mixture in bottom of buttered 11x7 inch pan. Cover with peach slices. Sprinkle with remaining crumb mixture. Bake at 350° for 30 to 40 minutes or until peaches are just cooked; peaches should not be mushy. Serves 6.

Variation 1: Add 1 teaspoon brandy, rum, or almond extract or 1 teaspoon grated orange rind to melted margarine before tossing with crumbs.

Variation 2: Substitute 1 cup fresh raspberries for 1 cup peaches.

Variation 3: Substitute ½ cup unsweetened pineapple tidbits, sliced pared apple, sliced strawberries, or chopped pears for ½ cup peaches.

Variation 4: Substitute ½ cup unsweetened applesauce for ½ cup peaches; season applesauce with almond extract to taste.

PEACH DELIGHT
Mary Ponas

2 (3 oz.) pkg. peach or apricot
   gelatin
1 (No. 2) can crushed pineapple
1 c. miniature marshmallows
2 bananas, sliced
½ c. pineapple juice

¼ c. sugar
1 egg, slightly beaten
2 Tbsp. margarine
1 (3 oz.) pkg. cream cheese
1½ c. whipped topping

Dissolve gelatin as directed on package. Drain pineapple; use syrup as part of liquid added to gelatin. Add pineapple, marshmallows, and bananas to gelatin; mix. Refrigerate in 13x9x2 inch pan until set. In saucepan, combine pineapple juice, sugar, egg, and margarine; cook until slightly thickened, about 2 minutes. Remove from heat; cool. Add cream cheese which has been whipped until smooth. Add whipped topping; stir until blended. Spread over set gelatin.

BAKED RHUBARB PUDDING
Eloise Maliwacki

3 c. diced rhubarb
1 c. sugar
2 Tbsp. water
2 Tbsp. shortening
½ c. sugar

1 egg
1 c. sifted flour
2 tsp. baking powder
½ tsp. salt
½ c. milk

Combine rhubarb, 1 cup sugar, and water; put in greased 1½ quart casserole. Place in 350° oven while mixing remaining ingredients. Combine shortening and ½ cup sugar; add egg, beating until light. Sift together flour, baking powder, and salt; add alternately with milk to egg mixture. Remove casserole from oven. Pour mixture over rhubarb. Bake at 350° for 30 to 40 minutes. Serve warm with cream.

BREAD PUDDING WITH BRANDY SAUCE

Anna Chyl

12 slices white bread
4 eggs
1 c. sugar
1 tsp. cinnamon
½ tsp. salt

2 tsp. vanilla
3 c. milk
1 (1 lb.) can applesauce
2 Tbsp. butter or margarine

Slice bread into ½ inch wide strips. Combine eggs, sugar, cinnamon, salt, vanilla, milk, applesauce, and butter. Place one-third of the bread strips in an 11x7x2 inch baking dish, making a lattice pattern. Top with half the applesauce mixture. Repeat layers of bread strips and applesauce mixture, making bread strips the last layer. Bake at 325° for 1 hour or until center is set and bread is lightly browned. Serve with Brandy Sauce.

Brandy Sauce:

1 egg white
2 Tbsp. sugar
1 egg yolk, slightly beaten

1 c. heavy cream, whipped
⅓ c. brandy

Beat egg white until stiff peaks form. Add sugar, gradually beating until stiff peaks form. Add beaten egg yolk and whipped cream; fold in until thoroughly combined. Stir in brandy.

LEMONADE PUDDING

Ann Dobransky

2 egg yolks, slightly beaten
1½ c. milk
1 (3¼ oz.) pkg. vanilla pudding
1 (3 oz.) pkg. cream cheese, softened
1 (6 oz.) can frozen lemonade concentrate, thawed

2 egg whites
¼ c. sugar
½ c. vanilla wafer crumbs
2 Tbsp. chopped walnuts
2 Tbsp. butter, melted

Combine egg yolks and milk. Prepare pudding according to package directions, using the egg-milk mixture as the liquid. Add cream cheese; beat with electric beater. Stir in lemonade concentrate. Cover; let stand 10 minutes. Beat smooth again. Beat egg whites to soft peaks; gradually add sugar, beating to soft peaks. Fold egg whites into pudding. Combine crumbs, nuts, and butter. Sprinkle half the crumb mixture into 6 sherbet glasses. Spoon in pudding; top with remaining crumbs. Chill. Just before serving, stand a vanilla wafer in each. Makes 6 servings.

NOODLE PUDDING

Sue Blue

1 (12 oz.) pkg. wide noodles
¼ lb. butter
1 lb. cottage cheese
1 pt. cottage cheese
1 (16 oz.) can crushed
   pineapple, drained

3 eggs, well beaten
3 Tbsp. sugar (optional)
½ c. raisins (optional)
Cinnamon

Cook noodles according to package directions. Add remaining ingredients to noodles; mix until thoroughly combined. Sprinkle with cinnamon. Bake at 350° for 45 minutes or until set and light brown on top.

PENNSYLVANIA DUTCH CRACKER PUDDING

1 qt. milk
2 egg yolks
½ c. sugar
1 c. saltine cracker crumbs

1 tsp. vanilla
½ c. coconut
2 egg whites, beaten

Heat milk in double boiler. Beat egg yolks; add sugar and cracker crumbs. Add to hot milk; cook until mixture boils and is thick. Add vanilla, coconut, and egg whites. Cool.

PINEAPPLE MARSHMALLOW PUDDING Sophia Malowicky

1 (No. 2½) can sliced pineapple
   or tidbits
½ lb. miniature marshmallows
¼ c. sugar
1 Tbsp. flour

1 egg
1 Tbsp. butter
Pinch of salt
½ pt. heavy cream

Drain pineapple; reserve liquid. Cut pineapple into small pieces; combine with marshmallows. Refrigerate overnight. In top of double boiler, mix sugar with flour; add egg, butter, and salt. Add reserved pineapple liquid; cook until thick. Refrigerate. Whip cream; fold into cooled custard. Pour over pineapple-marshmallow mixture. Garnish with chopped nuts if desired. Serves 8.

APRICOT RAISIN RICE PUDDING

Marie Brink

1½ c. apricot nectar
1 c. cooked rice
⅔ c. evaporated milk
2 eggs, slightly beaten

¼ c. sugar
¼ tsp. salt
½ c. seedless raisins
Nutmeg

Scald nectar; add rice and milk. Combine eggs with sugar, salt, and raisins; add slowly to rice mixture, stirring constantly. Pour into 1½ quart baking dish. Sprinkle with nutmeg. Set in pan with water 1 inch deep. Bake at 350° for 1 hour or until firm. Serve hot or cold, topped with whipped cream.

CREAMY RICE PUDDING I
Helen Charnetsky

½ c. rice
1 qt. milk, scalded
4 Tbsp. sugar
4 Tbsp. butter

¼ tsp. salt (optional)
2 eggs
¼ c. raisins (optional)
½ tsp. cinnamon

Wash rice; put in double boiler with scalded milk. Cook until tender. Add 2 tablespoons sugar, 2 tablespoons butter, and salt. Beat eggs; add a small amount of milk, stirring constantly. Add egg mixture to milk mixture gradually, stirring constantly. Cook 1 minute. Add raisins. Pour into serving dish. Combine remaining sugar with cinnamon; sprinkle on top of pudding. Cut remaining butter into small pieces; put on top of pudding. Serve hot.

CREAMY RICE PUDDING II
Ann Dobransky

2½ c. cooked rice
1 c. sugar
½ c. raisins
5 eggs

2 c. milk
Pinch of salt
1 tsp. vanilla
Cinnamon

Combine rice, ½ cup sugar, and raisins. Beat eggs; add milk, remaining ½ cup sugar, salt, and vanilla. Stir. Add rice mixture; mix. Pour into buttered 2 quart baking dish. Bake at 350° for 35 minutes or until set. Sprinkle with cinnamon while warm. Chill before serving.

CREAMY RICE PUDDING III
Natalia Boser

½ c. uncooked rice
½ tsp. salt
¼ c. sugar

5 c. milk
1 c. raisins
½ tsp. cinnamon

Wash rice thoroughly. Combine all ingredients in 2 quart casserole. Bake, uncovered, at 300° for 2 hours.

RICE PUDDING IV
Jane Ellsworth

1 qt. milk
1 qt. water
1 pt. half & half
1 c. River Rice

4 eggs
2 c. sugar
1 pt. half & half
1 tsp. vanilla

In a large saucepan, combine milk, water, 1 pint half & half, and rice. Cook over medium heat 1 hour or until rice is soft. Beat eggs, sugar, 1 pint half & half, and vanilla. Add hot rice mixture to egg mixture, stirring constantly. Cook 20 minutes more, stirring occasionally.

RICE PUDDING V
Marion Kaspryk

½ c. rice
¼ c. margarine or butter
1 c. water
Pinch of salt
1 qt. milk

2 eggs, beaten
½ c. sugar
1 tsp. vanilla
Raisins (optional)
Nutmeg

In a saucepan, combine rice, margarine, water, and salt; bring to a boil. Simmer until all water is absorbed. Add milk; bring to a boil. Simmer 40 minutes, stirring often. Beat together eggs, sugar, and vanilla; stir into rice mixture. Remove from heat; add raisins. Pour into a bowl; sprinkle with nutmeg. Refrigerate.

STRAWBERRY VANILLA PUDDING
Helen Zellers

4½ to 5 c. (6 oz.) angel cake
  cubes
1 (3¾ oz.) pkg. vanilla instant
  pudding
1 c. cold milk

1 pt. vanilla ice cream, softened
1 (3 oz.) pkg. strawberry gelatin
1½ c. boiling water
1 (10 oz.) pkg. frozen
  strawberry slices

Place angel cake cubes in a 9x9x2 inch pan. In a mixer bowl, combine instant pudding and milk; add ice cream. Beat at low speed until well blended. Pour over cake cubes; chill until firm. Dissolve gelatin in boiling water; add frozen strawberries. Stir until gelatin begins to thicken. Pour over pudding. Do not stir. Chill until set.

PUMPKIN TORTE
Jane Ellsworth

3½ c. graham cracker crumbs
⅓ c. sugar
½ c. butter or margarine,
  melted
12 oz. cream cheese
¾ c. sugar
3 eggs
2 c. pumpkin
3 egg yolks

½ c. sugar
½ c. milk
½ tsp. salt
1 Tbsp. cinnamon
1 env. unflavored gelatin
¼ c. cold water
3 egg whites
¼ c. sugar

Combine graham crackers and ⅓ cup sugar; add melted margarine. Mix with fork until crumbs are well coated. Press crumbs into greased 13x9 inch pan.

Beat cream cheese and ¾ cup sugar; add 3 eggs. Beat until smooth and creamy. Pour over crust. Bake at 350° for 20 minutes.

Cook pumpkin, egg yolks, ½ cup sugar, milk, salt, and cinnamon until mixture thickens. Remove from heat. Dissolve gelatin in cold water; add to pumpkin mixture. Beat egg whites with sugar until peaks form; fold into cooled pumpkin mixture. Pour over cooled, baked cheese layer. Refrigerate several hours before serving. Top with whipped cream when ready to serve. Serves 15.

RASPBERRY CREME

Sophia Malowicky

1 (8 oz.) pkg. cream cheese
½ c. sugar
1 env. unflavored gelatin
⅓ c. cold water
1 c. milk
1 tsp. lemon juice
1 tsp. vanilla
1 c. heavy cream

Beat cream cheese and sugar on medium speed until fluffy. Soften gelatin in cold water; dissolve over hot water, stirring constantly. Remove from heat. Gradually add milk, lemon juice, and vanilla, beating with mixer on low. Beat in dissolved gelatin. Whip cream to form soft peaks; fold into gelatin mixture. Turn into heavily greased Bundt pan; refrigerate. Serve with Raspberry Sauce.

Raspberry Sauce:

1 (10 oz.) pkg. frozen
  raspberries
1 Tbsp. cornstarch

Heat thawed raspberries; add cornstarch. Cook until raspberries come to a boil; boil one minute. Cool.

RHUBARB CRUNCH

Ann Dobransky

½ c. margarine
1 c. rolled oats
1 c. flour
1 c. brown sugar
Pinch of salt
4 c. diced rhubarb
1 c. fresh strawberries or 2
  Tbsp. strawberry jam
1 c. sugar
2 Tbsp. cornstarch
½ tsp. cinnamon
1 c. water

Melt margarine. Combine oats, flour, brown sugar, and salt; add melted margarine. Mix with fork until crumbly. Pat half the crumb mixture in bottom of greased 13x9 inch pan. Put rhubarb over crumbs; sprinkle with strawberries or jam. In a saucepan, combine sugar, cornstarch, and cinnamon. Add water;

bring to a boil. Cook until thick and clear. Pour over rhubarb. Sprinkle with remaining half of crumbs. Bake at 350° for 40 minutes.

NANCY'S RHUBARB CUSTARD KUCHEN Sophia Malowicky

Crust:

¾ c. butter or margarine
¼ c. + 1 Tbsp. sugar
2 egg yolks

1¾ c. + heaping Tbsp. flour
1½ tsp. salt

Cream butter and sugar until very creamy. Add egg yolks; mix thoroughly. Add flour and salt; blend with pastry blender. Pat on bottom and up sides of an ungreased 9x13 inch pan.

Filling:

1½ Tbsp. sugar
1½ Tbsp. flour

Rhubarb, cut in ½ inch pieces

Combine sugar and flour; sprinkle on crust. Fill (about 1 inch deep) with rhubarb.

Custard:

2 eggs
1 egg white
1½ c. sugar

½ c. light cream
Dash of salt

Combine eggs and egg whites; beat well. Add sugar, cream, and salt; beat. Pour over rhubarb.

Streusel:

½ c. flour
½ c. sugar

¼ tsp. salt
¼ c. margarine

Combine all ingredients in small bowl; blend with pastry blender. Sprinkle over rhubarb and custard. Bake at 350° for 45 minutes or until lightly browned.

RHUBARB FRUIT CRISP   Ann Dobransky

3 c. chopped rhubarb
1 (3 oz.) pkg. strawberry gelatin
1½ c. flour
1 c. quick rolled oats

1 c. brown sugar
1 tsp. cinnamon
¾ c. margarine

Place chopped rhubarb in buttered 9 inch cake pan. Sprinkle with gelatin. Combine oats, brown sugar, and cinnamon; cut in margarine until mixture is crumbly. Sprinkle over fruit. Bake at 375° for 40 to 45 minutes.

RHUBARB-PINEAPPLE CRISP

Eloise Maliwacki

¼ c. flour
½ c. sugar
¼ tsp. salt
6 c. (1 inch pieces) rhubarb
1 (1 lb. 4 oz.) can pineapple
  chunks, drained

¾ c. rolled oats
½ c. light brown sugar
¼ c. butter or margarine

Sift together flour, sugar, and salt; mix thoroughly with combined rhubarb and pineapple. Turn into buttered 1½ quart baking dish. Combine oats, brown sugar, and butter until crumbly. Sprinkle over rhubarb. Bake at 350° for 30 to 35 minutes. Serve warm or cool, with or without whipped topping.

RICE WITH APPLES

Teklia Farynyk

2 c. rice
1 c. sugar
¼ c. butter or margarine

6 large apples
Milk
Cinnamon

Parboil rice; drain. Add sugar and butter; mix. Peel apples; slice thin. Add to rice; mix. Put rice mixture in a buttered 2½ quart round casserole. Add milk to cover. Sprinkle with cinnamon. Bake at 350° for 1 hour. Serve hot or cold.

MARY H'S SHORTCAKE CRUST

Anne Pufky

1½ c. Bisquick
3 Tbsp. margarine

4 Tbsp. boiling water

Cut margarine into Bisquick with pastry blender. Add boiling water; mix with fork. Pat mixture into 9 inch pie pan. Bake at 425° for 8 minutes. Use for any filling recipe that calls for a baked crust.

STRAWBERRY BAVARIAN

Shirley Buchma

1 (10 oz.) pkg. frozen sliced
  strawberries
1 (3 oz.) pkg. strawberry gelatin

1 c. boiling water
Cold water
1 c. whipped topping

Drain thawed strawberries; reserve syrup. Pour boiling water over gelatin in bowl; stir until dissolved. Add enough cold water to reserved syrup to make 1 cup; add to gelatin. Stir. Chill until almost set. Beat gelatin until foamy; fold in strawberries and whipped topping. Pour into individual molds or serving dishes; chill until firm. Garnish with fresh strawberries and whipped topping. Serves 8.

TELL KADAYIF

Carol Wasylko

2 c. sugar
1 c. water
½ tsp. lemon juice
12 Shredded Wheat biscuits
1½ c. milk

1½ c. finely chopped walnuts
1 tsp. cinnamon
1 tsp. sugar
½ c. butter or margarine,
  melted

In a saucepan, combine 2 cups sugar and water. Bring to a boil; boil 10 minutes. Remove from heat; add lemon juice. Cool. Dip each biscuit in milk; drain on paper towel. With 2 forks, separate moist biscuit in center to make a sizable dent. Place on buttered 15x9x2 inch jellyroll pan. Combine walnuts, cinnamon, and 1 teaspoon sugar. Spoon 2 tablespoons of mixture into center of each biscuit. Drizzle a spoonful of melted butter over each biscuit. Bake at 350° for 30 minutes. Pour cooled syrup over hot biscuits; cover. Let stand 1 hour before serving - even better the next day. Serves 12.

DESSERT TRIFLE

Sophie Smyk

Pound cake
Wine (your favorite)
Raspberry jam
1 (3 oz.) pkg. raspberry Jell-O
1 c. boiling water
1 c. cold water

1 (3¾ oz.) pkg. vanilla pudding
2 c. milk
½ pt. heavy cream
2 Tbsp. confectioners sugar
1 tsp. vanilla
Slivered almonds

Line a 9x13 inch Pyrex pan with pound cake slices. Pour wine over cake until soaked. Spread with raspberry jam. Set aside. Dissolve Jell-O in boiling water; stir until completely dissolved. Add cold water; stir. Refrigerate until slightly set. Spread over wine-soaked cake. Refrigerate. Combine pudding with milk; cook according to package directions. Cool. Spread over Jell-O layer. Whip heavy cream until thick enough to stand in peaks. Add confectioners sugar and vanilla; mix. Cover pudding layer with whipped cream; sprinkle with almonds. Serves 16.

UKRAINIAN DELIGHT

Mary Mihalko

½ c. butter or margarine
¾ c. shortening
½ c. confectioners sugar
1 tsp. vanilla
2½ c. flour
½ tsp. salt
½ tsp. baking powder
2 (8 oz.) pkg. cream cheese

1 c. blackberry or raspberry
  preserves
1 pt. heavy cream
5 Tbsp. confectioners sugar
1 tsp. vanilla
1 (8 oz.) can crushed pineapple
Chopped nuts

Beat together butter, shortening, ½ cup confectioners sugar, and 1 teaspoon vanilla. Combine flour, salt, and baking powder; add to butter mixture. Mix well. Pat mixture into bottom of a greased 15½ x 10½ x 1 inch pan. Bake at 350° for 18 to 20 minutes. Cool completely. Combine cream cheese and preserves; beat until smooth. Spread on cooled crust.

Beat heavy cream, 5 tablespoons confectioners sugar, and 1 teaspoon vanilla until cream holds peaks. Drain pineapple very well; fold into whipped cream. Spread over cream cheese layer. Sprinkle with chopped nuts. Refrigerate until ready to serve.

Notes

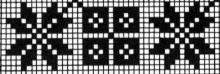

FISH

COD FISH CAKES

Anna Chyl

2 lb. cod fillets
1 large potato, peeled and
  cubed
1 onion

Pepper to taste
½ pkg. Sweet 'N Low
½ to ¾ c. matzo meal

Place fillets and potato in saucepan; add enough water to cover. Bring to a boil; boil 10 minutes. Drain. Grind fish, potato, and onion. Add eggs, pepper, sweetener, and matzo. Mix thoroughly. Form into patties. Fry to brown both sides.

FISH IN CHEESE SAUCE

Stephanie Gorick

6 Tbsp. butter
1 lb. fish fillets

American cheese slices
Salt and pepper

In large skillet, melt butter; add fish fillets and layer with cheese slices. Cover. Cook on medium heat about 5 minutes; uncover. Cook until done, about 10 to 15 minutes. Salt and pepper to taste.

FISH IN SOUR CREAM

Dot Skellett

Thin lemon slices
1 to 2 lb. fish fillets
Salt

Pepper
1 c. sour cream
Paprika

Cover bottom of a 9x13 inch pan with lemon slices. Arrange fillets over lemon slices; season with salt and pepper. Cover; bake at 350° about 30 minutes or until fish flakes easily. Uncover; add salt to sour cream. Spread over fillets; sprinkle with paprika. Place under broiler until bubbly and light brown.

FISH BAKED IN TOMATO JUICE

John and Vera Cibulsky

2 lb. haddock, cusk, turbot, or
  pollock (fresh or frozen)
½ tsp. garlic salt
Pepper
Flour
⅓ c. oil
3 medium onions, sliced

½ c. flour
24 oz. tomato juice
1 c. water
Salt and pepper
2 Tbsp. chopped fresh or
  dehydrated parsley
½ tsp. Italian seasoning

Wash fish; damp dry with paper towels. Cut in serving size pieces; season with garlic salt. Place fish in a bag with some flour; shake bag to coat fish. Heat oil in skillet; quickly sear fish on both sides to a light brown. Remove fish to baking dish in a single layer. Saute onion in remaining oil in skillet. Add ½ cup flour to onion mixture; stir to make smooth. Cook, letting it bubble for 1 minute, stirring as it's cooking. Add tomato juice and water. Season with salt and pepper to taste; add parsley and Italian seasoning. Simmer 5 minutes. Pour over fish. Cover; bake at 350° for 20 to 30 minutes.

Variation: A less tart taste is obtained by decreasing tomato juice to 16 ounces and adding a can of tomato soup plus a can of water.

If using frozen breaded fish, do not dip in flour.

PICKLED FISH
Helen Rucky

2 Tbsp. salt
7 Tbsp. sugar
2 tsp. whole pickling spice
1½ oz. dry white wine

1 medium onion, sliced
Cider vinegar
Fish, cut up to desired size

Fill quart jar ¾ full of fish, loosely packed. Add salt, sugar, pickling spice, wine, and onion. Fill rest of quart with vinegar. Put lid on jar and shake well to mix ingredients. Refrigerate 5 days. Shake twice a day.

FISH STEW
Olga Tarcha

2 pkg. frozen flounder fillets,
  thawed, cut in large pieces
3 medium onions, chopped
1 c. chopped celery
4 large potatoes, cubed
1 clove garlic, minced
1 Tbsp. salt

2 whole cloves
¼ tsp. pepper
1 c. water
½ c. white cooking wine
2 c. light cream or milk
¼ c. butter or margarine
1 bay leaf

Place all ingredients, except fish, milk, wine, and butter, in a large pan; simmer about 25 minutes or until veggies are tender. Add fish, another cup of water, then milk, wine, and butter. Cook 10 minutes, stirring occasionally.

MOCK LOBSTER
Carol Williams

1 lb. frozen flounder, cod, or
  perch

⅓ c. vinegar
Melted butter

Place fish in pan; add enough water to cover fish. Add vinegar; boil 10 minutes. Drain. Pour melted butter over fish.

SEAFOOD PAELLA

Anna Smyk

2 medium stalks celery, sliced
  thin
1 medium onion, sliced thin
1 medium green pepper, diced
6 Tbsp. oil
6 Tbsp. butter
½ tsp. garlic powder
1 bay leaf
1 Tbsp. parsley
1 c. crushed tomatoes
1 to 2 bouillon cubes
1 c. hot water
1½ c. rice

Chicken (1 piece per serving)
Hot Italian sausage (1 piece per
  serving)
Shrimp (2 per serving)
Scallops (2 per serving)
Clams (2 per serving)
Lobster (2 bite-size pieces per
  serving, optional)
Halibut (2 bite-size pieces per
  serving (optional)
A.1. Sauce
Salt and pepper

Saute celery, onion, and green pepper in oil and butter; do not brown. Add garlic powder, bay leaf, and parsley; cook on low heat for 10 minutes. Add tomatoes and bouillon which has been dissolved in hot water. Add rice; cover. When almost done, about 10 minutes, add precooked chicken and sausage. Add all seafood raw; cover. Cook 10 to 15 minutes. Stir with a fork. Season with A.1. Sauce, salt, and pepper.

BAKED SALMON

Dot Skellett

Salmon fillets
Salt and pepper to taste
¼ c. melted butter

Juice of 1 lemon
Paprika

Place fillets in a 9x13 inch baking pan; season with salt and pepper. Combine melted butter with lemon juice; drizzle over fillets. Sprinkle generously with paprika. Bake at 350° for 30 minutes.

BRAISED SHRIMP

Mary Kostyun

1 lb. shelled and deveined
  shrimp
½ lb. chopped onion
½ c. olive oil
2 Tbsp. tomato paste or 1 lb.
  fresh tomatoes, chopped

½ c. dry white wine
½ c. chopped parsley
½ stalk celery, chopped
Salt
Pepper

Boil shrimp in small amount of water for 2 minutes. Saute onion in olive oil until golden. Add tomato paste or tomatoes and simmer 5 minutes, stirring constantly. Add wine, parsley, celery, and salt and pepper to taste. Cook until celery is tender. Add precooked, cleaned shrimp and cook until shrimp are done. Serve hot over rice pilaf.

COCONUT SHRIMP

Phyllis Hatala

⅓ c. peanut oil
½ c. flaked coconut
¼ c. fine dry bread crumbs
3 Tbsp. chopped parsley
1 Tbsp. minced garlic
¾ tsp. salt

¼ tsp. paprika
Dash of cayenne
2 lb. uncooked shrimp, shelled
  and deveined
½ c. sherry

Combine peanut oil, coconut, bread crumbs, chopped parsley, minced garlic, salt, paprika, and cayenne. Reserve ¼ cup of the mixture for topping. Toss shrimp lightly in the remaining mixture until shrimp are well coated. Place shrimp in a lightly oiled 1½ quart casserole. Pour sherry over shrimp; sprinkle with reserved ¼ cup coconut mixture. Bake, uncovered, at 375° about 40 minutes or until shrimp are tender.

LOUISIANA SHRIMP

Millie Finch

1 lb. butter
1 medium onion, chopped
½ green pepper, sliced
2½ c. hot water

1 env. Lipton tomato vegetable
  soup mix
1 lb. shelled, deveined raw
  shrimp

In a large saucepan, melt butter. Add onion and green pepper; saute about 5 minutes. Add water and soup mix, stirring until blended. Cover; simmer 10 minutes, stirring occasionally. Add shrimp; simmer until shrimp are done. Serve over rice.

Note: Mushrooms can be added if desired.

OYSTER STEW

Mildred Charnetsky
Evelyn Kanazawich

¼ c. butter or margarine
1 tsp. Worcestershire sauce
Dash of paprika
2 qt. oysters

1½ qt. milk
1½ tsp. salt
Dash of pepper

Melt butter in deep saucepan; add Worcestershire sauce and paprika. Stir until smooth. Add oysters with the oyster liquor. Cook over low heat until edges of oysters curl; add milk, salt, and pepper. Heat thoroughly over low heat, but do not boil.

SMELT SEVARG

Evelyn Kanazawich

36 smelt
½ c. butter
¼ c. dry white wine

Salt
Black pepper
2 Tbsp. chopped parsley

Clean smelt, but do not remove head or bones. Melt butter in large skillet. Add wine; heat, but do not brown butter. Season smelt with salt and pepper; slide into skillet. Fry until golden brown; turn and brown on the other side. Drain on paper towels; transfer to hot platter. Sprinkle with parsley.

TROUT IN WINE

Marie Pufky

6 frozen rainbow trout, skinned
  and thawed
2 Tbsp. lemon juice
Salt and pepper
1 c. dry white wine
2 Tbsp. chopped fresh parsley

¼ c. sliced green onions
2 Tbsp. fine dry bread crumbs
¼ c. melted butter or
  margarine
Fresh dill for garnish
Lemon slices for garnish

Wash trout; pat dry with paper towels. Brush inside of fish with some of the lemon juice; sprinkle with salt and pepper. Arrange trout in a shallow baking dish; brush with remaining lemon juice. Sprinkle with salt and pepper; pour wine into baking dish. Sprinkle each trout evenly with parsley and onions; sprinkle lightly with bread crumbs. Drizzle melted butter evenly over trout. Bake, uncovered, at 325° for 25 minutes or until fish flakes easily with a fork. Arrange fish on a serving platter; garnish with fresh dill and lemon slices. Serves 6.

Notes

Meatless Dishes

MEATLESS DISHES

CASHEW NUT TIMBALES

Olga Gooley

½ c. chopped green onions
2 Tbsp. oil
¾ c. tomatoes (fresh or canned)
1½ c. evaporated milk

2 eggs, beaten
2 c. toasted bread cubes
1 c. chopped cashew nuts
½ tsp. salt (or to taste)

Saute onions in oil; add tomatoes and cook until tender. Add milk to beaten eggs. In mixing bowl, combine all the ingredients and blend well. Bake in buttered custard cups at 350° for 20 minutes. Yields 6 servings.

CREAM CHEESE BALLS

Olga Gooley

8 oz. cream cheese
1 c. chopped nuts
1 c. cracker crumbs

3 eggs, beaten
1 pkg. Lipton onion soup mix

Combine all ingredients. Roll into small balls and roll in cracker crumbs. Fry until golden brown.

Sauce:

1 (8 oz.) can tomato sauce
1 can mushroom soup

½ tsp. monosodium glutamate

Heat combined tomato sauce, mushroom soup, and monosodium glutamate and pour over cream cheese balls. Serves 6 to 8.

ENGLISH MONKEY

Marie Brink

1 c. bread crumbs or cubes
1 c. milk
2 Tbsp. butter
½ lb. grated sharp Cheddar
cheese

2 eggs, beaten
Salt and pepper
Dash of dry mustard

Soak bread crumbs in milk. In double boiler, melt butter and cheese together. Slowly add beaten eggs to cheese mixture; add salt and pepper to taste and a dash of dry mustard. Combine cheese mixture and bread crumb-milk mixture and blend. Serve "hot" on toast-bread or crackers.

COTTAGE CHEESE LOAF

Olga Gooley

1 c. cottage cheese
1 c. finely ground nuts (pecans, walnuts, or cashews)
2 c. corn flakes
1 medium onion, diced
2 Tbsp. butter

1½ c. tomato puree
4 eggs, beaten
2 Tbsp. soy sauce
¼ tsp. celery salt
Salt to taste

Saute onion in butter. Mix with other ingredients. Put in 9x13 inch greased pan. Cover. Bake at 350° for 45 minutes. Uncover and brown slightly. Serve with mushroom gravy. Yield: 6 to 8 servings.

COTTAGE CHEESE AND WALNUT LOAF

Olga Gooley

1½ c. cottage cheese
1 c. bread crumbs
1 c. chopped walnuts, pecans, or almonds
¾ c. chopped celery
¼ c. chopped onions

3 eggs, beaten
1 Tbsp. oil
½ tsp. salt
½ tsp. poultry seasoning
1 tsp. monosodium glutamate

Combine all the ingredients and place in a buttered casserole. Bake at 350° for 45 to 60 minutes.

Note: Good served with cranberry sauce or gravy.

SPECIAL "K" COTTAGE CHEESE LOAF

Olga Gooley

1 medium onion, chopped
1 stick butter
5 eggs, slightly beaten
3 c. Special "K" cereal
2 lb. cottage cheese

½ c. walnuts, finely chopped
2 env. vegetable broth seasoning
¼ tsp. garlic powder

Saute the onion in butter. Combine the rest of ingredients and add to onions. Pour into greased casserole; bake at 350° for 1 hour.

CHEESE ONION PIE

Charles Sarnoski

9 inch unbaked pie shell
½ to ¾ lb. sharp Cheddar cheese
1 Tbsp. flour
1 large Spanish onion, chopped
2 Tbsp. butter or margarine

1 c. milk
1 egg
1 egg yolk
½ tsp. salt
½ tsp. pepper
Paprika

Grate cheese and toss with flour. Put in pie shell. Saute onions in butter. Spread on top of cheese. Mix milk, egg, egg yolk, salt, and pepper together. Drizzle over cheese and onion in pie shell. Sprinkle with paprika. Bake in preheated 400° oven for 15 minutes. Reduce heat to 325° and continue to bake for 25 to 30 minutes or until knife inserted comes out clean.

CORN SOUFFLE
Olga Gooley

¾ c. soy flour
¾ c. water or milk
1 c. canned tomatoes
2 Tbsp. ground peanuts or
   peanut butter
4 Tbsp. oil

½ tsp. salt
1 tsp. onion powder
Dash of paprika
1 c. cooked, drained corn
½ c. soft bread crumbs

Blend first 7 ingredients until smooth. Fold in corn and bread crumbs. Pour into an ungreased casserole. Set casserole in pan of water, 1 inch deep. Bake a 350° for 1 hour.

EGG PUFF
Dot Skellett

3 Tbsp. margarine
½ c. chopped onion
½ c. chopped green pepper
1 (2 oz.) jar pimientos, drained
   and diced
5 eggs

2 c. (8 oz.) shredded Monterey
   Jack cheese
1 c. cottage cheese
¼ c. flour
½ tsp. baking powder

In a small skillet, melt margarine over medium heat; saute onion and green pepper until tender. Add pimientos. In a large bowl, with electric mixer at medium speed, beat eggs, all cheese, flour, and baking powder until well blended. Stir in vegetable mixture. Pour into a greased 1½ quart oblong baking dish. Bake at 350° for 40 minutes or until set.

GNOCCHI
Melodye Onysko

2 c. flour
2 c. Ricotta cheese

2 eggs
Spaghetti sauce

In a mixing bowl, combine the flour, cheese, and eggs. Knead. Roll into thin cigar shape logs and cut into ½ inch pieces. Drop into salted, boiling water; cook for 2 to 4 minutes or until they float to the top. Roll in spaghetti sauce and serve.

GREEN CLAM SAUCE

Marie Richardson

3 to 4 cloves garlic, chopped
3 scallions, chopped
½ c. margarine or 2 Tbsp. olive
  oil
2 c. broccoli, chopped
2 small zucchini, sliced
1 c. water

¼ c. white wine (optional)
2 (6½ oz.) cans chopped clams
½ c. chopped fresh parsley
1 Tbsp. cornstarch
Salt and pepper to taste
Your favorite pasta

Saute garlic and scallions in margarine or olive oil. Add broccoli, zucchini, and water. Cover; cook until vegetables are tender. Add wine, clams, and parsley; stir. Dissolve cornstarch in a small amount of water; add to vegetables, stirring constantly until thickened. Cover; simmer 1 minute. Add salt and pepper. Serve over your favorite pasta.

LENTIL NUT ROAST

Olga Gooley

1 c. uncooked lentils
½ c. chopped nuts
1 egg
1 can evaporated milk
½ tsp. salt

1 c. cooking oil
1½ c. corn flakes
½ tsp. sage
1 medium onion, chopped (or 2
  Tbsp. minced onion)

Boil lentils until well done. Add chopped onion, nuts, and slightly beaten egg. Combine all remaining ingredients and mix well. Bake in greased casserole at 350° for 45 to 60 minutes.

LINKLETTER LOAF

Olga Gooley

2 eggs
1⅓ c. milk
½ c. peanut butter
1¼ c. carrots, chopped fine

¾ c. raw brown rice
¼ c. parsley, chopped fine
2 Tbsp. oil
½ tsp. salt

Cook rice according to directions on package. Combine eggs, milk, and peanut butter; beat until smooth. Add remaining ingredients; mix well. Bake at 350° in greased 9x5x3 inch pan for 1 hour and 15 minutes. Serve with celery soup gravy or mushroom soup gravy or Cheddar cheese soup gravy.

ANGEL HAIR WITH BROCCOLI

Linda Zapach

1 bunch fresh broccoli
1 Tbsp. butter
2 scallions, cut into ¼ inch
  pieces
1 clove garlic, peeled and
  crushed

2 Tbsp. white cooking wine
½ stick unsalted butter, melted
¼ c. light olive oil
1 lb. angel hair pasta
Grated Parmesan cheese to
  taste

Cook broccoli flowerets in boiling water 3 to 4 minutes; drain. Saute scallions and garlic in 1 tablespoon butter, about 2 minutes; add wine. Cook 5 minutes; add melted butter and olive oil, then broccoli. Heat thoroughly. Cook pasta according to package directions. Drain. Toss broccoli mixture with pasta. Serve at once with Parmesan cheese.

CABBAGE AND NOODLES

Dot Skellett

1 (8 oz.) pkg. egg noodles
1 medium onion, sliced
6 Tbsp. butter
2 Tbsp. olive or vegetable oil
1 lb. shredded cabbage

¼ c. cider vinegar
1 Tbsp. brown sugar
1 Tbsp. paprika
½ tsp. salt

Cook noodles according to package directions; in a large skillet over high heat, heat 2 tablespoons butter and oil. Add onions; stir-fry until onions begin to brown, about 6 minutes. Add remaining 4 tablespoons butter and cabbage; reduce heat to medium. Cook about 5 minutes; add vinegar, sugar, paprika, and salt. Bring to a boil. Reduce heat. Cover; simmer until cabbage is completely wilted. Toss the noodles with the cabbage. Serves 6.

HOMEMADE PASTA DOUGH

Helen Charnetsky

4 c. sifted flour
1 tsp. salt
4 eggs, lightly beaten

¼ c. lukewarm water
2 tsp. oil

Sift flour with salt; make a well in center. Pour in eggs, water, and oil; blend ingredients. Dough will be fairly stiff. Knead dough on a lightly floured surface for about 10 minutes (until smooth and elastic). Cover with dry cloth; let rest for about ½ hour. Quarter dough and roll each piece paper thin into a 14 inch square on a lightly floured surface, keeping edges straight. Let dry slightly. Cut into noodles for soup, lasagna, or spaghetti. Cover with dry cloth; let dry at room temperature for 1 hour. Noodles may be dried overnight; turn now and then. Store in an airtight container. Makes 1½ pounds of noodles.

Note: Homemade noodles cook faster than store bought ones. This pasta dough may be used in a pasta machine.

FETTUCCINE WITH VEGGIES

Dot Skellett

1 (10 oz.) pkg. frozen chopped
  spinach
½ c. frozen peas
1 c. frozen chopped broccoli
½ lb. fettuccini
3 Tbsp. butter
3 Tbsp. olive or vegetable oil

8 scallions, chopped
5 cloves garlic, minced
¾ tsp. salt
½ tsp. pepper
1¼ c. sour cream
⅔ c. grated Parmesan cheese

Thaw spinach, peas, and broccoli; drain as much as possible. Press spinach between layers of paper towels to dry. Cook pasta according to package directions; drain. In a large skillet, melt butter; add oil. Heat; add scallions and garlic. Saute over medium heat about 5 minutes, stirring while cooking. Stir in sour cream; remove from heat. Combine vegetables, cheese, and pasta; mix well. Serves 6.

JIFFY MACARONI AND CHEESE

Dot Skellett

2 c. large elbow macaroni
½ c. milk

1 (10½ oz.) can Cheddar cheese
  soup

Cook macaroni as directed on package; drain. Blend milk with soup. Over medium heat, cook until heated through. Pour over macaroni; mix well. Serves 4 to 6.

MACARONI AND TOMATOES

Charles Sarnoski

1 to 1½ c. macaroni
1 medium onion, diced
1 tsp. Accent

4 Tbsp. margarine
Salt and pepper
1 (15 oz.) can tomatoes, mashed

Add macaroni and diced onion to boiling, salted water and cook until macaroni is almost done. Drain and rinse a little. Mash tomatoes and add to macaroni, onions, Accent, margarine, salt, and pepper. Over low heat, continue cooking until macaroni is done.

NOODLES WITH CREAMY POPPY SEED SAUCE

Dot Skellett

¾ lb. medium egg noodles
2 Tbsp. olive or vegetable oil
2 medium onions, sliced
2 cloves garlic, minced
2 Tbsp. butter
½ lb. mushrooms, sliced

⅓ c. lemon juice
¾ tsp. salt
½ tsp. pepper
⅔ c. sour cream
2 Tbsp. poppy seed
1 Tbsp. grated lemon rind

Just before serving, cook noodles according to package directions; drain. Place in a serving bowl. In a skillet, place oil; heat. Add onions and garlic; cook until onions begin to brown. Add butter. When melted, add mushrooms; cook 5 minutes. Add lemon juice, salt, and pepper; bring to a boil. Reduce heat to low; cover. Simmer about 6 minutes. In a medium bowl, combine sour cream, poppy seed, and lemon rind; add mushroom mixture. Mix well; pour over noodles.

PENNE WITH BEANS AND PEPPERS
Dot Skellett

1 (8 oz.) pkg. penne pasta
3 Tbsp. olive or vegetable oil
1 medium onion, sliced
3 cloves garlic, minced
1 green pepper, chopped
1 red pepper, chopped
1 (1 lb.) can white beans, rinsed
 and drained

2 Tbsp. lemon juice
1 tsp. thyme
¾ tsp. salt
¼ tsp. pepper
2 Tbsp. butter

Cook penne according to package directions. In a large skillet, heat 2 tablespoons oil; add onions and garlic. Saute until onions begin to brown; add remaining tablespoon of oil and green and red peppers. Cook 5 minutes, stirring while cooking; also, add rinsed and drained beans, lemon juice, thyme, salt, and pepper. Cook until beans are heated through. Remove from heat; drain pasta. Toss with butter; combine pasta with vegetables.

OLGA'S SAUERKRAUT AND NOODLES

1 lb. noodles
¼ c. oil or margarine
1 medium onion, chopped

1 (27 oz.) can sauerkraut,
 drained
Caraway seeds to taste

Cook noodles according to package directions; drain. Heat oil in skillet. Add onion and sauerkraut; cook until slightly browned. Add noodles and caraway seeds; heat thoroughly.

PECAN LOAF
Olga Gooley

1 c. Italian bread crumbs
1½ c. evaporated milk
⅔ c. chopped pecans
2 Tbsp. chopped parsley

2 eggs, beaten
1 Tbsp. chopped onion
2 Tbsp. melted butter
1 tsp. salt

Combine bread crumbs and evaporated milk. Separately combine remaining ingredients, then combine both mixtures. Bake in a well buttered baking dish at 350° for 30 to 40 minutes. Yield: 6 servings.

AMERICAN PIROHI

Colleen Rucky

10 to 12 potatoes, boiled and
  mashed
1 c. Cheddar cheese, grated
2 sticks margarine

3 onions, finely chopped
Salt and pepper to taste
1 lb. lasagna noodles

Cook lasagna noodles as package directs. Mash potatoes; add cheese. Saute onion in margarine until soft. Add ⅓ onion mixture to potatoes; add salt and pepper. Butter 9x13 inch dish; layer noodles, then potatoes. Repeat until all potatoes and noodles are used up. Pour evenly remaining butter. Bake at 350° for 30 minutes.

CABBAGE AND CHEESE PIROHI

Helen Charnetsky

Pirohi Dough:

4 c. flour
2 eggs, beaten
½ c. sour cream

Pinch of salt
⅛ to ¼ c. water

Into a large mixing bowl, sift flour and salt. Make a well in center of flour; add eggs and sour cream. Work into flour. Add water, as needed, to make a soft dough. Knead dough about 10 minutes until dough no longer sticks to your hands. Cover dough; let rest at least 30 minutes. Cut dough into 4 sections. Roll each section out on a slightly floured surface and cut into 3 inch circles or squares. Fill with one tablespoon of your favorite filling. Seal edges very carefully.

Cook 1 dozen pirohi in salted, boiling water with 2 tablespoons oil added, for about 15 minutes. Stir gently so they don't stick to the bottom of pan. Remove pirohi with slotted spoon when they rise to the top of the water and they puff up. Saute onion in butter and pour over hot, drained pirohi and serve.

Filling:

1 (1 lb. 11 oz.) can sauerkraut
1 tsp. oil
2 scallions (including tops)
1 clove garlic, mashed fine
Pinch of basil

1 bay leaf
½ lb. Farmer's cheese
1 egg, beaten
2 Tbsp. sour cream with onion

Rinse sauerkraut in cold water; hand squeeze as dry as possible. Saute scallions and garlic in oil; add sauerkraut, salt and pepper, basil, and bay leaf. Add cheese, egg, and sour cream; cook just until heated through, about ½ hour. Works very well if made the day before and refrigerated overnight.

PIROHI DOUGH I

Vera Cibulsky

6 c. flour
2 tsp. salt
2 small or medium eggs,
  slightly beaten

⅔ c. sour cream
¾ c. lukewarm water

Into a large mixing bowl, sift together flour and salt. Blend together eggs, sour cream, and water until smooth. Combine egg mixture with flour and salt. If there is any dry flour in bowl, moisten it by adding drops of water and start kneading in bowl. Knead dough to get all ingredients together. Lightly flour board and knead dough about 5 minutes. If dough is sticky, knead in a little more flour. Pat a little more flour on dough and place in a lightly floured plastic bag and let dough rest for at least 20 minutes. Cut off as much dough as you can roll out on a floured board. Keep unused dough in plastic bag until used. Cut in round circles and fill with your favorite filling.

Note: Do not overboil pirohi as dough is delicate.

PIROHI DOUGH II

Mary Mihalko

4 c. flour
3 eggs
½ pt. sour cream

½ tsp. salt
1½ Tbsp. oil

Beat eggs, sour cream, salt, and oil together. Add flour and knead. Let rest for short time; roll out dough. Cut in circles and fill with favorite filling.

QUICK PIROHI

Linda Zapach

6 lasagna noodles
1 lb. cottage cheese
1 egg yolk
Onion salt to taste
1½ c. mashed potatoes

½ c. shredded Cheddar or
  American cheese
2 Tbsp. butter, softened
Salt and pepper to taste

Cook noodles as directed on package. Drain and allow to sit in cool water to keep from sticking. In buttered 9x5x3 inch loaf pan, lay down 2 noodles lengthwise. Combine cottage cheese, egg yolk, and onion salt. Pour over first layer. Set in 2 more noodles. Combine mashed potatoes, Cheddar cheese, and 1 tablespoon butter. Pat gently over noodles. Top with 2 noodles; dab with 1 tablespoon butter. Cover and bake at 375° for 30 minutes. Uncover; turn off oven and let sit for 5 minutes to steam dry slightly. To serve, cut into squares and top with cold sour cream.

POTATO PANCAKES

Teklia Smyk

3 large potatoes, grated
1 small onion, grated
1 clove garlic, grated
Salt to taste
2 eggs, beaten

2½ c. flour
½ c. hot milk
1 tsp. baking powder
Cooking oil

Drain grated potatoes. Add remaining ingredients except oil; mix well using a wooden or stainless steel spoon. Heat oil in fry pan. Spoon batter in fry pan; fry on each side until golden brown. Serve with sour cream.

MY MOM'S POTATO PANCAKES

Julie Sadowitz

4 large potatoes
1 medium onion, grated
2 eggs, slightly beaten
⅓ c. flour

2 tsp. salt
⅛ tsp. white pepper
Salad oil for frying

Peel and grate potatoes. Drain off excess liquid; add onion, eggs, flour, salt, and pepper. Blend well. Heat salad oil in skillet (about ¼ inch deep). Drop about ¼ cup potato mixture into skillet, about 3 inches apart; flatten each to make a 4 inch pancake. Cook pancakes until golden brown on each side (about 4 minutes each side). Drain on paper lined cookie sheet; keep warm in low temperature oven. Makes about 12 pancakes. Serve with cottage cheese-sour cream topping or applesauce.

FRIED PIES (PHILIPPINES)

3 c. uncooked rice
1 green pepper
2 onions
3 tomatoes

2 stalks celery
2 tsp. Accent
3 Tbsp. butter
Dash of salt

Cook rice according to package directions. Finely chop all vegetables and saute in butter until tender. Add salt, Accent, and rice. Fry mixture for about 5 minutes. Dot with butter and serve.

POTATO PIE I

Julie Sadowitz

2 lb. russet potatoes, peeled, cut
 into 1 inch cubes
Cooking spray
1 Tbsp. unseasoned bread
 crumbs
½ c. chopped onion
1 clove garlic, minced
2 tsp. olive oil

2 large egg whites
⅓ c. plus 1 Tbsp. grated
 Romano cheese
½ tsp. salt
¼ tsp. pepper
¼ c. shredded part-skim
 Mozzarella cheese

Place potatoes in medium saucepan; add cold water to cover. Bring to boil; cook 20 minutes or until tender. Reserve ¼ cup of the cooking water. Drain potatoes; return to saucepan. Preheat oven to 350°. With cooking spray, lightly coat 9 inch pie plate. Dust with bread crumbs. In small nonstick skillet, over medium heat, cook onion and garlic in oil, covered, 5 minutes. Uncover; increase heat to high. Cook, stirring 2 to 3 minutes, until onions are lightly browned.

To potatoes, add egg whites, ⅓ cup of the Romano cheese, the salt, pepper, and reserved cooking water; beat with mixer until smooth. Stir in onion mixture and Mozzarella cheese. Spoon into prepared plate, spreading evenly; sprinkle with remaining Romano. Bake 50 minutes or until lightly browned. Let stand 10 minutes. Cut into 8 wedges. Makes 8 servings.

POTATO PIE II

Charles Sarnoski

8 large potatoes, peeled
1 large onion, diced
2 to 3 Tbsp. butter
Milk
Salt

Pepper
Pinch of rosemary
1 Tbsp. parsley, chopped
2 (9 inch) pie crusts

In a large saucepan, add enough water to cover cut up potatoes; boil until soft enough to mash. Saute onion in butter. Add to mashed potatoes. Add parsley and enough milk to make a smooth mashed potato. Add salt and pepper to taste; add rosemary. Mix. Put seasoned, mashed potatoes in pie shell in a 9 inch pie plate and top with pie crust. Bake at 350° for 45 minutes.

Notes

MEATS

MEATS

SOUR HAM BALLS

Mary Kostyun

3 c. ground cooked ham
½ c. fine dry bread crumbs
1 egg, slightly beaten
¼ c. vegetable oil
1 (14 to 15 oz.) can pineapple
   chunks in syrup
3 Tbsp. soy sauce

1 Tbsp. brown sugar
Water
2 Tbsp. cornstarch
¼ c. cider vinegar
2 large green peppers, seeded,
   cut in strips
Cooked rice

In large bowl, combine ham, bread crumbs, and egg; shape into 12 large balls. Brown in oil in a large fry pan. Remove from pan. Drain pineapple syrup into a quart measure; add soy sauce and brown sugar, then enough water to make 2 cups; stir to thoroughly mix. Stir into pan drippings in fry pan. Place ham balls in sauce; cover. Simmer 15 minutes. Blend cornstarch with vinegar. Remove ham balls from fry pan. Stir vinegar-cornstarch mixture into sauce in fry pan, stirring constantly until sauce thickens and boils 3 minutes. Stir in pineapple, peppers, and ham balls. Heat until bubbly. Serve over rice if desired.

MY SISTER'S MEATBALLS

Pani Julia Lawryk

1 lb. ground beef
1 tsp. salt
⅛ tsp. pepper
¼ tsp. garlic salt
¼ tsp. celery salt
½ c. cracker crumbs

½ c. water
2 Tbsp. chopped onion
1 (10½ oz.) can cream of
   mushroom soup
½ can hot water
2 beef bouillon cubes

Combine ground beef, seasonings, cracker crumbs, water, and onion; mix thoroughly. Form into balls; roll in flour. Brown in oil; drain on paper towels. Empty can of mushroom soup into a large saucepan; dissolve beef bouillon in hot water. Add to mushroom soup, stirring to make smooth. Add meatballs to gravy; cover. Simmer 30 minutes.

OVEN MEATBALLS

Anna Smyk

1 egg
1 lb. ground chuck
½ lb. ground pork
½ lb. ground veal
½ tsp. salt
1 c. packed corn flake crumbs

1 (1½ oz.) pkg. spaghetti sauce
   mix
¾ c. milk
2 (10½ oz.) cans mushroom
   gravy

In a large bowl, beat egg; add ground chuck, pork, veal, and salt. Blend well. Add crumbs and ½ the package of spaghetti sauce mix; blend. Add milk; blend. Shape level measuring tablespoon of meat mixture into balls; place in a single layer in a shallow baking pan. Bake in a 375° oven 30 minutes. In a bowl, whisk together the remaining ½ package spaghetti sauce mix and 2 cans of mushroom gravy; spoon over almost cooked meatballs. Continue baking 15 more minutes. Serve over hot rice, noodles, or mashed potatoes. May also be served as a hot hors d'oeuvre from a chafing dish.

SAUSAGE BALLS
Mary Kostyun

1 lb. sharp Cheddar cheese, grated

1 lb. hot breakfast sausage
3 c. Bisquick

Mix together cheese and sausage; add Bisquick, working all of it in. Shape in one inch balls. Bake at 350° for 15 to 20 minutes or until golden brown. Serve warm.

SWEDISH MEATBALLS I
Jody Dimitriou

20 lb. hamburger
10 lb. Italian sausage
20 c. uncooked quick oatmeal
20 eggs, beaten
½ Tbsp. salt
½ Tbsp. brown sugar
5 tsp. pepper

5 tsp. allspice
5 tsp. nutmeg
3 tsp. ginger
3 tsp. cloves
20 env. gravy mix
20 c. cream

Combine hamburger, sausage, uncooked oatmeal, eggs, salt, brown sugar, pepper, allspice, nutmeg, ginger, and cloves; mix thoroughly. Shape into 1 inch balls. Bake at 350° for 15 minutes; turn meatballs so they brown evenly on all sides. Bake 5 to 10 minutes more. Prepare gravy according to package directions; add cream to gravy. Pour over meatballs; return to oven to heat through. Serves approximately 100.

SWEDISH MEATBALLS II
Mary Kostyun

3 slices bread, crumbled
1 Tbsp. instant minced onion
1½ tsp. salt
¼ tsp. pepper
¼ tsp. nutmeg
¾ c. milk

2 lb. meatloaf mixture
4 Tbsp. butter or margarine
2 Tbsp. flour
1 can condensed beef broth
1 c. light cream

In a large bowl, combine bread, onion, salt, pepper, nutmeg, and milk; let stand 10 minutes. Add meatloaf mixture; mix until well blended. Form into

1½ inch balls; brown in butter or margarine in a large fry pan. Remove with slotted spoon, placing them in a 10 cup baking dish. Add flour to drippings in fry pan; blend well. Cook, stirring constantly, until bubbly. Stir in beef broth and cream. Continue cooking and stirring until sauce thickens and boils 1 minute. Pour sauce over meatballs. Bake at 325° for 30 minutes.

SWEDISH MEATBALLS III
Julie Sadowitz

4 eggs, slightly beaten
2 c. milk
1 c. packaged dry bread crumbs
4 Tbsp. butter or margarine
1 c. finely chopped onions
2 lb. ground chuck
½ lb. ground pork
2 (10½ oz.) cans condensed beef broth (undiluted)

1 c. light cream
¼ tsp. allspice
¼ tsp. nutmeg
¼ tsp. ground cardamom
⅓ c. flour
¼ tsp. pepper
Salt
Dill weed to taste

In a large bowl, combine the eggs, milk, and dry bread crumbs. In two tablespoons of hot butter, in large skillet, saute onion until soft. Lift out with slotted spoon; add to bread crumb mixture along with ground meats, 3 teaspoons salt, ½ teaspoon dill weed, allspice, nutmeg, and cardamom. Mix well to combine. Refrigerate one hour. Shape chilled mixture into 60 meatballs. Preheat oven to 325°F. In remaining hot butter, saute meatballs about one-third at a time until browned all over. Remove to two 2 quart casseroles.

Remove skillet from heat. Pour off all but ¼ cup drippings; stir in flour, ½ teaspoon salt, and the pepper. Gradually stir in beef broth. Bring to boil, stirring constantly. Add cream and 1 teaspoon dill weed. Pour over meatballs in casseroles. Bake, covered, 30 minutes. Garnish with fresh dill if desired. Yields approximately 20 servings.

Can also bake meatballs in large baking pan; add hot bouillon (2 cups). Bake at 350° about 30 minutes or until broth is absorbed.

BEEF BOURGUIGNON I
Mildred Charnetsky

2 Tbsp. vegetable oil
5 medium onions, sliced
2 lb. lean beef cubes
1½ Tbsp. flour
½ tsp. pepper
½ tsp. salt

1 tsp. thyme
1 c. dry wine
½ c. bouillon
Additional wine
½ lb. fresh mushrooms
Additional bouillon

Heat oil in large, heavy skillet. Add onion; cook until tender. Remove onions; set aside. Saute beef in skillet until browned. Sprinkle meat with flour mixed with seasonings. Add bouillon and wine (1 part bouillon to 2 parts wine) as necessary to keep beef barely covered. Return onions to skillet after meat has cooked 1½ to 2 hours. Add mushrooms; stir. Cook 30 minutes longer. Again, add more bouillon and wine if necessary. Sauce should be thick and dark brown.

BEEF BOURGUIGNON II
Josephine Vimislik

2 slices bacon
1½ lb. 1 inch beef cubes
1 (10½ oz.) can condensed
  golden mushroom soup
½ c. burgundy or other dry red
  wine

1 large clove garlic, minced
1 medium bay leaf
2 Tbsp. chopped parsley
12 small whole white onions

In a large, heavy pan, cook bacon until crisp; remove bacon. In the bacon drippings, brown beef cubes; add soup, wine, garlic, bay leaf, parsley, and bacon. Cover; cook over low heat 1 hour, stirring occasionally. Add onions; cook 1 more hour or until meat is tender and onions are of desired doneness. Remove bay leaf.

CARNE ASADO (SPANISH ROAST BEEF, MARINATED)
Evelyn Kanazawich

6 lb. boneless rib roast
1 Tbsp. salt
1 tsp. black pepper
1 tsp. paprika
3 cloves garlic, minced
1 c. dry red wine
½ c. red wine vinegar

¼ c. olive oil
2 c. chopped onion
1 c. chopped green pepper
2 c. peeled and diced tomatoes
1 bay leaf
½ c. sliced, stuffed olives

Place roast in a large glass bowl or dish. Combine salt, pepper, paprika, and garlic; rub into meat on all sides of roast. Combine wine and vinegar; pour over roast. Marinate 24 hours in refrigerator, turning meat occasionally. Just before roasting meat, drain marinade from meat, saving the marinade. Pat meat dry with paper towels. Heat olive oil in roasting pan over medium heat. Brown roast on all sides. Add onion, green pepper, tomatoes, and bay leaf; pour reserved marinade over roast. Place in a 300° oven; roast to desired doneness. Transfer to a heated platter; let stand 15 minutes before carving.

In the meantime, remove bay leaf from roasting pan; discard it. Pour all drippings from pan into a saucepan. Pour a small amount of boiling water into the roasting pan to remove bits which may have stuck to the bottom; pour this into the saucepan with the drippings. This will be the gravy; if lumpy, force through a sieve or puree it in a blender. Add the sliced olives to the gravy; heat and serve on the side.

BEEF CHOUFLEUR

Mary Ann Klish

1 lb. round steak, cut into ½
   inch squares
1 small head cauliflower
2 Tbsp. butter
1 green pepper, cut into pieces

¼ c. soy sauce
1 clove garlic, minced
2 Tbsp. cornstarch
½ tsp. sugar
1½ c. beef broth

Separate cauliflower into flowerets. Brown meat in butter for 5 minutes. Add soy sauce, cauliflower, peppers, and garlic. Stir to coat vegetables with sauce. Cover pan and simmer about 10 minutes. Blend cornstarch, sugar, and beef broth. Add to meat mixture. Cook, stirring constantly, until thickened. Serve over hot rice.

CHUCK ROAST WITH MUSHROOMS AND WINE

Olga Tarcha

4 lb. chuck roast (2 inches
   thick)
¼ tsp. pepper
Salt to taste

1 (¾ oz.) env. mushroom gravy
   mix
½ c. dry red wine

Place roast on 2 sheets of aluminum foil; sprinkle with pepper, salt, and mushroom gravy mix. Pour wine over meat. Wrap and seal tight by folding ends of foil so contents won't leak out. Place on grill over hot charcoal; cook 2 to 3 hours. Could be roasted in covered roaster for 2 hours or more at 350° in an oven.

REUBEN STYLE HAMBURGERS

Julia Malewiacki

1 lb. ground beef
Prepared mustard
1 c. drained sauerkraut

4 slices Swiss cheese
8 slices toasted rye bread

Shape beef into 4 oval patties about ¼ inch thick and spread each patty with mustard. Broil for 3 minutes on one side only. Spread a layer of sauerkraut on each patty. Top with a slice of cheese and broil until cheese is melted. Serve between slices of toasted rye bread. Makes 4 servings.

LEE'S CHINESE BEEF WITH PEPPERS   Helen Chubinsky

1½ Tbsp. oil
1 clove garlic, crushed
1 lb. beef (round or sirloin
    steak frozen)
1 tsp. salt
Pepper to taste
1 chicken bouillon cube

1 c. hot water
2 Tbsp. corn starch
1 Tbsp. soy sauce
2 Tbsp. water
1 c. green peppers, sliced
    lengthwise
¼ tsp. ground ginger

Heat oil and garlic; discard garlic when it turns brown. When beef is partly defrosted, cut in small, thin pieces and fry a few minutes. Add salt and pepper. Add bouillon cube dissolved in hot water and continue to cook a few minutes. Combine cornstarch, soy sauce, and 2 tablespoons water; add to beef and cook until sauce thickens, stirring constantly. Add peppers and ginger. Heat thoroughly. Serve over hot steamed rice.

MEAT LOAF   Anna Chyl

2 lb. ground beef
½ c. chopped onion
1 clove garlic, minced
1 Tbsp. minced parsley
Salt and pepper
1 small green pepper, chopped

1 c. applesauce
1 egg
8 slices bread, crumbled
Catsup to cover top of loaf
¼ c. flour to cover

Combine all ingredients except catsup and flour; mix well. Make a loaf and roll in flour to cover. Put loaf in pan and cover meat loaf with catsup. Bake at 350° for 1½ hours.

BEST MEAT LOAF   Mary Charnetsky

1 egg, beaten
¾ c. milk
1 tsp. poultry seasoning
1½ tsp. salt
Dash of pepper

2 c. soft bread crumbs
1 onion, minced
1 lb. ground pork shoulder
1 lb. ground veal shoulder
5 to 6 strips bacon

Preheat oven to 350°. In mixing bowl, combine egg, milk, poultry seasoning, salt, pepper, and bread crumbs. Let stand for 5 minutes. Add onion and meat; mix well. Line an 8x5x3 inch loaf pan with bacon strips across the width of pan. Pack mixture into bacon lined pan. Bake 1½ hours. Remove from oven and invert meat loaf onto a baking sheet. Return meat loaf to a hot 400° oven for 10 minutes to crisp bacon. Serves 6 to 8 people.

MY MAN'S MEATLOAF

Evelyn Kanazawich

4 to 5 slices bread
3 lb. ground beef
¼ c. instant dried onion
¼ c. ketchup
2 Tbsp. prepared mustard

2 to 3 Tbsp. horseradish
1 Tbsp. Worcestershire sauce
1 to 2 Tbsp. mushroom powder
1 egg
Salt and pepper

Quickly pass bread under running water; squeeze out excess water. Tear apart into small pieces and place in a bowl with remaining ingredients; mix well. Place mixture in a baking dish. Bake at 400° for ½ hour, then cover with your favorite tomato sauce and bake ½ hour more.

SPECIAL MEAT LOAF

Millie Finch

1½ lb. lean ground beef
½ c. soft bread crumbs
2 eggs
1 pkg. Italian salad dressing
    mix
½ c. water

½ tsp. curry powder
2 c. herb Stove Top stuffing mix
½ c. mayonnaise
½ c. finely chopped celery and
    leaves

Combine first four ingredients. Press into a rectangle on foil. Bring water to a boil; add next four ingredients, tossing well. Place in a strip down center of meat rectangle. Ease meat from one side to center, then do same with other side to center. Refrigerate. Flip, placing seam side down in baking dish. Cover. Bake at 350° for 1 hour. Serves 6.

AUTUMN GOLD BEEF POT ROAST

Ann Dobransky

¼ c. flour
2 tsp. salt
¼ tsp. pepper
3 to 4 lb. beef arm or blade
    roast
2 Tbsp. cooking oil
¼ c. water
½ tsp. oregano

¼ tsp. celery seed
½ c. orange juice concentrate
1¼ c. water
4 medium size sweet potatoes,
    pared and halved lengthwise
8 small onions, peeled and
    halved lengthwise
1 Tbsp. brown sugar

Combine flour, salt, and pepper. Dredge meat in seasoned flour, reserving remaining flour mixture for gravy. Brown meat in oil; pour off drippings. Add ¼ cup water, oregano, and celery seed. Cover tightly; cook slowly 2½ hours. Combine orange juice concentrate and 1¼ cups water; add 1¼ cups of this mixture to meat. Add potatoes and onions. Cover tightly; cook slowly 1 hour or until meat and vegetables are tender. Remove meat and vegetables to heated platter. Blend reserved seasoned flour with orange juice and brown sugar;

gradually add to the cooking liquid, stirring constantly until thickened. Serve with pot roast. Serves 6 to 8.

DEANO'S ROAST BEEF

Pani Lawryk
Marianne Thies

1 beef roast
1 can beer
1 can beef broth

1 tsp. garlic
1 jar chopped Greek peppers
   with juice

Place roast in crock pot on HIGH setting. Pour ingredients on top. Cook for 8 hours until meat falls apart. Serve on kaiser buns with a big dill pickle.

Also may be done in oven. Place in 9x13 inch pan, covered. Bake at 325° until meat falls apart.

SIMPLE SALISBURY STEAK

Charles Sarnoski

1 (10½ oz.) can cream of
   mushroom soup
1 lb. ground beef
½ c. dry bread crumbs

1 egg, beaten
¼ c. chopped onion
1½ c. fresh mushrooms, sliced

In a bowl, mix thoroughly ¼ cup soup, beef, bread crumbs, egg, and onion. Shape into 6 patties. In a skillet, over medium-high heat, cook patties, a few at a time, until browned on both sides. Spoon off fat. Stir in remaining soup (mixed with dry wine if desired) and mushrooms. Stir a few minutes. Return patties to pan. Reduce heat to low. Cover and simmer 20 minutes or until done. Turn patties occasionally during cooking. Yields 6 servings.

BARBECUED SHORT RIBS

Mary Ann Klish

3 to 4 lb. lean short ribs, cut
   into serving size pieces
1 Tbsp. flour
½ c. flour
1 tsp. salt

Pepper to taste
½ c. barbecue sauce
½ c. chopped green pepper
½ c. chopped onion
½ c. chopped celery

Trim excess fat from ribs. Combine ½ cup flour with salt and pepper; rub into ribs. Shake 1 tablespoon flour into a Reynolds oven bag; place in a 9x13 inch pan. Pour barbecue sauce into bag; mix with the flour. Add green pepper, onion, and celery; mix with the barbecue sauce. Place ribs in bag with sauce; follow cooking directions which are given with the oven bags. It will take about 2 to 2½ hours at 350°.

DELICIOUS SHORT RIBS

Olga Tarcha

3 lb. beef short ribs
1½ tsp. salt
¼ tsp. pepper
2 medium onions, sliced
½ tsp. dry mustard
2 Tbsp. lemon juice
2 bay leaves

1½ c. water
¼ c. brown sugar
1 (10 oz.) pkg. frozen lima beans
3 carrots, cut in strips
1 Tbsp. flour
½ c. water

Brown ribs in own fat; pour off drippings. Season with salt and pepper; add onions, dry mustard, lemon juice, bay leaves, and 1½ cups water. Cover lightly; cook slowly 2 hours. Add brown sugar, lima beans, and carrots; cook 45 minutes longer. Discard bay leaves; remove meat and vegetables to a warm platter. Combine flour with ½ cup water; dissolve flour so there are no lumps. Add this to the liquid remaining in the pan where ribs were cooked. Stir constantly while adding and cooking to make a nice smooth gravy. Pour over meat on the platter. Serves 4 to 6.

SWEET AND SOUR SHORT RIBS

Anna Chyl

4 lb. beef short ribs
2 tsp. salt
4 medium onions, chopped

6 tsp. flour
⅛ tsp. pepper
4 Tbsp. shortening

Sauce:

3 c. water
4 tsp. Worcestershire sauce
5 Tbsp. vinegar
3 Tbsp. brown sugar

1 tsp. chili powder
⅔ c. chili sauce
1 tsp. dry mustard

Brown short ribs in seasoned flour and shortening. Combine sauce ingredients and pour over meat. Cover and simmer 2½ hours in heavy kettle. Serve over wide noodles.

STEAK AU POIVRE (PEPPER STEAK)

Carol Wasylko

⅛ c. fresh peppercorns
4 individual steaks, trimmed
2 to 3 Tbsp. oil
Salt

3 Tbsp. butter
¼ c. cognac
½ c. heavy cream

Crush peppercorns using bottom of heavy skillet; coat both sides of steaks with crushed peppercorns. Let stand at room temperature 15 minutes. Heat oil in skillet. Saute steaks over medium-high heat; salt. Remove steaks from pan. Discard drippings. Add butter to pan; return steaks to pan. Add cognac; ignite. Allow to cook until flames cease. Remove steaks to serving platter; keep warm. Add cream to pan over medium-high heat, stirring with a wooden spoon while heating. Cream will boil and thicken. Add 1 teaspoon cognac and salt to taste.

FLANK STEAK ROSÉ

Carol Wasylko

1 to 1½ lb. flank steak
¾ c. rosé wine
1 large clove garlic, crushed

1 tsp. salt
1 tsp. pepper
¼ tsp. dried dill or rosemary

Place meat in a medium size bowl. Combine remaining ingredients; pour over meat. Cover. Refrigerate 1 to 2 hours, turning meat frequently. Drain, saving marinade. Brush meat with oil; broil or BBQ quickly until rare or medium rare. Cut meat into thin slices, diagonally across grain of meat. Add 1 or 2 tablespoons butter to reserved marinade; bring to a boil. Spoon over meat.

STUFFED FLANK STEAK

Evelyn Kanazawich

2 Tbsp. butter or margarine
1 medium onion, chopped
3 c. soft bread crumbs
½ tsp. poultry seasoning
½ tsp. salt
Dash of pepper

3 Tbsp. hot water
1 egg, well beaten
2 lb. flank steak
2 Tbsp. oil
½ c. boiling water

Melt butter in large skillet; add onion, cooking until golden brown. Add next 6 ingredients; mix well. Spread on steak; roll up like jelly roll. Tie securely with string. Heat oil in skillet. Season steak with salt and pepper; brown in skillet in heated oil. When brown, remove from pan to baking dish; add the boiling water. Cover. Bake at 325° for 1½ hours or until tender.

MARINATED STEAK

Jeanne Sankowski

1 (3 lb. - 1½ inch thick) sirloin
   steak
⅔ c. oil
⅓ c. vinegar
½ tsp. salt
½ tsp. garlic salt
½ tsp. sugar

½ tsp. crumbled thyme
¼ tsp. pepper
2 medium onions, sliced into
   rings
3 Tbsp. butter
1 (6 oz.) can whole mushrooms,
   drained

At room temperature, slash fatty edge of steak to keep from curling. Place steak in deep dish. Pierce with fork. In small bowl, combine oil, vinegar, salt, garlic salt, sugar, thyme, and pepper. Pour over steak and let stand for 1 hour. Brush hot grill with oil to prevent sticking. Place steak 6 inches above coals.

Pour marinade into a deep cup. Grill steak. Brush with marinade and turn. While grilling steak, melt butter in a frying pan on edge of grill and saute onions until soft. Add mushrooms and leftover marinade. Cover. Remove from grill and keep warm. Place steak in platter and pour mushroom-onion mixture over steak. Let stand for 5 minutes before slicing.

STUFFED ROUND STEAK
Anne Girnis

1 to 1½ lb. hamburger
1 large onion, diced
¼ c. chopped parsley
Salt and pepper

1 (4 oz.) can chopped
   mushrooms, drained
2 Tbsp. Gravy Master
1 large round steak

In a large bowl, combine all ingredients except steak and Gravy Master; mix well. Spread mixture on the steak. Roll up the steak and tie with string to hold it together. Brown the steak; place in a baking pan or dish to which you have added a small amount of water and 2 tablespoons Gravy Master. Bake, covered, at 350° until tender. Serve with mashed potatoes and gravy made from drippings.

STEAK SAN MARCO
Evelyn Kanazawich

2 lb. chuck steak (1 inch thick),
   cut in serving size pieces
1 env. dry onion soup mix
1 (1 lb.) can Italian peeled
   tomatoes

1 tsp. oregano
Fresh ground pepper and garlic
   powder to taste
2 Tbsp. oil
2 Tbsp. wine vinegar

In a large skillet, arrange meat; cover with onion soup mix and tomatoes. Sprinkle with oregano, pepper, garlic powder, oil, and vinegar. Simmer, covered, for 1½ hours or until meat is tender.

ITALIAN HUNTER STEW
Mary Ponas

½ c. flour
1 tsp. salt
2 lb. cubed chuck
3 Tbsp. oil
3 large onions, chopped
2 cloves garlic, chopped

1 large can tomato puree
½ c. water (add more if needed)
1 tsp. oregano
½ c. chopped parsley
⅓ c. Parmesan cheese
½ lb. macaroni or noodles

Combine flour and salt in a bag; shake to mix. Place meat in bag with flour; shake to thoroughly coat meat. In a large pot, brown meat in oil; remove meat. Add onion and garlic; saute until light brown. Add meat, tomato puree, water, oregano, parsley, and cheese. Simmer until meat is tender, about 2 hours. Serve over macaroni or noodles.

BEEF STROGANOFF

Mary Kostyun

1½ lb. round steak
1 onion, chopped
3 Tbsp. shortening
2 heaping spoons flour
1 c. sour cream

3 c. water
4 Tbsp. catsup
½ lb. mushrooms (fresh or
canned)

Pound steak with knife or glass. Fry onions until golden brown. Set aside. Cut steak in small strips and brown in shortening. Add water and cook about an hour or until meat is tender. Add seasonings to taste. Add catsup. Take about 1 cup of liquid from pan and slowly add 1 cup sour cream and flour. Add mushrooms and fried onions. Add mixture to meat and stir until heated through. More water can be added if needed. Serve over noodles or rice.

BAKED CHICKEN

Ann Dobransky

Chicken breasts, legs
1 pkg. Lipton onion soup mix

1 can cream of mushroom soup
1 c. sour cream

Wash chicken and place in pan. Combine remaining ingredients and pour over chicken. Bake at 325° for 1½ to 2 hours.

BARBECUED BROILERS

Evelyn Kanazawich

2 (2 lb.) broilers, halved or cut
up
1 c. oil
1 pt. cider vinegar

3 tsp. salt
1 Tbsp. poultry seasoning
1 tsp. pepper
2 eggs

Clean broilers; place in shallow pan or baking dish. Combine remaining ingredients, blending well. Pour over chicken. Marinate at least 2 hours. Drain marinade from chicken, reserving the marinade. Place chicken on grill over medium hot coals, skin side up. Grill until well-done, turning and basting with marinade frequently.

A MAN'S BARBECUED CHICKEN

Sophia Malowicky

2 (2½ to 3½ lb.) quartered
chickens
3 large sliced onions
1 to 2 tsp. salt
¼ tsp. pepper
1½ c. tomato juice
¼ tsp. cayenne pepper

¼ tsp. dry mustard
4½ tsp. Worcestershire sauce
¾ c. vinegar
1 tsp. sugar
3 minced cloves garlic
3 Tbsp. butter, margarine, or oil

In a saucepan, combine salt, pepper, tomato juice, cayenne pepper, mustard, Worcestershire sauce, vinegar, sugar, garlic, and butter. Simmer, uncovered, for 10 minutes and refrigerate. About 2¼ hours before serving, arrange chicken, skin side up, in a single layer in a shallow, open pan. Sprinkle lightly with salt and pepper. Add a little water to bottom of pan. Arrange onions on chicken to cover. Bake, uncovered, at 350° for ½ hour; turn chicken and bake ½ hour.

Remove chicken from oven. Pour off all but ¾ cup liquid. Turn chicken, skin side up, and pour warmed barbecue sauce over chicken. Bake 1 hour or until tender, basting with sauce. Yield: 4 to 6 servings.

CHICKEN BREASTS

Mary Ann Klish
Rose Klodowski

4 to 6 chicken breasts
  (boneless)
1 pkg. Pepperidge seasoned
  stuffing
1 (16 oz.) sour cream onion dip

1 tsp. paprika
1 tsp. salt
½ tsp. celery salt
½ tsp. pepper
1 (4 oz.) stick margarine

Combine sour cream, paprika, salt, celery salt, and pepper. Dip chicken breasts in mixture. Roll in seasoned stuffing; cover well. Place in buttered casserole. Refrigerate 6 to 8 hours or overnight. Melt 1 stick of margarine and pour over chicken. Bake, uncovered, at 350° for 55 minutes.

CHICKEN AND RICE

Marie Pufky

1 c. rice (uncooked)
1 can cream of chicken soup

1 can milk
Chicken pieces

Add all ingredients to small roaster or cake pan. Season pieces of chicken with salt, pepper, and parsley. Lay pieces of chicken on top of rice mixture. Cover with enough water to cover chicken. Bake, covered, at 350° for 1 hour.

CHICKEN AND SAUERKRAUT

Charles Sarnoski

1 or 2 whole chickens
1 (15 oz.) can sauerkraut

Melted butter
Salt and pepper

Rinse sauerkraut. Place chicken in a roasting pan. Stuff with rinsed sauerkraut. Brush chickens with melted butter; salt and pepper to taste. Cover and bake for 1 hour and 15 minutes. Uncover; bake 15 minutes longer.

Extra sauerkraut can be added to the pan with a little salt and pepper.

CHEESED CHICKEN KIEV

Anna Chyl

¼ c. butter, softened
1 (3 oz.) pkg. cream cheese
½ tsp. salt
½ tsp. instant minced onion
½ tsp. salad herbs
½ tsp. lemon pepper seasoning

4 c. shortening
4 double chicken breasts, split
¼ c. flour
2 eggs, beaten slightly with 1
   Tbsp. water and ½ tsp. salt
1 c. fine bread crumbs

Cream butter, cheese, and seasonings together; place in freezer while preparing chicken breasts. Skin breasts; split and remove bone. Flatten between waxed paper by pounding with the edge of a saucer or a rolling pin. Divide chilled butter-cheese into 8 parts. Place a spoonful on widest side of each breast; roll up, folding ends to hold filling firmly. Secure with wooden toothpicks. Dip rolled breasts in flour, then in beaten egg and then bread crumbs, coating well. Melt shortening at 370° in electric fry pan. With tongs put chicken in hot fat; reduce temperature to 360°. Fry chicken until a deep brown, turning often.

ONION-TOPPED CHICKEN

Emily Klish

4 boneless chicken breast
   halves
1 (10¾ oz.) can cream of potato
   soup (undiluted)
1 c. sour cream

1 (4 oz.) can mushroom pieces
   and stems, drained
1 (2.8 oz.) can French fried
   onions

Place chicken in greased 9 inch square baking dish. In a bowl, combine soup, sour cream, and mushrooms; spread over chicken. Bake, uncovered, at 350° for 1¼ hours. Sprinkle with French fried onions; bake another 10 minutes.

CHICKEN BREASTS WITH BACON

Anna Chyl

12 chicken breast halves
   (boneless and skinless), salted
8 oz. cream cheese
2 bunches green onions,
   chopped

24 slices bacon
Toothpicks

Cream together cream cheese and chopped green onion; form into 12 walnut size balls. Wrap half a chicken breast around each cream cheese ball. Wrap 2 slices of bacon around each chicken-cream cheese roll, securing with toothpicks. (Cover as much of chicken as possible with bacon.) Broil chicken-bacon rolls on a rack about 6 to 8 inches from broiler unit. Place a drip pan under rack. Turn chicken breasts occasionally; broil about 30 minutes or until bacon is well done.

CHICKEN WITH SWISS CHEESE

Dorothy Skellett

8 split, boneless chicken breasts
4 slices Swiss cheese
1 (10¾ oz.) can cream of
   chicken soup
⅓ c. butter, melted

1 (4 oz.) can mushrooms,
   drained
1 c. plain bread crumbs
¼ c. wine

Place chicken on bottom of an 8x12 inch pan. Place cheese on chicken. Combine soup with wine; set aside. Place sliced mushrooms on top of cheese. Pour soup-wine mixture over chicken. Sprinkle bread crumbs over chicken; drizzle with the melted butter. Bake, uncovered, at 350° for 55 minutes.

IMPERIAL CHICKEN

Charles Sarnoski

Approx. 6 pieces of chicken,
   skin removed (leg, thighs, or
   breasts)
¼ lb. margarine, melted
1 c. finely crushed bread
   crumbs

1 clove fresh garlic, minced
Salt and pepper
½ c. Parmesan cheese
Parsley flakes (optional)

Mix bread crumbs, Parmesan cheese, and garlic. Salt and pepper to taste. Dip chicken pieces in margarine, then coat with crumb mixture. Place on cookie sheet or baking pan. Pour remaining margarine over. Bake at 350°, uncovered, for 1 hour and 15 minutes. Turn once while cooking.

CHICKEN LIVERS

Julie Sadowitz

1½ c. chicken livers
½ c. canned lima beans
1 stick butter
½ c. chopped green pepper
½ c. chopped green onion

½ c. sliced white onion
2 Tbsp. mushrooms
¼ c. sliced pimento
1 tsp. salt
1 dash of cayenne pepper

Remember that the chicken livers must be fresh to obtain the best results. Cut them into the natural halves. Heat the butter in a heavy 9 inch skillet. Add the green pepper, green onion, and white onion, then add the chicken livers and saute until the livers are browned. It will take from 8 to 10 minutes. Add the mushrooms, pimento, and lima beans. Dust with salt and cayenne pepper. Heat through, tossing occasionally. Serves 4.

CHICKEN MARENGO

2 lb. fryer chicken, disjointed
3 Tbsp. oil
1 (10¾ oz.) can tomato soup
1 (10¾ oz.) can golden
   mushroom soup

1 (4 oz.) can mushrooms
16 small onions

Fry chicken in oil until golden - about 15 minutes. Drain fat. Drain chicken on paper towel. Place chicken in heavy skillet. Combine tomato soup, golden mushroom soup, mushrooms, and onions. Pour over chicken. Cover; cook over low heat for about 45 minutes or until tender. Season to taste. Serve over rice or noodles. Will serve 3 to 4 people.

CHICKEN IN MUSHROOM SAUCE   Carol Williams

Chicken parts
3 Tbsp. oil
1 can cream of mushroom soup
1 can water
¼ c. white wine (optional)

1 onion, sliced
1 chicken bouillon cube
Pepper to taste
1 Tbsp. parsley flakes

In a large skillet, brown chicken in oil on both sides. Combine soup, water, wine, and bouillon cube. Pour over browned chicken. Pepper to taste. Place sliced onion and parsley on top of chicken. Cover and simmer one hour.

CHICKEN WITH MUSHROOM CREAM SAUCE   Emily A. Klish

2 pkg. chicken tenders or
   skinless, boneless chicken
   breast halves
2 Tbsp. butter or margarine
1 (10¾ oz.) condensed cream of
   mushroom soup (undiluted)
1 c. sour cream onion dip

1 (4 oz.) can mushroom stems
   and pieces, drained
¼ c. white wine
½ tsp. garlic powder
½ tsp. salt
½ tsp. pepper
Hot cooked noodles or rice

In a skillet, melt butter or margarine; brown chicken on both sides. Drain. Place in a greased 7x11x2 inch baking dish. In a bowl, combine soup, sour cream, mushrooms, wine, garlic powder, salt, and pepper; pour over chicken. Bake, uncovered, at 375° for 20 minutes or until juices run clear. Serve chicken and sauce over noodles or rice. Serves 4.

CHICKEN NAPOLI

Evelyn Kanazawich

½ c. oil or melted margarine
1 env. Italian salad dressing
  mix

⅓ c. lime juice
1 broiler-fryer, cut into serving
  size pieces

Combine oil, salad dressing mix, and lime juice; mix well. Brush both sides of chicken pieces with the oil mixture. Grill about 6 inches from source of heat, brushing with oil mixture and turning frequently. Cook about 40 to 50 minutes or until tender.

GOLDEN CHICKEN NUGGETS

Marie Pufky

4 whole chicken breasts, boned
  and skinned
½ c. fine bread crumbs
¼ c. Parmesan cheese
2 tsp. Accent

1 tsp. salt
1 tsp. thyme
1 tsp. basil
½ c. melted butter

Cut each breast into 12 pieces. Combine all ingredients. Dip each piece of chicken into melted butter and then into crunch mixture. Place on ungreased cookie sheet. Bake at 400° for 15 minutes or until brown. Serve hot or cold. Makes 4 dozen.

OVEN CHICKEN

Celia Matias

1 broiler fryer chicken, cut up
2 Tbsp. oil
2 Tbsp. white wine vinegar
¼ tsp. garlic salt
1 c. Bisquick mix
1 tsp. salt

1 tsp. paprika
¼ tsp. white pepper
¼ tsp. celery salt
¼ c. shortening
¼ c. butter

Wash and dry chicken. Marinate chicken in mixture of oil, vinegar, and garlic salt for ½ hour; drain. Coat chicken with mixture of Bisquick, salt, paprika, pepper, and celery salt. Melt shortening and butter in baking dish. Lay chicken pieces in dish. Bake at 425° for about 1 hour.

OVEN BARBECUED CHICKEN

Genevieve Sadowitz

1 (3 lb.) frying chicken
2 Tbsp. olive oil
¼ c. chopped onion
1 tsp. Worcestershire sauce
1 Tbsp. brown sugar

½ tsp. salt
¼ tsp. paprika
2 Tbsp. lemon juice
1 Tbsp. burgundy wine
1 c. chili sauce

Cut chicken into serving size pieces; set aside. In a saucepan, saute onion, in olive oil for about 10 minutes or until tender; stir in Worcestershire sauce, brown sugar, and salt. Mix well. Add paprika, lemon juice, wine, and chili sauce. Simmer over low heat for 15 minutes, stirring to keep mixture well blended. Brush chicken pieces with some olive oil; arrange in a shallow baking pan. Place in a 375° oven; bake about 45 minutes, turning once or until lightly browned. Pour sauce over chicken. Bake about 45 minutes more or until chicken is done.

CHICKEN PAPRIKASH

Julia Dudik

1 (3 lb.) frying chicken, cut up
3 to 4 Tbsp. butter or
  margarine
½ c. water
3 Tbsp. paprika

1 small onion, chopped fine
¼ tsp. pepper
1½ tsp. salt
3 to 4 Tbsp. flour
1½ c. milk

Fry chicken pieces in the butter or margarine until browned. Add all the ingredients, except flour, milk, and ½ teaspoon salt, to the chicken in the pot. Cover pot; simmer until chicken is done. Remove chicken from pot. Blend flour with milk so that it is very smooth, no lumps. Add the milk-flour mixture to the drippings in the pot, stirring while adding with heat on medium; add the remaining ½ teaspoon salt. Cook until the gravy bubbles. If too thick, add milk until desired consistency. Put chicken back in pot with gravy. Coat all chicken with the gravy. Serve with hot mashed potatoes.

POULETTE PARISIENNE

Carol Wasylko

2 lb. chicken
1 Tbsp. shortening
1 (10¾ oz.) can cream of
  mushroom soup
⅛ tsp. dill

1 (16 oz.) can stewed tomatoes
Generous dashes of crushed
  basil and parsley
1 (9 oz.) pkg. frozen artichoke
  hearts, cooked and drained

In a large skillet, brown chicken in shortening; drain fat from pan. Add soup, tomatoes, and seasonings. Cover. Cook over low heat until chicken is tender. Add artichokes; heat through. Serves 4.

Note: For a gourmet touch, add ½ cup cooking sherry with the soup and tomatoes.

PARTY CHICKEN

Jeanne Sankowski

8 chicken breasts, skinned and
  deboned
8 slices smoked bacon
2 (3 oz.) pkg. chipped beef

1 can undiluted cream of
  mushroom soup
½ pt. sour cream

Roll each chicken breast and wrap with smoked bacon. Spread the chipped beef in a greased baking dish. Arrange chicken over the beef. Combine soup and sour cream and spoon mixture over chicken. Bake at 275° for 3 hours. Serve over wild rice.

PATIO BROILED CHICKEN

Lidia Madejchyk Cox

2 (2 lb.) chickens
1 c. salad oil
⅓ c. lemon juice
3 Tbsp. soy sauce

1 clove garlic, minced
1 tsp. Accent
½ tsp. salt
¼ tsp. pepper

Break drumsticks, thigh, and wing joints so birds will stay flat during broiling. Combine oil, lemon juice, soy sauce, garlic, Accent, salt, and pepper for marinade. Marinate chicken at least 4 or 5 hours, but better overnight, turning occasionally. Place chicken on grill with bones side nearest heat. Broil slowly 20 to 30 minutes; turn and brown skin sides. Baste occasionally with marinade. Cook about 30 minutes or until tender. May also be broiled in oven. Yield: 4 servings.

CHICKEN PICCATA

Jean Klodowski Geresi

1½ lb. chicken
5 Tbsp. butter
2 Tbsp. oil
Flour
Salt

Pepper
3 Tbsp. lemon juice
2 Tbsp. minced fresh parsley
2 Tbsp. dry white wine

Pound chicken thin and cut into small serving pieces. Dredge chicken in flour, shaking off excess. Heat 3 tablespoons butter and oil in a skillet. Add a few pieces of meat at a time after the fat starts foaming. Brown quickly on both sides about 2 minutes. When chicken is done, remove to a warm platter and salt and pepper to taste. Remove skillet from heat; add lemon juice and wine to the pan to deglaze. Swirl in remaining butter. Add parsley. Return chicken to the sauce and heat through very briefly. Garnish with lemon slices and chopped parsley.

CHICKEN WITH POTATOES IN TOMATO SAUCE

Julia Dudik

3 lb. frying chicken, cut-up
3 to 4 Tbsp. butter
2 small onions, chopped
1 clove garlic
1 green pepper, chopped

1 (8 oz.) can tomato sauce
Salt and pepper to taste
6 to 7 medium potatoes, peeled
   and cubed

In a chicken fryer, brown chicken in butter. Add one chopped onion, clove of garlic, and ¼ of the green pepper. When all are lightly browned, add tomato sauce, ½ can water, salt and pepper. Simmer ½ hour. When chicken is nearly done, add potatoes and remainder of green pepper and onions. Cook until potatoes are done. The gravy should be thick as most of the water boils out and potatoes thicken the sauce.

SKILLET CHICKEN

6 thin sliced chicken cutlets
   (1½ lb.)
Cooking spray
2 tsp. olive oil
2 cloves garlic, minced

1 c. sliced mushrooms
2 c. crushed tomatoes
½ c. dry red wine
½ tsp. oregano
1 tsp. basil

Coat both sides of cutlets with cooking spray; place in heated skillet. Saute on each side 2 minutes; remove from skillet. Keep warm. Add oil to skillet; saute garlic and mushrooms 5 minutes. Add crushed tomatoes, wine, oregano, and basil; cook 10 minutes. Return chicken to skillet; simmer 5 minutes. Yields 3 to 4 very low fat servings.

SKILLET CHICKEN ITALIANO

1 lb. chicken breasts, skinned
   and cut into strips
1 small can mushroom pieces,
   drained
½ c. Italian salad dressing
¼ c. chopped onion

2 Tbsp. margarine
2 c. sliced zucchini
1 large tomato, cut into wedges
½ c. cheese (American,
   Cheddar, or Muenster),
   chopped or grated

In shallow baking dish, marinate chicken and mushrooms in Italian salad dressing for 30 minutes. Drain and reserve marinade. In large skillet, cook onion in margarine until tender. Add chicken and mushrooms and cook, covered, over medium heat until chicken is tender, about 5 minutes. Add zucchini, tomatoes, and reserved marinade; cook and stir until zucchini is tender. Remove from heat; sprinkle with cheese. Cover. Let stand until cheese begins to melt. Garnish with parsley; serve.

SOUR CREAM SAUCE CHICKEN

Donna Bobrick

2 whole chicken breasts
1 (2 oz.) can mushrooms
1 can cream of mushroom soup
(undiluted)

1 (8 oz.) sour cream
Paprika

Place chicken breasts in baking dish, not overlapping. Sprinkle mushrooms on top of chicken breasts. Combine sour cream and mushroom soup and pour over chicken, covering completely. Sprinkle heavily with paprika. Bake, uncovered, at 350° for 1½ hours. Delicious served with rice.

STIR-FRY CHICKEN AND BROCCOLI

Linda Zapach

2 whole chicken breasts, cut in
pieces
2 Tbsp. soy sauce
1 Tbsp. vegetable oil
4 c. broccoli flowerets or 1 (20
oz.) pkg. frozen broccoli
Dash of garlic powder

1 (4 oz.) can mushrooms,
drained or 6 to 8 fresh
mushrooms, sliced
1 (6 oz.) can bamboo shoots
1 c. chicken broth
1 Tbsp. cornstarch
1 Tbsp. lemon juice

In a bowl, combine chicken, soy sauce, and oil. Put broccoli and ½ cup chicken broth in a wok at 300°; cook 5 minutes. Push up sides of wok. Set temperature at 375°; add chicken mixture and garlic powder. Stir-fry 3 minutes; push up sides. Add mushrooms. Cook 1 minute. Add bamboo shoots; cook 1 minute. Combine lemon juice and cornstarch with ½ cup chicken broth; stir into wok. Stir and heat until thickened, about 2 minutes. Reduce heat to warm; serve with bean sprouts, rice, or chow mein noodles.

CHICKEN TERIYAKI

Julieanne Marra

8 chicken breast halves, boned
½ c. soy sauce
½ c. sherry
½ c. burgundy wine
1 c. water

1 tsp. garlic powder
1 tsp. onion powder
1 tsp. ground ginger
⅓ c. oil

Mix all marinade ingredients well. Pour over chicken breasts and marinate overnight. Broil or grill.

CHICKEN TETRAZZINI
Anna Smyk

3 whole chicken fryer breasts
1 stalk celery
2 sprigs parsley
1 small onion, chopped
Salt and pepper to taste
1 (1 lb.) pkg. thin spaghetti
½ lb. mushrooms, sliced

¼ lb. butter
3 Tbsp. flour
2½ c. chicken broth
1 c. cream
½ Tbsp. sherry wine
Buttered bread crumbs
¾ c. Parmesan cheese

In a saucepot, simmer chicken in enough water to cover with the celery, parsley, onion, salt and pepper about 45 minutes or until tender. Remove chicken from broth when tender, saving the broth to use for the sauce. Cook spaghetti according to package directions; drain. Rinse in cold water; drain well. Saute mushrooms in butter; remove mushrooms. Stir flour into butter remaining in pan; let it bubble for 1 minute. Add 2½ cups of the chicken broth and the cream, stirring while adding; cook until thick and smooth, stirring constantly.

Shred chicken; add to thickened sauce with sherry and sauteed mushrooms. Mix well. Place cooked spaghetti in a greased casserole, pouring sauce over top; sprinkle with buttered bread crumbs, then Parmesan cheese. Bake ½ hour at 350°.

MILANO'S CHICKEN TETRAZZINI
Olga Gooley

8 oz. thin spaghetti, cooked and
    drained
2 Tbsp. melted butter
1 can cream of chicken soup
½ c. milk

2 c. cooked, cubed chicken
1 (4 oz.) can mushrooms
2 Tbsp. pimento, cut fine
3 Tbsp. minced parsley
¾ c. grated Parmesan cheese

Combine all ingredients and pour into a buttered casserole. Bake in a 400° oven for 15 minutes. Makes about 4 servings.

Optional: Two tablespoons sherry wine can be added to the above ingredients.

CHICKEN WITH TOMATO DILL SAUCE Evelyn Kanazawich

6 large tomatoes, peeled,
    seeded, and chopped
1 medium onion, chopped
⅓ c. chopped celery
1 Tbsp. chopped fresh dill
1½ tsp. salt

1 tsp. sugar
⅛ tsp. pepper
1 broiler-fryer chicken, cut in
    serving size pieces
Butter or margarine

In a medium saucepan, combine tomatoes, onion, celery, dill, salt, sugar, and pepper. Simmer for 10 minutes over medium heat. In a large skillet, brown chicken pieces in butter or margarine, then place chicken in a 2 quart casserole or small roaster. Pour sauce over chicken. Bake at 350° for 1 hour or until tender.

PORK CHOPS AND RICE BAKE

Evelyn Kanazawich
Genevieve Sadowitz

6 pork chops
2 Tbsp. shortening
1 c. uncooked rice
1 env. onion soup mix

1 (4 oz.) can sliced mushrooms
2 Tbsp. diced pimento
Hot water

In a skillet, brown pork chops in shortening. Spread rice on bottom of a 9x13x2 inch baking dish. Sprinkle all but 1 tablespoon of the onion soup mix over the rice. Drain mushrooms, reserving the liquid. Distribute mushrooms and pimento evenly over rice. Add enough hot water to reserved mushroom liquid to make 3 cups; pour over rice. Arrange browned pork chops on top of rice; sprinkle chops with the reserved tablespoon of onion soup mix. Cover lightly with foil; bake at 350° until just tender. Remove foil; bake 10 minutes more or until all liquid is absorbed by the rice.

PORK CHOPS AND STUFFING

Charles Sarnoski

4 pork chops or steaks
2 c. soft bread cubes
2 Tbsp. chopped onion
2 Tbsp. water
2 Tbsp. melted butter or
  margarine

¼ tsp. poultry seasoning
1 (10¾ oz.) can cream of
  mushroom soup
⅓ c. water

Grease bottom of fry pan with a small piece of fat cut from the chops. Brown chops over medium heat, turning once; place chops in a shallow casserole or baking pan. Mix together bread cubes, onion, melted butter, 2 tablespoons water, and seasoning. Top each chop with one-fourth of the mixture. In the fry pan used for browning the chops, combine mushroom soup with ⅓ cup water; heat. Pour over stuffing-topped chops. Bake, uncovered, at 350° for 1 hour or until chops are tender.

PEACH 'N PORK CHOP BARBEQUE

Helen Charnetsky

6 pork chops, cut 1 inch thick
1 Tbsp. shortening or oil
¼ c. brown sugar
1 tsp. cinnamon
½ tsp. cloves

1 (8 oz.) can tomato sauce
6 canned cling peach halves,
    drained (reserve)
¼ c. syrup
¼ c. cider vinegar

Brown chops in large, heavy skillet in hot fat. Combine brown sugar, cinnamon, and cloves; add to tomato sauce, syrup, and vinegar. Mix well. Sprinkle chops with salt and pepper; drain fat from pan. Place a peach half on each chop. Pour sauce over all. Simmer about 30 minutes or until pork is tender, basting while cooking.

PORK CHOPS ON CORN STUFFING

Olga Tarcha

1 qt. soft bread cubes
¼ c. chopped onion
1 tsp. salt
¼ tsp. pepper
¼ tsp. poultry seasoning
1 (12 oz.) can corn, drained
    (reserve liquid)

½ sweet pepper, chopped
1 egg, beaten
6 (¾ inch thick) pork chops,
    seasoned

Combine bread cubes, onion, salt, pepper, poultry seasoning, corn, and sweet pepper. Add enough water to the liquid drained from the corn to make ½ cup; add the liquid to beaten egg. Add to bread cube mixture; mix well. Transfer to a large, greased baking dish. In a fry pan, lightly brown seasoned chops; arrange over stuffing. Cover; bake at 350° about 45 minutes or until tender. Remove cover; bake 5 minutes longer. Serves 6.

CREAM OF MUSHROOM PORK CHOPS

Audrey Klym

150 lean pork chops
4 large containers flavored
    bread crumbs
1 doz. eggs
Salt and pepper

9 (10¾ oz.) cans cream of
    mushroom soup
1 gal. cooking oil
Milk

Bread pork chops; season with salt and pepper. Brown in a skillet in hot oil. Place 2 layers of chops in 3 large roasters; mix milk and soup (1 soup can milk per can of soup). Pour over chops. Bake at 350° for 2 hours.

Variation: One package dry onion soup can be mixed with each can of mushroom soup.

FANCY PORK CHOPS
Linda Zapach

6 pork chops
6 lemon slices
¾ c. catsup

¾ c. water
3 Tbsp. brown sugar

Brown pork chops; place in a baking dish. Place a lemon slice on each chop. In a small saucepan, combine catsup, water, and brown sugar; stir to combine thoroughly. Heat sauce, bringing it to bubble; pour over pork chops. Bake at 350° for 1 hour.

PORK CHOPS WITH ORANGE RICE
Mary Charnetsky

6 (¾ inch thick) pork chops
Salt and pepper
⅔ c. uncooked rice
¾ tsp. salt
1 tsp. granulated sugar
¼ c. raisins

1 Tbsp. grated orange rind
1½ c. boiling water
⅔ c. orange juice
3 orange slices, cut in halves
3 tsp. brown sugar

Brown chops well; drain off fat. Season with salt and pepper; set aside. In a 3 quart casserole, combine rice, salt, granulated sugar, raisins, and grated orange rind. Pour boiling water and orange juice over rice; bake, covered, at 350° for 10 minutes. Remove from oven; stir rice. Lay chops on top of rice. Top each chop with half an orange slice and ½ teaspoon brown sugar. Bake, covered, at 350° for 45 minutes or until chops are tender.

PORK CHOPS WITH ORANGE SAUCE
Charles Sarnoski

6 loin pork chops
Oil
1 Tbsp. butter or margarine
1 medium onion, diced
1 Tbsp. flour
2 bouillon cubes (beef)
1 c. hot water

½ tsp. minced parsley
1 tsp. dry mustard
1 Tbsp. lemon juice
1 c. orange juice
1 tsp. salt
½ tsp. pepper

Brown chops in oil. Remove from pan; drain grease from pan. Melt butter in the pan; add onion. Saute 5 minutes. Stir in flour; cook until it bubbles 5 minutes. Dissolve bouillon cubes in the cup of hot water, slowly, stirring constantly. Add bouillon; add to flour mixture in pan. Cook 5 minutes. Add rest of the ingredients and blend thoroughly. Return chops to the pan with liquid. Cover; cook over low heat 1 to 2 hours or until chops are tender.

STUFFED PORK CHOPS
Donna Bobrick

4 pork chops
8 toothpicks

Seasoned stuffing (prepared
commercial herb)

In a small saucepan, prepare stuffing as instructed on seasoned stuffing package. Place cooked stuffing in center of pork chop and place another pork chop on top to cover. Hold pork chops together by inserting toothpicks on both sides of stacked pork chops. Place pork chops in skillet with water lining the bottom. Bake in uncovered skillet at 350° for 1 hour and 10 minutes (35 minutes on each side). Serve with applesauce and creamed potatoes.

SPARERIBS AND SAUERKRAUT
Evelyn Kanazawich

3 lb. (or more) country style
  spareribs
Water
3 lb. sauerkraut
Caraway seeds

Small chunk salt pork, diced
1 medium onion, chopped
3 Tbsp. flour
Salt and pepper

Place ribs in a large stock pot; cover with water. Bring to boiling, removing scum as ribs are cooking. Rinse sauerkraut; set aside. Add to ribs after they have cooked 1 hour; add caraway seeds to your liking. In a fry pan, saute salt pork and onion until onion is soft; sprinkle flour over salt pork and onion in fry pan. Mix and cook until brown; add some water from the ribs, stirring constantly until you have a thick roux. Boil 1 minute; add to the ribs and sauerkraut. Cook 1 more hour. Season with salt and pepper. Canned kidney beans or dried mushrooms may be added before the final hour of cooking.

BARBEQUE SPARERIBS I
Jody Dimitriou

5 or 6 ribs
2 bouillon cubes
1 c. water
1 Tbsp. Worcestershire sauce

2 Tbsp. brown sugar
1 Tbsp. ketchup
¼ tsp. nutmeg
1 tsp. mustard

Brown ribs. Dissolve bouillon cubes in boiling water; add remaining ingredients. Bring to a boil. Simmer browned ribs in sauce 1 hour.

BARBEQUE SPARERIBS II
Julia Dudik

2 lb. spareribs, cut into 2 inch
  pieces
1 tsp. garlic powder
1½ tsp. dry mustard
½ c. sherry wine

2 Tbsp. soy sauce
3 Tbsp. vinegar
1 tsp. ginger
3 Tbsp. brown sugar

302

Brown ribs to melt off fat. Combine remaining ingredients. Place ribs in baking pan; pour sauce over ribs. Bake, covered, at 350° for 1 hour, basting every 20 minutes.

NEW YORK STYLE BARBEQUE SPARERIBS
Carol Wasylko

½ c. catsup	½ tsp. dry mustard
1½ tsp. salt	1½ Tbsp. brown sugar
¼ tsp. Tabasco sauce	½ tsp. lemon juice
½ tsp. Worcestershire sauce	2 Tbsp. soy sauce
⅛ tsp. chili powder	1 c. water

Mix together all ingredients. In a medium sized roasting pan, lined with foil (saves scouring), place a layer of meaty spareribs and cover with a layer of sliced onions. Season well with garlic salt, pepper, parsley flakes, and sweet basil. Pour barbeque sauce over top. Repeat layers. Cover. Bake at 325° for 2 to 2½ hours. Uncover at least ½ hour. Baste ribs frequently and serve hot!

SWEET AND SOUR PORK
Olga Tarcha

1 lb. pork or other meat cubes	Oil for deep-frying

Batter:

1 egg	½ c. flour
½ tsp. salt	¼ c. water

Combine batter ingredients; beat until smooth. Dip meat cubes in batter. Deep-fry; drain on paper.

Sauce:

1 c. pineapple cubes	1 green pepper, diced
½ c. vinegar	¼ c. brown sugar
1 Tbsp. molasses	2 Tbsp. cornstarch
¼ c. water	

Combine pineapple, green pepper, vinegar, brown sugar, and molasses; heat over medium heat. Combine cornstarch and water; mix to dissolve cornstarch. Add to pineapple mixture, mixing while adding to prevent lumps. Add fried meat cubes to the sauce. Serve with rice.

SAUSAGE AND PEPPERS

Carol Wasylko

1 lb. Italian sweet sausage with
fennel
½ lb. Italian hot sausage
2 large onions, thinly sliced
2 c. drained canned tomatoes
2 Tbsp. tomato paste
1 tsp. basil
½ bay leaf

Salt and pepper
¼ tsp. crushed fennel seeds
(optional)
6 to 8 Italian green peppers,
seeded and cut into bite size
pieces
Grated Parmesan cheese

Cut each sausage into 3 parts on slant; saute in pan until browned on all sides. Add onion; continue to cook slowly until onion is tender and golden and sausage is cooked through. If dry, add 1 to 2 tablespoons olive oil; add tomatoes, paste, basil, bay leaf, salt and pepper, crushed fennel seeds, and green peppers. Bring to a boil; simmer, uncovered, 20 to 30 minutes or until tender and mixture is thick.

FRESH KOLBASI

John Cibulsky

3½ lb. pork butts
1½ lb. veal shoulder (boneless)
1 small head garlic, chopped
½ c. water
2 Tbsp. coarse ground black
pepper

3 Tbsp. salt
1 c. water
½ lb. salted hog casing

Peel and chop garlic and puree with ½ cup water in a blender. Cut meat into 1 inch pieces; grind as coarse as possible. Combine ground meat, pureed garlic, pepper, salt, and water; mix thoroughly. Make a small patty; fry and taste for salt and pepper. Add more if desired. Wash casing in cold water by running water through the inside. With a sausage stuffing attachment on a grinder, stuff the casing slowly, evenly and carefully so as not to burst casing. Before stuffing, tie one end of casing with twine and after stuffing, tie other end.

Place ring of kolbasi in a flat pan with enough water to just cover the bottom of pan. Cover. Bake at 350° for 1 hour on one side. Turn over and bake 15 to 20 minutes on other side.

SPIEDIES

Marie Richardson

¾ c. vinegar
1 c. oil
3 Tbsp. garlic salt

3 Tbsp. onion powder
3 Tbsp. parsley flakes
3 Tbsp. oregano

Marinate 5 pounds of cubed meat overnight. Use chicken, beef, or pork. Place marinated cubes of meat on skewers. Cook over hot coals or in broiler of oven.

TURKEY CUTLETS PICCATA

Carol Williams
Linda Zapach

1 lb. turkey cutlets
1 egg
1½ c. plain or Italian bread
  crumbs
4 Tbsp. butter or margarine

1 medium lemon
¾ c. water
1 env. chicken bouillon
¼ tsp. salt

On a cutting board, pound turkey cutlets to ⅛ inch thickness. In a pie plate, beat egg and milk with fork. Dip cutlets in egg, then bread crumbs, coating both sides. In a 12 inch skillet, over medium-high heat, brown cutlets in butter or margarine. Remove cutlets to plate. Reduce heat to low; squeeze juice of one-half the lemon into drippings in skillet. Stir in water, bouillon, and salt until blended, scraping to loosen brown bits from skillet. Return cutlets to skillet; cover. Simmer 5 minutes or until cutlets are fork tender. To serve, thinly slice remaining half lemon. Arrange cutlets on warm platter with lemon slices; pour sauce from skillet over cutlets.

TURKEY DIVAN

Anna Smyk

1 pkg. frozen broccoli spears
3 Tbsp. butter or margarine
⅓ c. flour
¼ tsp. salt
⅛ tsp. pepper

½ c. turkey broth
1 c. milk
¾ c. grated Cheddar cheese
6 portions sliced turkey

Cook broccoli according to package directions; drain. Lay in a greased, shallow baking dish. In a saucepan, melt butter or margarine; stir in flour and salt and pepper which have been combined. Bring butter-flour mixture to a bubble and let bubble 1 minute; add turkey broth, stirring constantly while adding milk. Stir and cook until thick; add cheese, stirring until cheese is melted. Lay sliced turkey over broccoli; pour cheese sauce over turkey. Bake in a 300° oven 30 minutes.

TURKEY LOAF

Mary Ponas

4 c. coarsely ground cooked
  turkey
1½ c. soft bread crumbs
1 (6 oz.) can evaporated milk
⅓ c. chicken broth

⅔ c. finely chopped celery
2 eggs, slightly beaten
Dash of pepper, nutmeg, and
  dried marjoram

Lightly combine all ingredients. Line bottom of an 8½ x 4½ x 2½ inch loaf pan with greased foil. Turn turkey mixture into prepared pan. Bake at 350° for 45 minutes or until center is firm. Invert onto a serving platter; remove foil. Serve with Pimento Sauce.

Pimento Sauce:

1 (10¾ oz.) can cream of
   chicken soup

⅓ c. milk
2 Tbsp. chopped pimento

Combine soup, milk, and pimento in a saucepan. Heat; serve with the Turkey Loaf.

GROUND TURKEY MEATLOAF
Mary Mihalko

3 lb. ground turkey
1 c. bread crumbs (fine)
1 egg or ¼ c. Egg Beaters
¾ c. chopped onions
1 tsp. salt

2 tsp. molasses
¼ tsp. pepper
¼ tsp. garlic powder
¼ c. milk (skim)

In a large bowl, mix turkey with rest of ingredients; blend well. Form into a loaf and bake at 350° for 1 hour. (If a loaf pan is used, bake 1 hour and 15 minutes.)

VEAL AND PEPPERS
Olga Tarcha

1 lb. stewing veal
Salt and pepper to taste
4 Tbsp. shortening
1 c. burgundy wine
2 c. tomatoes

½ tsp. garlic salt
½ tsp. oregano
1 small onion, chopped
4 medium peppers, sliced

Season veal with salt and pepper; brown in hot shortening in fry pan. Add wine; cook 10 minutes. Add tomatoes, garlic salt, oregano, and onion; cook about 45 minutes or until meat is tender. Add peppers; cook until barely tender.

VEAL PARMESAN
Eugenia Krawecki

Veal steaks
Salt and pepper
1 egg, beaten
⅓ c. grated Parmesan cheese
⅓ c. bread crumbs
¼ c. oil

2 Tbsp. butter
1 onion, minced
1 can tomato paste
2 c. hot water
1 tsp. salt
½ lb. sliced Mozzarella cheese

Season veal with salt and pepper. Beat egg with 2 tablespoons water. Dip veal in egg, then in bread crumbs and finally in Parmesan cheese. Fry until golden and place in a baking dish; set aside. Saute onions in butter until soft. Add tomato paste, hot water, and salt. Stir until well blended. Pour sauce over veal and top each veal steak with a slice of Mozzarella cheese. Bake at 350° for 35 to 40 minutes.

Notes

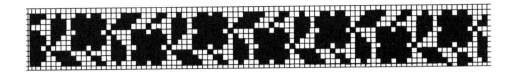

Miscellaneous

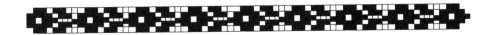

MISCELLANEOUS

ALMOND NUT

The almond nut tree originated in the areas of Ukraine, China, and Japan and is a small tree of the Rose family with flowers and young fruit resembling those of a peach. Centuries before Christ, the tree was brought to the Mediterranean area and is mentioned in the Bible - Aaron's rod being of the almond tree. The eaten nut is actually the seed within the pit; it is very nutritious.

APPLE

Central Asia and the Caucasus are said to be the birthplace of the apple; cultivation preceded the dawn of history. The apple was imported into North America in the beginning of the 17th century. There are now thousands of varieties throughout the world. The American folk hero, Johnny Appleseed, was a real person. He was born in Leominster, Massachusetts in 1775 Johnny Chapman, nicknamed "Appleseed," because he collected appleseeds from cider mills and gave them to everyone he met who was going West. For 40 years he wandered Ohio, Indiana, Illinois, and Iowa, distributing and planting apple seeds. According to the World Encyclopedia of Food by L. Patrick Doyle, "some of which are still bearing fruit to this day."

ASPARAGUS

Although its origins are obscure, it appears to be native to the Ukrainian steppes. The asparagus we eat is the immature spear. If allowed to mature, the plant produces a fernlike leaf which is not edible.

BACON

Bacon is pig's flesh (back and sides), salted and cured and is one of the oldest meats which for centuries was a staple for the poor and working classes. According to legend, the phrase, "Bring home the bacon," dates from Norman times in England when at the monastery of Dunmow a side of bacon was offered as a prize to any man who could swear before the Church, that for a year and a day he had not quarreled with his wife, nor wished himself to be single again.

BANANA

The sweet and nourishing fruit of a gigantic tree - the banana is believed to be native to Africa. According to legend, after the fall, Adam and Eve covered their nakedness with a banana leaf. Bananas were little known in the United

States before 1870, yet today Americans eat more bananas than any other fruit. This fact is largely due to their prolific cultivation in Central America, improved technology in transportation, particularly refrigeration and the knowledge that it is one of the most complete life sustaining foods.

BARLEY

A hardy grass believed to be the first grain cultivated in Egypt between 5,000 to 6,000 B.C. Food value of barley is similar to that of wheat; it makes a dark, heavy bread enjoyed by the Slavic people.

Barley today is used for animal fodder, manufacture of beer and whiskey, milling of flour for bread, breakfast foods, and the "pearl" is used for soups.

BEANS

Beans belong to the family of legumes, plants whose fruits grow in pods, several at a time in a single row, and are rich in protein. Beans have been cultivated for over 7,000 years. The kidney bean is of American origin.

BEET

The beet is native to the Mediterranean area and is a nutritious food. Thick, fleshy red root and edible leaves.

Borscht (beet soup) was originated by the Ukrainians and today has as many different recipes as the nations that enjoy this hearty fare.

BRUSSEL SPROUTS

They are miniature cabbages, originated in Brussels, Belgium in the 13th century - and named for their place of origin.

CUCUMBER

One of the oldest cultivated plants - as early as 9750 B.C. and its origin is in Thailand. The Spaniards brought them to the New World.

BUTTER

Butter is a prehistoric word. It was used as a medicine for burns and as a food. It is frequently referred to in the Bible: "The words of his mouth were smoother than butter, but war was in his heart." Psalms 7:21. "Behold a virgin shall conceive, and bear a son, and shall call him Immanuel. Butter and honey shall he eat." Isaiah.

CANDY

Egyptian hieroglyphics from 3,000 years ago record their candy making - which has not changed to this date.

COCOA

The most valuable tree crop in the world, originating in the wilds of Peru and Brazil. A Swiss, M.D. Peters in 1876 developed a method for making milk chocolate. For the first time, chocolate was eaten in solid form.

CELERY

Native to the Mediterranean areas, it grew in seaside soils filled with brackish water. Romans cultivated the celery plant and discovered its use as a table vegetable. They also believed that wearing a wreath of celery prevented a hangover. In 1874 Dutch farmers in Michigan initiated commercial cultivation of celery in the United States.

CHEESE

The history of cheese can be documented as far back as 4,000 B.C. Egyptians recorded this fact on clay tablets. Cheese making spread to all parts of the Western world and especially in Europe where it permeated the culture to such an extent that each district of each country has its own distinct cheese or variation on a well-known cheese. Many local cheeses resulted from happy accidents that occurred using tried and true methods and others from peculiarities of climate or bacteria that changed a standard taste or texture.

CHICKEN

Two thousand B.C. in India, the modern chicken was a jungle bird that was tamed; the domesticated chicken came East and West and became commonplace in the world, becoming the most universally eaten meat.

COCONUT

Fruit of the palm, the coconut is one of the most useful plants in the world. Thought to have originated in the area of Malaysia and Indonesia, it now grows throughout the world's tropics. There is a saying, "He who plants a coconut tree, plants food and drink, vessels and clothing, habitation for himself, and a heritage for his children."

COFFEE

Native to Ethiopia - it now grows in the tropics. According to legend, one day an Ethiopian goat herder noticed that his normally lethargic goats were dancing on their hind legs and bleating for joy. He also noticed that they had been feeding on some bright red berries. He sampled the berries himself and experienced an immediate boost in his spirits and energies. Impressed, he took some berries to the local monastery, where the head monk, on hearing the goat herder's story, condemned the berries as the devil's work. He flung them into the fire, whereupon a heavenly aroma came forth from the fireplace, filling the air. The head monk was inspired to rescue the berries from the fire and infuse them in hot water. So pleased was he with the taste and effects of the fragrant beverage, that he proclaimed it heaven-sent and gave it to the monks in the evenings to keep them from falling asleep during prayers.

DILL

Important plant since ancient times, medicinally as well as in the kitchen. The seeds are a favored seasoning in Ukrainian cooking.

HONEY

Honey is a syrupy food produced by bees from plant nectar and has been the chief sweetener for humans from remote times. When Moses led his people out of captivity in Egypt, the Promised Land was described as *a land rich and broad, where milk and honey flow.* (Exodus 3:8)

OLIVE

The olive is a long-lived tree and extremely hardy, thriving in poor soil and arid conditions that would kill most other plants. It is alleged that on the Mount of Olives in Jerusalem, Christ was betrayed amidst trees that are still standing today. Three-thousand B.C. olive oil was an important export for Greece. The olive branch is a symbol of peace.

ONION

Originated in Central Asia and is older than history.

CABBAGE

Ancient Greeks and Romans cultivated this leafy plant and it ranks as the world's most popular vegetable, next to the potato.

CORN

Cultivated in southern Mexico before recorded history, reaching what is now the United States more than 2,000 years ago, corn is cultivated all over the world. It played an important role in the survival of the colonies.

Because the strains of wheat that the Europeans brought with them would not grow in the American soil, salvation came on the very day the Pilgrims landed from the Mayflower at Plymouth Rock in 1621. Captain Miles Standish came across an Indian cache of corn and beans that fed the group through the winter and saved their lives. Corn remained the primary grain of the colonies for 200 years.

POTATO

The most precious gift Peru gave to the world over 3,000 years ago is the potato which provides nearly perfect nutrition. The potato can grow almost anywhere and yields more food energy per acre than grains do. Three great nations of Indians - the Incas of Peru, the Mayas of Central America, and the Aztecs of Mexico developed and cultivated wild plants and grasses into the corn, potatoes, beans, tomatoes, squash, coca, tapioca, and fruits that we enjoy today.

RICE

Rice cultivation in Asia began as early as 3500 B.C. It is one of the world's most important foods. It arrived in America in 1694, when a ship was blown off course and forced to land in Charleston, South Carolina. To thank the colonists for their hospitality, the ship's captain gave the governor a handful of rough rice grains which the colonists used for seed.

TOMATO

Tomatoes were found growing in the wild. Because the seeds were easy and light to carry, tomatoes spread from tribe to tribe as far north as Mexico. The Spaniards took the seeds home and planted the first tomatoes grown outside the New World. An 1893 U.S. Supreme Court ruled that the tomato was not a fruit (although botanically it is) but a vegetable. In 1876 Heinz bottled catsup and made the tomato popular.

WHEAT

Wheat, as a human food, leads all others and has played a major role in history. Wheat was the economic mainstay of ancient Egypt. Its overwhelming importance is made clear in the story of Joseph from the Bible. Joseph, who foresaw a catastrophic drought, averted famine and achieved power second only to the Pharaoh's by storing up enough grain during the 7 fat years to see the population through the 7 lean years.

HAPPY EASTER POEM

Fill a baby jar full of jelly beans. Tie with a ribbon; add the following explanation.

Jelly Beans:

> Red is for the blood He gave.
> Green is for the plants God made.
> Yellow is for the sun so bright.
> Orange is for the edge of night.
>
> Black is for the sins we do.
> White is for the Grace He offers us.
> Purple is for His hours of sorrow.
> Pink is for the new tomorrow.
>
> A bag full of jelly beans,
> Colorful and sweet,
> It's a prayer and a promise
> And a small Easter treat.

A RECIPE FOR A HAPPY NEW YEAR

Take 12 fine full-grown months; see that these are thoroughly free from old memories of bitterness, rancor, hate, and jealousy.

Cleanse them completely from every clinging spite; pick off all specks of pettiness and littleness. In short, see that these months are freed from the past. Have them fresh and clean as when they first came from the Storehouse of Time.

Cut these months into 30 or 31 equal parts. Do not attempt to make the whole batch at one time (so many people spoil the entire lot in this way), but prepare one day at a time as follows:

Into each day, put equal parts of Faith, Patience, Courage, Work (some people omit this ingredient and so spoil the flavor of the rest), Hope, Fidelity, Liberality, Kindness, Rest (leaving this out is like leaving the oil out of the salad - don't do it), Prayer, Meditation, and one well-selected Resolution.

Put in about a teaspoon of Good Spirits, a dash of Fun, a pinch of Folly, a sprinkling of Play, and a heaping cup full of Good Humor. Pour Love over the whole and mix with Vim.

Cook thoroughly in a fervent Heat; garnish with a few Smiles and a sprig of Joy, then serve with Quietness, Unselfishness, and Cheerfulness.

CAN SIZE EQUIVALENTS

Eight ounce can equals 1 cup.

No. 1 flat equals 1 cup or 8 to 9 ounces.

No. 300 equals 1⅓ cups or 1 pound.

No. 303 equals 2 cups or 16 to 17 ounces.

No. 2 vacuum equals 1¾ cups or 12 ounces.

No. 2 equals 2½ cups or 20 ounces.

No. 2½ equals 3½ cups or 28 ounces.

No. 3 cylinder equals 5¾ cups or 46 ounces.

No. 10 equals 13 cups or 6 pounds, 10 ounces.

CHESTNUT DRESSING
Olga Gooley

2 lb. chestnuts
6 to 8 medium onions
½ lb. butter
1 Tbsp. poultry seasoning

1 large loaf white bread
1 qt. milk
Salt and pepper to taste

Cook chestnuts in boiling water for 20 minutes. Peel and chop (can be done ahead and refrigerated). Slice onions and saute until soft and translucent. Cut loaf of white bread in cubes and combine all ingredients. Bake in ungreased deep casserole dish at 350° for 1 hour.

EGG DUMPLINGS
Mary Charnetsky

1 egg
½ egg shell of water

¼ tsp. salt
¾ c. flour

Beat egg with water and salt; add flour and beat until smooth. Drop mixture by ½ teaspoon into boiling water and boil for about 20 minutes or until tender. Use in soups or as a side dish, buttered.

ELEVEN SPICE MEAT COATING   Pani Julia Lawryk

2 c. flour
2 Tbsp. salt
1 Tbsp. celery salt
1 Tbsp. pepper
2 Tbsp. dry mustard
2 Tbsp. paprika

2 Tbsp. garlic powder
1 tsp. ginger
½ tsp. thyme
½ tsp. sweet basil
½ tsp. oregano

Combine all ingredients in a bowl; stir well. Store in an airtight container. May be used to coat liver, hamburgers, chicken, or meatballs for frying.

CRUNCHY GRANOLA   Dorotha Cenesky

5 c. old-fashioned oats
 (uncooked)
1 c. cut almonds
1 c. unrefined sesame seeds
1 c. sunflower seeds
1 c. unsweetened shredded
 coconut

1 c. soy flour
1 c. powdered milk (not instant)
1 c. wheat germ
1 c. raisins
1 c. honey
1 c. vegetable oil
2 tsp. vanilla

In a large bowl, combine oats, almonds, seeds, coconut, flour, milk, wheat germ, and raisins. In a separate bowl, combine honey, oil, and vanilla; stir to blend. Pour over dry ingredients; mix to coat all. Spread on 4 greased cookie sheets. Bake at 275° about 40 minutes or until lightly browned, stirring once or twice during baking.

MILANO'S GRANOLA   Olga Gooley

5 c. oatmeal
1 c. unsweetened coconut
¼ c. sesame seeds
¾ c. shelled sunflower seeds
½ c. wheat germ

⅔ c. honey
¼ c. corn oil
1 tsp. vanilla
½ c. raisins (added after
 baking)

Combine dry ingredients in a large bowl. Combine honey, corn oil, and vanilla in a small bowl; add to dry ingredients and mix. Pour ingredients into a greased 9x13 inch pan. Bake in 250° oven for 1 to 1½ hours, stirring about every 15 minutes at first, then sooner after granola starts to brown. Let cool; add raisins. Delicious with yogurt.

HOMEMADE NOODLES

Anne Petras

2¼ c. flour
1 tsp. salt
1 Tbsp. salad or olive oil

3 eggs
1 Tbsp. water

Place the flour and salt on a board and make a well in the center. Add the oil, eggs, and water to the well. With the fingers, gradually draw the flour into the wet ingredients and combine together. Flours vary in their ability to absorb mixture, so it may be necessary to add an extra teaspoon or two of water to make a stiff dough that can be kneaded. Knead the dough on a lightly floured board until smooth and satiny, about 10 minutes.

Roll out dough using as little extra flour as possible to a rectangle about 12x30 inches long. The dough will be thin and hang over the board. Set on a towel and let dry about 20 minutes. Roll from the short side like a jelly roll. For fine soup noodles, cut ⅛ inch slices or for wider noodles, ¼ inch slices. Separate the coils of noodles. Spread out and let dry completely, about 1 hour, before using or storing in a closed container. Yield: About ½ pound.

ZIPPY MUSTARD

Josephine Vimislik

2 c. flour
1 Tbsp. salt
¼ lb. dry mustard

1 egg
2 Tbsp. melted butter
1½ c. cider vinegar

In a bowl, combine flour, salt, and mustard; mix to evenly distribute ingredients. In another bowl, combine egg, melted butter, and cider vinegar; add to ingredients combined in first bowl. Beat with electric mixer until smooth. Needs to age at least 2 weeks before using.

PARTY MIX I

Olga Gooley

¾ c. margarine
1 tsp. (rounded) seasoned salt
3 tsp. Worcestershire sauce
4 c. Cheerios

1 (8 oz.) box Rice Chex
2 c. thin pretzel sticks
1 (13 oz.) can mixed nuts

Melt margarine in roasting pan; add salt and Worcestershire sauce. Stir. Add remaining ingredients; stir to coat with margarine mixture. Bake at 325° for 20 minutes, stirring every 5 minutes.

PARTY MIX II

Marie Richardson

2 c. Corn Chex
2 c. Wheat Chex
2 c. Rice Chex
½ c. walnuts

6 Tbsp. margarine
1 tsp. seasoned salt
4 tsp. Worcestershire sauce
Dash of garlic salt

Combine cereals and nuts. Melt margarine; add seasonings. Pour over cereal mixture, mixing thoroughly. Put mixture on cookie sheet. Bake at 250° for 1 hour, stirring every 15 minutes. Place on brown paper to absorb fat until cool.

Note: Pretzels, corn chips, peanuts, or other snacks may be used in addition to or in place of cereals.

SALSA

Millie Finch

1 large can whole tomatoes, diced
1 (3½ oz.) can medium hot green chiles, diced

1 clove garlic, minced fine
½ tsp. salt
Pepper to taste
Dash of Tabasco sauce

Combine tomatoes with the juice and remaining ingredients. Refrigerate overnight. Serve with tortilla chips or potato chips.

Pies
Pastries

PIES, PASTRIES

PIE CRUST I

Helen Charnetsky

3 c. flour
¾ tsp. salt

¾ c. butter
1 c. water (approx.)

Blend with blender flour, salt, and butter. Keep blending while adding water, a little at a time, until pie dough is desired consistency. Refrigerate for 2 to 36 hours. Divide dough in 2 parts. Roll out on floured board or pastry cloth and place dough in 2 (10 inch) pie pans.

PIE CRUST II

Ann Dobransky

2 c. sifted flour
1 tsp. salt

½ c. salad oil
5 Tbsp. ice water

Sift flour and sugar together. Beat together salad oil and water until thick and creamy. Pour over entire surface of flour and immediately mix with fork to form ball. Makes pastry for an 8 or 9 inch double crust pie.

PIE CRUST III

Jane Ellsworth

4 c. flour
1 Tbsp. sugar
1 tsp. salt
1¾ c. shortening

1 egg, beaten
1 c. cold water
1 Tbsp. vinegar

Combine flour, sugar, and salt. Cut in shortening, beaten egg, water, and vinegar; add to flour mixture. Mix to form a ball. Chill. Roll out and fill with your favorite filling and bake accordingly. Makes 2 double crust pies.

CORN FLAKE PIE CRUST

Ann Dobransky

1 c. crushed corn flakes
¼ c. sugar

⅓ c. melted margarine

Combine crushed corn flakes, sugar, and melted margarine. Press firmly into a buttered 9 inch pie pan. Chill for 45 minutes before filling with your favorite pie filling.

Rice Krispies, vanilla, or chocolate wafers (38 wafers) can be substituted for corn flakes.

NEVER FAIL PIE CRUST

Anna Chyl
Linda Zapach

(2 crust pie)

2 c. flour
½ tsp. salt
1 c. shortening

2 tsp. vinegar
¼ c. milk

Mix with fork flour and salt. Cut in shortening with 2 knives or pastry blender. Add vinegar to milk and add to dry ingredients. Mix until a ball is formed. Roll out on a heavily floured pastry cloth or board.

ZWIEBACK PIE CRUST

Ann Dobransky

1 c. Zwieback, crushed
¼ c. confectioners sugar

2 Tbsp. melted margarine

Combine Zwieback, sugar, and margarine. Press firmly into a buttered 9 inch pie pan. Chill.

EXOTIC AFTER DINNER PIE (SCOTCH WHISKEY AND DRAMBUIE PIE)

Marianne Lawryk

1 env. unflavored gelatin
½ c. cold water
3 egg yolks
⅓ c. sugar
⅛ tsp. salt
¼ c. (2 oz.) Scotch whiskey
¼ c. (2 oz.) Drambuie

3 egg whites
¼ c. sugar
1 c. heavy cream
1 Tbsp. Drambuie
Whole nutmeg
9 inch graham cracker pie shell

Sprinkle gelatin over cold water to soften. Let stand for 5 minutes. In top of double boiler, beat egg yolks; add ⅓ cup sugar and salt, blending well. Stir in softened gelatin. Cook over barely simmering water in bottom section of double boiler, stirring constantly, only until mixture begins to thicken. (It should not be cooked until it is a custard.) Remove from heat. Stir in whiskey and Drambuie. Chill until mixture begins to thicken around the edges, but not lumpy.

Beat egg whites until soft peaks form, then slowly add ¼ cup sugar while continuing to beat until egg whites are stiff. Carefully fold in whiskey mixture into egg whites. Beat ½ cup heavy cream until whipped and fold into whiskey mixture. Pour mixture into pie shell. Chill until pie filling is firm. Beat remaining ½ cup heavy cream until whipped. Stir 1 tablespoon Drambuie into cream. Spread evenly over top of pie filling. Grate nutmeg lightly over pie. Chill.

SISTER PAULINE'S ANGEL PIE
Julia Dudik

Crust:

4 egg whites
1 c. sugar

1 tsp. vanilla
¼ tsp. cream of tartar

Beat egg whites until stiff. Gradually add sugar; add vanilla and cream of tartar. Place in a buttered 9 or 10 inch pie pan. Bake for 1 hour at 300°. This pie shell will rise while baking; let it settle and cool for about 1 hour before filling.

Filling:

1 (3 oz.) pkg. lemon pie filling

1 c. heavy cream, whipped

Prepare lemon pie filling according to directions. Pour into cooled pie shell. When cooled, put whipped cream on top of lemon filling and refrigerate for 12 hours or overnight.

APPLE CAKE PIE
Ann Dobransky

3¾ c. flour
3 tsp. sugar
1½ c. shortening
1½ tsp. salt
2 egg yolks (add milk to make 1 c.)
1 c. crushed corn flakes

3 lb. apples, peeled and cut into thin slices
2 c. sugar
1 tsp. cinnamon
2 egg whites
1 c. confectioners sugar
4 Tbsp. lemon juice

Combine flour, sugar, and salt; cut in shortening. Add egg yolk and milk mixture to make a soft dough. Divide dough in half. Roll dough out and put half in a 15 x 10½ inch pan. Sprinkle crushed corn flakes on dough, then put apples in; sprinkle with 2 cups sugar and a teaspoon of cinnamon. Roll out the other half of dough and put on top of apples. Beat egg whites until stiff and spread over top of dough. Bake at 400° for 40 minutes. Mix 1 cup confectioners sugar (sifted) and 4 tablespoons lemon juice together and drizzle over top of hot cake when baked.

APPLE CRUMB PIE
Linda Zapach

5 to 7 tart apples
9 inch unbaked pastry shell
½ c. sugar
¾ tsp. ground cinnamon

⅓ c. sugar
¾ c. flour
6 Tbsp. butter

Pare and core apples; slice. Arrange in unbaked pastry shell. Combine ½ cup sugar and cinnamon; sprinkle over apples in pastry shell. Combine ⅓ cup sugar and flour; cut in butter until crumbly. Sprinkle over apples. Bake at 400°

for 35 to 40 minutes or until done. If crust is browning too quickly, cover edge with foil.

BOB'S PIE CRUST AND APRICOT-APPLE FILLING
Marianne Lawryk

Crust:

2 Tbsp. apple cider vinegar
¼ c. milk

2 c. flour
⅔ c. Mazola oil

Combine vinegar and milk and refrigerate for 1 hour. Combine flour and oil with vinegar/milk mixture. Mix. Divide into 2 parts. Roll out thin; will make bottom and top crust.

Filling:

1 (16 oz.) can drained apricot
 halves (reserve liquid)
½ c. sugar
4 Tbsp. cornstarch

4 c. peeled, chopped tart apples
1 Tbsp. lemon juice
½ tsp. cinnamon

In large saucepan, combine reserved apricot liquid, sugar, cornstarch, apples, lemon juice, and cinnamon. Cover. Cook gently until apples are soft, stirring occasionally. Remove from heat. Fold in apricot halves. Spoon into pastry-lined 9 or 10 inch pie pan. Arrange pastry over filling. Fold edge of top pastry under edge of bottom crust. Press together to seal. Flute edge. Bake at 350° for 45 minutes or until golden brown. Place pie pan on a larger tray to catch escaping juices while baking.

SOUR CREAM APPLE PIE
Audrey Klym

Filling:

2 Tbsp. flour
⅛ tsp. salt
¾ c. sugar
1 egg (unbeaten)
1 c. dairy sour cream

1 tsp. vanilla
¼ tsp. nutmeg
2 c. diced apples
9 inch pastry pie shell

Sift together flour, salt, and sugar; add egg, sour cream, vanilla, and nutmeg. Beat until smooth, thin batter. Stir in apples. Pour into pastry-lined pie pan. Bake in hot oven at 400° for 15 minutes, then turn down oven to 350° and bake for 30 minutes. Remove from oven.

Top with - Spicy Topping:

⅓ c. sugar
⅓ c. flour

1 tsp. cinnamon
¼ c. butter or margarine

Combine sugar, flour, cinnamon, and butter or margarine. Mix well. Sprinkle over pie and return to oven and bake at 400° for 10 more minutes to brown.

BLUEBERRY PIE
Ann Dobransky

1 c. sugar
¼ c. flour or 2½ tsp. Minute
  tapioca
1 Tbsp. lemon juice
2½ c. fresh blueberries

Dash of salt
1 Tbsp. butter
2 unbaked pie pastries for 2
  crust pie

Combine sugar, flour or tapioca, lemon juice, and salt. Set aside. Add lemon juice to blueberries; add sugar mixture to blueberries. Pour berry filling into unbaked pie shell. Dot filling with butter. Cover with top crust. Bake at 400° for 40 to 50 minutes. Watch carefully so as not to burn crust.

OLGA'S BLUEBERRY LEMON PIE
Anna Chyl

24 vanilla wafers
1 (4 oz.) pkg. lemon pie filling
2 egg yolks
⅓ c. sugar
2 c. water

2 egg whites
¼ c. sugar
2 c. fresh blueberries, rinsed
  and drained
1 c. heavy cream

Use wafers to line bottom and sides of 9 inch pie pan. Prepare pie filling according to package directions using the egg yolks, ⅓ cup sugar, and water. Cover and cool. Beat egg whites until stiff. Gradually beat in ¼ cup sugar, a tablespoon at a time. Fold egg whites and half the blueberries into cooled lemon pudding. Pour in wafer lined pie pan. Chill several hours until firm. Whip heavy cream until stiff; sweeten if desired. Spoon cream in circles on top of pie. Spoon remaining blueberries between cream circles. Chill until ready to serve.

Note: Frozen blueberries can be used.

BLUEBERRY MALLOW PIE
Ann Dobransky

Filling:

2½ c. (1 lb. 5 oz. can) blueberry
  pie filling*

1 (9 inch) graham cracker
  crust, chilled

Pour pie filling into crust. Chill.

Topping:

2 c. miniature marshmallows
¼ c. milk

½ tsp. vanilla
½ c. heavy cream, whipped

Melt marshmallows with milk in double boiler; stir until smooth. Add vanilla (mix until well blended). Chill until slightly thickened. Fold in whipped cream. Spread over pie filling. Chill until firm.

* Any other favorite pie filling can be used - strawberry, raspberry, etc.

WONDERFUL CHERRY PIE
Linda Zapach

½ pt. heavy cream
1 (8 oz.) pkg. cream cheese, softened
½ c. confectioners sugar

1 tsp. vanilla
1 baked pie shell or Ready crust graham cracker
1 can cherry pie filling

Whip cream until very stiff; cream together cream cheese, sugar, and vanilla. Add to whipped cream; blend together. Turn into pie shell. Spoon cherry pie filling over top. Chill overnight.

CHERRY TOPPED CHEESE PIE
Marianne Lawryk

1 (8 oz.) pkg. cream cheese, softened
½ c. sugar

2 c. thawed Cool Whip
9 inch graham cracker crust
1 can cherry pie filling

Beat together softened cream cheese with sugar until creamy. Blend in thawed Cool Whip. Pour into unbaked graham cracker crust. Top with cherry pie filling. Chill at least 3 hours before serving.

PISTACHIO CHEESE PIE
Anna Chyl

Crust:

¼ c. chopped or ground nuts
1 c. flour

1 stick margarine

Combine flour and margarine; cut in with 2 knives or pastry blender until particles are the size of peas. Blend in chopped nuts. Press crust into bottom and sides of a 10 inch pie pan. Bake for 10 minutes at 350°. Cool.

Filling:

1 (8 oz.) pkg. cream cheese
1 c. confectioners sugar
1 (8 oz.) container Cool Whip, thawed

2 (3 oz.) pkg. instant pistachio pudding
3 c. milk (cold)

Cream together cream cheese and confectioners sugar. Blend in 4 ounces of Cool Whip. Pour mixture into cooled pie shell. Pour cold milk into a bowl; add pistachio pudding and beat for 1 minute with a rotary beater or electric mixer. Pour over cream cheese mixture and spread remaining 4 ounces of Cool Whip on top. Refrigerate for at least 1 hour before serving.

AMAZING COCONUT PIE

Linda Zapach

Makes its own crust.

2 c. milk
¾ c. sugar
½ c. biscuit mix
4 eggs

¼ c. butter or margarine
1½ tsp. vanilla
1 c. Angel Flake coconut

In a blender, combine milk, sugar, biscuit mix, eggs, butter, and vanilla; place cover on blender. Blend on low speed 3 minutes. Pour into a greased 9 inch pie pan; let stand 5 minutes. Sprinkle with coconut. Bake at 350° for 40 minutes. Serve warm or cold.

CREME DE MENTHE PIE

Mary Buckingham

Crust:

24 Oreo cookies, crushed fine
¼ c. melted butter or
   margarine

Combine crushed cookies and melted butter. Save ½ cup for the top. Pat mixture in 9 inch pie pan.

Filling:

¼ c. creme de menthe
1 small jar marshmallow creme

2 c. whipped cream (1 pt.)

Combine creme de menthe with marshmallow creme. Fold in whipped cream and put on top of cookie crumb crust. Sprinkle reserved ½ cup cookie mixture on top of filling. Freeze.

CUSTARD PIE - MAKES OWN CRUST

Sophia Malowicky

3 eggs, beaten
4 Tbsp. flour
½ c. sugar

Dash of nutmeg
2½ c. milk
Dash of salt

Combine eggs, flour, sugar, nutmeg, milk, and salt; beat until smooth. Pour into a 9 inch buttered pie plate. Bake at 350° for 45 minutes.

ANN HONSHIRGER'S CONCORD GRAPE PIE

Dorothy Skellett

Filling:

1½ lb. (4 c.) Concord grapes
1 c. sugar
1 c. flour

1 Tbsp. lemon juice
1½ Tbsp. butter, melted
1 (9 inch) unbaked pastry shell

Crumb Topping:

½ c. flour
¼ c. sugar

6 Tbsp. butter

Slip skins from grapes; set skins aside. In a saucepan, bring pulp to boiling; reduce heat and simmer for 5 minutes. Press pulp through sieve to remove seeds. Add skins to pulp. Combine sugar, flour, and salt; add lemon juice, butter, and grape mixture. Pour into unbaked pastry shell.

Combine topping ingredients - flour and sugar; cut in butter until crumbly. Sprinkle over filling. Bake at 400° for about 40 minutes.

Filling can be frozen.

FAMOUS LEMON PIE

Ann Dobransky

3 Tbsp. cornstarch
1¼ c. sugar
¼ c. lemon juice
1 Tbsp. grated lemon rind

3 eggs, separated
1½ c. boiling water
6 Tbsp. sugar
1 (9 inch) baked pie shell

Combine cornstarch, 1¼ cups sugar, lemon juice, and lemon rind. Beat egg yolks; add to cornstarch mixture. Gradually add boiling water. Heat to boiling over direct heat and then boil gently for 4 minutes, stirring constantly. Pour into baked pie shell.

Beat egg whites until stiff, but not dry. Gradually beat in 6 tablespoons sugar, one tablespoon at a time, until egg whites stand up in peaks. Spread meringue to touch all edges of crust. Bake in hot oven at 425° for 4 to 5 minutes or until lightly browned. Cool on a cake rack away from drafts. Serve cold.

HEAVENLY LEMON PIE

Ann Dobransky

1 env. unflavored gelatin
¾ c. sugar
1 tsp. salt
1 c. water
⅓ c. lemon juice

2 egg yolks, slightly beaten
1½ tsp. grated lemon rind
1 pt. Cool Whip
1 (9 inch) graham cracker crust
    or baked pie crust

In a saucepan, mix gelatin, sugar, and salt; add water and lemon juice. Blend in egg yolks. Place saucepan over medium heat and cook, stirring constantly, until gelatin is dissolved, about 5 minutes. Remove from heat. Add lemon rind. Pour into a bowl and chill until slightly thickened, about 1½ hours; stir occasionally. Place thickened bowl of gelatin in larger bowl of ice water and whip with electric beater until double in volume. Blend in 1½ cups of Cool Whip and pour into pie shell. Chill until firm, 3 to 4 hours. Top with remaining Cool Whip.

LEMON MERINGUE PIE   Natalia Boser

Filling:

6 Tbsp. flour	1 lemon rind
3 Tbsp. cornstarch	½ c. lemon juice
1 c. sugar	1 Tbsp. butter
3 c. boiling water	¼ tsp. salt
3 egg yolks	9½ inch baked pie shell

Combine flour, cornstarch, and sugar; add to boiling water, stirring while adding. Cook over low flame for 15 minutes, stirring constantly. Beat the egg yolks slightly and add part of the hot mixture to them; mix well and return to the remainder of the sugar and cornstarch mixture. Stir and cook over low flame until the egg yolks are thickened. Remove from the heat; add the grated lemon rind, lemon juice, butter, and salt and mix well. Cool. Pour into a 9½ inch baked pastry shell.

Meringue:

3 egg whites	½ tsp. vanilla
¼ tsp. salt	½ tsp. almond extract
6 Tbsp. sugar	

Add salt to egg whites and beat until stiff. Fold in sugar gradually and add vanilla and almond extract. Spread on top of lemon filling and brown in oven at 300° for 15 to 20 minutes.

BETTY'S PECAN PIE   Dorothy Skellett

3 eggs	1 c. Karo syrup
½ c. brown sugar, firmly packed	½ tsp. vanilla
	1 c. pecans, broken up
¼ tsp. salt	1 (8 inch) pie shell

Mix together eggs, brown sugar, salt, Karo syrup, vanilla, and pecans. Pour into pie shell. Bake at 350° for 45 minutes. (Pecans rise during baking.) If you use a glass pan, bake pie at 300°.

PINEAPPLE PIE

Ann Dobransky

1 (20 oz.) can crushed pineapple
2 Tbsp. cornstarch
¼ tsp. salt

¼ c. sugar
2 Tbsp. butter or margarine
Dough for 2 crust pie

Drain pineapple. Combine cornstarch, salt, and sugar; stir into pineapple juice. Cook until thickened. Add drained pineapple and butter to thickened mixture. Pour into pastry lined pie tin. Put on top crust and bake for 25 to 30 minutes or until crust is brown in moderate oven (350°).

PAPER BAG PLUM PIE

Ann Dobransky

Filling:

4 c. quartered purple plums
½ c. sugar
¼ c. flour
¼ tsp. salt

¼ tsp. nutmeg
1 Tbsp. lemon juice
9 inch pastry shell (unbaked)

Remove pits from plums and cut each half crosswise. Combine sugar, flour, salt, and nutmeg; add to plums and mix well. Heap into pastry shell; sprinkle with lemon juice.

Topping:

½ c. flour
½ c. sugar

½ tsp. cinnamon
½ c. butter or margarine

Cut butter into blended flour, sugar, and cinnamon; sprinkle topping over filling. Slip the pie into a heavy brown paper bag large enough to cover the pie loosely. Fold open end over twice and fasten with paper clips or staples. Place on a large cookie sheet for easier handling. Bake at 425° for 1 hour. Remove from oven and let rest a few minutes to give juice time to stop bubbling. Remove bag and place pie on cake rack until ready to serve. Good served with vanilla ice cream or dollops of whipped cream or dairy sour cream.

PUMPKIN PIE I

Helen Charnetsky

3 c. steamed pumpkin
1 c. brown sugar
½ c. white sugar
2 Tbsp. molasses or Karo syrup
¼ tsp. cloves

2 tsp. cinnamon
1 tsp. ginger
1 tsp. salt
4 eggs, beaten
2 c. scalded milk

Combine pumpkin, sugars, spices, molasses, eggs, and milk; blend well. Pour into 2 (10 inch) pie shells. Bake for 10 minutes in preheated oven at 400°, then lower temperature to 300° for about 45 minutes. Bake on lower rack.

PUMPKIN PIE II

Sophie Cox

1½ c. cooked, mashed pumpkin
1 tsp. cinnamon
½ tsp. cloves
¼ tsp. nutmeg
1 tsp. salt
1 c. dark brown sugar
3 egg yolks, beaten

5 Tbsp. flour
1 c. milk
½ tsp. vanilla
½ tsp. grated orange rind
1 baked 9 inch pie shell
⅓ c. sugar
3 egg whites

Combine pumpkin, cinnamon, cloves, nutmeg, salt, brown sugar, egg yolks, and flour; add milk and cook in double boiler. Add vanilla and orange rind. Pour into baked pie shell. Add sugar to egg whites and beat until creamy. Spread over pumpkin. Bake at 325° for 20 minutes.

PUMPKIN PIE III

Ann Dobransky

1½ c. pumpkin
¾ c. brown sugar
½ tsp. salt
½ tsp. ginger
1 tsp. cinnamon
¼ tsp. cloves

¼ tsp. nutmeg
3 eggs, beaten
⅔ c. evaporated milk
1 c. milk
1 (9 inch) pie shell

Combine all ingredients; pour into pastry lined 9 inch pie pan and bake at 400° for 50 minutes.

WILMA'S PARADISE PUMPKIN PIE

Jane Ellsworth

1 (8 oz.) cream cheese
¼ c. sugar
½ tsp. vanilla

1 egg
9 inch unbaked pie crust

Combine cream cheese, sugar, and vanilla, mixing until well blended and creamy. Add egg and blend. Spread over bottom of unbaked pie crust.

Top Filling:

1¼ c. canned pumpkin
½ c. sugar
1 tsp. cinnamon
¼ tsp. ginger

¼ tsp. nutmeg
Dash of salt
1 c. evaporated milk
2 eggs, slightly beaten

Combine pumpkin, sugar, cinnamon, ginger, nutmeg, salt, milk, and beaten eggs. Blend until smooth. Carefully pour over cheese mixture. Bake at 350° for 50 to 60 minutes. Test with cake tester or with a knife inserted into pumpkin mixture and if it comes out clean, pie is baked.

RHUBARB MERINGUE PIE

Nancy Tarcha

Filling:

3 c. sliced rhubarb
1 c. sugar
2 Tbsp. butter

2 Tbsp. flour
2 egg yolks
1 baked 9 inch pie shell

Combine rhubarb, sugar, butter, flour, and egg yolks in a saucepan and cook about 15 minutes until it is a thick pudding. Pour into a baked pie shell.

Meringue:

2 egg whites
¼ tsp. cream of tartar

4 Tbsp. sugar

Beat egg whites with cream of tartar until frothy. Gradually beat in sugar, a little at a time; continue beating until stiff and glossy. Pile meringue on hot pie filling. Bake at 350° for 20 minutes, until light brown.

If you want a higher meringue, increase recipe by 1 more egg. Add yolk to pudding and white of egg to meringue, plus 2 tablespoons of sugar per egg white.

GLAZED STRAWBERRY RHUBARB PIE

Ann Dobransky

1¼ c. sugar
⅛ tsp. salt
⅓ c. flour
2 c. fresh strawberries
2 c. fresh rhubarb, cut in 1 inch
   pieces

2 Tbsp. butter or margarine
1 Tbsp. sugar
Pastry for 2 crusts (10 inch
   pan)

Arrange half of strawberries and rhubarb in pastry-lined pan. Combine 1¼ cups sugar, salt, and flour; sprinkle half of this mixture over fruit. Repeat layers with remaining fruit and sugar mixture. Dot with butter or margarine. Adjust top crust of pie; brush with cold water and sprinkle with 1 tablespoon sugar. Bake in a hot oven at 400° to 450° for 40 to 50 minutes. Serve with sour cream.

OLGA'S ITALIAN RICE PIE

Anna Chyl

Crust:

1 c. flour
2 Tbsp. sugar
½ tsp. baking powder
½ tsp. vanilla

1 Tbsp. cooking oil
¼ c. milk
1 egg

Mix ingredients together in a bowl. Roll out dough and line a 9 inch pie plate.

Filling:

½ c. rice
1 c. milk
1 tsp. melted butter
½ c. sugar

2 Tbsp. citron
½ lb. Ricotta cheese
4 eggs
¼ tsp. cinnamon

Cook rice in boiling water for seven minutes; drain and set aside. Mix together milk, butter, citron, and sugar. Cook for 10 minutes; remove from heat. Add rice, cheese, and well beaten eggs. Blend well; add cinnamon. Pour mixture into pie shell and bake for 35 minutes at 325°. (Pie freezes well.)

FROZEN STRAWBERRY-YOGURT PIE Natalia Boser

2 (8 oz.) containers vanilla
  yogurt
1 (8 oz.) container Cool Whip,
  thawed

2 c. sweetened, diced
  strawberries
1 (9 inch) graham cracker or
  pastry pie shell

Fold yogurt into Cool Whip; blend well. Fold in strawberries. Spoon into pie shell. Freeze until firm (4 hours or overnight). Remove from freezer 30 minutes before serving - keep chilled in refrigerator. Garnish with whole strawberries. Serve.

SHONEY'S STRAWBERRY PIE Mary Kostyun

1½ c. sugar
1½ c. boiling water
¼ c. cornstarch

1 (3 oz.) pkg. strawberry Jell-O
1 qt. fresh strawberries
1 (9 inch) baked pie shell

Dissolve sugar in boiling water; combine cornstarch with strawberry Jell-O. Add to sugar mixture; mix thoroughly until Jell-O is dissolved. Cool. Arrange fresh strawberries in baked pie shell. Pour thickened mixture over strawberries. Chill. Serve with whipped cream.

TOLL HOUSE PIE Helen Rucky

1 (9 inch) unbaked pie shell
2 eggs
½ c. flour
½ c. sugar
½ c. firmly packed brown sugar
1 c. margarine

1 (6 oz.) pkg. semi-sweet
  chocolate chips
1 c. chopped walnuts
Whipped cream or Cool Whip
  (optional)

Line pie pan with unbaked shell. In large bowl, beat eggs until foamy. Add flour and sugars; blend well. Add melted margarine (cooled to room temperature); stir in chips and nuts. Pour into pie shell. Bake at 325° for 1 hour. Serve with whipped cream or Cool Whip.

ZUCCHINI CRUMB PIE
Jane Ellsworth

Crumb Mixture:

4 c. flour
1 c. sugar
½ tsp. salt

3 sticks margarine
2 tsp. cinnamon

In bowl, combine flour, sugar, and salt. Cut in margarine with pastry blender or 2 knives until crumbly. Place half of crumb mixture in an ungreased 9x13 inch pan. Bake for 10 minutes at 350°. Cool.

Filling:

**8 c. diced zucchini, peeled and
  seeded**
⅔ c. lemon juice

1 c. sugar
1½ tsp. cinnamon

Cook zucchini with lemon juice until tender. Add sugar and cinnamon; simmer 1 minute. Add ½ cup crumb mixture to zucchini filling. Cool. Pour cooled filling over baked crumb mixture. To remaining crumb mixture, add 2 teaspoons cinnamon; sprinkle over zucchini filling. Bake at 375° for 30 to 35 minutes.

Salads

Dressings

SALADS, DRESSINGS, SAUCES

TANGY BEET SALAD
Celia Matias

1 (3 oz.) pkg. raspberry gelatin
1 (1 lb.) can beets, drained well
  (save liquid)

½ bottle horseradish
¼ c. vinegar

Chop beets fine; drain. Combine beet juice, vinegar, and enough water to make 2 cups of liquid. Heat to boiling point; add gelatin and stir well. Refrigerate until slightly jelled; add beets and horseradish. Beets will sink to the bottom if you mix them in too soon. Refrigerate until well set. Serve with ham.

BROCCOLI SALAD
Julieanne Marra

2 heads broccoli florets
1 small red onion, sliced
½ lb. bacon, cooked crisp
½ c. chopped walnuts
½ c. raisins
½ c. Craisins

8 oz. shredded Mozzarella
  (optional)
1 c. Miracle Whip salad
  dressing
½ c. sugar
2 Tbsp. vinegar

Combine broccoli, onion, bacon, cheese, walnuts, raisins, and Craisins; set aside. Cream together salad dressing, sugar, and vinegar and add to rest of ingredients. Chill for one-half hour before serving.

LOW CALORIE CABBAGE SALAD
Linda Youmans

1 medium head cabbage,
  shredded
1 onion, chopped
1 c. celery, chopped
1 green pepper, diced
1 tsp. salt

1 tsp. celery seed
1 tsp. white mustard seed or ½
  tsp. ground mustard
½ c. cider vinegar
Sugar substitute to equal 1 tsp.
  sugar

Combine all vegetables. In a small bowl, combine seasonings, vinegar, and sugar. Pour over cabbage mixture; stir well. Refrigerate. When ready to serve, 2 teaspoons oil may be added to each serving.

COLESLAW I

Sue Blue Charnetsky

1 small head cabbage, shredded
½ c. mayonnaise
2 Tbsp. sugar
1 Tbsp. lemon juice
¼ c. raisins
¼ c. carrots, shredded

1 Tbsp. vinegar
1 onion, chopped
1 Tbsp. oil
Salt to taste
Pepper to taste
Cinnamon to taste

In a bowl, combine all ingredients except onion. Saute onion in the oil; add to cabbage mixture. Refrigerate overnight.

COLESLAW II

Sophie Malowicky

1 small head cabbage
1 small onion
1 green pepper
½ c. sugar

¼ c. salad oil
½ c. cider vinegar
¼ c. water
Salt to taste

Shred cabbage very fine; dice onion very fine. Dice green pepper; combine all vegetables. Combine sugar, oil, vinegar, water, and salt; stir until dissolved and well blended. Pour over cabbage mixture; refrigerate at least 3 hours before serving. Stays crisp for at least a week.

FREEZER COLESLAW

Anna Chyl

1 gal. shredded cabbage
1 Tbsp. salt
2 carrots, chopped
1 green pepper, chopped

1 c. vinegar
½ c. boiling water
2 c. sugar
1 tsp. celery seed

Mix cabbage and salt well and allow to stand for one hour. Add vinegar and sugar to boiling water. Boil one minute and cool. Squeeze salt water from cabbage; discard liquid. Add chopped vegetables, celery seed, and cooled vinegar mixture; mix well. Let stand ½ hour. Package and freeze.

LUCHOW'S COLESLAW

Mary Kostyun

1 medium head cabbage,
   shredded
2 qt. boiling water
2 onions, shredded fine
1 to 2 green peppers, shredded
   fine

¼ c. vinegar
2 egg yolks, beaten
1 tsp. salt
½ tsp. pepper
3 Tbsp. olive oil
1 c. sour cream

Scald cabbage for 5 minutes in boiling water. Drain well; press out all the water. Mix onions, green pepper, and vinegar. In a small bowl, beat eggs, salt, and pepper. Add oil gradually, beating steadily. Pour over cabbage mixture and mix well. Add sour cream and stir until well mixed.

SPICY MARINATED PEPPER SLAW   Marianne Lawryk

3 large red bell peppers, cut
   into matchstick strips
2 jalapeno chilies, minced

½ c. red wine vinegar
3 Tbsp. sugar
12 c. cabbage, thinly sliced

Put peppers and chilies in a large bowl. In a heavy saucepan, over medium heat, bring oil, vinegar, and sugar to a boil, stirring often. Pour over pepper mixture; toss to coat. Cool. Add cabbage and toss. Cover and refrigerate.

COLESLAW SUPREME   Anne Girnis

1 c. sour cream
3 Tbsp. lemon juice
1 tsp. diced onion
1 tsp. prepared mustard
1 tsp. celery seed

1 tsp. sugar
1 tsp. salt
Dash of pepper
5 c. shredded cabbage

In a small bowl, combine sour cream, lemon juice, onion, mustard, celery seed, sugar, salt, and pepper; blend well. Pour over cabbage in a large bowl.

WARM SLAW   Marie Brink

2 egg yolks, beaten
2 Tbsp. sour cream
1 c. white vinegar
1 Tbsp. butter

1 medium head cabbage,
   shredded fine
Salt and pepper to taste

In a small saucepan, combine egg yolks, sour cream, vinegar, and butter; blend well. Cook over medium heat; bring to a boil. Pour over cabbage in a large bowl. Add salt and pepper to taste.

CARROT SALAD I   Natalia Boser

2 lb. carrots, peeled and sliced
1 small onion, chopped
½ green pepper, chopped
1 stalk celery, chopped
1 c. tomato juice

½ c. white vinegar
½ c. honey
½ c. salad oil
1 tsp. dry mustard
¼ tsp. celery seed

Cook carrots in small amount of water until tender. Drain carrots and combine onions, peppers, and celery. In a medium saucepan, combine tomato juice, vinegar, honey, oil, dry mustard, and celery seed. Bring to a boil. Pour sauce over vegetables. Mix thoroughly. Allow mixture to stand in refrigerator overnight before serving.

CARROT SALAD II

Olga Gooley

2 lb. carrots, sliced
1 (10¾ oz.) can tomato soup
½ c. sugar
½ c. vinegar

½ c. oil
1 onion, chopped
1 small green pepper, chopped
1 stalk celery, chopped

Cook carrots until crisp-tender, about 12 minutes; drain. Combine remaining ingredients. Add to carrots; mix well. Refrigerate at least 24 hours.

CARROT SALAD III

Sophia Malowicky

2 c. carrots, ground
1 lemon, ground
½ c. sugar

Dash of salt
Raisins (optional)

In a salad bowl, combine all the ingredients; mix well. Refrigerate.

CARROT SALAD IV

Helen Rucky

4 c. shredded raw carrots
2 Tbsp. sugar
1 tsp. salt
2 c. celery, diced

1 c. raisins
¼ c. mayonnaise
Salt to taste

Mix shredded carrots, sugar, and salt. Let stand 1 hour. Place in large colander or strainer. Add celery and raisins; mix and let stand 30 minutes in colander or strainer. Stir in mayonnaise; mix well. Let stand in colander 15 to 20 minutes so extra mayonnaise can drain. Makes 6 to 8 servings.

CARROT SALAD V

Eugenia Skarvinko

3 to 4 carrots, grated
1 apple, grated
1 orange, chopped

1 c. crushed pineapple
½ c. concentrated orange juice, thawed

In a bowl, combine all ingredients; mix well. Chill and serve.

CHICKEN SALAD

Anna Smyk

2 c. chicken, cooked and cubed
½ c. celery, diced
¼ c. mayonnaise or salad
  dressing

½ tsp. salt
½ tsp. poultry seasoning
⅛ tsp. onion salt
Dash of pepper

In a medium bowl, combine chicken and celery. In another bowl, combine mayonnaise, salt, poultry seasoning, onion salt, and pepper. Pour over chicken and celery. Toss and cover. Chill 2 or 3 hours, preferably overnight.

DELUXE CHICKEN SALAD

Shirley Buchma

4 c. chicken breast, cooked and
  cubed
1 (16 oz.) can crushed
  pineapple, drained
2 c. seedless grapes, halved

2 c. celery, diced
Hellmann's mayonnaise
  (enough to moisten)
Salt and pepper to taste

In a salad bowl, combine chicken, pineapple, celery, salt, pepper, grapes, and mayonnaise. Mix well; cover and refrigerate. Serves 8 to 10.

JAPANESE CHICKEN SALAD

Carol Williams

3 to 4 cooked chicken breasts,
  chopped
1 head lettuce, torn
3 green onions, sliced

1 (3 oz.) can chow mein noodles
1 (4 oz.) pkg. slivered almonds,
  toasted
¼ c. poppy seeds

Combine chicken, lettuce, and onions in a large bowl. Add noodles, almonds, and poppy seeds just before tossing with the following dressing.

Dressing:

4 Tbsp. wine vinegar
4 Tbsp. sugar
2 tsp. salt

½ tsp. pepper
½ c. salad oil

Combine all ingredients in a covered container; shake to blend. Pour just before serving over chicken combined with the other ingredients. Toss to cover all ingredients in bowl.

EGG SALAD SANDWICHES

Jody Dimitriou
Beth Harendza

1 doz. hard-boiled eggs
1½ c. mayonnaise
3 Tbsp. Indian relish

½ tsp. pepper
1 tsp. salt
2 loaves bread

Peel shell from eggs; chop eggs. Combine mayonnaise with relish, salt, and pepper; mix well. Add to eggs; mix thoroughly. Spread some on a slice of bread; top with another bread slice. Cut in half or quarters. Continue using all bread and salad. Serves approximately 50.

FRUIT SALAD
Julia Dudik

1 c. fruit cocktail, drained
1 c. crushed pineapple, drained
1 c. miniature marshmallows
1 c. fresh orange slices, seeds
   removed

½ c. chopped walnuts
½ c. coconut flakes (optional)
1 c. sour cream
2 fresh bananas, sliced

Combine all ingredients except bananas which are sliced and added just before serving.

FRUIT SALADA
Eugenia Skarvinko

1 apple, chopped
1 banana, chopped
1 orange, chopped
½ c. chopped walnuts

½ c. raisins
½ c. low fat yogurt
1 Tbsp. honey

In a bowl, combine apple, banana, orange, raisins, and walnuts. In a small bowl, combine yogurt and honey; pour over fruit. Mix to thoroughly combine and coat all the fruit. Chill before serving.

LOW CALORIE FRUIT SALAD TOPPING
Millie Finch

1 c. fresh strawberries or other
   fruit
¾ c. cottage cheese

3 Tbsp. lemon juice
2 Tbsp. honey

Place all ingredients in a blender; blend until very smooth. Spoon over a fresh fruit salad.

BLACK CHERRY SALAD
Jeanne Sankowski

1 (3 oz.) pkg. black cherry
   Jell-O
1 c. boiling water
1 Tbsp. orange juice
1 (1 lb.) can dark pitted
   cherries

2 Tbsp. mandarin orange juice
1 (11 oz.) can mandarin orange
   sections

Dissolve Jell-O in boiling water. Drain cherries in measuring cup; add cold water to make 1 cup. Add cherry juice, orange juice, and mandarin juice to the Jell-O. Chill until slightly thick. Fold in cherries and mandarin orange sections. Chill until firm.

Dressing:

½ c. whipping cream, whipped, or Cool Whip
½ c. mayonnaise

¼ c. chopped or slivered, toasted almonds

Combine all ingredients. Top each serving of salad with a dollop of dressing.

BLACKBERRY SURPRISE SALAD
Helen Rucky

2 (3 oz.) pkg. raspberry Jell-O
1 c. boiling water
1 c. blackberry wine
1 (1 lb.) can black cherries, drained (save juice)

1 (3 oz.) pkg. cream cheese, cut in small pieces
½ c. broken walnuts

In a medium bowl, dissolve Jell-O with boiling water. Add wine and cherry juice. Mix well. Refrigerate until slightly thickened. Stir in cherries, cream cheese, and walnuts. Pour into a mold. Refrigerate.

FRESH BLUEBERRY SALAD
Dorothy Skellett

2 (3 oz.) black cherry Jell-O
3 c. boiling water
1 (8½ oz.) can crushed pineapple, drained

¼ c. maraschino cherries, halved
2 c. fresh blueberries

Place gelatin in a large bowl; add boiling water. Stir gelatin until it is completely dissolved. Add crushed pineapple and chill until thickened. Fold in maraschino cherries and blueberries. Chill until firm.

DELUXE CHEESE MOLD
Mary Ponas

1 (3 oz.) pkg. orange gelatin
1 c. boiling water
1 c. orange sherbet
1½ c. cottage cheese with pineapple or 1 c. plain cottage cheese and 1 (8¾ oz.) crushed pineapple, drained

Dissolve gelatin in boiling water; add sherbet. Blend. Chill until very thick. Add cottage cheese; stir. Chill until firm in ring mold.

COTTAGE CHEESE SALAD I

Anne Girnis

1 (12 oz.) can evaporated milk
1 lb. cottage cheese
1 (20 oz.) can crushed
   pineapple, drained

2 c. boiling water
1 (3 oz.) pkg. lemon gelatin
1 (3 oz.) pkg. lime gelatin
1 tsp. salt

    In a bowl, combine milk, cheese, and pineapple. Mix well. Set aside. Dissolve the lemon and lime gelatin in the boiling water. Add the salt. Mix until dissolved. Add to cottage cheese mixture; chill until ready to serve.

COTTAGE CHEESE SALAD II

Mary Mihalko

24 oz. small curd cottage cheese
15 oz. canned crushed
   pineapple, drained

1 (6 oz.) pkg. strawberry gelatin
1 (8 oz.) Cool Whip

    Combine cottage cheese and pineapple; sprinkle with gelatin. Fold in Cool Whip. Refrigerate.

CRANBERRY RELISH MOLD

Helen Rucky

1 (8 oz.) can crushed pineapple
1 (3 oz.) pkg. strawberry gelatin
1 env. unflavored gelatin
½ c. sugar
1 c. hot water
1 Tbsp. lemon juice

1 c. ground fresh cranberries
1 c. chopped celery
1 small orange, ground (seeds
   removed)
½ c. chopped walnuts

    Drain pineapple, reserving syrup. Add enough water to syrup to make ½ cup. Dissolve gelatin and sugar in hot water. Add reserved syrup and lemon juice. Chill until partially set. Add pineapple and remaining ingredients. Pour into 5 cup ring mold. Chill overnight.

FRESH CRANBERRY RELISH

Mary Mihalko

2 (12 oz.) pkg. fresh cranberries
2 large or 3 small Sunkist
   oranges
3 Granny Smith apples, peeled
   and cored
1 (20 oz.) can crushed pineapple

4 (3 oz.) pkg. raspberry or
   strawberry jello
1 c. sugar
1 c. boiling water
2 c. cranberry juice

    Grind cranberries, oranges with the peel, and apples; mix all together. Add crushed pineapple; mix thoroughly. Dissolve sugar and jello in boiling water and cranberry juice; add to combined fruit. Mix thoroughly. Refrigerate. Serve with any meat, but especially good with turkey or pork.

DIVINE DESSERT SALAD

Evelyn Kanazawich

¾ c. whole natural almonds
1 (1 lb. 4½ oz.) can crushed
   pineapple
Water
1 (3 oz.) pkg. lemon gelatin
1 (3 oz.) pkg. lime gelatin

1 c. heavy cream
1 c. mayonnaise
2 Tbsp. prepared horseradish
½ tsp. salt
1½ c. small curd creamed
   cottage cheese

Coarsely chop almonds; place in shallow pan in 300° oven for 15 minutes or until golden brown. Drain pineapple well; reserve liquid. Add enough water to make 2 cups. Combine liquid and gelatin in saucepan; heat, stirring until dissolved. Cool slightly in bowl. Beat in cream, mayonnaise, horseradish, and salt. Chill until mixture mounds on spoon. Fold in almonds, pineapple, and cottage cheese. Turn into 6½ cup ring mold; chill until firm. Unmold onto serving plate; garnish with additional almonds.

HEAVENLY SALAD

Anne Girnis

1 (3 oz.) pkg. lemon or lime
   gelatin
1½ c. boiling water
1 (3 oz.) pkg. cream cheese
1 (20 oz.) can crushed
   pineapple, drained

½ c. diced almonds
1 pkg. Dream Whip
1 tsp. almond flavoring
Maraschino cherries for
   garnish

In a large bowl, dissolve gelatin in boiling water; add cream cheese to dissolved gelatin. Mix until well blended; refrigerate until thickened. Add pineapple and almonds; mix well. Refrigerate until almost firm; prepare Dream Whip according to package directions, adding almond flavoring. Combine Dream Whip with gelatin mixture; top with sliced cherries. Chill until firm and ready to serve.

HOLIDAY JELLO SALAD

Mildred Charnetsky

1 (1 lb.) can pitted Bing
   cherries
1 (11 oz.) can mandarin oranges
1 (6 oz.) pkg. raspberry Jell-O

½ c. Port wine
½ c. coarsely chopped pecans
Salad greens

Drain cherries and oranges, reserving the juices. Pour juices into a 1 quart measuring cup. Add enough water to make 3¼ cups liquid. Heat juice mixture to boiling; add gelatin and stir until gelatin is dissolved. Cool slightly; stir in wine. Chill until mixture is the consistency of unbeaten egg whites. Fold in cherries, orange segments, and nuts. Pour into a 1½ quart gelatin mold. Chill several hours until set. Unmold on salad greens. Serves 8 to 10.

JEANNIE'S HAPPY SALAD

Dorothy Skellett

1 (3 oz.) pkg. instant pistachio
  pudding
1 (8 oz.) ctn. Cool Whip

1 (20 oz.) can crushed pineapple
  (undrained)

Mix pudding with Cool Whip. Add pineapple and juice and mix well. Refrigerate until firm.

JELLO ICE CREAM SALAD

Marion Kaspryk

1 (3 oz.) raspberry gelatin
1 c. hot water
1 c. vanilla ice cream
1 small can crushed pineapple,
  drained

½ c. nuts, chopped
1 medium banana, sliced

Combine gelatin and hot water; stir until dissolved. Add ice cream; stir until ice cream is melted and evenly distributed throughout mixture. Set aside until partially thickened. Combine pineapple, nuts, and banana; add to partially thickened gelatin. Pour into a 1 quart mold. Chill until firm.

JELLO PRETZEL SALAD

Linda Zapach

¾ c. butter or margarine
Very thin pretzels, broken to
  make 2 c.
1 Tbsp. sugar
1 (8 oz.) pkg. cream cheese
1 c. sugar
1 (12 oz.) container whipped
  topping

1 (6 oz.) pkg. strawberry gelatin
2 c. boiling water
2 (10 oz.) pkg. frozen
  strawberries, partially
  thawed

Melt butter in a 9x13 inch glass pan; combine pretzels with 1 tablespoon sugar. Add to butter in pan; mix to coat pretzels. Press down into pan to cover bottom to form a crust. Bake at 350° for 8 minutes. Cool completely. In a large bowl, beat cream cheese with 1 cup sugar; fold in whipped topping. Spread over cooled pretzel layer. Dissolve gelatin in boiling water. Stir in strawberries; mix thoroughly. Chill in refrigerator about 20 minutes or until mixture begins to thicken. Pour over cream cheese layer. Refrigerate. To serve, cut into squares.

LAYERED GELATIN

Helen Rucky

1 (3 oz.) pkg. lemon Jell-O
1 (3 oz.) pkg. lime Jell-O
1 (3 oz.) pkg. strawberry Jell-O
1 (3 oz.) pkg. orange Jell-O
4 c. boiling water
2 c. cold water

2 c. milk
1 c. sugar
2 env. unflavored gelatin
½ c. cold water
2 c. sour cream
2 tsp. vanilla

Dissolve lemon Jell-O in 1 cup boiling water; add ½ cup cold water. Pour into greased 9x13 inch pan; chill. Spoon ⅓ cup milk mixture; cool 20 to 30 minutes or until set. Repeat with lime Jell-O, ⅓ cup milk mixture, and then strawberry with remaining milk mixture and ending with orange.

Milk Mixture: Bring milk to a boil; add sugar. Dissolve unflavored gelatin in ½ cup cold water and add to milk. Beat until fluffy. Cool slightly; add sour cream and vanilla. Blend well. Keep at room temperature while waiting for layers to harden.

LEMON-LIME TROPICAL MOLD

Helen Rucky

1 (8¼ oz.) can crushed
   pineapple
1 (3 oz.) pkg. lime Jell-O
1 c. boiling water
1 c. cold water

¼ c. chopped nuts
1 (3 oz.) pkg. lemon Jell-O
1½ c. boiling water
1 (8 oz.) pkg. cream cheese

Drain pineapple, reserving ¼ cup syrup. Dissolve lime Jell-O in boiling water; add cold water. Chill until partially set; fold in pineapple and nuts. Pour into oiled 1½ quart mold; chill until almost set. Dissolve lemon Jell-O in water; add reserved syrup. Gradually add to softened cream cheese, mixing until well blended. Pour over lime layer. Chill until firm.

MANDARIN ORANGE MOLD

Anna Chyl

2 (6 oz.) orange gelatin
3 c. boiling water
3 c. cold water
1 (20 oz.) can crushed
   pineapple, drained (reserve ½
   c. juice for topping)
2 small cans mandarin oranges
   (undrained)

Miniature marshmallows
¾ c. sugar
1 egg, beaten
2 Tbsp. flour
1 (8 oz.) cream cheese
1 (12 oz.) ctn. Cool Whip
Coconut

Dissolve gelatin in boiling water. Add cold water; stir. Add pineapple; stir. Pour into a 9x13 inch pan. Top with enough marshmallows to cover. Refrigerate until firm.

In a medium saucepan, combine pineapple juice, sugar, egg, and flour. Cook over medium heat, stirring constantly, until thick. Remove from heat. Add cream cheese to hot mixture; stir until smooth. Cool completely. Add Cool Whip; stir. Spread over firm gelatin. Sprinkle with coconut. Refrigerate.

CREAMY ORANGE SALAD
Helen Rucky

1 (3 oz.) pkg. orange Jell-O
1½ c. boiling water
1 (8 oz.) pkg. cream cheese

¼ c. orange juice
1 Tbsp. lemon juice
1 Tbsp. grated orange rind

Dissolve Jell-O in boiling water. Gradually add to softened cream cheese, mixing until well blended. Stir in juices and rind; chill until partially set. Pour into oiled 1 quart mold; chill until firm.

ORANGE-PINEAPPLE SALAD MOLD
Mary Kostyun

1 c. boiling water
1 (3 oz.) pkg. orange gelatin
1 pt. vanilla ice cream, softened
1 small can mandarin oranges, drained
1 small can pineapple tidbits, drained

1 to 2 bananas, sliced
⅓ bag miniature marshmallows
½ c. chopped walnuts
¼ c. maraschino cherries, chopped

Dissolve gelatin in boiling water. Add ice cream; stir well. Chill until thickened. Combine mandarin oranges, pineapple, bananas, marshmallows, walnuts, and cherries. Add to gelatin mixture; stir. Pour into mold; refrigerate. Serves 6 to 8.

PARTY SALAD
Mary Ponas

1 (3 oz.) pkg. lemon or lime gelatin
1 c. boiling water
1 (20 oz.) can crushed pineapple

½ c. cottage cheese
1 c. whipped topping
¼ c. chopped maraschino cherries

In a bowl, combine gelatin and boiling water; stir until completely dissolved. Drain pineapple, reserving the juice; add ½ cup of the juice to the gelatin. Chill until very thick; fold in pineapple, cottage cheese, whipped topping, and maraschino cherries. Pour into a 9x5x3 inch loaf pan. Chill until firm.

PEACH PARTY LOAF

Sophie Malowicky

2 (1 lb.) cans sliced peaches
1½ c. grapefruit juice
2 (3 oz.) pkg. lemon Jell-O
¼ tsp. salt

1½ c. cottage cheese
½ c. celery, diced
1 Tbsp. chopped fresh parsley
½ tsp. onion, grated

Drain peaches, reserving the juice. In a bowl, combine Jell-O and salt; heat 1 cup peach juice and the grapefruit juice. Pour over Jell-O; stir until completely dissolved. Place in refrigerator until thickened, but not set. Place 1½ cups of the drained peaches on the bottom of a Pyrex baking dish; pour half of the thickened Jell-O over peaches. Place dish with peaches and Jell-O in refrigerator to set. Combine remaining half of thickened Jell-O with remaining ingredients; pour over peach layer. Refrigerate until set. Serves 8 to 10.

RASPBERRY SALAD DESSERT

1 (6 oz.) can frozen lemonade
1 (10 oz.) pkg. frozen red
  raspberries

2 c. water
1 (6 oz.) pkg. raspberry gelatin
1 pt. vanilla ice cream

Thaw lemonade and raspberries; set aside. Place water in 2 quart casserole; microwave on HIGH 5 minutes. Add gelatin; stir until dissolved. Add lemonade and raspberries. Add ice cream, a spoon at a time, stirring to melt. Pour into an 8x8x2 inch pan or 2 quart mold. Refrigerate until set.

STRAWBERRY PEAR GELATIN

Linda Zapach

1 (29 oz.) can pears
1 (6 oz.) pkg. strawberry gelatin
1 (8 oz.) pkg. cream cheese,
  cubed

8 oz. frozen whipped topping,
  thawed
Mandarin oranges (optional)

Drain pears, reserving juice. Chop pears; set aside. Add water to the juice to measure 3 cups. Place in a saucepan; bring to a boil. Transfer to a large bowl. Add gelatin; stir until dissolved. Whisk in cream cheese until smooth. Refrigerate until slightly thickened. Whisk in whipped topping until smooth. Add chopped pears. Pour into a 9x13 inch dish. Cover; refrigerate until firm. Garnish squares with mandarin oranges.

TRIPLE LAYER MOLD

Marion Kaspryk

1 (3 oz.) pkg. orange gelatin
1 c. boiling water
1 c. cold water
¼ tsp. almond extract

1 c. fresh, frozen, or canned
  peaches, sliced and drained
2 c. Cool Whip

Dissolve gelatin in boiling water. Add cold water and almond extract. Chill until slightly thickened, about 1½ hours. Measure ⅓ cup; pour into a 4 cup mold and chill about 5 minutes. Measure ¾ cup gelatin; blend into 1½ cups of the Cool Whip. Carefully spoon into the mold and chill 5 minutes. Add peaches to remaining gelatin; carefully spoon into the mold. Chill 4 hours or overnight. Dip mold just to rim in warm water for 20 to 30 seconds; unmold. Garnish with remaining Cool Whip and additional fruit if desired. Makes 4 cups or 8 servings.

Alternate fruit combinations:

Black cherry gelatin with 1 c. sliced bananas

Strawberry gelatin with 1 c. sliced strawberries

Lime gelatin with 1 c. melon balls

MOLDED VEGETABLE RELISH   Mary Ponas

1 (3 oz.) pkg. lemon or lime
  gelatin
¾ tsp. salt
1 c. boiling water
¾ c. cold water
2 Tbsp. vinegar

2 tsp. grated onion
½ c. finely chopped cabbage
½ c. grated carrot
¼ c. finely chopped celery
3 Tbsp. chopped green pepper

Dissolve gelatin and salt in boiling water. Add cold water, vinegar, and grated onion. Chill until thickened. Fold in vegetables. Pour into a 3 or 4 cup mold. Chill until firm, about 3 hours. Unmold onto a platter; garnish as desired.

HAM AND PINEAPPLE SALAD   Helen Rucky

7¼ oz. (2½ c.) mostaccioli
8 oz. cream cheese, softened
1 (2 oz.) can crushed pineapple
  (reserve liquid)
1 Tbsp. sugar
1 tsp. salt

1½ c. cubed cooked ham
1 c. celery, sliced
1 (16 oz.) can mandarin
  oranges, drained
Sliced almonds (optional)

Cook mostaccioli as directed. Drain; rinse with cold water. In large bowl, beat cream cheese, reserved pineapple liquid, sugar, and salt until smooth. Stir in mostaccioli, ham, pineapple, celery, and orange segments. Refrigerate 2 to 3 hours. Garnish with sliced almonds.

HAM SALAD SANDWICHES

Jody Dimitriou
Beth Harendza

Serves approximately 50 people.

4 lb. ham, ground
6 hard-boiled eggs
½ tsp. pepper

1½ c. mayonnaise
1 tsp. onion powder
2 loaves bread

Combine ham with eggs which have been peeled and chopped. Combine mayonnaise, onion powder, and pepper; mix thoroughly. Add to ham and egg mixture; mix thoroughly. Spread some on a slice of bread; top with another slice of bread. Cut in half or in quarters. Continue using all bread and salad.

KOREAN SALAD

Pam Scannell

1 lb. fresh spinach, washed and
   dried
1 can water chestnuts, drained
1 lb. fresh mushrooms, sliced

6 hard-boiled eggs, sliced
1 lb. bacon, cooked and
   crumbled
Bean sprouts

Layer above ingredients in a large bowl.

Dressing:

1 c. ketchup
1 c. cooking oil
¼ c. vinegar
½ small onion, grated fine

½ c. sugar
2 Tbsp. Worcestershire sauce
¼ tsp. salt

Blend the above ingredients. Chill for one hour. Pour over salad just before serving.

LAYERED SALAD

Rose Klodowski
Dorothy Skellett

1 head lettuce, torn into bite-
   size pieces
½ c. chopped celery
½ c. chopped green pepper
1 (10 oz.) pkg. frozen peas
1 red onion, sliced thin

2 c. mayonnaise
1 Tbsp. sugar
¼ lb. Cheddar cheese, grated
8 slices bacon, fried crisp and
   crumbled

Layer the first five ingredients in a 9x13 inch pan. Spread top layer with mayonnaise; sprinkle with sugar, then with grated cheese and last with crumbled bacon. Cover with foil. Refrigerate 24 hours.

Variation: Can substitute 1 cup mayonnaise and 1 cup sour cream for the 2 cups mayonnaise. Can also cook the peas for 3 minutes and drain before serving.

CAROL'S PICKLED MACARONI
Dorothy Skellett

1 box spirals
5 to 6 drops yellow food
  coloring
2 to 3 Tbsp. cooking oil
3 c. cider vinegar
1½ c. sugar
2 Tbsp. prepared mustard
1 scant Tbsp. coarse pepper

1 Tbsp. salt
1 tsp. garlic salt
1 tsp. Accent
2 Tbsp. chopped fresh parsley
½ (4 oz.) jar pimentos, chopped
1 onion, chopped
1 medium cucumber

Cook spirals according to package directions, adding the yellow food coloring to the water. When cooked to the desired tenderness, drain in colander; rinse and drain well. Transfer to a large bowl; drizzle with the cooking oil. Mix to coat pasta to prevent spirals from sticking together. In a 4 quart bowl, combine cider vinegar, sugar, mustard, pepper, salt, garlic salt, Accent, chopped parsley, pimentos, cucumber, and onion; mix well. Pour over pasta; mix. Cover and refrigerate for 24 hours.

ITALIAN MACARONI SALAD
Mary Buckingham

1 lb. macaroni
½ lb. bacon
8 oz. green olives, sliced

1 chopped onion
¼ tsp. coarse black pepper

Cook macaroni according to directions on package. Fry bacon until crisp. Remove bacon from pan. Add onions and saute until golden color, then add macaroni and olives. Stir well. Crumble bacon over mixture; add coarse black pepper. Mix and serve hot.

LINGUINI SALAD
Marion Kaspryk

1 lb. cooked linguini
1 (8 oz.) bottle Seven Seas
  Italian dressing
½ bottle McCormick Salad
  Supreme*

2 tomatoes, diced
1 large cucumber, diced

Cook linguini according to package directions. Rinse with cold water; drain well. Combine all ingredients; marinate overnight.

* McCormick Salad Supreme can be found at most grocery stores in the spice aisle.

QUICK 1 DISH SALAD

Olga Drost

3 c. macaroni shells, cooked
1 (1 lb.) can kidney beans
1 (12 oz.) can luncheon meat, diced
2 c. cucumber, diced

¾ c. mayonnaise
1 Tbsp. prepared mustard
½ tsp. Tabasco sauce
½ c. sour cream
2 Tbsp. minced parsley

In a salad bowl, combine the macaroni, beans, meat, and cucumber. Mix well. In a small bowl, combine the mayonnaise, Tabasco sauce, and sour cream. Pour over the macaroni and mix well. Sprinkle with parsley. Makes 6 servings.

PASTA SALAD

Linda Zapach

1 (5 oz.) pkg. medium pasta
2 c. cucumbers, thinly sliced
1½ c. diced tomato
1 (7 oz.) can tuna or shrimp, drained and flaked
½ c. chopped celery
¼ c. chopped green pepper

1 c. mayonnaise
½ c. Italian-style salad dressing
1 tsp. prepared mustard
1 tsp. dill weed
1 tsp. salt
⅛ tsp. pepper
1 hard-cooked egg, sliced

Prepare pasta according to package directions for salad use; drain. Combine macaroni with cucumbers, tomato, tuna, celery, and green pepper; blend mayonnaise, salad dressing, mustard, dill weed, salt, and pepper. Toss salad mixture with dressing. Chill. Garnish with egg slices. Serves 8 to 10.

RAVIOLI SALAD

Julieanne Marra

2 (8 oz.) pkg. Celentano mini cheese ravioli or 1 (13 oz.) pkg. regular ravioli, cooked according to pkg. directions
2 carrots, cut in julienne strips

2 c. broccoli florets
1 c. red and green peppers, chopped
2 green onions, finely sliced
½ c. ripe olives, sliced

Salad Dressing:

½ c. olive oil
½ c. red wine vinegar

2 tsp. Dijon mustard
2 tsp. garlic powder

In bowl, blend dressing ingredients. Blanch carrots and broccoli in boiling water 1 minute; rinse in cold water. Drain. Add to dressing ingredients. Toss gently, but well. Chill 2 hours.

ROSA MARINA SALAD

Jane Ellsworth

1 lb. Rosa Marina pasta (No. 30)
2 (No. 2) cans crushed
   pineapple
1 can mandarin oranges
2 Tbsp. flour

¾ c. sugar
1 tsp. salt
2 eggs, slightly beaten
1 large container whipped
   topping (such as Cool Whip)

Cook pasta according to package directions; set aside. Drain pineapple and oranges, reserving juices. In a saucepan, combine sugar, flour, salt, eggs, and reserved juices; cook until thick. Set aside to cool; add pineapple, oranges, and pasta. Mix. Refrigerate overnight. The next day, add whipped topping; mix.

SPAGHETTI SALAD

Helen Rucky

1 lb. spaghetti
1 (8 oz.) bottle Zesty Italian
   dressing
½ bottle Salad Supreme
   seasoning

1 green pepper, chopped
1 medium onion, chopped
2 tomatoes, chopped
1 can black olives, sliced

Break raw spaghetti in ⅓; boil as package directs. Drain. Add remaining ingredients. Chill overnight before serving.

MUSHROOM SALAD

Helen Rucky

2 lb. fresh mushrooms
1 c. Italian salad dressing
½ tsp. garlic powder
½ tsp. onion powder
1 tsp. parsley flakes

8 oz. torn, fresh spinach
2 tomatoes, diced
3 slices bacon, cooked and
   crumbled

Clean and slice mushrooms. Combine with salad dressing, garlic, and onion; toss gently. Sprinkle with parsley. Cover and refrigerate overnight. Drain well and serve on spinach. Garnish with tomatoes and bacon. Serves 6.

MARINATED MUSHROOM SALAD PLATTER

Olga Gooley

1 lb. fresh mushrooms or 2 (6 to 8 oz.) cans whole mushrooms
1 c. celery, thinly sliced
½ green pepper, coarsely chopped
½ onion, finely chopped
1 c. olive or salad oil

¼ c. dry red wine or wine vinegar
2 tsp. basil leaves, crumbled
1 tsp. salt
½ tsp. garlic, finely minced
½ tsp. pepper, coarsely ground
½ tsp. sugar

Rinse, pat dry, and halve fresh mushrooms or drain canned mushrooms. In a large bowl, combine mushrooms, celery, green pepper, and onion; set aside. Mix remaining ingredients. Pour over mushroom mixture; toss well. Refrigerate 6 hours or longer. Serve as salad with assorted, sliced luncheon meats if desired. Yields 6 to 8 servings.

POTATO SALAD

Nancy Tarcha

6 c. potatoes, cooked, diced
½ c. cucumbers, diced
½ c. onions, diced
¼ c. green peppers, diced
½ c. celery, diced
3 Tbsp. pimiento, drained
2 eggs, hard cooked, diced

1 c. sour cream
½ c. mayonnaise
1 Tbsp. prepared mustard
2 Tbsp. vinegar
1½ tsp. salt
⅛ tsp. pepper

In a large salad bowl, combine potatoes, cucumbers, onions, green pepper, celery, pimiento, and eggs. Mix well. In a medium bowl, combine sour cream, mayonnaise, mustard, vinegar, salt, and pepper. Mix thoroughly and pour over the potato mixture. Mix well. Chill thoroughly; serve on salad greens or line the salad bowl with greens.

EASY POTATO SALAD

Carol Williams

½ env. Italian dressing mix
1 Tbsp. vinegar
5 c. potatoes, diced

4 hard cooked eggs, chopped
1½ c. mayonnaise
1 c. chopped celery

Combine salad dressing mix and vinegar. Let stand 20 to 30 minutes. Combine with mayonnaise mixture. Sprinkle potatoes with salt. Add celery and mayonnaise mixture. Fold in chopped eggs. Chill.

EV'S POTATO SALAD

Evelyn Kanazawich

6 or 7 medium potatoes,
  cooked, peeled, diced
3 hard-boiled eggs, chopped
1 large stalk celery, chopped
1 medium onion, chopped

1 c. mayonnaise
1 c. sour cream
2 Tbsp. vinegar
Garlic salt to taste
Salt and pepper to taste

In a large bowl, combine potatoes and eggs. Add celery and onions; mix well. Sprinkle vinegar over potato mixture. In a small bowl, combine mayonnaise, sour cream, garlic salt, salt, and pepper. Pour over potato mixture; mix well. The salad is delicious served warm, but is equally good when served cold. Other vegetables may be added to the salad, such as cucumbers and carrots.

GERMAN POTATO SALAD I

Helen Rucky

Potatoes
1 onion, sliced paper thin
Salt
Pepper

Vinegar
Boiling water
Oil
Cooked bacon (optional)

Boil potatoes in jackets; skin and slice rather thin. Put onion slices over potatoes. Season with salt and pepper. Add a little boiling water and vinegar and mix. Taste for correct seasoning, water, oil, and vinegar. Sprinkle with optional bacon.

GERMAN POTATO SALAD II

Anna Smyk

1 lb. pork sausages, sliced
4 strips bacon, cooked and
  crumbled
½ c. onion, chopped
½ c. celery, diced
1 tsp. salt

½ tsp. sugar
¼ tsp. dry mustard
½ c. water
⅓ c. cider vinegar
4 c. potatoes, cooked and diced
2 Tbsp. mayonnaise

Cook sausage according to directions on the package, then slice in ⅛ inch slices. In a medium skillet, cook bacon until crisp. Remove bacon from pan. Add onions and celery; saute in bacon drippings until limp. Add salt, sugar, pepper, dry mustard, water, and vinegar. Bring to a boil. Boil 2 minutes. In a greased 2½ quart casserole, combine bacon, potatoes, and mayonnaise. Pour the seasoned sauce over the potatoes. Top with sausages. Heat in a 300° oven for 20 minutes.

GERMAN POTATO SALAD III

Carol Williams

6 to 8 potatoes
6 strips bacon
3 Tbsp. bacon grease
1 Tbsp. flour

⅔ c. sugar
⅔ c. vinegar
⅓ c. water
1 medium onion, chopped

Cook potatoes with skins. When cooked, peel and slice. Place potatoes in a large bowl; set aside. Cook bacon until crisp; drain. Save 3 tablespoons bacon fat. Add flour, sugar, vinegar, and water. Bring to a boil; pour over potatoes. Crumble bacon; mix with onion. Sprinkle over top of potatoes. Serve at room temperature.

GREEK POTATO SALAD

Mary Kostyun

1 lb. potatoes, boiled, peeled,
  cooked, and diced
¼ c. onions, chopped
½ c. celery, chopped
1 medium carrot, grated
1 Tbsp. pickles, chopped

1 Tbsp. parsley, chopped
2 Tbsp. salad oil
2 Tbsp. vinegar
Salt and pepper to taste
Black olives and green pepper
  slices for garnish

To the prepared potatoes, add the onions, celery, parsley, carrot, and pickles. Season to taste. Sprinkle oil and vinegar and mix carefully. Place in a salad bowl and garnish with slices of olives and green peppers.

HOT POTATO SALAD

Anna Smyk

3 Tbsp. margarine
3 Tbsp. flour
1 tsp. salt
¾ tsp. dry mustard
¼ tsp. pepper
1½ c. milk

¾ c. mayonnaise
6 medium potatoes, cooked and
  diced
1 medium onion, chopped fine
¼ c. bread crumbs, buttered

In a medium saucepan, melt the margarine. Add flour, salt, mustard, and pepper. Gradually add milk. Bring to a boil; boil 1 minute. Add mayonnaise to the flour mixture; mix well. Pour over potatoes and onion; mix well. Pour into a 2 quart casserole and sprinkle with buttered bread crumbs. Bake, uncovered, at 350° for 1 hour.

MANHATTAN CRANBERRY RELISH
Anna Chyl

1 (16 oz.) can whole cranberry
  sauce
1 (20 oz.) can crushed
  pineapple, drained
½ c. diced orange peel

2 inch cinnamon stick or ½ tsp.
  ground cinnamon
½ tsp. ginger
3 oz. bourbon or whiskey
1 oz. sweet vermouth

Combine all ingredients; mix well. Refrigerate 24 hours before serving. Makes 4 cups.

SAUERKRAUT SALAD I
Anna Grech

½ qt. sauerkraut, squeezed
  until almost dry
1 onion, chopped fine

3 Tbsp. oil
Salt and pepper to taste

In a bowl, combine sauerkraut, onion, salt, pepper, and oil. Mix well.

SAUERKRAUT SALAD II
Mary Mihalko

1 (1 lb.) can sauerkraut,
  drained
½ c. sugar
½ large onion, finely chopped
½ large green pepper, finely
  chopped

½ c. celery, diced
2 to 3 Tbsp. carrot, grated
¼ c. salad oil
2 Tbsp. wine vinegar

Combine sauerkraut and sugar. Let stand 15 to 20 minutes. Drain. Combine chopped vegetables. Mix oil and vinegar thoroughly; pour over vegetables. Add sauerkraut and mix well. Chill several hours or overnight.

SAUERKRAUT SALAD III
Charles Sarnoski

1 (1 lb.) can sauerkraut,
  drained
1 c. green peppers, diced
1 c. celery, diced
1 large onion, diced

1 (7 oz.) jar pimiento, drained
  and diced
¾ c. sugar
⅔ c. cider vinegar
½ c. salad oil

Squeeze juice from sauerkraut. In a bowl, combine sauerkraut, peppers, celery, onion, and pimiento. Mix well. Combine sugar, vinegar, and oil. Pour over cabbage mixture and mix well. Chill before serving.

SHRIMP SALAD

Anne Girnis

1 (1 lb.) can peas, drained
1 (1 lb.) can beets, drained and
  diced

1 lb. cooked shrimp, diced
½ tsp. salt (optional)

In a salad bowl, combine peas, beets, shrimp, and salt. Add enough mayonnaise to blend into the ingredients. Chill before serving.

SHRIMP SUNSHINE SALAD

Mary Kostyun

1 lb. shrimp, cooked and
  deveined (save liquid)
1 (3 oz.) pkg. lemon gelatin
1 c. boiling water

¼ c. carrots, grated
½ c. crushed pineapple, drained
½ c. celery, diced

Dissolve gelatin in boiling water. Pour shrimp liquid into a 1 cup measuring cup. Add water to 1 cup level. Pour into gelatin mixture; stir. Add shrimp; blend. Combine carrots, pineapple, and celery. Add to gelatin mixture. Chill until slightly thickened. Pour into 6 individual molds; chill until firm. Unmold onto crisp salad greens. Garnish with carrot curls.

SPINACH SALAD IN TOMATO CUPS

Helen Rucky

Salad:

1½ c. cooked rice
1 (10 oz.) pkg. frozen chopped
  spinach, thawed and
  squeezed to drain
1 c. chopped tomato
½ c. sliced green onion

½ c. sliced celery
6 large tomatoes, cut in tulip
  shape*
2 Tbsp. sunflower nuts
  (optional)

Dressing:

2 Tbsp. tarragon vinegar
2 Tbsp. oil
1 tsp. dill weed
¾ tsp. salt

¼ tsp. garlic powder
¼ tsp. dry mustard
Dash of pepper

In small bowl, combine dressing ingredients; mix well. In medium bowl, combine rice, spinach, tomato, onion, and celery; mix well. Pour dressing over salad; toss. Refrigerate 1 hour to blend flavors. Spoon about ⅔ cup salad mixture into each tomato tulip. Sprinkle with sunflower nuts.

* To prepare tulip: Hollow out stem portion of center of each tomato. Make 6 cuts from center of each tomato to outside, making sure not to cut through bottom skin.

SHIRLEY'S SPINACH SALAD

Dorothy Skellett

1 lb. fresh spinach
6 slices bacon
3 hard-boiled eggs, sliced
1 onion, sliced

½ c. mayonnaise
½ c. milk
½ c. sugar
3 Tbsp. vinegar

Wash spinach; dry. Tear into bite-sized pieces. Place in a large bowl. Cook bacon until crisp; crumble. Add bacon, eggs, and onion to the spinach; toss well. In a blender, combine mayonnaise, milk, sugar, and vinegar. Pour over spinach mixture at serving time.

TACO SALAD I

Jane Ellsworth
Marie Richardson

1 lb. ground chuck
2 tsp. chili powder
Salt and pepper to taste
1 head lettuce, torn
2 tomatoes, chopped
1 red onion, sliced thin
1 (16 oz.) can red kidney beans,
  drained

½ lb. Cheddar cheese, grated
1 (5 oz.) pkg. tortilla chips,
  crushed
1 (8 oz.) bottle Italian dressing
1 (4 oz.) jar taco sauce

Brown ground chuck and drain grease. Add chili powder, salt, and pepper; mix well. Set aside. In a large bowl, combine tomatoes, onion, beans, and cheese. Add ground chuck mixture and mix well. Refrigerate until ready to serve. Just before serving, place lettuce on a serving dish. Put crushed tortilla chips on lettuce. Place beef mixture over chips. Mix Italian dressing and taco sauce together. Pour over salad.

TACO SALAD II

Linda Zapach

1 lb. ground beef
1 (15 oz.) can kidney beans,
  drained
½ tsp. salt
2 Tbsp. dry minced onions
½ c. tomato paste
1 head iceberg lettuce

2 to 4 tomatoes, cut in wedges
4 to 8 oz. grated Cheddar
  cheese
8 oz. Italian dressing
Taco seasoning to taste
1 small bag taco flavored chips,
  crumbled

Brown ground beef; add beans, salt, onions, and tomatoes to paste. Simmer 10 to 15 minutes. Cool. Chop lettuce and add tomatoes. Toss with cheese, dressing, and meat mixture. Add taco seasoning. Cover with crumbled chips.

TEQUILABERRY'S LOFT SALAD

Pani Julia Lawryk

1 washed head lettuce, chopped
¼ c. shredded carrots
½ c. shredded red cabbage
2 c. mayonnaise
½ c. buttermilk

¼ c. sugar
¼ c. Parmesan cheese
¼ c. real bacon bits
1 c. cauliflower, chopped fine

In a very large bowl, combine lettuce, carrots, and cabbage. In a large jar, combine mayonnaise, buttermilk, sugar, bacon bits, cauliflower, and Parmesan cheese. Shake to blend thoroughly. Pour over salad; toss quickly and serve immediately on chilled plates.

TOMATO ASPIC

Eugenia Skarvinko

1 env. unflavored gelatin
¼ c. cold canned tomato juice
1¾ c. hot tomato juice

2 Tbsp. fresh lemon juice
1 tsp. Worcestershire sauce
1 tsp. dried basil

Sprinkle gelatin over cold tomato juice; set aside to soften. Add hot tomato juice; stir to dissolve. Add remaining ingredients; stir. Pour into a mold. Refrigerate until set. To unmold, put mold in warm water up to the rim; invert on a plate. If it doesn't slide out, take the point of a knife and put it between the aspic and the side of the mold to allow some air to get in to loosen it. Garnish with parsley or other greens.

TOMATOES VINAIGRETTE

Evelyn Kanazawich

4 large tomatoes, peeled
6 Tbsp. chopped fresh parsley
1 clove garlic, crushed
6 Tbsp. olive oil

2 Tbsp. cider vinegar
1 tsp. salt
½ tsp. basil
⅛ tsp. pepper

Slice tomatoes into a bowl; sprinkle with parsley. Combine garlic, olive oil, vinegar, salt, basil, and pepper; pour over tomatoes. Cover. Chill 3 hours or overnight.

DELICIOUS TUNA SALAD

Olga Drost

2 c. macaroni, small elbow, or
    small shells
½ c. mayonnaise
½ c. sour cream
½ tsp. celery seed
½ tsp. salt
1 tsp. grated onion

1 (7 oz.) can tuna fish
1 (17 oz.) can peas, drained
¾ c. mild Cheddar cheese,
    diced
2 Tbsp. green pepper, minced
1 Tbsp. pimiento, diced

Cook macaroni as directed on package; set aside to cool. Combine mayonnaise, sour cream, and seasonings. Gently stir in peas and remaining ingredients as well as macaroni. Chill. Serves 4 to 6 people.

O'S LINGUINI TUNA SALAD
Dorothy Skellett

¼ c. ReaLemon concentrate
¼ c. vegetable oil
¼ c. green onions, sliced
2 tsp. sugar
1 tsp. Italian seasoning
1 tsp. seasoned salt
1 tsp. Tabasco sauce

7 oz. linguini, broken in half, cooked
1 (12½ oz.) can tuna, well-drained
1 (10 oz.) pkg. frozen peas, thawed
2 medium tomatoes, chopped

In a large bowl, combine lemon juice, oil, onions, and seasonings. Mix well. Add hot linguini; toss. Add remaining ingredients; mix well. Chill in refrigerator. Refrigerate leftovers.

WILTED LETTUCE
Dorothy Skellett

1 lb. leaf lettuce or head lettuce
1 onion, thinly sliced
3 Tbsp. bacon drippings

1 tsp. salt
1 Tbsp. sugar
4 Tbsp. vinegar

Wash, drain, and coarsely tear lettuce. Mix onion rings with lettuce. Place in warmed earthen bowl (4 quart). Heat bacon drippings. Blend in salt, sugar, and vinegar. When steaming, pour over lettuce; mix thoroughly.

Note: I break up the bacon I used for the drippings and sprinkle it over the lettuce.

BLUE CHEESE DRESSING
Helen Charnetsky

½ c. crumbled Blue cheese
⅔ c. half & half
½ tsp. dry mustard
1 tsp. paprika

Salt and pepper to taste
⅔ c. salad oil
2 Tbsp. lemon juice

Note: Have all ingredients cold.

Combine all ingredients; place in electric blender. Process until thoroughly blended. Refrigerate. Yield: About 2½ cups.

DRESSING FOR CABBAGE

Celia Matias

¾ c. sugar
⅔ c. vinegar
⅓ c. salad oil

1 tsp. salt
1 tsp. pepper

Combine all ingredients in a jar with a tight fitting lid; shake well to thoroughly blend. Pour over shredded cabbage.

FRENCH DRESSING I

Natalia Boser

½ c. mineral oil
½ c. lemon juice or vinegar
Dash of paprika and cayenne
    pepper

1 Tbsp. catsup
½ Tbsp. Worcestershire sauce
1 clove garlic, minced

Combine all ingredients in a jar with a tight fitting lid; shake well to blend ingredients. Keep refrigerated.

FRENCH DRESSING II

Mary Charnetsky

1 c. salad oil
⅓ c. vinegar
1 clove garlic, slashed
1 Tbsp. vinegar
½ tsp. salt

1 tsp. paprika
½ tsp. dry mustard
¼ tsp. coarsely ground black
    pepper

Combine all ingredients in a jar with a tight fitting lid. Let stand several hours. Shake thoroughly before serving. Yield: 1½ cups.

Blue Cheese Dressing: Add 3 ounces crumbled Blue cheese to the French Dressing.

Zesty Dressing: Add one teaspoon minced onion and one teaspoon Worcestershire sauce to the French Dressing.

RUBY FRENCH DRESSING

Josephine Vimislik

⅔ c. salad oil
⅓ c. red wine vinegar
½ tsp. salt

2 tsp. paprika
1 tsp. dry mustard

Combine all ingredients in a jar with a tight fitting lid; shake until well blended. Refrigerate.

CREAMY GARLIC SALAD DRESSING   Eugenia Skarvinko

1 c. buttermilk
¼ c. low fat yogurt
1 clove garlic, pressed
1 Tbsp. Worcestershire sauce

2 Tbsp. wine vinegar
Pinch of sugar
Salt and pepper to taste

Combine all ingredients in a jar with a tight fitting lid; shake vigorously. Chill. Shake before serving.

RUSSIAN DRESSING   Eugenia Skarvinko

1 c. low fat plain yogurt
½ c. ketchup

1 c. low fat mayonnaise

Combine all ingredients; blend until smooth. A good dressing for greens and vegetables.

CREAMY SALAD DRESSING   Pam Scannell

½ c. finely chopped parsley
1 c. finely chopped carrots
½ c. buttermilk
1½ c. mayonnaise

1 tsp. garlic powder
1 tsp. onion powder
¼ tsp. garlic salt
¼ tsp. salt

Combine and mix all ingredients together; chill 1 hour. Serve over green salad.

CREAMY CUCUMBER SAUCE   Olga Tarcha Drost

1 c. sour cream
2 Tbsp. mayonnaise
¾ c. finely diced cucumbers
1 Tbsp. vinegar

¾ tsp. salt
¾ tsp. chopped fresh dill
Dash of garlic salt

Combine all ingredients; cover. Refrigerate at least 1 hour before serving. Makes about 1½ cups. Serve with any meat, but especially good with beef or chicken. May also be used as a salad dressing.

CHICKEN MARINADE I   Pam Scannell

½ c. soy sauce
½ c. sherry
½ c. burgundy
½ c. salad oil

1 c. water
1 tsp. garlic powder
1 tsp. onion powder
¾ tsp. ginger

Marinate 8 split chicken breasts for 48 hours and grill.

CHICKEN MARINADE II

Anna Smyk

½ c. soy sauce
1 c. pineapple juice
1 clove garlic, mashed
2 Tbsp. minced onion

1 tsp. ground ginger
½ c. brown sugar
1 c. beer

Combine all ingredients; makes enough marinade for 2 or 3 chickens. Marinate chicken pieces overnight. Drain chicken; brown in oil or margarine. Place chicken in a roaster; pour ½ cup marinade over chicken. Bake 20 to 30 minutes or until done.

MARINADE FOR SPARERIBS

Donna Bobrick

¾ c. vinegar
½ tsp. dry mustard
2 Tbsp. chopped onion
1 Tbsp. light brown sugar
¼ c. Worcestershire sauce

½ c. catsup
¼ c. chili sauce
1 Tbsp. lemon juice
1 clove garlic

Combine the above ingredients; simmer for ½ hour. Pour over browned spareribs and bake at 300° for 3 hours, basting occasionally.

MARINADE FOR VENISON

St. John's Sportsman's Club

1 qt. vinegar
2 qt. Crisco oil
6 eggs, beaten
6 Tbsp. salt
3 Tbsp. pepper
4 pkg. Good Seasons Italian
   salad dressing or 1 restaurant
   size pkg.

6 large onions, sliced
2 oranges, sliced with skins on
2 lemons, sliced with skins on
1 qt. beer

Combine all above ingredients; mix well. Marinate meat for 1 to 3 days. Turn meat once a day. Quantity: Enough for 5 large roasts. Marinade can be used to make Spiedies.

Notes

SOUPS

BARLEY SOUP
Teklia Smyk

1 c. barley
½ c. cracked peas (dry)
½ c. dried beans
4 qt. water
½ tsp. baking soda
1 soup bone or soup meat

1 small carrot, cubed
1 small onion, chopped
2 stalks celery, chopped
1 clove garlic (whole)
3 whole peppercorns
1 small can mushrooms

Place barley, peas, and beans in a saucepan and wash well in hot water; drain and add 1 quart of water and ½ teaspoon baking soda. Let come to a boil for 2 minutes; drain and rinse. Place in saucepan and add 3 quarts of water and 1 soup bone or soup meat and cook until meat and lentils are almost cooked. Add carrots, onion, celery, garlic, peppercorns, and mushrooms. Cook until vegetables and lentils are soft. If soup becomes too thick, add water.

STRING BEAN SOUP
Mary Gormish

1 lb. string beans, cut up
3 carrots, diced
4 potatoes, diced
1 celery rib, diced

2 Tbsp. butter or margarine
2 Tbsp. flour
Salt
Pepper

Fill a 6 quart saucepot ¾ full with water and add string beans, carrots, potatoes, and celery; cook until vegetables are tender. Melt butter in a small frying pan and slowly stir in flour to make a roux; make as brown as you like it. Slowly add to soup to thicken and add flavor. Add salt and pepper to taste.

BOUILLABAISSE MARSEILLAISE
Anna Smyk

3 lb. fresh firm fish (red snapper, halibut, black or striped bass)
2 lb. lobster*
½ c. olive oil
2 c. julienne onions
2 c. julienne leeks (use white part)
6 c. tomatoes, peeled, seeded, cubed

3 cloves garlic, crushed
½ c. chopped parsley
1 tsp. saffron
2 bay leaves
1 sprig fresh thyme
2 Tbsp. salt
½ tsp. freshly ground pepper
2½ qt. water
2 c. dry white wine

Wash and cut fish into 1 ounce pieces. Wash lobster; crack claws. Remove stone bag and black vein. Pour olive oil into brazier; add onions, leeks, tomatoes, garlic, parsley, saffron, bay leaves, thyme, salt, and pepper. Arrange lobster and fish over vegetables; cover. Simmer 8 to 10 minutes or until juices have been extracted. Add water and wine. Cover; bring to a fast boil. Lower heat; boil gently 15 to 20 minutes.

To serve: Place a thin dry slice of French bread in a soup dish. Place fish and lobster on a serving platter; pour broth from pan over bread in soup dishes. Serve hot. Fish and lobster may be eaten with the soup. Yields 10 portions.

* Any combination of seafood can be used (preferably shrimp, scallop, clams, oysters).

BROCCOLI SOUP I
Evelyn Kanazawich

1 large bunch broccoli, cut up
1 onion, chopped
½ c. butter
½ c. flour

2 c. milk
1 c. grated Cheddar cheese
2 cans chicken broth
Salt and pepper

Cook broccoli; drain and mash ½ of the broccoli. Set aside. Saute onion in butter; add flour and cook for 5 minutes, stirring constantly. Gradually add milk, constantly stirring. Add cheese and blend until smooth. Gradually add chicken broth, then add mashed broccoli and pieces. Blend well. Salt and pepper to taste and simmer for 20 to 30 minutes.

Cauliflower can be used instead of broccoli or both broccoli and cauliflower can be used in this recipe.

BROCCOLI SOUP II
Dorothy Skellett

1 head broccoli, chopped, or 1
   (10 oz.) pkg. frozen chopped
   broccoli, thawed
1 tomato, chopped
1 clove garlic, chopped

6 c. water
4 chicken bouillon cubes
¼ lb. linguini, broken into 1
   inch pieces
2 Tbsp. olive oil

In a 3 quart saucepan, measure 6 cups water and add 4 chicken bouillon cubes and bring to a boil. Add the chopped broccoli, tomato, and garlic; simmer 15 minutes. Add the linguini and simmer for 20 minutes. Remove from heat and add the olive oil. Serve with grated Parmesan cheese sprinkled on top.

Thin spaghetti can be substituted for linguini.

BROCCOLI AND CHEESE SOUP

Dorothy Skellett

1 large bunch broccoli
2 Tbsp. unsalted butter
1 Tbsp. olive oil
2 medium onions, sliced
2 garlic cloves, chopped
2 Tbsp. flour
6 c. homemade chicken stock
1/4 c. heavy cream
1 Tbsp. lemon juice
1 tsp. Worcestershire sauce
1/8 to 1/4 tsp. Tabasco sauce
1/4 lb. sharp Cheddar cheese,
  grated (1 c.)
Salt and pepper

Trim ends of broccoli stems; peel thick stalks and slice into 1 inch pieces and separate florets. In a large saucepan (6 quart), melt butter and add olive oil over moderate heat. Add onions and saute until softened, but not brown (3 minutes). Add garlic and cook for 1 minute longer. Sprinkle flour in and cook, stirring, for 1 to 2 minutes; do not brown. Add stock and bring to a boil over moderate heat. Add broccoli stems and boil for 5 minutes; add florets and leaves and cook until tender - 3 minutes. Remove from heat.

Let soup cool slightly. Puree in batches in blender. Return to saucepan; add cream, lemon juice, Worcestershire sauce, and Tabasco sauce. Simmer, uncovered, 3 to 5 minutes. Just before serving, stir in cheese and season with salt and pepper to taste.

CREAM OF BROCCOLI SOUP

Jean Klodowski Geresi

1 medium bunch broccoli
1 medium potato
2 Tbsp. butter or margarine
1 onion, chopped
2 Tbsp. flour
1 c. chicken broth, warmed
1 c. milk, warmed
Salt and freshly ground pepper

Cut broccoli into 1 inch pieces. Peel and thinly slice the potato. Cook broccoli and potato in water until tender. Drain. Reserve a few broccoli florets for garnish. Heat butter in saucepan and add onion; cook until transparent, but not brown. Add flour and cook until well blended and bubbly. Add chicken broth and milk, stirring until smooth. Place the broccoli and potatoes in a blender and puree, gradually adding the milk-broth mixture. Salt and pepper to taste.

BEEF 'N CABBAGE SOUP

Julie Sadowitz

1½ lb. lean beef, cubed
Oil
4 c. beef broth or bouillon
4 c. shredded cabbage
1 c. chopped onion
¼ lb. bacon, chopped
2 tsp. salt
1 large garlic clove, minced
½ tsp. pepper

½ tsp. dry mustard
3 c. water
1 bay leaf
2 large potatoes, peeled and
  cubed
2 large sweet potatoes, peeled
  and cubed
2 Tbsp. ketchup

In a large pot, brown beef in hot oil; add broth, 2 cups of the cabbage, onion, bacon, salt, garlic, pepper, and mustard. Simmer 1 hour; skim foam. Add water, potatoes, ketchup, bay leaf, and remaining 2 cups of cabbage; continue to simmer another hour or until potatoes are tender.

MOM'S CABBAGE SOUP

Lesia Klysh
Nancy Tarcha

1 (1 lb.) can sauerkraut
2 c. sliced cabbage
4 qt. water
Garlic powder to taste
Salt and pepper to taste
2 c. diced onion

4 Tbsp. oil
2 (11¼ oz.) green pea soup
1 (15½ oz.) can butter beans,
  drained
1 (3 oz.) can mushrooms,
  drained

Drain and wash sauerkraut once; place sauerkraut, cabbage, water, garlic powder, salt, and pepper in a stockpot. Simmer 1 hour. Saute onion in oil until a light golden brown; add to sauerkraut and cabbage in stock pot. Add pea soup, butter beans, and mushrooms; cover. Simmer 30 minutes. Add roux; simmer 10 minutes. Serve with rye bread.

Roux:

10 Tbsp. oil   **18 Tbsp. flour**

In a fry pan, combine oil and flour; cook over medium heat, stirring constantly until brown and smooth. Add to soup.

UKRAINIAN CABBAGE BORSCHT

Julie Sadowitz

Broth:

2 lb. beef soup bones
2 lb. boneless beef chuck, cut
  into 2½ inch strips

4 qt. water

In an 8 quart stainless steel saucepot, cover beef bones with water and bring to a boil. Skim. Remove beef and bones and put in a strainer and rinse in warm water. Return beef and bones to pot and add 4 quarts of water. Bring water to a boil over high heat; reduce heat to moderately low. Cover pot and simmer 2½ hours, until meat is tender when pierced with a fork. Using a slotted spoon, remove and discard bones. Measure broth; add water to make 4 quarts. Cover and refrigerate up to 3 days.

Soup:

2 c. julienne strip peeled carrots	10 c. coarsely shredded cabbage
1 c. julienne strip celery	1 Tbsp. salt
3 c. sliced onions	3 Tbsp. tomato paste
1 bay leaf	2 tsp. sugar
1 clove garlic, chopped	½ c. chopped parsley
1 Tbsp. chopped, fresh dill or ½ tsp. dried dill	¼ c. vinegar
	6 c. julienne strips cooked beets
	6 c. beets, pureed

Skim and discard fat from broth. Bring broth to a boil; add carrots, celery, onions, bay leaf, garlic, parsley, and dill. Simmer for 20 minutes. Stir in cabbage, salt, tomato paste, vinegar, and sugar; simmer for 30 minutes or until cabbage is tender. Add beets and beet puree and simmer 20 minutes. Makes about 24 cups or 8 main-dish servings.

CARROT BISQUE   Pani Elizabeth Hutnick

5½ c. chicken stock	¼ tsp. dried thyme or 1 tsp. fresh thyme
3 to 5 slices bacon, chopped	1 small bay leaf
1¼ lb. carrots, pared, coarsely chopped	1¼ c. half & half
5 oz. fresh mushrooms, coarsely chopped	Salt
½ c. scallion, coarsely chopped (with tops)	Freshly ground pepper
1 c. celery, coarsely chopped (with leaves)	Chopped scallion tops

Make chicken stock using your own recipe or canned broth may be substituted. Saute bacon in large, heavy saucepan over medium heat until crisp. Stir in carrots, mushrooms, scallion, and celery until thoroughly coated with bacon drippings; saute, stirring frequently, until scallion and celery are wilted, about 5 minutes. Cover; reduce heat to low. Simmer vegetables 10 minutes.

Uncover saucepan and stir in 5½ cups chicken stock; add thyme and bay leaf. Increase heat to high; heat soup to boiling. Reduce heat to low; simmer, covered, 50 minutes. Remove saucepan from heat; let soup cool slightly. Remove and discard bay leaf. Puree soup, in two batches, in blender or food processor.

Return soup to saucepan; stir in half & half. Heat just until heated through; do not allow to boil. Remove from heat; stir in salt and pepper to taste. Ladle soup into warmed bowls and serve immediately; garnish with chopped scallion tips.

CREAM OF CARROT SOUP
Dorothy Skellett

4 Tbsp. butter or margarine
2 to 3 c. sliced carrots
1 large onion, finely sliced
½ clove garlic or dash of garlic
  powder
2 Tbsp. uncooked rice
3 to 4 sprigs fresh parsley or 1
  Tbsp. dried parsley

Thinly peeled rind of ½ orange
  or ¼ tsp. dried orange peel
4 c. chicken broth
¼ tsp. sugar
Juice of ½ orange

Melt butter; add carrots, onion, crushed garlic, and rice. Mix well over gentle heat for 5 minutes without browning. Add parsley, orange rind, chicken broth, and sugar; bring to a boil. Lower heat and simmer 30 to 40 minutes or until vegetables are tender. Put soup into blender and blend until smooth. Return to pot and reheat, adding orange juice.

CREAM OF CELERY SOUP
Olga Gooley

2 c. celery, chopped (leaves too)
1 large onion, chopped

1½ c. boiling water
½ tsp. salt

In a saucepan, boil water and add the celery, onion, and salt. Simmer for 10 minutes.

White Sauce:

¼ c. butter or margarine
¼ c. flour

3 c. milk
Salt and pepper

Melt butter or margarine; slowly add flour and brown (roux). Blend in milk and salt and pepper to taste. Add to celery mixture and simmer for 15 minutes. Do not boil.

CHICKPEA SOUP ITALIAN STYLE
Marie Pufky

1 (1 lb.) can chickpeas
1 qt. water
4 bouillon cubes
1 (8 oz.) can tomato sauce
1 clove garlic, crushed

Salt and pepper to taste
2 c. shredded cabbage
¼ c. cooked, small noodles
Grated cheese

In large saucepan, combine chickpeas, water, bouillon cubes, tomato sauce, garlic, salt, and pepper. Heat to boiling; cover and simmer for 10 minutes. Add cabbage and cook until wilted. Add cooked, small noodles. Serve topped with grated cheese. Makes 4 servings.

CHICKEN-BROCCOLI CHOWDER
Linda Zapach

2 c. chicken broth
⅓ c. chopped onion
1 (10 oz.) pkg. frozen chopped
   broccoli
1⅓ c. mashed potato mix

2 c. cut-up cooked chicken
2 c. shredded Cheddar cheese
2 c. milk
½ tsp. salt

Heat chicken broth, onion, and broccoli to boiling in 3 quart saucepan. Reduce heat; cover. Simmer 5 minutes. Stir in potatoes until well blended. Stir in remaining ingredients. Heat over low heat, stirring occasionally, until hot and cheese is melted, about 5 minutes.

GRANDMA CHARNETSKY'S CHICKEN SOUP
Mary Charnetsky

1 large breast of chicken
1 or 2 carrots, sliced
2 or 3 ribs celery, cut in 1 inch
   lengths
1 whole small onion

1 tomato, finely cut
1 tsp. parsley
Dash of paprika
Salt and pepper

Fill a Dutch oven ⅔ full of cold water and chicken breast; bring to a boil. Skim; reduce heat and add carrots, celery, onion, and tomato. Simmer until vegetables and chicken are tender. Season with parsley and salt and pepper. Serve with egg noodles. Chicken can be cut into small pieces and returned to the soup or made into a salad.

CHICKEN NOODLE SOUP
Anne Petras

Backs, necks, and wings from 6
   to 8 chickens or 2 lb. chicken
   wings
2½ qt. water
1 onion, sliced
2 ribs celery with leaves, diced
3 parsley sprigs
1 Tbsp. salt

1 bay leaf
1 carrot, quartered
½ tsp. ground cumin
½ tsp. ground coriander
6 peppercorns, roughly crushed
1 c. homemade ⅛ inch noodles
1 Tbsp. chopped parsley
½ tsp. caraway seeds

Place all ingredients, except noodles and chopped parsley, in heavy kettle or casserole. Bring to a boil; cover and simmer 1 hour or until chicken pieces

369

are very tender. Strain the broth into a clean saucepan and reduce it by boiling until it measures about 2 quarts. Remove the meat from chicken pieces and reserve. Add noodles and salt to taste. Boil rapidly until noodles are tender, about 10 minutes. Add reserved chicken and chopped parsley. Season to taste. Makes 4 servings.

AUNT RUTH'S CLAM CHOWDER   Sue Blue Charnetsky

28 oz. canned tomatoes
½ c. finely shredded cabbage
3 chopped onions
1 c. chopped celery
3 cubed carrots
2 cubed potatoes
3 qt. water

2 cans clams, drained (reserve juice)
2 Tbsp. margarine
2 tsp. salt
Pepper to taste
1½ tsp. thyme
Pinch of baking soda

In a large saucepot, bring tomatoes, cabbage, onions, celery, carrots, potatoes, water, clam juice, margarine, salt, pepper, and 1 teaspoon thyme to a boil; lower heat and simmer for 1 hour. Add pinch of baking soda; simmer for ½ hour more. Add 2 cans of drained clams and ½ teaspoon thyme. Bring to a rolling boil. When reheating, do not boil.

MANHATTAN CLAM CHOWDER   Doris Okrepkie
Mary Buckingham

3 strips bacon, diced
1 c. onion, diced
2 c. celery, diced
2 c. carrots, diced
2 c. potatoes, diced
16 oz. whole tomatoes in juice
16 oz. tomato puree
2 c. clam broth
3 c. hot water

2 c. chopped clams and juice
2 Tbsp. margarine
½ tsp. thyme
1 tsp. garlic salt
2 tsp. salt
¼ tsp. pepper
2 Tbsp. parsley flakes
1 bay leaf

Brown bacon; add margarine and onions and cook until transparent. Add all other ingredients except clams with juice and potatoes. Cook ingredients for 30 minutes, then add clams with juice and potatoes. Cook 20 minutes or until vegetables are tender.

NEW ENGLAND CLAM CHOWDER

Linda Zapach

1½ c. potatoes, cut in ½ inch
   cubes
1 c. water
¾ c. thinly sliced carrots
½ c. thinly sliced celery
1 c. coarsely chopped onion
3 tsp. butter

3 tsp. flour
1 pt. half & half
2 (6½ oz.) cans minced or
   chopped clams
1 tsp. sugar
¼ tsp. pepper
¼ tsp. powdered thyme

Cook potatoes and carrots in 1 cup water for 15 minutes; do not drain. In a fry pan, saute celery and onion in butter; add flour, mixing to make it smooth. Let bubble for 1 minute. Add about 2 tablespoons half & half, stirring to make a smooth sauce; bring to a boil. Boil for 1 minute. Add remaining half & half; heat through, but do not boil. Add this to cooked potatoes and carrots; add remaining ingredients. Heat through. Serve with crusty bread.

CORN CHOWDER

Linda Zapach

6 slices bacon, cubed
2 to 3 ribs celery, sliced
1 large onion, chopped
3 whole chicken breasts, cubed
1 (49½ oz.) can chicken broth
2 (15 oz.) cans whole kernel
   corn

5 medium potatoes, peeled and
   cubed
2 Tbsp. parsley flakes
1 (12 oz.) can evaporated skim
   milk
Salt and pepper to taste

Brown bacon on bottom of stock pot; after bacon is browned, remove all but 2 tablespoons of bacon fat. Add celery and onion to bacon fat in stock pot; brown slightly. Add cubed chicken; brown. In a blender, puree half the can of chicken broth with one can of corn; add to ingredients in stock pot. Bring to a boil; add potatoes. Simmer 20 minutes; add remaining can of corn, evaporated milk, parsley flakes, salt and pepper, and remaining half can of chicken broth. Heat to serving temperature. Serve.

GAZPACHO (GAZ-PAH-CHO)

Carol Wasylko

1 can stewed tomatoes
1 c. cucumber, peeled
½ c. onion
¾ c. green pepper
1 clove garlic
1½ c. tomato juice

¼ c. olive oil
2 Tbsp. vinegar
1 tsp. salt
⅛ tsp. pepper
A few drops hot pepper sauce

Using a blender, combine and chop for ½ minute stewed tomatoes, cucumber, onion, green pepper, and garlic; add the rest of the ingredients. Chill until serving time. (Make in early afternoon; serve for supper on a hot summer day.)

For hotter flavoring, add ¼ cup of Mexican jalapeno sauce to soup - *Oidel Paso by Pet Product).* If desired, add an ice cube to each serving; top with toasted bread cubes. Makes 6 servings.

Optional: More finely chopped cucumber and green pepper can be added.

HAMBURG SOUP I

Doris Okrepkie
Mary Buckingham

2 lb. ground round
1 qt. canned tomatoes
1½ qt. water
1 c. chopped onion
1 c. chopped celery
2 Tbsp. parsley
1 c. chopped carrots

1 c. chopped potatoes
1 can corn
1 box frozen peas
1 box frozen lima beans*
¼ tsp. pepper
1 tsp. garlic salt

Brown hamburger and drain. In a large pot, add browned hamburg, tomatoes, water, onions, celery, parsley flakes, salt, pepper, and garlic salt and simmer for 2 hours. Add carrots and potatoes. Cook for 30 minutes, then add the remaining vegetables and heat through.

* String beans may be used in place of lima beans.

HAMBURG SOUP II

Helen Rucky

1 tsp. Crisco
1 lb. ground chuck
½ c. chopped onion
½ c. diced celery
2 c. (or one 1 lb. can) tomatoes
1 tsp. salt

¼ tsp. pepper
½ c. elbow macaroni
6 c. water
2 bouillon cubes
1 (20 oz.) can mixed vegetables
1 (8 oz.) can mushrooms

Saute onions and celery until tender; add ground meat. Saute until brown. Combine with remaining ingredients. Cover; simmer 1 hour.

QUICK BEEF MINESTRONE SOUP

Marie Pufky

½ lb. hamburger, browned and
  drained
½ c. onion, chopped
1 clove garlic, crushed
1 can beef broth
1 can water
1 (20 oz.) can cannellini beans
  (undrained)

1 (16 oz.) can tomatoes, cut up
1 bay leaf
Salt and pepper to taste
1 tsp. basil
1 (10 oz.) pkg. frozen mixed
  vegetables
1 c. cooked elbow noodles
Parmesan cheese

Place all ingredients (except elbow noodles and Parmesan cheese) in saucepan; bring to a boil. Simmer until vegetables are tender. Add elbow noodles and serve topped with Parmesan cheese. Makes 4 servings.

MUSHROOM SOUP
Vera Cibulsky

2 small carrots	3 Tbsp. flour
2 celery stalks	1½ c. cold water
2 onions (2 inch diameter)	½ c. sour cream
4 c. cold water	1 Tbsp. parsley, chopped
1 lb. fresh mushrooms, chopped fine	1 Tbsp. dill, chopped
	Salt and pepper to taste
3 to 4 Tbsp. butter or oil	Cooked barley, noodles, or rice

Chop carrots, celery, and 1 onion very fine. Simmer in 4 cups water for 10 minutes. Add mushrooms and cook for 10 minutes more. Meanwhile, chop the other onion; add to butter or oil in frying pan. Saute until golden. Add flour; fry until medium brown, stirring constantly. Remove from heat. Add 1½ cups water, mixing until smooth; place back on heat and stir constantly until thick. This is your gravy or zaprashka. Add to soup; blend thoroughly and lower heat to simmer for 3 to 4 minutes. Add sour cream which is at room temperature. Also add dill and parsley. Add salt and pepper to taste. Keep warm, but do not boil after adding sour cream. Serve with cooked barley, noodles, or rice.

MUSHROOM-BARLEY SOUP I
Pani Elizabeth Hutnick

2 c. fresh mushrooms, thinly sliced	3 qt. water
	1 Tbsp. salt
1 c. pearl barley	½ tsp. pepper, freshly ground
1 lb. beef bones (in small pieces)	4 Tbsp. margarine
	1 c. onion, finely chopped
1 carrot, sliced	2 Tbsp. fresh parsley, chopped
2 ribs celery, sliced	2 or 3 dried mushrooms, broken up (optional)
1 lb. chicken backs and necks or wing tips	

Place the beef bones, carrot, celery, and chicken pieces in a soup pot. Add the water, salt, and pepper. Bring to a boil; reduce heat and simmer for 2 to 3 hours. In 2 tablespoons margarine, saute half of the barley until it starts to turn yellow and gives a crackling sound. Add the onion and continue cooking, stirring constantly, until the onion turns limp and glossy. Melt the remaining margarine in another pan and quickly saute the fresh mushrooms with the parsley. Set aside.

Strain the broth through a sieve. Discard the bones and vegetables. Add to the broth the remaining uncooked barley. Add the dried mushrooms, if using, and cook for 30 minutes. Add the sauteed barley-onion mixture and cook for 30 minutes more. Add the mushroom-parsley mixture and simmer for 10 additional minutes. Let the soup stand, covered, for at least 30 minutes before reheating and serving. The sauteed barley will keep its shape; the rest will cook to a pulp and give thickness to the soup.

MUSHROOM BARLEY SOUP II
Carol Wasylko

10 fresh mushrooms
4 Tbsp. large pearl barley
½ c. dried lima beans
¼ c. celery, diced
¼ c. carrots, diced
¼ c. onion, diced
3 Tbsp. butter

2 tsp. salt
¼ tsp. pepper
2 qt. water
½ c. milk
2 Tbsp. flour
Chopped dill

Wash mushrooms, barley, and lima beans. Slice mushrooms finely. To 2 quarts boiling water, add the mushrooms, barley, beans, celery, carrots, salt, pepper, and 1½ teaspoons butter. Simmer for 1 hour. While soup is simmering, stir slowly every 20 minutes until barley is tender. In a saucepan, melt butter over low heat and saute onion. Add flour slowly; stir to fine consistency. Add milk, making a smooth white sauce. When soup is done, add white sauce and mix well. Adjust seasoning to taste. Serve hot; garnish with chopped dill.

CREAM OF MUSHROOM SOUP
Julia Dudik

½ c. butter
1 onion, chopped
1 lb. mushrooms, sliced
½ c. flour

1 qt. milk
1 c. cooked, diced potatoes
  (optional)
Salt and pepper to taste

Saute onion and mushrooms in butter for about 5 minutes; add flour. Blend; cook about 2 or 3 minutes, stirring constantly. Add milk slowly, stirring while adding; season with salt and pepper to taste. Add the cooked potatoes if desired.

FRENCH ONION SOUP
Shirley Buchma

4 medium onions, diced
½ c. margarine
1½ Tbsp. oil
½ c. flour

6 c. very hot water
1 tsp. salt
1 c. Swiss cheese, grated

Saute onions in margarine until they are soft and start to turn brown. Add oil and flour, stirring quickly to make paste (roux). Pour in very hot water and add salt. Bring to a boil and simmer for 25 minutes. Fifteen minutes before serving, add grated cheese and put soup in ovenproof serving dish and put in oven at 350° for 10 minutes or until cheese is melted. Serve with toasted bread cubes on top.

POTATO SOUP
Marianne Lawryk

Potatoes, peeled and cut
Cold water to cover potatoes
Milk (enough to give soup a
   thick consistency)
Margarine (as desired for
   flavor)

Salt and pepper to taste
Warm corn bread or dark rye
   bread

Fill pot half full with cut up potatoes; add cold water to cover potatoes. Cover and cook until almost done. Skim off starch. Add enough milk to give the soup a thick consistency. Add margarine and salt and pepper to taste. Simmer 30 to 45 minutes. Should appear thick and white, not watery, and may have potato chunks. Serve with warm cornbread or dark rye bread. Can serve cold as a vichyssoise or hot during inclement weather.

BAKED POTATO SOUP
Marianne Lawryk

2½ lb. baby red potatoes,
   quartered
½ lb. raw bacon, diced
1 jumbo yellow onion, diced
¼ bunch celery, diced
1 qt. water
2 oz. chicken base

1 qt. milk
1 tsp. salt
1 tsp. pepper
1½ sticks margarine
6 oz. flour
1 c. whipping cream
¼ bunch fresh parsley, chopped

Boil potatoes in water for 10 minutes. Drain and set aside. In a large, heavy pot, saute bacon, onions, and celery over medium-high heat until celery is tender. Drain off bacon grease and return bacon, onions, and celery to pot. Add milk, water, chicken base, salt, and pepper. Heat over medium-high heat until very hot. *Do not boil.*

In a heavy, large saucepan, melt margarine and add flour; mix well and allow to bubble, stirring for 1 minute (called roux). While constantly stirring soup, add the flour-margarine mixture (roux) slowly. Continue stirring the soup until thick and creamy. Stir in potatoes, parsley, and cream. Garnish with shredded Colby cheese, fried bacon bits, chopped green onions, or all three.

CREAM OF POTATO SOUP

Helen Rucky

2 medium onions, diced
2 stalks celery, diced (including leaves)
⅓ c. oleo
5 to 6 potatoes, peeled and sliced thin

2 chicken bouillon cubes
1 tsp. parsley
6 c. water
1 tsp. salt
Dash of pepper
1 (13 oz.) can evaporated milk

Saute onions and celery in oleo; set aside. Add potatoes to water and cook until tender; mash a little bit. Add remaining ingredients except milk. Simmer ½ hour. Correct seasoning. Add evaporated milk just before serving; blend well.

GARLIC POTATO SOUP

Mary Gormish

8 medium potatoes, diced
1 large onion, diced
2 cloves garlic, diced fine

2 Tbsp. butter
Salt
Pepper

Fill a 6 quart saucepot ¾ full with water; add potatoes, onion, garlic, and butter. Bring to a boil; skim and cook until potatoes are done. Salt and pepper to taste.

ZUCCHINI SOUP

Dorothy Skellett

1 lb. Italian sausage (mild)
½ c. onion, chopped
½ c. celery, chopped
½ c. green pepper, chopped
1 (20 oz.) can whole Italian tomatoes and juice
1 lb. zucchini, sliced or cubed

½ tsp. oregano
½ tsp. basil
½ tsp. garlic powder
1 tsp. sugar
Salt to taste
Pepper to taste

Brown sausage and drain fat; saute onion and green pepper with meat. In a large saucepan, combine rest of ingredients with sausage mixture; stir and cover. Simmer for 45 minutes, stirring occasionally. Sprinkle with Parmesan cheese when served.

VEGETABLES

ASPARAGUS WITH HORSERADISH SAUCE

Mary Kostyun

2 (10 oz.) pkg. frozen asparagus
1 c. sour cream
1 Tbsp. prepared horseradish

1 Tbsp. butter
¾ c. soft bread crumbs

Cook asparagus according to package directions. Combine sour cream and horseradish; heat at a very low temperature. Keep warm until asparagus is served. Melt butter in shallow baking pan in a 300° oven. Add bread crumbs; bake until crisp and golden. Drain asparagus; put in serving dish. Pour sauce over asparagus; sprinkle with bread crumbs.

BACON BEANS

Marie Richardson

3 slices bacon
2 to 3 c. fresh or frozen green beans

¼ c. water

Fry bacon until crisp; drain off fat. Break bacon into small pieces; put back in pan. Add beans and water; cook on medium heat until done.

DUTCH STYLE GREEN BEANS

Mary Ponas

3 strips bacon
1 small onion, sliced
2 tsp. cornstarch
¼ tsp. salt

¼ tsp. dry mustard
1 (No. 3) can green beans
1 Tbsp. brown sugar
1 tsp. vinegar

Fry bacon until crisp. Remove bacon from pan; crumble. Drain off all but 1 tablespoon drippings. Add onion; brown lightly. Stir in cornstarch, salt, and mustard. Drain beans, reserving ½ cup liquid. Stir reserved liquid into pan. Cook, stirring, until mixture boils. Blend in brown sugar and vinegar. Add beans; heat.

FRESH GREEN STRING BEANS WITH TOMATOES

Julia Dudik

2 lb. green beans
4 medium onions
3 cloves garlic

½ to ¾ c. cooking oil
1 (14½ oz.) can tomatoes
Salt and pepper to taste

Clean and wash beans. Chop onions; leave cloves of garlic whole. Saute in enough oil to cover. Cook until golden. Add beans; cook until beans test done. Add tomatoes and salt and pepper; simmer a few minutes.

ITALIAN BEANS
Marie Richardson

1 clove garlic
1 medium onion, sliced
2 Tbsp. butter

1 (1 lb.) pkg. green beans
1 (28 oz.) can tomatoes

Saute garlic and onions in butter. Add beans and tomatoes; cook until beans are done. Flavor is best when served the next day.

CANDIED BEETS
Jody Dimitriou

12 medium beets, sliced or
   diced
2 Tbsp. flour
¼ c. sugar

¼ tsp. salt
½ c. orange juice
2½ Tbsp. butter

Place beets in greased 11x9 inch baking dish. Combine remaining ingredients; pour over beets. Dot with butter. Cover. Bake at 400° for 30 minutes or until tender.

HARVARD BEETS
Julia Dudik

½ c. sugar
1½ tsp. cornstarch
¼ c. vinegar or lemon juice
2 Tbsp. cooking oil or melted
   butter

¼ c. water
12 small cooked beets or 1 (No.
   2) can, sliced or diced
Salt

Combine sugar and cornstarch in saucepan. Add vinegar, oil, and water; boil 5 minutes, stirring constantly. Add beets and salt to taste; cover. Simmer 30 minutes. Serves 4.

BROCCOLI AND CHEESE
Jayne Maliwacki

1 to 2 bunches broccoli
1 (6 oz.) pkg. Stove Top stuffing
8 oz. Cheddar cheese, cubed

1 (10½ oz.) can cream of
   mushroom soup

Cut broccoli into florets; rinse. Cook until partially done. Cook stuffing according to package directions. Combine broccoli and stuffing; place in 9x13 inch pan. Set aside. Combine cheese and undiluted soup in saucepan; heat until cheese melts. Pour over broccoli and stuffing; cover with foil. Bake at 350° for 1 hour.

BAKED CABBAGE

John Cibulsky

1 lb. sauerkraut
1 large head cabbage
½ lb. salt pork, diced fine or ½
  lb. fat back, diced fine, or ½ c.
  vegetable oil

3 large onions, diced
Salt and pepper

Drain and squeeze sauerkraut; reserve juice. Rinse sauerkraut in cold water; squeeze dry. Shred cabbage same consistency as sauerkraut. In large pan, mix cabbage with sauerkraut. Saute diced salt pork; add onions. Saute until light brown. Add to cabbage; season to taste with salt and pepper. Mix thoroughly. Place in roasting pan; cover. Bake at 350° for 2 hours; mix occasionally. If any time during the cooking you feel the taste isn't sour enough, add some sauerkraut juice; mix. Complete baking.

STEWED CABBAGE

Anne Pufky

1 medium onion
2 Tbsp. butter
¼ c. water
1 small head cabbage, shredded

Salt and pepper
3 Tbsp. catsup
1 Tbsp. vinegar

Saute onion in butter until golden. Add water and cabbage; bring to a boil. Add salt and pepper to taste and catsup; simmer, stirring occasionally, about 45 minutes or until cabbage is tender. Add vinegar; bring to a boil. Serve.

CARROTS

Julia Bycz

2 lb. carrots, sliced
1 c. sugar
½ c. vinegar
½ c. salad oil
1 tsp. salt

½ tsp. pepper
1 tsp. dry mustard
1 (10½ oz.) can tomato soup
1 green pepper, sliced
1 onion, sliced thin

Cook carrots until tender. Drain; set aside. In saucepan, combine sugar, vinegar, salad oil, salt, pepper, dry mustard, and tomato soup; bring to a boil, then simmer 5 minutes. Remove from heat. Add carrots, green pepper, and onion; mix well. Cool. Refrigerate.

GLAZED CARROTS

Mildred Charnetsky

2 bunches small carrots
1 Tbsp. lemon juice
⅓ c. sugar

½ c. water
1 tsp. salt
2 Tbsp. butter or margarine

Scrape carrots; cut in fourths lengthwise. Place in heavy skillet. Add remaining ingredients. Cover. Cook over low heat, turning often, until tender and glazed. Serves 6.

TANGY MUSTARD CAULIFLOWER

Anna Smyk

1 (10 oz.) pkg. frozen
  cauliflower
½ c. mayonnaise
1 tsp. chopped onion

1 to 1½ tsp. prepared or dry
  mustard
½ c. shredded Cheddar cheese

Cook cauliflower according to package directions; drain. Put in casserole. Combine mayonnaise, onion, and mustard; spread on hot cauliflower. Sprinkle with cheese. Bake at 350° until cheese melts. Serve immediately.

FIESTA CORN BAKE

Mary Ponas

1 (1 lb.) can cream style corn
1 c. cooked, diced carrots
¼ c. chopped onion
¼ c. sliced ripe olives
2 eggs, beaten

Salt and pepper
Dash of hot pepper sauce
1¾ c. bread crumbs
3 Tbsp. butter or margarine,
  melted

Combine corn, carrots, onion, and olives. Add eggs, salt and pepper, hot pepper sauce, and 1 cup bread crumbs; mix. Pour into 1 quart casserole. Toss remaining ¾ cup bread crumbs with melted butter; sprinkle on corn mixture. Bake at 350° for 50 minutes. Remove from oven. Let stand 5 minutes before serving.

CORN PEPPER BAKE WITH CHEESE SAUCE

Dorothy Skellett

6 large green peppers
4 slices bacon
1 Tbsp. butter
2 Tbsp. finely diced onions
2 Tbsp. flour
1 tsp. sugar

1½ tsp. salt
¼ tsp. pepper
1½ c. milk, scalded
2 c. cooked corn
½ c. soft bread crumbs
1 egg, beaten

Wash peppers; cut a slice from top of each. Remove seeds and fibrous parts. Put in saucepan; cover with boiling water. Simmer 5 minutes. Cook bacon; fry.

Dice. Melt butter in saucepan; add onion. Cook until tender. Add flour, sugar, salt, and pepper; blend. Add milk gradually; cook over low heat until thick, stirring constantly. Add corn, bread crumbs, and bacon. Add beaten egg; mix. Fill peppers. Place pan of stuffed peppers in a pan to which about 2 inches of hot water has been added. Bake, uncovered, at 325° for 45 minutes or until filling is set. Serve with Cheese Sauce.

Cheese Sauce:

3 Tbsp. butter	⅛ tsp. pepper
3 Tbsp. flour	1½ c. milk
¾ tsp. salt	1 c. grated American cheese

Melt butter; add flour, salt, and pepper. Blend. Add milk gradually; cook until bubbles form and break, stirring constantly. Cook 1 minute. Add cheese; stir until melted. Serve hot on Corn Pepper Bake. Makes 1½ cups sauce.

CUCUMBERS 'N CREAM
Genevieve Sadowitz

½ c. vinegar	1 large cucumber, sliced thin
½ c. water	1 medium onion, sliced thin
1 tsp. salt	1 c. sour cream
5 peppercorns	Tomato wedges

Combine vinegar, water, salt, and peppercorns. Add cucumber slices; chill 2 hours. Drain. Combine cucumbers with onion and sour cream. Garnish with tomato wedges.

OLD TIME CUCUMBERS
Genevieve Sadowitz

1 medium cucumber	1 Tbsp. sugar
2 small green peppers	1 tsp. salt
2 Tbsp. white vinegar	

Pare cucumber; slice thin. Remove seeds from peppers; cut into thin strips. In a shallow serving dish, combine vinegar, sugar, and salt; stir to dissolve. Add cucumbers and green pepper. Cover; chill, stirring several times before serving. Serves 4.

CREAMED MUSHROOMS
Julia Dudik

2 Tbsp. butter	2 c. milk
½ lb. mushrooms	Salt and pepper
2 Tbsp. flour	

Melt butter in saucepan; add mushrooms. Saute. Add flour; blend. Cook until mixture bubbles; continue cooking for 1 minute. Add milk; cook over low heat until thick, stirring constantly. Season with salt and pepper.

POTATOES AU GRATIN
Linda Zapach

6 c. thinly sliced potatoes
1½ tsp. salt
2 Tbsp. butter or margarine, melted

1 c. shredded Cheddar cheese
½ c. fresh bread crumbs

Preheat oven to 425°. Toss potatoes with salt in a greased 9x13 inch pan; arrange potatoes in an even layer. Drizzle melted butter or margarine over potatoes; sprinkle with cheese and bread crumbs. Bake 20 minutes or until tender.

MOUNTAIN HOME POTATO SLICES
Mary Ponas

4 Idaho russet potatoes
¼ c. butter or margarine, melted

1 Tbsp. grated onion
1 tsp. salt
⅛ tsp. ground black pepper

Scrub potatoes. Slice unpeeled potatoes in ½ inch thick slices. Place single layer on greased baking sheet. In small skillet, combine butter, onion, salt, and pepper; brush mixture over potato slices. Cover with foil. Bake at 425° for 35 to 40 minutes or until potatoes are tender when pierced with a fork.

Variation - Puffed Potatoes: In small bowl, beat 1 egg white until stiff. Gently stir in ¼ cup mayonnaise, 1 tablespoon prepared horseradish, ¼ teaspoon grated onion, 1 teaspoon salt, and ¼ teaspoon paprika. Spoon mixture on top of each baked potato slice. Return potatoes to oven; bake 3 to 5 minutes or until topping puffs up and is golden brown. Serves 4 to 6.

MY SISTER'S WONDERFUL MASHED POTATOES
Pani Lawryk

5 lb. or 9 large potatoes, peeled
1 c. sour cream
¼ tsp. pepper

1 (8 oz.) cream cheese, cubed
2 tsp. onion salt
1 Tbsp. butter

Cook and mash potatoes; add all ingredients. Mash again to make smooth and fluffy. Turn into a greased 9x13 inch pan; dot with butter. Cover with foil; bake at 350° for 35 minutes.

May be prepared in advance and stored in refrigerator or freezer until the day you are serving.

OLGA'S BAKED STUFFED POTATOES Marion Sarnoski

6 medium baking potatoes	Salt and pepper
½ c. warm milk	½ c. grated Cheddar cheese
3 Tbsp. butter	

Scrub potatoes. Bake at 400° for 45 to 60 minutes or until done. Cut top off each potato; scoop out potato. Mash. Add milk, butter, salt and pepper to taste, and half the cheese; beat with electric beater. Spoon potato mixture into shells; sprinkle with remaining cheese. Bake at 350° for 30 minutes or until piping hot.

Potatoes may be prepared in advance and frozen. To serve, thaw potatoes. Bake at 350° approximately 45 minutes or until hot.

OVEN FRIED POTATOES Julia Malewiacki

8 large baking potatoes (unpeeled)	1 tsp. salt
½ c. oil	½ tsp. garlic powder
2 Tbsp. grated Parmesan cheese	½ tsp. paprika
	¼ tsp. pepper

Scrub potatoes; cut into wedges. Arrange in 2 shallow pans, peel side down. Combine remaining ingredients; brush over potatoes. Bake at 375° for 45 minutes, brushing occasionally with oil mixture. Serves 8.

RICK'S POTATO CAKE Celia Matias

1 lb. thick-sliced bacon	1 large onion, grated
10 to 12 medium potatoes, grated	1 c. flour
	1½ tsp. salt

Cut bacon into ½ x 1 inch strips; fry until crispy brown. Reserve fat. Grease a 10 inch cast iron fry pan with bacon fat. In a bowl, combine potatoes, onion, flour, salt, fried bacon, and all but 2 tablespoons bacon fat; pour into greased fry pan. Drizzle remaining 2 tablespoons bacon fat over the top. Bake at 350° for 1 hour 15 minutes. Serve with gravy or sour cream.

POTATOES SUPREME Phyllis Hatala

6 medium potatoes	1 tsp. salt
¼ c. melted butter or margarine	Pepper to taste
2 c. shredded Cheddar cheese	2 c. sour cream
⅓ c. chopped green onions	Paprika

Cook potatoes in their skins until just tender. Cool, peel, and shred coarsely. Mix cheese with melted butter or margarine; add to potatoes. Add green onion; season with salt and pepper. Fold in sour cream; put in greased baking dish and sprinkle generously with paprika. Bake for 30 minutes at 350°.

BRANDIED SWEET POTATOES
Patricia Hoover

6 large sweet potatoes
2 Tbsp. cornstarch
½ tsp. nutmeg
2 tsp. salt
½ c. light brown sugar

1 c. water
1 Tbsp. lemon juice
⅓ c. brandy
Marshmallows

Peel potatoes; cut in halves lengthwise. Cook in boiling water until tender, approximately 25 minutes. Combine cornstarch, nutmeg, salt, and sugar in a 1 quart saucepan. Gradually stir in water; cook until clear, stirring constantly. Stir in lemon juice and brandy. Place potatoes in buttered casserole; cover with sauce. Cover. Bake at 375° for 30 minutes. Baste occasionally. Sprinkle with marshmallows; broil until marshmallows melt and brown slightly.

RATATOUILLE (FRENCH VEGETABLE STEW)
Patricia Hoover

2 large onions, chopped
2 cloves garlic, diced
2 Tbsp. cooking oil
2 green peppers, cut in strips
1 lb. zucchini, sliced
1 lb. eggplant, diced

4 large tomatoes
3 Tbsp. chopped parsley
1 Tbsp. salt
1 tsp. sugar
½ tsp. oregano
¼ tsp. pepper

Saute onion and garlic in oil about 5 minutes. Add green peppers, zucchini, eggplant, tomatoes which have been skinned and cut in wedges, parsley, salt, sugar, oregano, and pepper. Simmer until vegetables are done.

SAUERKRAUT
Anna Grech

1 qt. sauerkraut
4 Tbsp. margarine

1 chopped onion
Salt and pepper

Rinse sauerkraut twice; place in saucepan. Add water to cover; cook until tender. Drain. Saute onion in margarine until golden. Add sauerkraut to onion; cook 10 minutes, mixing occasionally. Add salt and pepper to taste.

BAKED SPINACH

Charles Sarnoski

2 (10 oz.) pkg. frozen spinach
1 (3 oz.) pkg. cream cheese
¾ c. grated medium sharp
  Cheddar cheese

Bread crumbs

Cook spinach according to package directions; drain. Combine with cream cheese and Cheddar cheese; stir until melted. Turn into buttered casserole; sprinkle with bread crumbs. Bake at 350° for 30 minutes.

ANNETTE'S SQUASH CREOLE

Charles Sarnoski

2 c. diced yellow squash
2 c. diced zucchini
1 c. water
1 env. instant chicken bouillon
2 green peppers, diced
2 stalks celery, diced

1½ c. tomato juice
¼ c. chopped onion
1 clove garlic, crushed
½ tsp. salt
⅛ tsp. pepper

In saucepan, cook squash in water until tender. Add remaining ingredients; cover pan. Cook until all vegetables are of desired consistency and very little liquid remains.

FROZEN SQUASH

Anna Dobransky

Zucchini*
Egg, beaten

Italian bread crumbs
Cooking oil

Wash zucchini. Slice thin, leaving skin on. Dip in egg, then in bread crumbs. Fry in hot oil until brown. Cool. Package for freezer. To serve, heat for 10 minutes at 400°.

* Summer squash may be substituted for zucchini.

TOMATOES AND DUMPLINGS

Millie Finch

1 (28 oz.) can tomatoes
½ tsp. crumbled bacon or Baco-
  Bits
Salt and pepper

¼ tsp. dill seed or dill weed
½ tsp. minced onion or dry
  onion flakes

Combine all ingredients in large saucepan; simmer 5 minutes.

Dumplings:

1 c. Bisquick
½ c. milk

Salt and pepper to taste

Combine all ingredients; mix thoroughly. Drop by 1 tablespoon dough evenly on top of simmering tomatoes; cook 3 minutes, uncovered. Cover; cook 5 minutes. Test for doneness with toothpick; if done, toothpick will come out dry. Serve dumplings with tomatoes spooned over them.

SCALLOPED TOMATOES
Julia Dudik

2 c. chopped tomatoes
½ onion, chopped
1 Tbsp. sugar
½ tsp. salt

Dash of pepper
2 Tbsp. butter
2 c. bread crumbs

Combine tomatoes, onion, sugar, salt, and pepper. Melt butter in saucepan; remove from heat. Mix in bread crumbs. In a buttered casserole, put a layer of tomato mixture, then a layer of bread crumbs. Continue alternating layers until all tomatoes and bread crumbs are used, ending with bread crumbs on top. Bake at 400°, uncovered, until bread crumbs are brown.

STUFFED TOMATOES
Mary Charnetsky

4 tomatoes
½ c. finely chopped onion
2 Tbsp. butter or margarine

Bread crumbs or corn flake
crumbs

Scoop out centers of tomatoes; add onion. In a fry pan, melt butter; add tomato pulp with onion. Cook about 15 minutes or until onion is soft. If watery, add bread crumbs. Stuff tomato shell with prepared tomatoes; sprinkle with bread crumbs. Bake at 350° for 15 minutes.

ZUCCHINI AND TOMATOES
Charles Sarnoski

1 (15½ oz.) can tomatoes
1 to 2 cloves garlic, minced
Oregano

Parsley
Salt and pepper
1 large zucchini

Crush tomatoes; place in fry pan. Add garlic and oregano, chopped parsley, and salt and pepper to taste. Do not peel or remove seeds from zucchini; cut into cubes. Add to tomato mixture; stir. Cook, uncovered, until tender and most of the juice from tomatoes is absorbed.

OLGA'S BAKED ZUCCHINI
Anna Chyl

4 medium zucchini (1 lb.)
¾ c. seasoned bread crumbs
2 Tbsp. butter

2 Tbsp. grated Parmesan cheese
1 clove garlic, minced, or ⅛ tsp.
garlic powder

Peel zucchini; cut in cubes. Cook until tender. Do not overcook. Mash zucchini. Add bread crumbs, butter, cheese, and garlic; mix thoroughly. Spoon into casserole. Bake, uncovered, at 350° for 15 minutes.

ZUCCHINI GOULASH

Charles Sarnoski

1 lb. seasoned pan sausage
1 small onion, diced
2 cloves garlic, minced
2 large potatoes, peeled, diced
   or cut in chunks

1 medium zucchini (unpeeled),
   diced or cut in chunks
1 qt. spaghetti sauce

In large skillet, brown sausage with onion and garlic; drain fat. Add remaining ingredients; simmer until veggies are of desired doneness. Serve with Parmesan cheese.

ZUCCHINI ITALIANO

Millie Finch

4 to 5 zucchini
4 slices bacon
1 small onion, diced
2 Tbsp. Parmesan cheese

Salt and pepper
Dash of garlic powder
2 Tbsp. bread crumbs
1 egg

Cut zucchini in ¼ inch slices. Fry bacon; drain on paper towels. Crumble. Saute onion in bacon fat until tender. Add crumbled bacon and zucchini. Cook about 5 minutes or until fork tender. Add cheese, salt and pepper, and garlic powder; mix. Add bread crumbs. Scramble egg; add to zucchini mixture. Mix through.

ZUCCHINI ROUNDS

Charles Sarnoski

½ c. biscuit mix
¼ c. grated Parmesan cheese
⅛ tsp. pepper
2 eggs, lightly beaten
2 Tbsp. margarine, melted

2 c. shredded, unpeeled
   zucchini
1 Tbsp. shredded onion
Additional margarine for frying

Combine biscuit mix, cheese, and pepper; mix. Add eggs and melted margarine; mix. Fold in zucchini and onion. In a 10 inch skillet, melt margarine for frying; drop 2 tablespoons of mixture into pan. Cook 2 to 3 minutes on each side.

OLGA'S DILL-LIGHTFUL VEGETABLES   Marion Sarnoski

2 c. sliced carrots
1 (16 oz.) can cut green beans, drained
1 (16 oz.) can chickpeas, drained
1 (7 oz.) can whole kernel corn, drained

1½ tsp. dill weed
1½ tsp. mustard seed
¾ tsp. salt
2 cloves garlic, minced
1½ c. water
⅔ c. white vinegar
⅓ c. sugar

Cook carrots in boiling salt water 5 minutes or until crisp tender; drain. In large bowl, combine carrots, green beans, chickpeas, and corn. Combine dill weed, mustard seed, salt, and garlic; add to vegetables. Mix. In small saucepan, combine water, vinegar, and sugar; bring to a boil, stirring occasionally to dissolve sugar. Pour marinade over vegetables; cover securely. Chill 4 to 6 hours or overnight. Yield: 6 cups.

"QUESTIONS??????"

Puzzled about a recipe?
Don't hestitate, don't wonder -
Pick up your phone and call
The girl who signed her name down under.

If many errors do appear,
It's really not a blunder -
But just a scheme, for you to meet
The gal whose name's down under.

PRAYERS AFTER MEALS

We thank Thee, O Christ our God, that Thou has satisfied us with Thine Earthly Good Things; deprive us not also of Thy Heavenly Kingdom. As Thou wast present among Thy Disciples, O Savior, and gavest them Peace, come Thou also among us and save us. Amen.

Blessed be God, who is Merciful unto us, and nourishes us from His Bounteous Gifts by His Grace and Compassion, now and ever and unto ages of ages. Amen.

Blessed be Thou, O Our God, Who has Mercy on us and feeds us from our youth. Thou gives Food to all flesh, and fillest our hearts with Joy and Gladness. Having every satisfaction, we Thy servants shall abide in all good deeds in Jesus Christ our Lord and Savior, with Whom are due unto Thee Glory, Majesty, Honor and Worship, together with the Holy Spirit, now and ever and unto ages and ages. Amen.

INDEX

ALPHABETICAL INDEX OF RECIPES

392

S

T

Notes

INDEX OF RECIPES

DESSERTS

406

This Cookbook is a perfect gift for Holidays, Weddings, Anniversaries & Birthdays.

To order extra copies as gifts for your friends, please use Order Forms on reverse side of this page.

* * * * * * * * *

Cookbook Publishers, Inc. has published millions of personalized cookbooks for every kind of organization from every state in the union. We are pleased to have the privilege of publishing this fine cookbook.

ORDER FORM

Use the order forms below for obtaining
additional copies of this cookbook.

Fill in Order Forms Below - Cut Out and Mail

You may order as many copies of our Cookbook as you wish for the regular price.
Mail to:

Sisterhood of St. John's
1 St. John Parkway
Johnson City, NY 13790

Please mail _____ copies of your Cookbook @ _____ each.

Mail books to:

Name _____

Address _____

City, State, Zip _____

You may order as many copies of our Cookbook as you wish for the regular price.
Mail to:

Sisterhood of St. John's
1 St. John Parkway
Johnson City, NY 13790

Please mail _____ copies of your Cookbook @ _____ each.

Mail books to:

Name _____

Address _____

City, State, Zip _____